Praise for SELF-PRINTED:
The Sane Person's Guide to Self-Publishing

"An exceptional breath of realism, real knowledge and hard experience – don't dream of self-publishing your book without it. This is the self-publishing guide to read if you actually care about the quality of your writing and your readers." – *Nicola Morgan, author of around 100 books – including* Write to be Published *(and other writing advice on her website - www.nicolamorgan.com), award-winning YA novels such as* Wasted, *and books on the teenage brain and stress.*

"[*Self-Printed* has] been my bible! Whenever anyone asks me for a tip on self-publishing, I tell them to go buy it. I had it in digital version first and then in paperback so I could have it open next to the laptop." – *Kitty French,* USA Today *bestselling author of* The Knight Series

"*Self-Printed* is my self-publishing bible. It taught me how to format, create and upload my e-books and print-on-demand paperbacks. It showed me practical things such as how to build a website/blog and how to promote my books. More importantly, it taught me how to compete with the professionals. Just look at the results - The Estate Series has sold nearly 100,000 copies and following that I got a traditional book deal with Thomas & Mercer too, so I'm now a hybrid author. Jam-packed full of hints and tips all in one place, I'm always referring back to it. In a word, it's priceless." – *Mel Sherratt, author of* The Estate Series *and DS Allie Shenton Series*

"The BEST book on self-publishing … Seriously, GET THIS NOW!" – *David Wright, co-author of the bestselling* Yesterday's Gone *series*

Praise for SELF-PRINTED:
The Sane Person's Guide to Self-Publishing

"It's authoritative, engaging, and, like [Catherine's] blog, caffeinated. If you're thinking of self-publishing and you want to give your book a great start in life, get *Self-Printed*." – *Roz Morris, author of* Nail Your Novel: Why Writers Abandon Books and How You Can Draft, Fix and Finish With Confidence

"When I decided to self-publish my work, I didn't have the faintest idea how to do it. Fortunately, I came across Catherine Ryan Howard's guide to encourage, push, and prod me through the process. I doubt I would have achieved the success I've experienced without her down-to-earth, practical, meanwhile-here-in-the-real-world advice. I recommend *Self-Printed* to every writer I meet." – Martin Turnbull, author of the Garden of Allah novels, recently optioned by the producer of Disney's *Million Dollar Arm*

"The best thing about Catherine is that she not only lives the dream, but offers you a stepladder up to join her. The advice she gives is utterly practical – because she's done what she describes – and the whole [book] is suffused with humour. I am a fan." – *Associate Professor Alison Baverstock, author of* Is There a Book in You...? *and Course Leader, MA Publishing, Kingston University (UK)*

"Catherine explains clearly and concisely how to make self-publishing work for you. Laugh-out-loud funny in places, this book covers everything you need to know to make your book a success."
– *Vanessa O'Loughlin, founder of Writing.ie*

SELF-PRINTED

The Sane Person's Guide to Self-Publishing

*How to Use Digital Self-Publishing, Social Media and Common Sense
to Start Earning A Living as a Writer Through
E-Books and POD Paperbacks
(And Do It Without Ever Saying "Gatekeepers"
or Shouting "Down with the Big Five!")*

ISBN-10: 1502810158
ISBN-13: 978-1502810151

Catherine Ryan Howard © 2011-2014
This third edition published October 2014.

DISCLAIMER:

This book's aim is to serve as a guide for authors intending to make work available for sale through the print-on-demand service CreateSpace, Amazon's Kindle Direct Platform and the e-book publishing website Smashwords. It is not intended to be a comprehensive guide to self-publishing, a guide to self-publishing in any other form or a replacement for legal or other expert advice. While every effort has been made to ensure that the information in this book is accurate and up to date, mistakes or inaccuracies may well exist. The author accepts no liability or responsibility for any loss or damage caused, or thought to be caused, by following the advice in this book and recommends that you use it only in conjunction with other trusted sources and information. All foreign currency exchange calculations are approximate and were conducted in August 2014.

Follow Catherine on Twitter
@cathryanhoward
www.catherineryanhoward.com

SELF-PRINTED

The Sane Person's Guide to Self-Publishing

Also by Catherine Ryan Howard:

Mousetrapped:
A Year and a Bit in Orlando, Florida

More Mousetrapped:
A Little Bit More from That Year and a Bit*

Backpacked:
A Reluctant Trip Across Central America

*e-book edition only

SELF-PRINTED
The Sane Person's Guide to Self-Publishing

PART 3: Publishing Your E-books

PART 4: Publishing Your Paperback

PART 5: Selling Self-Published Books

PART 6: Everything Else

Introduction:

The Whose Guide to What Now?

Welcome to the third edition of *Self-Printed: The Sane Person's Guide to Self-Publishing*.

Perhaps I should start by explaining the thinking behind that title, and to do that I need to explain how and why I came to write this book.

My favourite piece of writing advice has always been "write the book you want to read" but in this case it was more like "write the book you *need* to read", or "write the book you'd need to read if you could find a quantum physicist to build you a time machine that would allow you to go back five years, to *before* you self-published, and thus instead of having to figure out all of this for yourself – and figure out some of it by making *very* costly mistakes – you could have read this book and got it right first time."

Writing things I could've done with reading once upon a time has become a bit of a theme with me. My first book, *Mousetrapped: A Year and a Bit in Orlando, Florida*, started life as the travel memoir I wish I'd read *before* I moved to Florida without a driver's licence, anywhere to live or indeed the first clue of what lay in store for me on the other side of the Atlantic.

It was back in early 2010 that I found myself and *Mousetrapped* at a crossroads. It had got the same rejection everywhere it went: "We like it, but there's no market for it." Publishing is a business and it would be bad business to spend money editing, designing, printing, distributing and promoting a book no one thought would sell in significant numbers. Only a publisher who didn't quite know what they were doing would disagree, and so I realised that continuing to submit it would be just like repeatedly hitting my head off a wall, only more painful.

It was time to take the hint. But what to do next, if anything? As I saw it, my options were these:

- Never mention it again, despite having told every *single* person I'd ever met that I was writing it.
- Recycle the 400 sheets of paper it was printed on (double-spaced 12 point Courier, of course) and try to forget about it.
- Have it bound in leather, leave it on the coffee table and tell guests – whether they asked about it or not – that it was my travel memoir, saying it in a French accent so that it sounded all posh, i.e. *mem-wah*.
- Use a print-on-demand (POD) service to, um, print a few copies on demand, so that I could attempt to sell it to the small group of people I knew would be at least *mildly* interested in buying it: my parents, my friends who were in it, my friends who'd think they were going to be in it, a handful of Disney fans, a handful of NASA fans and the 30 or so people I'd squeeze into the acknowledgements.

I couldn't face having to tell everyone that a summer locked in my bedroom and a credit card melted by a new computer had come to nothing. Since I didn't particularly care about the planet and my French wasn't great, that left just one option: using a POD service to print and sell copies of *Mousetrapped*.

(E-books, I should say at this point, were not yet on my radar. They would be soon enough.)

But that would be *self-publishing*, and for years I had been a certified self-publishing snob. I mean, who in their right mind would publish their *own book*? Only losers who knew nothing at all about getting published, the publishing industry or writing books, in my pre-2010 opinion.

Every week the local newspaper would highlight the latest delusional scribe to bind a few copies of their book ("It's called *The Loxatocki Protocol*," the author would be quoted as saying. "It's Victorian lesbian romance meets dystopian science fiction meets *P.S. I Love You*. I wrote it last Friday afternoon and my little brother made the cover on his Etch A Sketch. I've just sent a review copy to Michiko Kakutani of *The New York Times* ...") and my insides would contract at the sheer mortification of it all.

So how could I, the girl who by now had spent ten years of her life reading books like *500 Pages About How the Publishing Industry Works Even Though You'll Never Need to Know Unless You Stop Reading Books Like This and Write Your Own Book Instead* resort to self-publishing? And if I did, how could I differentiate my book from the likes of *The Loxatocki Protocol*?

Well, since I'd recklessly quit my job six months before to devote myself full-time to writing, and since my drug of choice was Nespresso coffee capsules (nearly €4 for a pack of ten!), I came around to the idea of self-publishing pretty *quick*, let me tell you. As for differentiating myself, I decided the only way to do that was to be unfailingly, unforgivingly, *brutally* realistic.

I would acknowledge that none of the following things were going to happen to me as a result of self-publishing: getting rich, getting famous, getting "properly" published, getting skinny, getting to meet Josh Groban, getting a condo with pool access somewhere in or near the town of Celebration, Florida, where I'd live out my days drinking mojitos and reading Apollo astronaut biographies on my iPad. (Or, it being the *Sunshine* State, perhaps on my Kindle. Screen glare and all that jazz ...) If anything, my Realistic Self reasoned, this endeavour was going to *cost* me money, not make it.

But I soon discovered that being realistic made me a rare creature in the dark and murky world of POD publishing – or so it seemed as I trawled through the information on Lulu and CreateSpace, two of the most popular POD sites. I ventured into their community forums, where the decorative scheme was five shades of crazy, the distinct scent of Eau de Delusional hung in the air and everyone seemed to be complaining, confused, or both.

One guy was particularly agitated because his 350,000-word novel about the adventures of Rafellius the Great, a talking purple unicorn who lives between this world and the next and has a penchant for Bird's Eye fish fingers, had only sold one copy in six months, which was a shock to him even though all he'd done was upload his files and click Publish. He was upset that, first of all, Lulu, the *distributor*, wasn't doing anything to sell his book (!) and second of all, that they'd as yet failed to pay him the $2.87 that was rightfully his.

Then there was this:

"I am very apprehensive. I am frightened. I wrote my first children's book five years ago and I still haven't figured out how to publish it. I don't have illustrations. My book is one of the best books I have ever read. I have read over 3,000 children's books."

Indeed.

In the midst of all this there appeared to be one or two sane people helpfully and patiently dispensing advice to the likes of Miss Apprehensive, but other than them I felt quite alone, what with my realistic expectations and, dare I say, modesty. I was embarrassed – almost apologetic – about self-publishing my book. How did I fit in with these people who clearly thought that the one thing the world was waiting for was a bound copy of their copyright-infringing *LOST* meets *Cheers* fan fiction sporting a cover that looked like several small house pets had enthusiastically vomited on it?

The answer was that I didn't.

I had yet to learn anything significant about the POD world, but thanks to *500 Pages About How the Publishing Industry Works Even Though You'll Never Need to Know Unless You Stop Reading Books Like This and Write Your Own Book Instead,* I knew enough about the book and publishing worlds to know that all clicking the Publish button would do for me was bind a copy of the PDF document I'd submitted to the POD service, slap the cover I'd designed on it (mistakes and all), list the book for sale in the darkest corner of Amazon.com and deduct $14.49 from my credit card for the privilege. It wouldn't benefit from the work of a graphic designer, an editor or a typesetter. Heck, the page numbers might not even be in sequence. And while it would be available on Amazon, it wouldn't grace the shelves of any bookstore, chain or independent – it *couldn't* because the wholesale cost per unit was way too high for anyone to consider stocking it. I thought my book was certainly a better read than the back of a cereal box but I didn't expect to sell more copies than I could find people easily bribed with chocolate. Without the backing of a marketing department or money to spend on advertising, very few people might end up even knowing my book *existed,* let alone handing over money in exchange for a copy. And it was about me, Disney World, Florida, NASA, the Space Shuttle, Bruce Willis, humidity-challenged hair and the Ebola virus – there wasn't a talking purple unicorn in sight.

In short, I wasn't publishing at all. I was just getting copies printed, and from there we'd have to see where it could go, if it could go anywhere.

So I wasn't self-publishing. I was self-*printing.*

Now I just had to figure out *how.*

Beyond the community forums, I struggled to find self-publishing advice that didn't come served with a generous helping of "Traditional publishing is dead!" propaganda, or that wasn't seemingly written by someone with a literary-agent-shaped chip on their shoulder who could clearly benefit from attending some kind of Resolving Your Bitterness self-improvement course.

It just all seemed so *angry.* There was talk of evil "gatekeepers" and a shadowy group known only as the Big Six. (I was surprised to learn that these weren't in fact horned demons but merely literary agents and major publishing houses.) These people weren't just self-publishing their novels or trying to sell e-books; they were sticking it to The Man, man! They were going to prove that their book was as good as anything Stephen King could produce. They were gonna show 'em all, just you wait and see. As soon as their novella, *Complicated Stuff That Happens in Space During a Bleak Time in the Future,* hit No. 1 on *The Sunday Times* bestseller list, they were going to send a snarky reply to every one of the 1,532 rejection letters the book had received, along with a photocopy of the bestseller list and a crayon drawing of a middle finger.

Yeah. Take *that*, Big Publishing. Take THAT.

In the section of the self-publishing world I'd stumbled into, it seemed that reality was as rare a commodity as it is in so-called reality TV. One website advised would-be self-publishers that writing a book actually wasn't all that hard – if you could *say* it, they claimed, then you could *write* it. Another said that agents, as a rule, never responded to unsolicited submissions and only used their slush piles for kindling. And don't bother pursuing your dreams of traditional publication – publishing is like a business class lounge us civilians aren't allowed into, and anyway all publishers want to do to aspiring writers is point and laugh at them. *Hard.* A parade of the usual "Bad" Writing, Big Selling suspects (Dan Brown, James Patterson, E. L. James) was regularly dragged out to prove the point that Big Publishing wouldn't know good writing if it set up camp on their desk, as were famous stories of missed opportunities, such as J. K. Rowling repeatedly being told there was no money to be made in children's books back when she and Harry Potter were getting rejected up the wazoo. And everyone seemed to think that by uploading a file to a website today, their book was going to be stacked in a pile just inside the door of every bookstore in the world no later than Tuesday.

I just wanted to self-publish (or rather, self-*print*). I wasn't angry or bitter or on a list of Persons Unwelcome at the security desk of a major publishing house. Yes, my book had been rejected, but I wasn't taking it personally. I was also brutally realistic and knew that by self-publishing a paperback with a print-on-demand site like CreateSpace and e-books with Amazon and Smashwords, I was *not* going to get rich, famous, or rich *and* famous. In all likelihood, I'd be lucky just to recoup the cost of the coffee I'd have to drink to get me through the formatting process. And I knew that despite what the self-publishing evangelists claimed with their James Patterson arguments and the like, most self-published books were just not up to scratch. This was just a fact, and a fact that could be easily proven with a quick trip to the store on any self-publishing service's website. While I would try to ensure that mine was as not-rubbish as it could possibly be, I wasn't under any illusions that it wouldn't get picked out as the impostor in a line-up of "properly" published books.

Where was the information for people like *me*?

I couldn't find it. I had to figure it out as I went along and that was difficult, so I tried to leave a trail of breadcrumbs for everyone else who might follow in my wake. Just as I had written *Mousetrapped*, the travel memoir I'd needed to read before I moved to Florida, I started posting about self-publishing on my blog, making it the blog I'd needed to read before I started this whole self-publishing adventure. Whenever I collected new information, I'd run it through a Delusions of Grandeur filter, spray it with common sense and post it under the heading Self-Printing. The posts became popular, and soon I was getting e-mails from other would-be self-publishers – or self-*printers* – asking for answers to questions I hadn't covered, or that they couldn't find in the ever-growing collection of posts I'd written on the subject.

Mousetrapped was out a year in March 2011 and my thoughts turned to writing its sequel. Before I got started on *that* though, I wanted to do something for the new visitors to my blog who perhaps didn't have the time or inclination to trawl through what was now more than a year's worth of posts. Maybe I could consolidate them into a downloadable document, copy and paste them into it in chronological order. A PDF maybe? A little e-book? I sat down one weekend to start doing just that, but I soon realised that there was so much more I wanted to share about this whole self-printing business than the stuff I'd had the time to blog about.

So I started writing a guide from scratch. That guide became this book, the guide that – yes, you've guessed it – I wished I could have read three years ago, back when I didn't know what POD meant, or what a Kindle was, or anything about the migraine-inducing horror that is formatting your manuscript for e-book conversion.

Self-Printed became my best-reviewed book and if I'm honest, it's also my personal favourite of the books I've released. (Let's not dwell on what this says about my *other* books, okay? Moving quickly along ...) Now here I am, almost five years after I first decided to self-publish, writing the third edition of it and, out there in the Big, Bad Self-Publishing World, everything looks *completely* different.

Self-publishing is no longer a last resort but a credible and worthwhile option for writers at all stages of their careers. We self-published authors have become savvy and smart about every stage of the publishing process, and many of us have started businesses providing the services this new industry needs, like cover design and e-book formatting. Some self-published books look better than their traditionally published counterparts, and self-published titles dominate the Kindle charts.

But the biggest change is that while late-2009 Catherine would've struggled to find any self-publishing instruction online that wasn't geared towards pre-digital methods, late-2014 Catherine is spoiled for choice. She can't *move* for the blogs and websites telling her how to self-publish – and that's a different kind of problem. There's so much information out there now that anyone just joining the self-publishing party is bound to feel incredibly overwhelmed and confused about where to even start.

That's where *Self-Printed* comes in.

What I really needed back in early 2010 was someone to sit me down and explain to me how this whole shebang works. What happens? When does it happen? *How* does it happen? A roadmap that I could clutch as I took my first tentative steps into the self-publishing world.

That's what I hope this book will be for you but, as you'll soon learn from these pages, having realistic expectations is one of the keys to self-publishing success. So while I'm hoping *Self-Printed* will lead you by the hand through this entire process until you get your first fat royalty cheque, I'm *aiming* for you just not wanting a refund.

Have you made yourself a big pot of coffee? Good.

Let's go.

Well, let's go in a minute.

Before we begin, there are some things you should know about me and some things you should know about this book.

The first thing you should know about me is that in the self-publishing world, I'm small fry. *Average* fry, if you will. The most books I ever sold in a one-month period was 1,000, and it only happened once. I know several self-published authors who've sold that number in a *week*. I also know a couple who've received high five-figure royalty cheques from Amazon, when the most I can boast is that they've been keeping me in Nespresso capsules since mid-2010.

Surely, you're saying to yourself now, if you wanted to make money from, say, selling coffee, and you wanted to learn how by buying a book, you'd start with *How I Made a Billion* by the guy who founded Starbucks, and leave *How I Pay My Bills* by the guy who owns the coffee shop on the corner for another day? In other words: why read a self-publishing guide written by someone like me if there are self-publishers out there selling a lot more books (and presumably writing how-to guides as well)?

I'm sure you've seen the headlines about Amanda Hocking, Colleen Hoover and Hugh Howey, among others – authors who self-published and hit the big time. But *millions* of self-published books are pushed into the world every year and yet I don't need all my fingers to count the number of No. 1 bestseller, household-name, money-soaked success stories that have emerged from among them.

The *good* news, however, is that I've lost count of the number of authors I know personally who are making good money from writing and self-publishing books. You may not see them in the headlines, but there are thousands of storytellers out there who are making a living (in part, at least) from doing what they love to do the most, often for the first time in their lives.

And you have every chance of becoming one of *them*.

Yes, it would be nice to be a millionaire by Monday, but chances are that's not going to happen. The odds are stacked against us – and that's okay. We'll focus on far more achievable dreams. This means that you don't have to read this book and think, "Well, that's great for *her*, but this couldn't happen for *me*." Instead you can read it and say, "What am I going to spend my first royalty cheque on?"

(Tip: I could do with some Nespresso capsules.)

The second thing you should know about me is that I have very strong views on self-publishing, namely that we *shouldn't* have very strong views on self-publishing.

You know when you're watching *Dragons' Den* (*Shark Tank* in the US) and you see someone pitch an idea for a problem that doesn't exist, like the guy who wanted to change the traffic light system even though (a) the existing system works fine and (b) the Road Safety Authority had told him it was the most dangerous thing they'd ever seen? And you know how, watching it, you marvel at the mind-boggling *pointlessness* of it all? Well, that's how I feel whenever someone brings up the so-called self-publishing versus traditional publishing "debate". Or when an author paints Amazon as the Big, Mean Capitalist Machine while, at the same time, happily collecting royalty cheques from them (see also: defending Amazon in a David-and-Goliath war with another corporation, seemingly forgetting that Amazon is a Goliath too). Or when anyone uses things like Stockholm Syndrome, World War II or the Irish Potato Famine as analogies for the publishing industry.

It makes me want to scream, "It's just books, people. BOOKS!"

If you think self-publishing is the first step in some sort of anti-establishment uprising, you are, of course, entitled to your opinion. And you might want to take a Xanax. But you should stop reading this right now, because this isn't the book for you. This book is for people who know that we're just talking about *books*, and *writing*, and *being authors*. (And coffee and Josh Groban, occasionally.) We're not interested in sticking it to The Man, proving something to the people who rejected us or coming up with new and ever more inappropriate ways to describe the publishing industry.

Nor do we care what anyone else is doing. This is the biggest mystery, for me, at the heart of the self-publishing "debate": why does anyone who is (delete as appropriate) self-publishing/traditionally publishing give a tiny rodent's rear end about whether *someone else* is (delete as appropriate) self-publishing/traditionally publishing? I can't figure it out.

Many of the people I've encountered are bitterly negative about one side in particular because *their* side is the other one, and now that they've made their decision they want you and me to validate it by making the same one. Others are genuinely trying to answer the question, *As a new writer, which is better for me: self-publishing or trying to get an agent?* But that's an impossible question to answer unequivocally, what with so many factors at play: type of book, length of book, timing, whether or not the author can/will self-promote, etc. etc. Publishing is not one size fits all. It *can't* be. So why are we bothering to debate it? Wouldn't our time be better spent writing more books?

Needless to say, selling a million copies of a book that got rejected by agents and editors all over town would certainly bring on a case of the warm and fuzzies. I'll admit I had the pleasure of being interviewed for a feature in a major national newspaper about *Mousetrapped's* success by a man who, in his previous role as a commissioning editor for a small press, had rejected it so fast I thought it was an out-of-office e-mail notification I was getting. But smugness is not our goal. Our goal is to self-publish our book well, build an audience for our work and, potentially, make a living (or at least coffee money) from this endeavour. So let's chillax about revenge for now.

The final thing you need to know about me is that I'm a little bit bossy. Okay, fine. I'm a lot bossy. That's, like, the *point*?

I'm not here to make suggestions. Check the cover: this book isn't called *If You're Going to Self-Publish, Here Are Some Things I Think You Should Potentially Maybe Do, You Know, If You Want To. Or Whatever.* I've seen what works and what doesn't. I'm a self-published author but I'm a reader too. A reader who buys a frightening number of books on a weekly basis, so I know what sells books to readers and what makes their eyes glaze over with disinterest and boredom. I've also been working as a freelance social media marketer for one of the world's biggest publishing houses for the past two years – a gig I was invited to do based on my self-publishing success – so I can say with some authority what's effective and what isn't in terms of selling books in the social media sphere.

That doesn't mean you have to agree with everything I say. Of *course* it doesn't. But please, don't bother sending me 3,000 words about why I'm wrong, and how you wish I would scratch out a certain section of my advice and replace it with your wisdom instead. It's my name on the cover of this book, sunshine. If you want everyone to take your advice, go write your own one.

"But," you'll cry, "what about that guy who not only put Comic Sans on his cover, but put the *entire text* into it as well? He sold ten million copies of his book *yesterday*. What do you know, Miss I Sold a Thousand in a Month Once, eh?!"

There are exceptions to *every single rule*, yes, but it's not helpful to dwell on them, or worse yet, model yourself on them. For instance, if you knew a writer who had just signed a six-figure deal after accidentally wrapping her son's ham sandwich in a page from her synopsis, a ham sandwich that her son then left in his desk at school over the Easter holidays, a desk that started to smell so much that the caretaker came to investigate, a caretaker who happened to read the synopsis page and think it might be something important, the synopsis page that he subsequently showed to his daughter, his daughter who was interning for a major literary agency and was desperate to prove herself, a major literary agency where they took things like synopsis sandwich wrappers seriously, from where an agent called your writer friend a week later to give her the good news: a six-figure, three-book deal, foreign rights sold in ten countries and a potential movie deal, what would you do? Would you continue to send out query letters, or would you start wrapping your children's sandwiches in Chapter Ones?

We shouldn't aspire to be an exception to the rule when, chances are, *we won't be it*. We should do what *works*. And I'm going to tell you what works, and works with little other than common sense, time and imagination. (Rest assured, *Self-Printed* is Jedi-mind-trick, cerebral-sales-strategy and spamtastic-tactics free. Also, I'm going to share with you all *my* ideas so you don't even have to use the imagination bit, if you prefer.) I may come off as a little bossy while I'm doing it – yeah, okay, a *lot* bossy – but you're just going to have to deal with it. Because yes, I'm here to hold your hand through this process, but that leaves my other hand free to slap you should I catch you putting Comic Sans anywhere near your book.

Now, on to things about this *guide*.

I can't stand it when I pick up a reference book and there's a section called How to Use This Book that takes the time to explain to me that I should read the book from start to finish without skipping bits. (Um … oh-*kay*. And should I also, like, read from left to right? Because I wasn't sure.) One time I opened a how-to book that warned me against highlighting text because, according to the author, there was *so* much useful information in it I'd just end up highlighting the whole thing.

Cue me deciding not to even bother *reading* it.

My point is, I don't need to tell you how to use this book. You had the good sense to buy it – or borrow it, at least – so my confidence in your ability to figure out how to use it is high.

But I will say this: find out about *everything* before you do *anything*. The information in this book isn't presented in the exact order you'll need it because if it was, the sections would be all over the place. For example, how we'll sell our books comes after the bit about how we publish them, even though a good chunk of our promotional efforts will take place *before* the book comes out. But it makes more sense to keep all the publishing bits together, rather than dividing them into two and separating them with a chapter about getting reviews.

Successful self-publishing is all about seeing the big picture, and you won't get to see that until you've read the whole book. So please don't be tempted to publish your paperback when you get halfway down page 142, or drop everything to create your blog somewhere around page 213. Just *wait*. Wait! Things will be *so* much easier that way. Trust me.

On to the second thing about this guide ... One of my favourite how-to-write-books books is *Wannabe a Writer?* by Jane Wenham-Jones. I *love* that book. It makes me laugh, it motivates me to write and it's full of practical advice too. (It also makes me want to drink wine, even though I hate the stuff.) It's essentially the wine-soaked tale of how Jane became a writer herself, spiced with plenty of hilarious anecdotes and insider tips about living the writing life. That's what makes it great. Which is why I was a tad confused to read a review of it that lambasted (oooh, good word!) Jane for repeatedly mentioning her own books. "It's all about *her*," the reviewer spat, "and what *she* did with *her* books."

I was then practically nauseous to read a review of the first edition of *this* book that said – and I quote/copy and paste – "Good information, but you really have to wade through a lot of stories ... about what the author did or did not do on her book ... to get to it."

Um, yeah. That's, like, the whole idea?

I have only self-published my own books. (The clue there is in the term *self-publishing*.) Therefore I'll be mentioning them and what I did with them throughout this book. The stories about what I did – or did not do – with them *is* "it". Apologies in advance, but I'm not quite sure how else I would do this, especially since I can only presume that you'd like to read a self-publishing guide by someone who has actually *done* it. Right?

The third and final thing about this guide – and the final point of this interminable introduction – is that when I say "self-publishing" I mean publishing an e-book with the likes of Amazon's Kindle Direct Publishing (KDP) and Smashwords, and a print-on-demand (POD) paperback with the likes of CreateSpace, Lulu and Blurb. (And I'll be saying "self-publishing" because that's the term we're all familiar with, but you'll know I mean "self-*printing*".) I won't be telling you anything about other types of self-publishing or how to use the other services, because this book is about how *I* did it, and how I did it was the cheapest and simplest way possible to get a book out into the world without said book being a total embarrassment, but in fact with said book looking pretty good, if I do say so myself. And *doing* pretty good as well. What I *will* be telling you is everything you need to know to do that.

Are you sitting comfortably? Good. Still got that coffee cup? Okay. Have some more caffeine-delivery-juice brewing in the kitchen? Wise.

Let's begin.

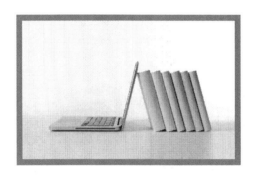

PART 1
Welcome to Self-Publishing

A Whole New World

Let's start with the good news: now is a *great* time to self-publish a book.

It wasn't that long ago that the self-published author cut a lonely figure on the outskirts of the publishing world, forced to drink juice from a plastic cup at the kids' table while the real writers sipped champagne from crystal flutes at the adults' one. He had self-published, most likely, for one of two reasons: either his writing room's ceiling was resting on columns of stacked rejection letters, or he had decided to circumvent the entire try-to-get-published process completely. Maybe he was even unaware that there was one. He'd paid thousands for hundreds of copies of his book, most of which were now gathering dust in boxes beneath his stairs because, even if he'd managed to avoid the pitfalls of bad cover design, lazy editing and prohibitively expensive unit costs, he *still* found himself with a major credibility problem. The term *self-published* was synonymous with *not good enough to get published,* and so convincing anyone of his book's merit, beyond his circle of obligated family and friends, had proved near impossible.

But it was the *logistics* of selling books that had ultimately doomed him to failure.

He might have managed to convince his local bookshops to stock a few copies – the independent ones, anyway; the chains rarely empowered their store managers to make stock decisions – but getting his book on the shelves of stores anywhere else would require the help of a distributor. If by some miracle a distribution company agreed to take on his book, they'd require thousands of copies of it and, as they'd sell them to bookshops on a sale-or-return basis, our self-publisher could end up getting them all back. *If* they sold them to bookshops, because with limited shelf space, a high unit price and competition from the world's bestselling and most highly lauded authors, it would be unlikely that any stores would bother to stock self-published works by writers unknown and, as yet, unproven. They'd know that there wouldn't be any marketing campaign or publicity push gently nudging customers into the store to buy it and that, in fact, the book was sure to be ignored by all print media, book reviewers and literary-prize judging panels.

But let's pretend our self-publisher caught a break and won a few sales in store. Out of the retail price comes the bookshop's cut, the distributor's cut *and* the cost of the book to the self-publisher himself, i.e. the manufacturing cost, leaving just a few pennies as profit. With the amount of time and effort it's taken to organise the book's distribution – the research, the paperwork, delivering the books to the warehouse, etc., our self-published author isn't sure if it's all worth it. Especially since he won't receive payment until *months* after the sales of his book have taken place.

And what of the rest of the world? What of the readers who don't live within driving distance of our self-published author or one of the stores stocking his book? What of readers in other countries? Well, our self-published author could, theoretically, sell his books directly from a website or blog, but that would bring about a whole new headache of processing credit card payments, packing and shipping books, and always keeping enough copies in stock to fulfil orders even when you've no guarantee that any will come in at all. And how are people going to find out that the book is for sale on his website? How is he going to convince them to buy it if and when they do? He could sell his book on Amazon, but with his choices being either to set himself up as a Marketplace Seller or to get his distributor to sell his book there on his behalf, it's a pain not too dissimilar to the one brought on by his bookshop experience. And again, how does he tell the world about it in the first place? How does he convince strangers to shell out more on his book than they would on a traditionally published book of the same length? How does he persuade them to take a chance on *The Loxatocki Protocol*?

The short answer is that he doesn't. And so, a few months or maybe a year in, our self-published author is left with no choice but to accept the failure of his book, to write off the thousands he invested in publishing it and to flog all the copies he has left at Sunday morning car boot sales for a fraction of what it cost him to print them.

I mean, really. Who'd have self-published?

Today – that is a whole, um, five years later – the landscape is completely different. Unrecognisable, even. And in this new world of digital self-publishing, *The Loxatocki Protocol* could have every chance of finding a readership and *earning* our self-published author friend some money, instead of just costing him lots of it.

(Although probably not with that title ...)

In this new world, our self-published author begins by spending a lot less. Two things require investment: editing, which is relatively expensive, and a cover design, which doesn't have to be. (A survey of self-publishers in 2012 found that on average, they spend around $500 getting a book to market. I think this is a bit low, and that $1,000–1,500 would be more like it. We'll talk money matters later.) He finds a professional editor and cover designer and while they get to work, he starts building anticipation about the release of his book on social networks, his blog, forums, etc. Once both book and cover are ready, he registers for free accounts on sites like Amazon KDP and CreateSpace, and uploads his files. Within twelve hours, a Kindle edition of his book is for sale in most parts of the Western world. Within a week, a paperback is too. (And whenever one of these paperbacks is sold, it's not from any stock he's had to provide; CreateSpace only prints a copy when a copy is ordered, Amazon ships it, both companies take their cut and our self-published author friend gets the rest – he can sell paperback editions of his book globally without ever holding a copy in his hands, if he likes.) On Amazon, his book virtually sits next to work by the world's bestselling authors, and gets treated no differently. Having no manufacturing costs to cover with his e-book price tag means he can use low prices to entice new readers to try his work, and programmes like KDP Select enable him to promote it as free for limited periods, bringing him thousands of downloads, and among them, hopefully, new fans as well. Eventually the Amazon customer reviews start rolling in, backed up by reviews from book bloggers he's sent digital copies to. Along with the blog posts, tweets and Facebook updates that serve as the coal in the steam engine of his promotion train (and with each purchase making his book more visible on sites like Amazon), sales begin to trickle in; then they pick up, and then they start to steadily *pour* in. All our self-published author friend need do is lodge the royalty cheques he receives once a month and start working on his next book.

Yes, that is a *very* rosy picture of self-publishing that I've painted there. But then I did say I'd start with the good news, didn't I?

Self-publishing is breaking into the mainstream. Readers who would never in a million years have considered trying a self-published book are now enticed to do so by cheap e-books, free promotions or online connections such as reading and liking the author's blog. Self-publishers can make their books available to readers all over the world, and do it without spending thousands or even leaving their house. Self-published titles sit atop bestseller lists, and some of the authors of them have gone on to sign six- and seven-figure traditional deals. Going it alone is now a badge of honour in some circles when, not long ago, it was evidence of stubborn delusion in all of them.

Self-publishing, dare I say it, has become *cool.*

(Gasp!)

We've pulled up a chair to the adults' table and we're holding out our own flute for some champagne. But it's not *all* good news. Some of our tablemates are eyeing us suspiciously, and the waiter is hesitating as he tries to work out whether or not we're gatecrashers who need to be asked to leave. It's not their fault; we can't blame them. Because the last self-publisher they invited to join them got messy drunk, threw food and accused the literary agent sitting next to him of moving all unsolicited submissions directly to the recycle bin and not being able to identify good writing if it smacked him across the face.

And then he smacked him across the face.

My point is, this new self-publishing world is amazing. It's wonderful. It's practically *glistening* with opportunity for authors at all stages of their careers. But not all of us are treating it with the respect it deserves. Not all of us are behaving ourselves. And whenever one of us behaves badly – be it by releasing a book we only started a week ago, or attempting our own Microsoft Paint cover design, or spamming other authors with "Buy my book!" tweets and e-mails – it affects *all* of us.

To quote Voltaire – and Spider-Man – with great power comes great responsibility. And so before you attempt to self-publish, you should ask yourself if you're *ready* for this responsibility, and if you're willing to act in accordance with it. Because I'm not here to help you bang out 100,000 words of typing over the weekend only to throw it up on the Kindle Store by Monday afternoon. If that's your plan, I'd really rather you didn't bother.

My advice is intended for what I call *The New Self-Publisher*.

The New Self-Publisher is dedicated to the craft of writing. They know that books are not written, but rewritten. They take their time. They wouldn't *dream* of putting anything out into the world that hadn't been at least professionally proofread, and ideally copy-edited too. They didn't decide to be a writer yesterday; they've wanted to do this for years. Perhaps they can't remember a time when they *didn't* want to be a writer. Self-publishing is maybe something they've come to after getting tantalisingly close to realising their publication dreams, only to be stopped by a niche market, an overcrowded genre or bad timing. Maybe they even have an agent, or had one. Or perhaps they're a mid-list author with an extensive backlist and no new contract visible on the horizon who wants to take their career into their own hands. Maybe they're a bestselling author who wants to cut out the middle man from here on in.

For them, this isn't an experiment or a project, but a step towards the realisation of their lifelong writerly dreams. They aren't fuelled by bitterness or resentment. They've got professional feedback on their book and so they don't just believe it's good, they *know* it is because unbiased experts have told them so. (And they recognise industry professionals with years of experience in the book world as *experts*.) They're realistic about what they can achieve and are professional in their approach. They ensure that their book doesn't look out of place side by side with traditionally published books. They're not just out to get rich quick, but their goal is to make a living from their writing. They're in this for the long run. They know that the only way to succeed is to assume the role of an entrepreneur as soon as they've typed "THE END", and to treat their book like the product it is. They're willing to get out there and sell their book. They know what that'll take. They appreciate the opportunities this new world brings, and they never take it for granted or abuse it. They don't get into long, rambling arguments about the future of publishing, use the word *gatekeepers* or publicly attack reviewers who didn't like their book with four-letter words. They don't do anything to bring the side down. On the contrary, the self-publishing world is delighted to have them.

The New Self-Publisher can be summed up with one of my favourite quotes about self-publishing, which comes from my blogging friend Roz Morris, author of *Nail Your Novel: Why Writers Abandon Books and How You Can Draft, Fix and Finish with Confidence* and *My Memories of a Future Life*:

"Self-publishing isn't for authors who couldn't get published. It's for authors who *could*."

In other words, self-publishing is for:

- books that under different circumstances would've *got* published
- authors who any publishing house or agent would be happy to have

Roz herself has an example of a book that under different circumstances would've got published. *Nail Your Novel* is a fantastically useful book, but it's short – too short to be worth the investment a publishing house would have to cough up in order to print and distribute it. So Roz released it herself as an e-book and POD paperback. My own book, *Mousetrapped*, got (some) positive feedback from each of the agents and editors I sent it to, but ultimately they all concluded the same thing: that there just wasn't a market for a book like that.

From what I've seen, almost all successful self-published authors are great at being authors. I don't mean the writing bit, although they're good at that too. I mean the bits of being an author where you have to *get out there and convince people to buy your book*.

Imagine for a minute that you're the publicity director at a major publishing house. You have a debut novel to promote and you're brainstorming ways to get the word out about it. You can try to get the book reviewed in the press, place advertisements, supply bookstores with special displays, but you know that's all a bit hit-and-miss and it costs a small fortune. What you *really* need is an author who can sail through a radio interview, or give a sparkling performance on a TV talk show; who gives great writing workshops, or is an entertaining public speaker; who is active on social media and motivated to find her own fans; who always carries business cards with her book's cover on them; who gets a bunch of friends together to make a fun book trailer; who sends daily e-mails to the publicity department outlining plans for new (cost-free) ways to promote her book; who is always professional and pleasant, someone you *like* to work with; who doesn't make diva demands, or have unrealistic expectations, or expect everyone else to sell her book while she sits back and relaxes because after all, she *wrote* the bloody thing, didn't she?

Now I'm not saying you can't successfully self-publish without also being able to confidently speak in public. Most writers don't like to, what with us generally being shy, retiring types comfier in our sweatpants than in our diamonds (or, this being *writers* we're talking about, our cubic-zirconias more like), and most of us won't get the opportunity anyway. Focus on my bigger picture, which is that the self-publisher destined for success is not only one the *self-publishing* world is happy to have, but one any *publishing house* would be happy to have, because they'd be confident she has the skills to get them a return on their investment. (And possibly will be sorry they *don't* have when the self-publisher goes on to sell a gazillion books. Let's hope, anyway.)

Is this you? Are *you* a member of The New Self-Publishing Club? Are you willing to do everything you must to make your book the best it can be, to become an entrepreneur, to devote as much time, energy and imagination as you can spare to get that book selling and then some?

If you are, read on.

If you're not, all this will be is an exercise in losing money, wasting your time and maybe even being humiliated in public about the quality of your work.

There are easier ways. For instance, you could drop this book right now, throw all your cash out the window, watch a few episodes of *I Didn't Know I Was Pregnant* and then run naked down your street, and you'd have basically achieved the same thing.

Don't say you weren't warned.

The Importance of Appeal

The first thing you'll learn the moment you step out, blinking, into the harsh light of the self-publishing world is that just because you wrote a book does not mean people are going to want to read it.

Sounds suspiciously like common sense, I know, but as I'll say elsewhere in this book, common sense isn't as common as you might think.

Read the sentence again and then have a little think about it. *Just because you wrote a book does not mean people are going to want to read it.* No one will give a damn. Even the people you thought would give a damn won't bat an eyelid. The fact that a book exists does not, sadly, equal people scrambling to read it. It needs more than that. *You* need more than that, or this will all be for naught. So before you even dip a toe into this self-publishing thing, consider spending five minutes making sure that your book comes packaged with a reason for me to read it that I just can't ignore.

This is a hard concept to explain and I have failed miserably to do so in the past, telling readers in the previous edition of this book that they had to have a "good" book, and that the best way to figure out whether or not they did was to try to get it traditionally published first and see what the feedback was like. I won't be saying that in this edition, but I do want you to stop and think about the book you are putting out there before you introduce it to the world. *Will people want to read it?* Will they choose to read it over all the other books out there too? If so, why? When someone encounters your book on the virtual shelf, what is it that's going to push them to hit the Buy button?

Does your book come with *appeal*?

Think of all the books you hear about on a daily basis. Think of all the books you see when you walk into a bookstore, or in the book aisles of supermarkets. Think of all the books that pop into your line of vision while you're on Amazon. Do you buy them all? Are you even *interested* in them all? Or are you like me – and, I'd suspect, most book buyers – buying and ultimately reading just the very cream of the crop, the top 0.5 per cent or less of the books we know about, just the ones that get us interested in them and wanting to read them, i.e. just the ones *we care about*?

At least once a day I receive an e-mail from an author I don't know saying "I've written a book. Will you review it?" If this author knew that every Friday Oprah's Book Club sends me an e-mail recommending several books – books that, this being Oprah's Book Club, are hugely publicised, high-advance, this-is-gonna-be-big traditionally published books – and that, on average, I make a note of maybe two of them and ultimately buy at most one of them for every five or six e-mails I get, do you think they'd do anything differently? At the very least, I hope they'd make an effort to get me to *care about their book*.

Good self-publishers are entrepreneurs. They treat self-publishing like a business, with their book being their first product launch. Going back to *Dragons' Den/Shark Tank*, think about some of the pitches the investors have been treated to. How many times do they say things like "You've answered a question no one was asking" or "You've come up with a solution to a problem that doesn't exist"? How many times have they just been utterly unimpressed with the product that's being pitched, to the point where they roll their eyes or sigh with boredom? What's different about the pitches that make them all sit up straight and then compete with one another to invest? When that happens, aren't you usually sitting in front of the TV screen agreeing with their enthusiasm, making a mental note to pick up the product when it hits the shelves?

It is very hard to get people to care enough about your book that they go and buy it. It's the hardest part. And before you can attempt to do that, you have to get them interested in it, and before that you have to let them know that it exists. It's a tall and steep mountain to climb but embracing this fact will help you scale it, because you'll know what lengths you have to go to in order to make it happen.

Start thinking about it now. Let it begin to fester in the back of your mind. If you were pitching your book, how would it fare? How would you convince me that I simply *had* to buy it and read it? You're going to have to figure out an answer and the fact that you wrote it just isn't enough.

While we're on the subject, there is something to be said about making sure you have a good book, if we take *a good book* to mean something that other people will find engaging and worthwhile. You know when you happen upon news of an upcoming book and the blurb, title and cover design just grab you, and you say to yourself, "I can't WAIT to read that!" That's what we want other people to say about our book. But here's the thing: we need to *make them* say that. That's our job. So consider using beta readers, or getting professional feedback from a manuscript critique service, or maybe even an agent if you're prepared to submit your work. Don't rely on friends and family to tell you your book is wonderful, interesting and/or "unputdownable". They'll be impressed you managed to *type* 100,000 words, let alone write them. Find an unbiased but qualified test audience and see what they think *before* you send your book out into the world.

To be frank, don't self-publish crap.

Consider the fact that once the book is out there, you will get feedback on it you never asked for – but by then, it'll be too late. Everyone gets both good and bad reviews but for some reason that's unclear to me, some readers feel the need to leave *baaaad* reviews, so filled with spite and hate that you wonder if you wrote a book they didn't like or killed their puppy. If you've never read a *baaaad* review of your work, I can't adequately explain to you how deep inside those words can go. *Eviscerating* is the only word that comes close. The worst lines will be forever tattooed on your brain and they'll overwrite any and all positive feedback you ever got. Trust me when I say that the only thing worse than reading an acidic, spiteful, hate-filled review of your book that's been posted in public is reading an acidic, spiteful, hate-filled review of your book that's been posted in public and suspecting, deep down, that the reviewer *might have a point*.

If you dream of writing becoming your career then you should take that into consideration as well; once you release the book, you can't take it back. (You can unpublish it, of course, but you can't scrub the magical interweb of its existence, or take it back from the people who bought it.)

You never know: a future interested agent or publisher might be on the verge of offering you a deal, only to google your name and find out about *The Loxatocki Protocol* and read about how the general consensus was that it was less entertaining than the instruction manual for a microwave oven.

There's also the issue of your self-published author responsibility, of not letting side down. Do you know how hard it is to get someone to read a self-published book? I think self-publishers lose their perspective when it comes to the answer to this question, because of course we're encountering scores of people every day who do read self-published books – *ours*. But in fact, most people don't read them. Most people *won't*. But let's say that one of us manages to break through and gets someone who never, ever, *ever* wanted to read a self-published book to read a self-published book. Maybe accidentally. Maybe they didn't realise that's what it was. If it's a good book then our new convert might buy another one. But what if it's a terrible book that reads like a Google Translate malfunction? Now this self-publishing toe-dipper has just confirmed what they thought about self-published books all along – that they're not worth it – and you can guarantee that they won't be buying any more. Maybe the book they would've bought next was mine. If the bad one was yours, *you've* cost *me* a sale. You haven't treated this opportunity with the respect it deserves and you've messed it up for more people than just yourself.

I know self-publishing is exciting and you feel an urge to get your book out there as soon as is humanly possible. I've felt that too. But I've also learned from experience that publishing your book 24 hours after typing "THE END" is a recipe for disaster and humiliation.

Take your time. There's no rush.

Why You (Yes, YOU!) Need an Editor

I've been blogging about self-publishing for five years now and I can tell you that the number one thing self-publishers don't like to be told is that every *single* self-published book needs a professional polish before its release. It's also the thing self-publishers need to be told the *most*.

Why does this matter? Because *writing* matters. Don't stick any old crap out there just because you can. Make your mistakes in private. Don't ask your readers to be the assessors *and* editors *and* spell-checkers of your work; they shouldn't have to be. By the time their eyes hit your pages, all of that should've been done already. And with another nod to our self-publishing-as-a-business idea, you are not merely self-publishing a book. You are *selling a product*. As unromantic as this may sound, it's the truth. It's reality. And just as you couldn't sell an apple pie that was in fact filled with thumbtacks, you can't sell a book that just isn't up to scratch. You are taking people's money and in exchange you must deliver the goods.

I don't care what excuses you're forming in your mind right now or your list of reasons for why you're different from everyone else and why this advice doesn't apply to you. Unless your book has no words in it, there is absolutely *nothing* you can tell me that will make the next sentence untrue.

You need an editor.

(Yes, *you*.)

(No, really. *You*.)

(Yes, this *does* include *you*.)

Why self-publishers get so angry at being told this is a bit of mystery to me, but they *do* get angry. Very angry. Whenever I mention this on my blog or at a talk or something, I get virtual sacks of bitchy e-mails accusing me of everything from forcing self-publishers into debt to insulting their intelligence. Maybe it's because they think that someone telling them "you have to get your book edited" is the same as someone telling them "your book isn't good" or "you don't know how to spell". But that's not the case at all. Giving our book a professional polish before it gets released is exactly the same thing as ensuring that it has a cover, sequential page numbers or that it reads from left to right. It's about *standards*.

I think this lack of understanding accounts for most of the Anti-Editing Syndrome I come across. These, for example, are typical responses from a self-publisher after being told that they absolutely *have* to get their book edited:

- "Who is an 'editor' to say that a book is good or bad for everyone? Just because one person doesn't like a particular turn of phrase does not mean the other six billion of us won't like it."
- "I'd love to hire an editor, but I can't afford it. I use spell-check and get my friend who, like, reads books all the time to read over it for me."
- "Most people will overlook a couple of typos if they like the story. I find typos in traditional books all the time and no one says anything about them."
- "I am perfectly capable of doing my own editing. I mean, I *am* a writer, aren't I?"

Now maybe you can see their points, or have even said some similar things yourself. But if we took these statements out of the book world, would you still agree with them?

- "Who is a 'mathematician' to say that two plus two equals four? Just because one person gets that answer doesn't the mean the other six billion of us will get the same one."
- "I'd love to hire a translator, but I can't afford it. I put all my text through Google Translate and then get my friend who, like, goes to France on her holidays every year to read over it for me."
- "Sometimes you order a salad in a restaurant and it comes out with a hair on it, and it's no big deal. No one says anything. So in my restaurant, there'll be no washing of hands, wearing of hair nets or cleaning the kitchen."
- "I am perfectly capable of doing my own brain surgery. I mean, I *have* a brain, don't I?"

What Is Editing?

So what *is* editing? Let's talk about that first, because the term "editing" actually covers a lot of different things, not all of which are relevant to self-publishers.

The first stage of the editing process is **structural editing**, where an editor looks at the book as a whole and notes any big-picture problems like a slow pace, a confusing plot or someone being pregnant for eleven months. If you paid for a manuscript critique, the report you got will contain the problems flagged or suggestions made after a structural edit of your book.

This is the one stage where the goal is to make the book generally better, and it's the only stage I'd allow a self-publisher to skip. This is because it's the most expensive, takes the most time and doesn't make much business sense if (i) we're charging very little for our book and (ii) we've already got positive feedback from an agent, enlisted beta readers or paid for a manuscript critique. If we were opening a coffee shop, paying for a structural edit is like putting Egyptian cotton tablecloths on our tables: we would if we could afford it, but it's unlikely we'd recoup the cost and our customers probably won't be able to tell the difference anyway.

I believe that people can either write and tell stories or they can't, and if the book is bad there's not much Band-Aiding a structural edit can do. If you write well, chances are you've told a good story and your beta readers will help you see and fix any big-picture problems – let's hope.

The next stage is **copy-editing** or line-editing, where an editor goes through your book line by line looking for typos, sentences that could be changed for clarity or correctness, misuse of words, missing words, misspellings, consistency (e.g. *e-mail* and *email*) and anything else that isn't correct use of the English language, be it British or American English. This is where the bulk of a self-publisher's budget should go, and I would strongly advise against skipping this. If you've written fiction, I'd beg you not to.

The final stage is **proofreading**, where a proofreader (or your editor; they usually do both) goes through the text with a fine toothcomb one last time to make sure that everything is perfect, and it is the absolute *minimum* a self-publisher should do before they release their book.

So to recap:

- Getting your book proofread will meet the basic requirement for books with price tags on them.
- Getting your book proofread and copy-edited will produce a professionally put together, polished product that meets accepted standards, which you can confidently release to the world.
- Getting your book proofread, copy-edited and structurally edited will make your book the best it can be, but at a cost.

You cannot do it yourself, or get a friend who, like, reads *all the time* to do it for you. Because:

1. *You can't edit your own work.* This isn't my opinion, but a universal truth. You are too close to the work and have read over it too many times to ever be able to look at it with fresh eyes. Even editors can't edit their own work, just like psychiatrists can't treat themselves. They'll tell you that themselves.
2. *You don't know what you don't know.* You may be convinced that with enough go-throughs, you'll find every last mistake there is to find in your book. But how can you find something you aren't looking for? How can you weed out the mistakes you don't know you've made? It's impossible.
3. *This isn't about spell-checking and typos.* A copy-editor is someone who has a special skill that they've acquired through study, training and experience. They cannot be replaced by your friend who reads all the time, even if your friend is so pedantic about the English language that they drop friends for using "your" instead of "you're".

Still not convinced? *Sigh* ... Well, let me take one last lash at it with my three scary get-an-editor stories:

- *The editor is the one who asks the questions.* An editor at Faber & Faber said this at a talk I attended a few years ago and it's stuck with me ever since. How often have you read a review of a book and seen a comment like "I don't understand why X did Y ... that was totally out of character" or "Whatever happened to X? That was never explained" or "I just don't buy that X ran into Y after the party – isn't that too much of a coincidence?" If your readers are asking questions like these, it's already too late. It should be the *editor* asking those questions, back when the book was only on your computer. You may think you will anticipate these questions but it is impossible because *you wrote the damn thing*. It all makes perfect sense in your head already because if it didn't, you would've written it differently. Hire an editor or at least a herd of beta readers so *they* can ask those questions *before* readers who've parted with their hard-earned cash do.

- *Consider the same process in a publishing house.* In a big publishing house, the commissioning editor (the one who bought the book) will spend a minimum of 2–3 months working with the author on structural edits. Sometimes this process goes on for years. This is usually after the author's agent has provided feedback, and the author herself has gone through several drafts getting the book to the best place she can. Then the copy-editor will go through the book line by line, checking the language, looking for inconsistencies, testing clarity, etc. Then the proofreader – a different person – will go through the book again. At the same talk where I heard the line "The editor is the one who asks the questions", I also heard that in some houses, there are *two* proofreaders who both go through the book at the same time. I also heard this: the final proofread finds no errors. As in, the book is proofread again and again until the proofreader can go through the entire thing and find not one single error. Can you replicate all that work and expertise all by your lonesome, on 100,000 words or so that you've written yourself and read again and again, to the point where the voice in your head is finishing the sentence before your eyes even reach the words? *Really?* I have my doubts.

- *Even with an editor, the text won't be perfect.* "But there are mistakes in traditionally published books!" That's what you're screaming at me now, isn't it? Here I am talking about all the work that goes into making a traditionally published book perfect, and yet you've seen typos in plenty of them. I have too. Why would you bother trying to emulate that, eh? Well, that's just my point. Even *with* all that professional input – even with three rounds of editing (structural, copy-edit, proofread) – mistakes *still* managed to sneak through. So how bad would it be if none of that work had been done? It is nigh on impossible to get 100,000 words exactly right. You won't believe it until you've tried to do it yourself. I used both a copy-editor and a proofreader for my self-published travel memoir, *Backpacked*, and there were still errors in the finished product. Not many, but they were there. It's just the nature of the beast. But while some might say so why bother, *I* say imagine how many there would've been if I *hadn't* hired any editors to work on it at all.

Hiring Professional Help

Freelance editors are easy to find online, but beware: there are plenty of people *saying* they're qualified editors, especially now that they know plenty of self-published authors are out looking for them. I would make sure I got a personal recommendation from another author, and/or that the editor in question was a member of a professional association like Ireland's Association of Freelance Editors, Proofreaders and Indexers (AFEPI) or the UK's Society for Editors and Proofreaders (SfEP).

You can also go to companies that offer a one-stop shop for editing services, like Bubblecow (www.bubblecow.co.uk) and the Inkwell Group (www.inkwellwriters.ie), based in the UK and Ireland respectively. It is unlikely terrible editors are working for a referral service when they can collect feedback from their clients but if you *do* have a bad experience, you at least have someone other than the editor to go back to. Everything is done by e-mail so as long as both author and editor are proficient in the same *type* of English, i.e. British or American, location isn't really an issue.

I'd be wary of "bargain" editing offers because just like building a house, this *isn't* the kind of job where you want everything to go to the lowest bidder.

SfEP has suggested minimum hourly rates and while they won't apply all over the world, they are a good reference point for self-published authors:

- Proofreading: $33/€26/£20 per hour
- Copy-editing: $40/€31/£24 per hour
- Developmental (structural) editing: $44/€35/£27 per hour

Why an hourly rate and not a per 1,000 words one? Because *my* 1,000 words might need a lot more work than yours does. To find out how much your project is going to cost, send your prospective editor a few pages and let them be the judge. You might also ask two or three of them – your shortlist – to edit the pages for you, so you can see what working with them is going to be like.

Payment is usually half before the job and the rest afterwards, or in full once the work has been delivered. Make sure you both agree on exactly what you're paying for. For example, is the proofread a once through the book, or will the proofreader go through it one more time after that to ensure it's perfect?

If you're writing science fiction with unusually spelled names or places, or have, say, a non-fiction book full of technical terms, it's helpful to make a definitive list of the correct spellings and send them to the editor along with your book. Then he or she can check them against your text to make you're spelling them right each time.

It goes without saying – but I'm going to say it anyway – that while it might be prudent to employ the services of an up-and-coming book cover designer, web designer or video trailer-maker to save money, it is certainly *not* a good idea to hire someone who's "just starting out in editing".

(EYE ROLL.)

Chances are that most self-publishers do not have bottomless pits of cash to spend on preparing their manuscript for publication. However, you must spend *some* money. You're starting a business after all. Would you still open that coffee shop if you had no money to invest? If you can't afford to employ an editor, you can't afford to self-publish. That's that.

But when your budget is limited, where's the best place to splash the cash?

I think this is a good plan for the average self-publisher:

1. Rewrite, rewrite, rewrite. Then rewrite some more.
2. Recruit a group of beta-writers and ask them for their feedback on your book. At this stage, it's big-picture questions like *does the plot make sense? Is the ending satisfying? Is the main character likeable?* Take their criticisms and suggestions and rewrite some more, OR hire a structural editor if you can afford it.
3. Get your book copy-edited. Once the copy-edit is complete, go through your manuscript again to see if you can eliminate any more errors. I like to change my font to something drastic – like Comic Sans – to help me see the text afresh.
4. Enlist the help of some reader friends and have them read through the manuscript. Ideally these will not be the same people we got to read it back in step 2; we want as many different eyes on our book as possible, and we want them looking at it afresh. Make sure they understand they're looking for mistakes like spelling errors or

missing words, and that the time for suggestions on the language used, plot, etc. has passed. Update your manuscript to eliminate any errors they find.

5. Hire a proofreader (or your editor again) to go through the manuscript.

6. Remember that friend who drops people for using "you're" instead of "your"? This is where you get *her* to go through the book. When she comes back to you having failed to find any mistakes, you'll know you're good to go.

If you've got to this point and you're still thinking, *my book's in pretty good shape; I think I'm good to go right now*, then please, reconsider.

Let me tell you that as a writer, there is no worse feeling in the world than reading a bad review. I don't mean a negative review, because we don't all like the same things and negative reviews are just par for the course, but a *baaaaad* review, one that rips your book (and your confidence) into tiny shreds. If you've had your book professionally edited, you can console yourself with the fact that you *know* your book is good, and that the reviewer must have a bee in their bitchy bonnet for some reason unrelated to you. If your book hasn't been professionally edited, you don't have this comfort.

Furthermore, the bitchy reviewer will undoubtedly point out any errors they've found in your book – and if you don't have an outsider look at it, there will be at least a couple – which will lead other potential readers looking to your reviews to help them decide whether or not to buy it to believe that, since this is clearly a fact, everything else in the bad review must be true too. And then they'll cease to be a potential reader of yours.

It's a sad fact that many if not most self-published books have errors in them, and it's a sadder fact that most people read self-published books *looking* for them. As self-published authors we haven't yet earned the reader's trust. So while my eyes might skip over a typo in a Michael Connolly novel – not that, to my knowledge, they've ever had to – a reader *will* spot and recall the errors in *your* book. Then, in all likelihood, the reader will mention them in their review.

Finally, this isn't just about you. You'll benefit hugely from having your book edited, yes, because you'll be able to carry everything you'll learn forward with you into your self-published career, but it's not you that you have to think about. It's your *readers*. When they buy a book, they want to *read* it. Not keep their eyes peeled for errors you couldn't be bothered to catch.

A few months back, I was reading an interview with a self-published author when I came across this quote: "Unfortunately I don't have the luxury of an editor." An editor is not a luxury, it's a necessity. And it's the *readers of her books* who'll have to do without it, along with the money they've spent on her badly produced book. Please don't do the same to yours.

Okay, I'll stop now.

(Get an editor!)

Sales Goals: What's Realistic?

I don't believe you should set out to do anything without having some goals in mind, but when it comes to self-publishing it can be hard to find the cold, hard numbers of success. It also depends on what *you* want for yourself. The vast majority of self-published books on a POD site like Lulu or CreateSpace only sell one or two copies, so if you sold ten you'd be considered an above average success. But would selling ten copies of your book make you happy? I know it wouldn't do it for me.

When I was setting my own goals, I searched for as many examples of sales figures as I could find and then tried to find a spot somewhere in the middle of them for me and *Mousetrapped*. I read on one publishing blog that very few POD books sell more than 200 copies, so I set that as my embarrassment level, i.e. I could avoid humiliation if I managed to sell that many but would have to dig a hole and hide in it if I sold any fewer.

But of course I wanted to sell more than *that*.

A pretty level-headed self-publishing book told me that a well-produced POD title could expect to sell between 50–200 copies per month, but would likely only achieve those sales after being on sale for a year, as it seemed to take that long for POD books to reach their full potential. So I took that into consideration as well, and finally decided on 100 copies in the first month, 500 copies by six months and 1,000 copies in the first year. If I managed to reach those targets, then I'd think up some new ones.

Two years in, I'd sold around 18,000 books. My goals were *way* off and there's a specific reason why: *e-books*. I didn't factor e-book sales into my goals because when I was getting ready to self-publish and deciding on things like my goals, I didn't even know I was going to release e-book editions. (Amazon KDP – or Amazon DTP as it was called then – had just opened to Word documents. *That's* how long ago this was.) E-books are easier to sell than paperbacks – mainly because they're priced much lower and so the purchaser takes less convincing – but how *well* your e-books will sell is anyone's guess.

There seems to be absolutely no way to tell in advance if sales will trickle through in dribs and drabs, or if they'll take off like a rocket, catapulting you and your book right to the top of the charts. For nearly a year after *Mousetrapped* was released, it sold only about 100 copies a month. That was in 2010. But when a blogging friend of mine released a 99¢ novel two years later, in 2012, she promptly shifted 30,000 copies of it in just a few weeks. On the other hand, I think the self-publishing market is now awash with new titles and standing out is harder than ever before. Some lament that the "gold rush" is well and truly over. So how can you even begin to estimate how many you'll sell?

Well, you can't. You can only aim for goals. Starting out, I think you should have three different sets of them.

The first should be the number you'll have to sell in order to recoup all of your costs. Let's say you spend $1,000 on editing and a cover design for your book that you then sell for $2.99. If you sell that on the Kindle Store, you'll earn about $2.09 from each sale. That means you'll have to sell 479 copies in order to break even. Let's call that figure our We'll Cry If We Don't Sell This Amount Goal. It doesn't need a time scale, but of course we'd like to reach it as soon as possible.

The second should be a number that is reasonable with a touch of aspiration, an amount that's within our grasp, but that would also make us really happy if we got there. An achievable goal, in other words, but not one that's *too easily* achievable. The parameters of this goal will depend on what kind of book you're self-publishing – you might want to find a similar self-published book and see if you can find out how well it's selling. It should be a nice, round figure, like 1,000, 10,000 or even 50,000 if you're feeling particularly lucky. This should also be the focus of your first year, i.e. the number of books you're aiming to sell within the first 12 months. We'll call this our We'll Crack Open the Champagne When We Sell This Amount Goal.

The third should be your Pinch Me, I'm Dreaming Goal, and I think this should be something *other* than cold, hard sales figures. We need something to daydream about, something to focus on *just in case* we reach that champagne moment and keep on going. What, if it happened to you, would make you feel like all your writing dreams had come true? If we were talking traditional publishing here, this would be the cherry on top of the book-deal cake. For me, it would probably be something like hitting No. 1 in the Irish charts, or appearing on *The Late Late Show* (a long-running talk show here in Ireland; if you're on it, you're deemed to have "made it"!), or having my book optioned for a movie. (We can also call this the Let's Not Admit to Anyone That We've Ever Even *Thought* About These Things, Okay? Goal.)

Here are some ideas for your Pinch Me, I'm Dreaming Goal:

- Get an e-mail from a fan (a *fan*!)
- See your book in a bookstore
- Hit No. 1 in the Kindle bestseller charts for your category

- Catch the attention of a publishing house
- Earn enough from self-publishing to quit the day job

Think about it, pick one and then tuck it away somewhere safe.

Readers of the first edition might be wondering who I am and what I've done with Catherine, the girl who loved to warn self-publishers off daydreams of success. Well, the whole idea of *Self-Printed* is to help you do better than the average self-publisher, and three years ago, when the first edition of this book came out, the numbers that equalled self-publishing success were smaller than they seem to be today. (I suspect this has a lot to do with the KDP Select programme and the increased professionalism of self-publishers, both of which we'll get into later.) The idea of a successful self-published book being one that sells 200 copies in total is about as relevant today as floppy disks; from what I've seen, many self-publishers who release good books and treat their promotion professionally sell more than that in their first month.

So I'm encouraging a *little* dreaming.

Having said all that, I still think a good baseline for all books is 100 books a month to begin with, or 1,200 books in the first year. If you managed that you would have something to be very proud of, but those sales are still achievable (with time and hard work) so you're not setting yourself up for disappointment. If you do sell more, well then, great!

And if you think 100 books a month would be a failure, then please come back out of the Forest of Self-Publishing Delusion. It *would* be a success, and no small achievement. That's 6,000 books in five years, more than most traditionally published books shift in their lifetime.

And remember: we're only talking about the *beginning*. Your sales may start to grow – they might even take off – and if they do, you can readjust your figures.

But let's stick to being (mostly!) realistic for now.

How Does All This Work?

If you know nothing about how self-published e-books and POD (print-on-demand, if you've forgotten already) paperbacks work, let's get a little overview out of the way now.

Hold your questions; there'll be more technical information later, when we're actually producing the books. This is just to give you an *idea* of what will happen.

E-books

For our e-books, we're potentially going to use two services simultaneously, **Amazon's Kindle Direct Publishing** (KDP) and **Smashwords**.

You will need:

- A cover image (just the front and with text big enough to be read in a thumbnail size)
- The book in a MS Word document, formatted to optimise e-book conversion (I'll tell you how) OR
- Money to pay someone else to do the formatting bit for you OR
- Money to pay someone else to turn your book into an e-book for you.

How it works:

1. You sign up for a free account at Amazon KDP and Smashwords
2. You set up a new title, i.e. enter description, price, etc.
3. You format your MS Word interior as per guidelines OR pay someone else to convert it
4. You upload your interior and cover files
5. The site's conversion software converts them into e-books for you if need be
6. You check everything looks okay, and if it does:
7. Your book appears for sale on e-book stores. Hooray!

What does my e-book look like?

Different on every single e-reading device, but fine if you've done the formatting correctly. More on *that* migraine later.

What happens when someone buys my e-book?

Nothing happens to you unless you're obsessively tracking your Amazon sales, in which case you'll probably experience a momentary high. Amazon or Smashwords will take care of everything. They collect the money, allow the customer to download the book to their e-reading device and set aside your profit to pay you later.

At any time you can log on to KDP or Smashwords and see how many copies you've sold. Amazon tends to update these in near enough real time but Smashwords can take months to do it.

How do I get paid?

Amazon KDP pays out royalties once a month by cheque or electronic transfer, depending on where you live. In this payment will be your earnings for the month that ended 60 days previously. Smashwords pays once a quarter by automatically transferring your profits into a PayPal account. You can then either spend them immediately on other people's books at The Book Depository, like I do (damn them for accepting PayPal!), or transfer them into a bank account.

Print-on-Demand (POD) Paperbacks

Paperbacks are a tad more complicated, but still relatively easy to produce. For them, we're going to use CreateSpace, a POD service owned by Amazon which, because I'm lazy, I'm going to call CS a lot from here on in.

You'll need:

- The interior of your book in a PDF file
- The cover of your book in a PDF file
- A credit card with which to pay for the proof copy, usually less than $20 including the cost of shipping it to you

How it works:

1. You register for a free CS account at www.createspace.com
2. You set up a new title, i.e. enter the description, decide on a size, number of pages, price, etc.
3. You take a note of the free International Standard Book Number (ISBN) CS have assigned you
4. You enter the ISBN into your interior file's copyright notice
5. You upload your PDF files
6. You submit your files for review (CS will check the cover is the right size, ISBN is correct, etc.)
7. You order and pay for a proof copy OR check a virtual edition online
8. You check the proof copy when it arrives, if applicable
9. If everything is okay, you approve the proof and the book becomes "Published"
10. If everything isn't okay, you repeat the process until it is
11. Within a few days, the book appears on Amazon.com, Amazon.co.uk, etc.

Part 1: Welcome to Self-Publishing

12. Eventually the book appears on additional online retailers like Barnes & Noble. This could take weeks or even months to happen.

What does my book look like?

Good, if you do it right. CS has a number of different trim sizes you can choose from and paper that's available in cream or white. I've found both their interior and cover printing to be of very high quality and I have to say I'm extremely pleased, overall, with the appearance of the end product. It is not, however, the same as a "properly" printed book and it doesn't wear as well, probably because the cover card is not as thick as it would be on a non-POD book.

I've noticed, for example, that POD books that are handled a lot end up with a front cover that curls back slightly.

But I was very happy with my CS-made books and would even go so far as to say I was surprised at how good they turned out.

Trust me, when it comes to what your book will look like, it isn't CS you have to worry about it. It's *you*.

Your book will not say "CreateSpace" anywhere unless you put it in there, and CS will automatically add a barcode for you.

FYI: If you're holding a paperback right now, it's one that CreateSpace made. So *this* is what it looks like.

What happens when someone buys a copy of my book?

Nothing happens to *you*; you can sit back and relax. Amazon and CS take care of everything for you. If I go online and order a copy of your book, it arrives, brand new and freshly printed, in my mailbox a few days later. Someone else has printed it, packaged it, shipped it and collected the cash. Amazon will then take their cut and give CS the rest, and CS will then take *their* cut (the manufacturing cost) and give *you* the rest.

Whenever a sale is made, you'll also see your sales jump up one on your CS Dashboard, the screen you see whenever you log on to the site.

If you want to order some copies of your book, either to, say, sell at a book launch or just to put on a shelf and gaze at adoringly (the best part of this whole thing, I've found), you can order them yourself at cost price direct from CS.

I should also say here that whenever you publish a book on CS, you automatically get your own "eStore", which is basically a page where anyone can go and buy your book directly from CS. But I'll be explaining later why we don't want *anyone* to do that.

47

How do I get paid?

Similar to KDP, CreateSpace pays once a month by cheque or electronic transfer, depending on where you live. In this payment will be your profits – or "royalties" as they call them, even though strictly speaking they're not – for the calendar month that ended 30 days previously.

Why are you pushing CreateSpace? Aren't there loads of other POD sites?

Yes, there are. Lulu is probably the most popular one. But I'm only talking about using CS for *two* reasons: firstly, this book, as I've already said, is about doing it the way I did; secondly, I looked at both Lulu and CS and even ordered proof copies from both sites so I could compare the quality and, for me, CS won hands down.

Then I compared the cost per unit. Again, CS won hands down. In fact, CS was so much cheaper than Lulu that even when I factored in CS's then astronomical shipping charges, CS was still *half the price* of Lulu. (I e-mailed Lulu about this huge discrepancy and they told me it was due to the "cost of doing business in the Eurozone". Whatever!) So I went with CS.

But if you do want to use someone else, you'll find that the process is broadly the same.

So that's great and all, but what about brick-and-mortar bookstores, eh?

Have a skim back over that section again and tell me, where do you see the phrase "Your book will appear in bookstores"? And the phrase "Your book can be ordered by wholesalers"? And "You should be on *The New York Times* list by Friday"?

I'll save you the bother: *they're not there.*

Your book will not be in bookstores unless you put it there. This will involve you ordering copies of your own book at cost price, getting them shipped to you and then persuading individual stores to take on your book, buying it from you at a discounted price. You will then have to invoice them, wait ages for them to pay you and take back at no cost any books they don't sell, even if they've been completely wrecked by careless browsers. And that's only if you can persuade the stores to take them; most bookstores, especially the larger ones, don't deal with authors on an individual basis because it messes up their accounting. They prefer just to deal with distributors, the link between publishing houses and bookshops. You could try to get a distributor to take on your book, but you'd have to provide them with a significant amount of stock, maybe a couple of thousand copies (which you'd have to pay CS for outright and you can't return *them*), and again, you'd have to be prepared to take them back if they didn't sell. You would also end up losing money because the POD cost per unit price isn't low enough to accommodate both a distributor discount *and* a bookshop discount. Bookstores may *theoretically* be able to order your book into stock directly, but they won't; the wholesale price won't be cheap enough for them and some chain stores don't order in POD books as a rule.

If you do what I describe in this book, you will end up with a paperback for sale on Amazon.com and all other regional Amazon sites (like Amazon.co.uk, which also covers Ireland, and the sites for Germany, Italy, France and Spain and so on.) Your book will also – eventually – appear for sale on sites like Barnes & Noble and The Book Depository. If you publish e-books with Amazon KDP and Smashwords, you will have e-books for sale on all Kindle Stores, the Smashwords website and, if you pass Smashwords's Premium Catalogue test, the likes of Apple's iBooks, Barnes & Noble's Nook e-book store, Kobo and Diesel.

If your eyes are glazing over about now, let me put it like this: by default, **your book will only be for sale online**. And this will be *enough*. So if you harbour notions of seeing your book in the display at your local Waterstones or Barnes & Noble, or even that kooky independent bookstore with the great coffee and comfy armchairs, you're going to have to get it in there yourself.

Do I need to do both an e-book and a paperback?

You certainly don't need to publish both an e-book and a paperback, although in this new digital-publishing world it seems pointless to publish a paperback but not an e-book. Producing only an e-book makes your life as a self-publisher a lot easier, and saves you some money as you won't have to fork out for a proof copy or a full cover design, but then you might lose sales because many readers – myself, ironically, included – still haven't wholly embraced e-books.

For all my books to date, I have released both editions simultaneously, but I think there's something to be said for releasing the e-book *ahead* of the paperback, making the e-book the equivalent of traditional publishing's hardback. This not only spreads the workload out into a more manageable schedule, but it also means that by the time you have to pay for proof copies and larger, more expensive jacket designs, you'll (hopefully) have already earned something from the book that you can reinvest – and if you haven't, you can reconsider the paperback altogether. Most importantly, it provides you with *two* online launch opportunities instead of just one.

However, if this is your first book, I'd recommend going the whole hog, e-book *and* POD paperback, right out of the gate, if only because seeing your name on the grey screen of a Kindle is nowhere *near* as exciting as seeing it on the spine of a book.

A word of warning before you pay a visit to CreateSpace. All the major POD sites and self-publishing services offer additional "author services" and bundle them into packages. The idea is that you hand over a wad of cash and in return they'll take care of things like editing, cover design and making flimsy postcards and bookmarks with a picture of your book on it, which will look terrible because they'll have designed the cover for you. They are, without exception, overpriced. From what I've seen other authors pay thousands and thousands of dollars for, they are also terrible. One self-published author had a cover he'd paid a POD service $1,000 for that my cover designer would use as an example of what *not* to do, and my cover designer charges a fifth of that. My advice: steer well clear of them.

And watch out, because some of the more sinister self-publishing sites arrange advertisements of these packages and services in such a way that you may believe you *have* to pay for them. You don't. The only thing you *have* to pay for to get your paperback for sale online is the price of your proof copy, which generally is less than $20 including shipping.

This book is not about paying through the nose to get someone else to project-manage your self-publishing adventure. It's about producing a high-quality self-published book for the least amount of money possible. This means finding your own editor and cover designer, and paying CreateSpace no money other than the price of your proof copy, shipping fees and your extended distribution plan charge, if you need it.

We're going to keep as much *self* in our self-publishing as possible.

ISBNs 101

In order for your paperback book to be distributed and sold through retail channels, it has to have an International Standard Book Number (ISBN). CreateSpace will give you one for free. Smashwords require ISBNs to be attached to all e-books sold through their Premium Catalogue, e.g. retailers such as Apple's iBooks, Barnes and Noble, etc., but they will also give you one for free. (Amazon KDP don't require ISBNs; they give you one of their own unique identification numbers instead, called ASINs. Also free.) My advice: **take the free ISBNs**. In fact, I'm *telling* you to take them. Self-publishing authors shunning freebies is fine, but when it comes to a free ISBN they always seem to be doing it for the wrong reason.

And it drives me a *tad* insane.

What Is an ISBN?

An ISBN is a 10- or 13-digit numerical identifier that helps catalogue, track and, um, *identify* various editions of books. Although not legally required, in order for your book to be distributed and sold through the same channels as a "properly" published book, you need to have one.

The ISBN appears above and below the barcode in this image.

It will be on the copyright page (because we're going to put it there, and we have to) and above the barcode on the back of your paperback book, which CreateSpace will add for you.

We don't have to put our ISBN anywhere in our e-books, but it will appear on our e-book's listing on sites like iBooks.

Peter Paranoia

An ISBN normally appears alongside the copyright notice, but it has *nothing* to do with ownership. The main purpose of an ISBN is to *identify*, whereas copyright serves to *protect*.

As long as the self-publishing service you use operates a non-exclusive agreement (and it should; all the ones I talk about in this book do), you have nothing to worry about with regards to ownership or your rights to your work. If you take a free ISBN from CreateSpace, they own the ISBN – you can't use it with anyone else – but they do *not* own your work. Same goes for Smashwords.

You can buy your own ISBN, of course, but it *costs money* and is kind of a pain in the arse. And since we're trying to do this for as little money as possible, why spend it on something we can get for free?

I have seen countless self-publishers get their independent knickers in a *right* twist over ISBNs, and while some concern (however unfounded) over the ownership of your work is perfectly natural, being wildly paranoid about scenarios that have about as much chance of transpiring as I do of getting an urge to run a marathon (or anything, or anywhere) is just plain crazy. For example, I recently encountered online an author who is considering self-publishing asking what would happen if she got a movie deal for her novel. Would taking the free ISBN affect that?

(Pause while I take a very deep breath and you brace yourself for the tirade that you suspect is coming.)

Okay, I won't resort to a tirade. (*This* time.) But can we take a minute here to have a glass of sanity juice? I mean, seriously. *Movie deals?* How about we take things one step at a time, sunshine? Stop worrying about whether or not taking a free ISBN will affect your future Universal Studios-movie-rights or NBC sitcom-development-deal contract negotiations and come back and join the rest of us here in the real world, where *we're* selling books.

And again, it's just *a number that identifies your book.*

I can only assume that this ISBN confusion stems from shady vanity publishing houses who get you to sign stuff and then claim that you can't publish your book with anyone else or in any other formats because they own the publishing rights to it now. But CreateSpace and the other services we'll be using are *not like that.* When we take their free ISBN, all we're doing is publishing with them. We're not giving them the rights to *anything.*

(And no, it wouldn't affect it, if you were wondering about your own future movie deal.)

The Publisher of Record

Not all self-publishers who don't want to take the free ISBN are crazy. Some of them don't want to take the ISBN from, let's say, CreateSpace because if they do, CreateSpace will be the publisher of record. I have no problem with CS being my publisher of record; my only concern is selling books, and one doesn't affect the other one bit.

The name "CreateSpace" appeared nowhere on *Mousetrapped* without me putting it there, inside or out. On the very last page was a barcode, the phrase "Made in the USA, Charleston, S.C." and the date on which that particular copy was printed. That was the only evidence of its POD beginnings, and even then you'd have to know what you were looking at to understand what it meant.

CreateSpace is listed as the publisher on *Mousetrapped*'s Amazon listing and other online retailer listings, but so what? When was the last time you looked up a book on Amazon and noticed who'd published it? And "CreateSpace" may be a name that's familiar to you and me, but what proportion of the book-buying public has heard of it? Not a lot, I'd suspect, and even fewer of them know what it is.

The Dishonest Self-Publisher

Maybe you don't want to take the free ISBN because you don't want anyone to know that you've self-published, or at least you don't want to advertise the fact. When I talk about making our book look like a traditionally published book and not like a self-published one, I'm talking about *quality* or the perception of it. We want to fit in with the big boys because they do it right, and because we want to be taken as seriously as they are. We also want to separate our book from the generally held opinion about self-published books, which is that they're bad or sub-standard. I'm not talking about *pretending we haven't self-published*, which is a completely different thing and utterly idiotic, because you'd have to be seriously *stoopid* to fall for it.

Scenario #1 (the most common): the writer buys their own ISBN, registers it to a publisher (themselves) with a name that almost always includes the word "books" or "press". They set up a website and go ahead with the self-publishing process, all the while pretending that they and the publisher are not one and the same, or attempting to give that impression.

Scenario #2 (the half-truth): the writer buys their own ISBN, registers it to a publisher (themselves) and sets off self-publishing. If questioned, they'll say that they've started a new publishing house that wants to specialise in publishing [insert group of writers perceived to be slighted by Evil Big Publishing]. Oh, and it just so happens that the first title they're going to produce is their own book. What a coincidence!

Scenario #3 (illegal): the writer claims they're being published with a major publishing house and attempts (miserably) to make their self-published book look like something that house would produce. I encountered a writer once who had copied the logo of a very well-known publishing house and pasted it onto the spine of her POD book. Um ... *really?*

If you are ashamed or embarrassed about self-publishing your book, if you're convinced people won't want to buy it when they find out it's self-published or you are considering any of the above scenarios, then don't bother self-publishing. Simples.

So what have we learned here? TAKE THE FREE ISBN!

Money Matters

Ah, money. Of all the questions I'm asked about self-publishing, *how much do you have to spend?* and *how much will you make?* are always sitting pretty in the top two spots. You've probably been speed-reading everything else up to now, wondering when I was going to get to this bit, or perhaps you've even skipped straight here from the table of contents. Either way, let's put you out of this misery right now.

And into a different one, because self-publishing – or writing of any kind – is not a get-rich-quick scheme. It's not even a get-slightly-less-poor-slowly scheme. I know it *seems* like it is, as we're presented almost daily with what seems like evidence to the contrary. J. A. Konrath gets monthly royalty cheques with lots of numbers on them; Amanda Hocking made millions on her own and then signed a seven-figure traditional deal; E. L. James is earning more in interest on her bank balance than most people earn in a lifetime of full-time work. That's *three* people we can name who got rich from self-publishing. Can you name any more? I think I can name three more, four if we count one duo as two individual writers. I also know a few people who aren't exactly millionaires but have still got some hefty royalty cheques, so I'll throw them in too. There's about 20 of them. What are we up to now – 27? Let's say 30 just to round it up. And let's pretend that you know 30 *different* writers who got rich by self-publishing. That makes it 60. And just to make it really fair, to make sure we're not rounding down at all, let's call it 100. Between the two of us, we know of 100 writers who have either got stinking rich or made a lot of money from this self-publishing lark.

One hundred writers.

Smashwords.com has published a couple of hundred thousand self-published books. Amazon doesn't release numbers, but there are over 2,000,000 books in the Kindle Store, and anywhere from 10 to 50 per cent of them could be self-published. Maybe even more. And that's not including e-books self-published through other services, like Barnes & Noble's Pubit or Kobo's Writing Life, or authors who've only self-published in paperback.

My point is that even though it seems like every day there's a new "WRITER SELF-PUBLISHES, BECOMES SICKENINGLY RICH IMMEDIATELY" headline, the number of self-published authors getting sickeningly rich is a very, *very* tiny fraction of the number of self-published authors. *Tiny*, I tell you! Like, not visible to the naked eye. Maybe even only visible to the type of electron microscopes top-secret government laboratories have.

The self-published millionaires are the exceptions to the rule and, as I've said already, it's not helpful to think you'll be one too when the odds are against you. While it's fine to *hope* you're going to strike it rich, *believing* that you will is only going to pave a path to bitter disappointment. Somebody buying your book is a wonderful thing and you should be able to celebrate each purchase, even if it's the only one you had this week. And it's actually *better* if you only make a handful of sales to begin with, because then you can frame your first royalty cheque, like Amanda Hocking did.

Hers was for $15.72.

As for the question *how much do you have to spend?*, it's really more a case of *how much* should *I spend?*

Sadly, the vast majority of would-be self-publishers I encounter do not want to spend any money at all. They have various reasons for this – they don't *have* any money, they don't want to spend money when they're only going to be charging 99¢ for the book, the whole point of doing this self-publishing thing is to make money, so by not spending any, they'll be in the black as soon as they make their first sale, blah, blah, blah. They all have one thing in common: *they shouldn't self-publish.*

Remember when I said that The New Self-Publisher treated self-publishing like a business and assumed the role of a dedicated entrepreneur? Let's return again to the idea that we're opening a coffee shop. Would you attempt it if you didn't have any money at all to invest? Would you say you didn't want to spend money on it because the coffees were only going to be $3.50? Would you say you *weren't* going to spend any money on it because the whole point of opening a coffee shop was to make money and by not spending any, you'll be in the black just as soon as you sell your first latte?

And even if you *would* say all that (God help us ...), do you think *I* would pay *you* anything at all for a cup of coffee served to me in a chipped mug you brought from home and brewed in lukewarm water with half a spoon of the cheapest instant blend, that I was then expected to drink without milk or sugar and in a space with no chairs, tables or countertops? No sane person would. And yet this is what bad self-publishers expect people to do every minute of every day. Just replace coffee with books, and a coffee shop with the Kindle Store.

Your book will soon be a product with a price tag on it, and you'll have a duty to deliver on the promises that product makes. If I was going to spend $3.50 on a latte, I'd expect the shop to be a pleasant place to be, with comfy chairs, nice cups and well-trained, friendly staff, and I'd want the coffee to come from good-quality, freshly ground beans and to be made in a suitable machine. When I spend $15 on a paperback, I want text that's big enough to read, tightly bound pages and an attractive cover. I want it to look like a real book, to match my expectations of what a book should look like. I want to see what I'm used to seeing when I open a book: title pages, page numbers, a standard font. When I spent $5 or $3 or even $1 on an e-book, I want the formatting to be perfect and I want to be able to navigate it like I do all my other e-books. In both cases, I want to be reading text in correct English, with few or no grammar or spelling mistakes.

You *have* to bring your book up to a minimum standard – the standard that's expected of it if you put a price tag on it and sell it as a book. If you don't, asking people to pay $2.99, $1.99 or even a handful of sofa change on your book is just *dishonest*. The reality is that in almost all cases, you'll need someone else's help to make this happen. Someone who's a professional, which by definition means that they won't be helping you for free.

Some self-publishers release a book in which they haven't invested any money in the hope that once sales pick up, they'll be able to use the profits to hire an editor or get a professional cover design or whatever. "I want to see if it'll sell," they say, "before I spend any money on it." This sort of thinking makes my head hurt and my wallet recoil in horror. The counter-arguments are all obvious ones – you have only one chance to make a first impression, so the first release of your book has to be the best version possible; whether or not your book sells as a crappy DIY version is no indication of how well it would sell as a professionally produced great version; you don't deserve to have people spending their hard-earned money on your book when you aren't even willing to invest in it yourself – but the main problem with it is that this book will be a *prototype*. It's an inferior version of the real thing. And would you sell people a prototype of something *other* than a book – a car, for example – in order to fund the finished product, when the prototype doesn't work as well and looks terrible? Of *course* you wouldn't. It's just books' bad luck that you can get a version of your product to market for free. Have a conscience and don't make it your *readers'* bad luck that they fell for it. Don't be a selfish self-publisher.

At the same time, we don't want to spend a fortune. You could sink thousands into a book if you liked. You could commission an original illustration for the cover, hire a typesetter to make the pages of your paperback dazzle and pay someone to convert your e-book for you instead of learning how to format it yourself. But it wouldn't make any business sense. Going back to the coffee shop – yes, I have to have tables and chairs, but having the chairs upholstered by Laura Ashley and the tabletops under Egyptian cotton cloths is overkill.

When it comes to our self-publishing budget, we need to achieve two things:

- Spend what we need to in order to bring our book up to the minimum standard required of it
- Spend as little as possible

I think you need to have a budget of around $1,500/€1,150/£925, which will be almost entirely spent on editing costs and potentially a cover design. We may not ultimately have to spend that much or we may require a few dollars more, but that's a good ballpark, in my opinion. It's also a *fraction* of what traditional publishing houses – the people producing the books that will compete directly with ours – spend getting a title to market, so if you think that's too much, you can probably guess what I'm going to say to you.

(*Don't self-publish*, if it wasn't clear.)

The Price Is Right

There's one other money-related question self-publishers need to ask: *how much should I charge for my book?*

Now, chances are you're not going to like what I have to say about this, but then chances are you're already annoyed with me after the whole "if you can't afford to self-publish, don't" so I'm just going to power through. Think of this like Dr Phil Does Self-Publishing Prices: you may not want to hear it, but you know I'm right. (Or at least *I* know I'm right.) There are only two places in this book where if you ignore what I say, you definitely *won't* be a successful self-publisher. *Pricing* is one of them.

Before we go any further I want you to read these next three sentences aloud: *I cannot expect each individual reader to compensate me for the years of blood, sweat and tears that went into writing this book. The price tag on my book is not a reflection of how much work went into it. I have to look at the big picture and acknowledge that if I insist on being greedy and overcharging people, I won't sell any copies at all.*

Pricing Your Paperback

Let's start with our paperbacks, because pricing our paperbacks is not entirely within our control; we have to cover the manufacturing costs. When it comes to deciding on your price, the most important thing you need to take into consideration is how much similar books that have been traditionally published cost. People will not buy your book if it's significantly more expensive than all the other books in the world. Keep in mind I'm talking about their *recommended retail price*, not how much Tesco (the UK and Ireland equivalent of Walmart) is selling them for, which could be half price. You'll find this printed on the back of the book, near the barcode, but not necessarily on the price tag. (In Ireland, this is about €9.99.) Obviously it will cost you more to produce a book than, say, Penguin Random House, and so some leeway is inevitable. However, I'd always try to stay within at least a euro – or a dollar or a pound – of the standard recommended retail price of similar sized books. Remember that doing this will also help you fit in with your traditionally published counterparts; the fewer "I'm a self-published book!" signals we can give off, the better.

The next thing you need to consider is that in all likelihood paperbacks will not be your main source of income. When I started out on this process I concentrated on my paperback and thought that any e-book sales would just be a bonus, but it's proved to be the other way around. I doubt there's a self-published author in the world making more from POD paperbacks than they are from e-books. If you're going to make money from this, you'll make it from your e-books. So don't fret too much about how much you're getting from paperbacks.

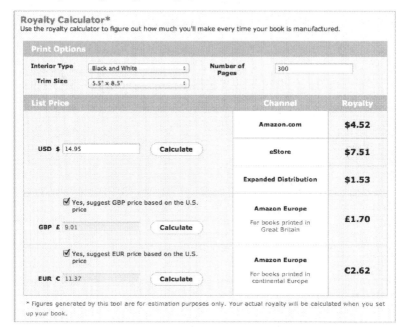

CreateSpace's royalty calculator

Lastly, think about what your aim is here – and then douse it with reality. *Lots* of it. What would be the worst-case scenario? Selling a book that costs *us* money. CS won't let you do that (they have a minimum list price), so that's not going to happen, and hopefully we'll manage to offset any money we spend prepublication with our e-book sales. What's the best case scenario? Turning a profit, making some money. In order to do that, we have to price our books reasonably. What's in the middle? Making more off our books than a traditionally published author would, which we will, as you'll soon see. So if we've satisfied all those requirements, we're doing well.

So let's see first how much it's going to cost you to create your paperback book. CS has a royalty calculator on their website that anyone can access (click on the Distribution and Royalties tab in the Book section on the homepage; see also image on previous page) and it allows you to get a rough cost estimate for your book based on the size and the number of pages. You may not yet know what size you want or how many pages it will be, so let's just use a generic example of a 5.5″ x 8.5″ trim size (the size of *Mousetrapped*), 300 pages (an average paperback) and a list price of $14.95 which is about the cost of the traditionally printed equivalent, give or take a buck or two.

If you did that, you'd get:

- $7.51 from every book sold from your eStore (CS takes $7.44)
- $4.52 from every book sold from Amazon.com (CS and Amazon take $10.43)
- $1.53 from every book sold on other online retailers under Expanded Distribution (CS, the distributor and the retailer take $13.42)

If you charged the British pound equivalent of £9.01 for your book on Amazon.co.uk, you'd earn £1.70 per sale, and if you charged the euro equivalent of €11.37 for your book on other European Amazon sites, each sale would earn you around €2.62.

Now if you're thinking that earning over a third of the list price off every paperback you sell is a bad deal, then clearly you've never had a publishing contract. And you're wrong. It's *great*. If you were traditionally published, the best you could hope for on a paperback is 10 per cent and even the smallest amount we can possibly earn, $1.53 from an Expanded Distribution sale, is more than that. What you need to focus on here is (i) the fact that other than your single proof copy, you don't need to hand over any money upfront, and (ii) the percentage of the list price you're earning rather than just the amount itself. What you're paying for here is the convenience of not having to spend a few thousand bucks on a print run of a few hundred copies that you may or may not sell, and organising things like a printer and a typesetter. Going to a printer yourself might bring the cost per unit down, but it's a far more complicated process and then you'll have the added headache of getting the book for sale on Amazon. Why bother, when in all likelihood your paperback sales will only account for a fraction of your sales overall? Trust me: it's a good deal.

Member Order Calculator

		Per Book	Order Subtotal
Interior Type	Black and Whit ÷		
Trim Size	5.5" x 8.5" ÷		
Number of Pages	300	**$4.45**	**$4.45**
Quantity	1	each	1 copies
	Calculate		

* Figures generated by this tool are for estimation purposes only. Your actual order costs will be calculated when you set up your book. This does not include shipping and handling, which can be calculated below.

Order Shipping Calculator

		Shipping Options		
Quantity	100	$112.99	**Standard**	31 business days
Country	Ireland ÷	$130.99	**Expedited**	20 business days
	Calculate	$145.99	**Priority**	2 business days

* See the rate tables used to calculate shipping and handling.
* Shipping times do not include the printing of your order.

CreateSpace's member order and shipping calculator, shipping to Ireland

You can buy as many copies of your own book from CreateSpace as you like. In our 300-page, 5.5″ x 8.5″ example, each book would cost us $4.45. There's no volume discount; buy one copy for $4.45 or buy a hundred for $445. And then there's shipping on top of that.

Continuing to use the same example, CreateSpace would charge us $43.00 to send us 100 copies of our $4.45-per-unit book to a continental US address. If we were selling those copies on to family and friends at $15 – I've added 5¢ to the list price because who is going to be bothered giving back that amount of change? – we'd be collecting a profit of $10.12 on each book. *($43 to ship 100 books equals 0.43 per book, plus unit price of $4.45 equals a total cost of $4.88; $15 minus $4.88 equals $10.12.)*

Unfortunately things don't look as good for those of us on the other side of the Atlantic. If you're living in the UK or Ireland, for example, CreateSpace will charge you $112.99 to ship 100 copies of your book, and then take up to 31 business days to get them to you. But it's still workable. If family and friends paid us $15 for a copy, we'd collect $9.42 worth of profit each time. *($112.99 to ship 100 books equals $1.13 per book, plus unit price of $4.45 equals a total cost of $5.58; $15 minus $5.58 equals $9.42.)*

I suspect better news for non-US-based CreateSpacers is on the horizon though. When the first edition of this book came out, your book was only guaranteed to appear on Amazon.com, and you had to pay $39 for the chance for it to possibly appear on other sites, including other

Amazons. If it did and you managed to sell a copy, you'd be making less than a couple of dollars off it, because everything but Amazon.com came under Expanded Distribution. But recently, CreateSpace began printing in the UK and Europe as well, guaranteeing free listing on European Amazon sites and increasing the amount of money you earn off sales there. Yet, if you place a personal stock order, it still ships from CreateSpace in South Carolina, which is why the shipping costs are so high and the times so lengthy. The next logical step is to begin printing stock orders in Europe and the UK as well, so fingers crossed.

The cost of shipping copies of your book to yourself is something I see a lot of self-publishers get their knickers in a twist over, and their knicker-twisting perplexes me. How many times are you planning on shipping books to yourself, eh? You'll be sending yourself one proof copy, maybe two if you fail to find all the mistakes first time round, and then you might want to order a box of them for family, friends and a prominent bookshelf. If you decide that you don't like having money all that much and throw yourself a book launch, you might have to order another box for stock. But that's pretty much it and even in the worst-case scenario, we're *still* landing on a profit-margin cushion thicker than the one we have on Amazon.com. So why the fuss about shipping costs? They're just not *that* big of a deal.

And what if Amazon discounts your book? I got an irate e-mail a while back from a blog reader spitting bullets because Amazon had started selling her book at 25 per cent off "without her permission". How much a retailer pays for a book *never changes*. No matter what they charge for it, you still get the agreed amount. Discounts or even price hikes won't affect you one way or the other, except for bringing you more or fewer sales.

I would've thought this was obvious, but let me spell it out just in case it isn't: if you are buying copies of your own book, buy them through CreateSpace's Member Order feature. As in, do not buy them from Amazon or from your CreateSpace e-store, where they'll be on sale for $14.95 or however much you've decided to charge for them. As the author, you can and should buy them at cost price from CreateSpace.

Pricing Your E-book

Now onto **e-books**, where the news is better but perhaps harder to take.

E-book royalties vary but the important ones – Amazon's Kindle Store, Smashwords and the majority of Smashwords' sales channels – offer you around 70 per cent of the list price.

There is some small print to go along with this, i.e. the Amazon 70 per cent royalty rate is only awarded if a customer purchases from their domestic store (i.e. if a UK purchaser buys from Amazon.co.uk); if they live somewhere else, the rate is only 35 per cent (i.e. if a Icelandic customer, who has no region-specific Amazon of their own, buys from Amazon.com). But honestly you'll barely notice this, as most of your sales will be US- and UK-based. (They have been in my experience, and from what I hear from other e-book self-publishers, most of their sales are in the 70 per cent bracket too.) So we're not going to worry too much about the 70/35 per cent thing, and likewise we're not going to worry too much about Smashwords, because most of your sales will be from Amazon's Kindle Direct Platform, or KDP from now on. They just *will*, because Amazon has a much bigger share of the e-book market than anyone else. Apple's iBooks is catching up but for now even people who have iPads seem to be using Kindle's Mac application to read their e-books on them.

(Yes, we'll ultimately upload to *both* services, but when we make decisions about our e-books, we'll focus on their consequences on KDP.)

In order to qualify for that 70 per cent royalty rate, your book has to be priced at *least* $2.99. Basically:

- Charge less than $2.99 or more than $9.99, earn 35 per cent of the price
- Charge between $2.99 and $9.99, earn 70 per cent of the price

My recommendation is that every self-publisher releases their book at $2.99.

You know all those mega-selling e-book authors you've been hearing about, the ones who have to store cash under their mattresses because they've made so damn much of it from selling their self-published work in electronic format? They're all writing fiction and they're all charging less than $5. Most are charging 99¢. You might bristle at selling your book for an amount of money you could probably raise in change that's fallen down the back of your sofa cushions, but this again is where we need to concentrate on the big picture. Charging 99¢ for a book encourages people to take a chance on it because, hey, even if it's the computer-code equivalent of soiled toilet paper, the most they're down is 99¢, and that's *exactly* the kind of thinking you want to take advantage of.

However, if you're reading the e-book edition of this, you didn't pay 99¢ for it (unless I've had a few too many mojitos and logged onto Amazon KDP, or you bought it in a promotion period, or you stole it, you naughty thing) and *Mousetrapped* and its sequel, *Backpacked*, are both priced $2.99 or more. So how come *I'm* not charging 99¢?

Well, there are a couple of factors in there. One is that if you've only one book to sell, charging 99¢ for it isn't exactly going to make a dent in your credit card bill. All those big-selling e-book self-publishers have multiple titles for sale, so unless you do too, I'd aim a little higher, like at

$1.99 or $2.99. The second factor is that I don't *need* to charge 99¢. When I brought out *Mousetrapped* as an e-book, I didn't have a clue how much to charge for it. I also didn't particularly care about how much money I'd make, because I didn't think I'd make any. Remember, I was (stupidly) focused on paperbacks as my main earner. So I set it at $4.99. But as luck would have it, I released it right before Read an E-Book Week, when Smashwords encourages its authors to enrol their books in discount promotions, e.g. 25 per cent off for the duration of the week. I enrolled *Mousetrapped* at 50 per cent off, and so it became about $2.50. Only then did it start to sell. I hadn't sold a single copy at $4.99 but at half that, it was selling steadily. So when the promotion was over, I changed it to $2.99 all over e-book town and it's been selling ever since. So I don't *need* to lower the price, not at the moment anyway. If sales stopped or slowed, I might drop it down to $1.99, and if and when I release another e-book, I might make *Mousetrapped* 99¢ after six months or so. But I don't want to because I don't get 70 per cent unless I price it at $2.99 or more, and I quite like getting $2 every time someone buys my e-book.

My recommendation to you is that you start off at $2.99 and see what happens. If it sells, up it to $3.99 or even $4.99 and see if it's *still* selling at a rate you like. If you aren't shifting many copies at $2.99, drop it to 99¢ for a while. Call it a special promotion or something. I should say here that I do *not* recommend you have your book priced at $2.99 on Monday, $4.99 on Tuesday and 56¢ on Wednesday. That would be Grade A Stoopid, which is my least favourite kind. To really test how well a book is selling at a certain price, you'd want to give it *at least* six weeks, and up to three months, ideally.

Another factor is that although you're setting your price in dollars (because both KDP and Smashwords are based in the US), not everyone is buying it in dollars. For example, *Mousetrapped* is $2.99 but if you see it on Amazon.com's Kindle Store and you live in, say, Ireland, it's actually $3.41. Why? Because in the EU we pay value-added tax (VAT) on e-books (but not print books) at a rate of 21 per cent and Amazon charges [exaggerated eye roll] "international delivery" when you purchase Kindle books outside the US. (Even though they're delivered by way of the internet. Go figure.) Conversely, €4.99 might sound reasonable for an e-book to you but when you convert it into dollars you get nearly $7, or way too much for a self-published e-book.

I will say this, though: I wouldn't be as quick to charge 99¢ for my book as I would've been when the first edition of this book came out. In the past year, while self-publishing has been shedding its stigma, 99¢ books have been collecting it.

Once upon a time, 99¢ was the go-to price for self-published authors – especially authors of fiction – but the tide appears to be turning against such low-priced books. Setting your price so low no longer guarantees sales, if it ever did. Whether or not it's true, having the lowest price tag possible attached to your work sends a message to potential readers that it may only be worth a sum they could make up in change found beneath their sofa cushions. I know it's extremely difficult for us self-published authors to get perspective when we are surrounded by other self-published authors all the livelong internet day, but you have to remember that the vast majority of readers do not read self-published books. You're kidding yourself if you think they do. So our next task, as self-publishers, is to show this group that our books can be as good as the ones they're used to. We must show them that our books are worth their attention. And I don't think 99¢ is the way to do that any more.

Sometimes we also have to consider the other books in our category. This happened to me with *Self-Printed*. I was charging $2.99 for it until I went looking for a reference guide about another subject and noticed that the No. 1 bestseller was $9.99, while the No. 2 was only $1.99. I thought two things: the No. 1 must be a fantastic book if it's so expensive and it's still No. 1, and the No. 2 must be pretty rubbish if it's so cheap and still can't manage to overtake the No. 1. When a book promises to contain valuable information, the price has to go some way to conveying that.

I believe that the less you charge for a book, the less time people spend hemming and hawing over their decision whether or not to click Buy. Therefore if your price tag is 99¢, you're likely to experience what I call the "I'll Give It a Go, I Suppose – and Then Hate It and Shred Your Insides With a Spiteful Amazon Review" factor. They didn't take the time to read the synopsis, or even the other reviews, because what's the worst that could happen? They're only down 99¢. It drives me mad to read one-star reviews that complain about things that either have been (a) covered in the product description, or (b) already highlighted by another reviewer. Why didn't they read that before they bought it? *Because we were charging so little for our work that we encouraged them not to.* $2.99 avoids all the bad associations of 99¢, while still being low enough to encourage readers to give it a chance, and it earns you 70 per cent of the price.

But Catherine, I'm sure at least one of you is saying now, and perhaps in a small voice because you've grown a bit scared of me and my "Make Your E-book Cheap!" ways, *why do I have to charge $2.99 for my e-book when HarperCollins or Little, Brown or Simon & Schuster or whoever is charging $9.99 for theirs? Are you telling me that my book isn't worth as much as theirs is? You won't allow me to stick it to traditional publishing, and yet you seem to be allowing traditional publishing to stick it to me. What's up with that?*

All over the traditional publishing world right now, a fight is going on about how much an e-book should cost. War has all but broken out about it between Amazon and Hachette, with no solution in sight as I type these words. This is partly because readers – and self-published authors, to some extent – have a perception that because there are no manufacturing costs involved in e-books (such as paper, printing, etc.), they should cost a lot less than their print equivalents, while publishers, knowing that things like paper and printing only ever represented a *tiny* percentage of what books were sold for, want to charge a similar price for both e-books and print books. E-book rights were also written into contracts before e-books made anyone any money, and so were put on a par with say, serialisation rights. Now with their market share growing more and more every day, authors are, understandably, thinking they should be paid more for them. Add in the perception that something you can hold in your hands is worth a lot more than something that comes from the internet in computer code, an industry already in flux and traditionally published authors turning to Amazon KDP to release their latest work because Amazon will give them seven times what their publisher would, and you have one fine mess on your hands.

As self-publishers this doesn't really concern us, except for the fact that the longer it goes on, the better it is for us and the more books we'll sell. Why? Because the only opinion that really matters is that of our potential readers and they have shown without question that they think e-books should be cheaper than print books. So if *Eat, Pray, Love* is $9.99 and its paperback is $12, they're not going to buy that e-book. But they've bought a Kindle or a Nook or an iPad, so they still need something to read on it, something they can buy without feeling swindled. Enter *your* book, priced at $2.99.

I'm not suggesting your writing is worth less than Elizabeth Gilbert's. I'm saying that the fact that her work is currently overpriced in the eyes and wallets of most e-book readers is a situation you can take advantage of. (This is why I am flabbergasted that any self-published author has taken the time to defend Amazon in their spat with Hachette. Amazon want Hachette to lower their e-book prices. Don't we want to increase our chances of competing with them? Isn't a low price an advantage our e-books have over traditionally published books? Smashwords conducted a research study in 2012 that showed that books priced at $2.99 sell on average 6.2 times more than books priced over $10. Shouldn't we be trying to *encourage* Hachette to remain at their $10 level? Or have I just been taking crazy pills?)

To summarise, when you decide on an e-book price, it should be:

- Focused on getting readers, not making pots of cash (although getting the first greatly increases your chances of achieving the second)
- Low enough to encourage people to take a chance on your book

- Not so low that people subconsciously get the impression your book is worthless or fail to research it before they buy
- Not lower than it needs to be (test the waters first, then raise or lower accordingly)
- Either $1.99, $2.99, $3.99 or $4.99 (although I'd recommend starting at $2.99)
- The same price on BOTH Amazon KDP and Smashwords (them's the rules)

The good news for you is that if you can be reasonable with your price, and so see the big picture and not just the price tag, you are already head and shoulders above most of your competition, who *can't*. A self-publishing author I met recently told me he was about to charge €20/$27/£17 for his 300-page paperback, or *double* the norm. I mentally rolled my eyes and asked how much his e-book was going to be, thinking that maybe he'd save himself there. But no: his e-book was going to be €9.99/$14/£9. I'd bet money that the reason he was doing this was because he was thinking how much he was going to make off these books on each individual sale, i.e. *if Mary buys a paperback, I get x amount. X? Really? For all that work? I don't think so. Let's double it … instead of, if 1,000 Marys buy that paperback, which they are more likely to do if the price bears some relation to, you know, the price of all the other books in the world, then I'll make X, which is actually quite a nice bit of compensation for all that work.* Best of all, he was telling me this with a condescending tone and a smirk that said, "I'm not silly enough to practically give my book away like you did." When I told him to drop the e-book to 99¢, he actually *laughed* at me, like I was a little child explaining my theory that babies come from storks. What's he doing now? I don't know, but I know what he's *not* doing, and that's selling books. (Ooh, burn!)

If the prices of books reflected their true value, they'd be hundreds of dollars each. Focus instead of getting readers to give your book a chance.

NB: Sales from Smashwords.com earn you on average 85 per cent of the list price, and their retail-partner sales a minimum of 60 per cent.

Designing a Cover

Remember how I said that there were only two places in this book where, if you didn't listen to me, you definitely *wouldn't* be a successful self-publisher? Well, pricing was one of them, and this, *cover design*, is the other.

You can write a bad book. You can write a truly *terrible* book that's also a little offensive. You can publish it chock full of grammar and spelling mistakes, lay it out sideways and do the whole thing in super-large print and upside down. You can call it something boring, do no promotion and claim in your book description that you're the next J. K. Rowling or something equally pompous and annoying. ("My book is the best book I've ever read," for instance.) You can do all these things and *still* sell books. It's unlikely, but it can happen.

But charge too much money for it or wrap it in a stinky cover and you *will not sell books*. Those two mistakes *cannot* be overcome, partly because they are so obvious and the telltale signs of a badly self-published book. Hopefully I've already convinced you that you need to be reasonable in your pricing, so now let me clatter you over the head with my arguments for why you need to have a good cover and why this may make or break your entire self-publishing career.

The good news is that covers are by far the trickiest thing in this whole process so if you can do this right, you're more than halfway to a successful self-publishing adventure.

You will need a "front" cover for your e-book (a JPEG of what would be just the front cover of your paperback, which is all an e-book needs) and a full front, back and spine cover for your paperback (in PDF and sized to specific requirements; more on that later) for your paperback.

We are now entering what I like to call the Bermuda Triangle of self-published cover design, because chances are everything you know about books is about to mysteriously disappear. Writers who've (hopefully) been reading books all their lives who then go on to make their own instantly forget every single thing they know about them. It amazes me on a daily basis how self-published authors create books that look absolutely *nothing* like the books they've been buying, borrowing, reading, stacking, stroking (or is that just me?) and gazing at adoringly for years and then, even *more* amazingly, don't see that they've done anything wrong.

Why does that happen? Well, first we have to consider that seeing your name on the spine of a book and your words running across its bound pages is a *very* exciting thing. I can still recall in minute detail the moment I opened the package from CreateSpace that contained the first proof copy of the finished version of *Mousetrapped*. I practically swooned. Then I danced around the house with it, seeing how it looked in various positions (on this bookshelf, on that bookshelf, etc.) before holding it aloft for others to behold it, *The Lion King* style. Would I have noticed if the text on the cover was too small to read from afar? Or if there was a blurred picture on the front? Or if the book looked absolutely nothing like the books I'd been buying and loving all the years of my life? Put it this way: have you ever heard a mother say her baby was butt-ugly?

So, objectivity is a problem. I mentioned already that your family will be impressed that you managed to type 100,000 words, let alone write them. Similarly, your eyes will tear up at the sight of your words in a bound book, regardless of whether or not that bound book looks like a big stinking pile of badly published poo. This is a landmine that you must work hard to avoid stepping on.

Another problem is that the importance of a good cover design is often underestimated, due to a lack of knowledge, a lack of understanding or a lack of giving a damn. You'll claim that you never buy books because of the cover. You'll claim you can't even recall the cover of the last book you bought. You'll claim that you rise above such marketing nonsense, and go straight for the blurb instead.

Puh-*lease*. Don't be ridiculous. If you don't notice the covers of the books you buy, it's because they're *good*. You would certainly notice if they looked to have been designed and created by a toddler who'd recently eaten something that didn't agree with them. You'd remember them if they stood out from the crowd in the worst possible way. And I've news for you: the cover *does* influence your purchase decision. It can't *not*.

Your cover is a shop window for your book; you want readers to stop in their tracks alongside it and take a moment to take a better look. Ideally, we want them to then come inside and spend some money and, unfortunately, we've very little time to try to make that happen.

If you don't already own a Kindle, buy or borrow one immediately.

(Go on. I'll wait.)

I didn't realise it until I owned one myself, but the purchase

experience is awful. Just *awful*. I have a Kindle Paperwhite so my screen is (fifty?) shades of grey, meaning I see every colour picture in what is essentially black and white. Worse again, I see every book cover in a teeny *tiny* thumbnail size (see image). Only when I click on a listing do I see a slightly larger version, but it's still small and it's still in black and white. Even when I've downloaded the book as a sample to my Kindle, I'm *still* only seeing the cover in a small and colourless version. The cover really has to pull out all the stops to compete in such an environment, while still looking good in full colour on Amazon.com and on Kindle Fire devices and iPads, and in the real world on the covers of our paperbacks.

So how do we do that?

Pick and Stick (to) a Genre

I love writers who claim to have written books that don't belong in any genre. We all need a good laugh from time to time. Tip: if you've written a book, you've written a book that can find a home in an existing genre.

Yes, it may be unlike the majority of books already considered to be in the genre, and/or it may be bending the genre's perceived rules, but it *is* in a genre. If you think it's not, fine, but you must shoehorn it into one or more of them when it comes to selling it. Otherwise you are making things far, far harder for yourself and your book than they need to be.

If your book was stocked in Waterstones or Barnes & Noble, what section would it be in? (And "Authors A–Z" is not allowed, smarty-pants.)

I get why authors don't want to say their book belongs in a genre. We're all just special unique snowflakes – yeah, yeah, I know. But genre isn't about saying that your book is formulaic, or more of the same of something that has gone before. Genre is about telling readers that if they liked *x*, chances are they'll enjoy *y*. This is extremely helpful to your cause if *x* sold five million copies.

People complain about cookie-cutter covers that tag all women's commercial fiction with disembodied legs standing in fields and swirly writing, but those covers are letting readers know that the books inside them are like other books they've loved in the past. And isn't that a great thing, when the books are brand new and by debut writers? Aren't we, as self-published authors, looking to take advantage of every trick in the book we can?

Say it with me, people: *genre is a shortcut to sales.* Whether it happens subconsciously or consciously, pushing your book into a genre and then creating a cover that makes it look at home there is cutting by half the distance between your book on sale and a copy of it sold.

Don't be precious. Be smart. Start by identifying which genre your book belongs in. Keep it as broad as possible, e.g. "crime" is good but "period steampunk erotic thriller" is perhaps overthinking it. Next: research. Go onto the Amazon charts and see what's selling in your chosen genre. Check out the competition. What do their covers look like? Are certain types of covers selling better than others? What types work the best? Pay a visit to your local bookshop and study the New Releases shelves. Are there any new trends in cover design that you can spot? One of my favourite Michael Connelly novels has a background picture of a window, tinged purple, and two lines of text: his name and the name of the novel. It's incredibly simple but incredibly effective too. Look for other examples of such simple covers. The fewer elements, the better. Use this information to form at least a vague notion of what your own cover design will look like.

A word of warning: if you see a Harlan Coben or Karin Slaughter cover that you like where the author's name is bigger than the title, don't do the same thing on yours. Their names are their *brands*. It's what primarily sells their books, before the titles or content. That's why their names are the largest element.

You, on the other hand, have a ways to go yet, so make the title the biggest space-taker on your cover design.

Making a Kindle Cover with Canva

Canva (www.canva.com) is an online design service akin to Photoshop or InDesign. Unlike them, however, it's free and easy to use. Think *InDesign for Budget Conscious Dummies.*

It's incredibly easy and cost-effective to make an e-book cover with Canva. Let me show you how in just a few quick steps.

Step 1: Go to www.canva.com and sign up for a free account. On the page you see when you log in (Your Designs) select Kindle Cover from the slidey option thingy list running across the upper part of your screen.

(Yes, that *is* the technical term …)

Step 2: Select a layout you like from the collection on display on the sidebar.

Step 3: Change the text to your name and title by clicking and typing. If you're happy with it as it is now, skip straight to Step 6. Otherwise:

Select a layout you like and edit the text to your title and name…

… and replace the template's default image if you like (see next step).

Step 4: Search (see the search box in the top left-hand corner?) for an image you like. When you find one, click on it. It will now appear on your existing design. You will probably have to stretch it and send it backwards (i.e. behind the title text and graphic) in order for it to fit nicely onto your cover as a background image. You can also change its appearance by clicking the Filter button.

Step 5: Change the colour of the title graphic too if you like.

Step 6: *Finished!* Click Download or Link in the upper right-hand corner of the screen and then select Image in the new window that appears. Canva

will now present you with a bill for any elements you have used in your design. Generally it's only their images that aren't free, so the bill for my cover – as you can see in the image – was only $1. (Yes, ONE DOLLAR!) I paid it and was instantly able to download my finished e-book cover to my computer, watermark-free. You can see what my finished Canva cover looked like on the next page and although it is called a "Kindle" cover, you can of course use it for other e-book editions too – plus a few other things, but as ever, we'll get to that.

How easy was *that*? Here's my word of warning though: all of Canva's layout options look really professional. Professional, modern and attractive. So if you're going to use Canva to make your e-book cover, best not to fiddle with it *too* much. The ideal amount of fiddling is enough to make it *not* recognisable as a Canva template but not so much that it doesn't look at all like a Canva design, if you know what I mean.

I think we should all make a Canva Kindle cover at this stage in our self-publishing operation. Even if it's not going to be your final cover design, having something this simple and swanky to represent your upcoming book in the meantime will prove *very* useful.

It's also kind of exciting, isn't it?

Look, there's *our book*!

Using KDP or CreateSpace's Cover Creator

Don't.

I'd leave it there, but I suppose you want to know *why*, right? Ugh. All right then ...

Both KDP and CreateSpace offer Cover Creator software where, during the upload process, you have the chance to fashion a cover by essentially picking a template and inserting your own text, etc. It's free to use too. But while it might sound just like making a cover with Canva, in reality it's far from it. The templates bear little resemblance to actual books, and what you can change within them is extremely limited.

For instance, with Canva I can move the text around. I can actually move around anything I want. With KDP's and CreateSpace's templates, I can only *replace or amend* text. No moving around allowed. There's also a preponderance of borders, which are not typically a feature of the covers of real, live books, hinting – or confirming – that yours is self-published.

In short, I have never been impressed by a cover that these Cover Creator programs have created. They all give themselves away as being rigid, limited templates. Avoid them if you can.

Hiring a Graphic Designer

If you can afford to, the best way to get a cover that works is to hire someone who knows how to make one for you. If you plan on publishing a paperback and you can't use or afford programs like InDesign, you'll probably have to.

Don't baulk; I initially didn't want to do this either. I thought that, first of all, finding a cover designer would be a right pain in the arse. And if I did find one, I assumed that getting a cover professionally designed would cost thousands and eat into any profit I might make from selling the book. Luckily I was *totally* wrong on both counts.

Cover designers are easier to find than you think. The best way to find them is to look on successful self-published authors' blogs or in their books (if you like the look of their covers, of course!) and find out who did it for them. Then contact them for a quote. This is ideal because you know they've worked with self-published authors before and you can see actual examples of their work. (If you like *my* covers and want to use my cover designer, his contact details are at the back of this book.)

Joel Friedlander, otherwise known as The Book Designer (www.thebookdesigner.com) runs the monthly E-book Cover Design Awards, and this is a great place to source *your* cover designer. Because Joel publishes all the entries, good and bad, it's also a great place to research what's working and what's not, as he offers his professional feedback on the unsuccessful entries. You can also enter your own cover once it's done and maybe even win some publicity for your book.

Get several quotes before deciding on who to go with and don't tell any of them what the others have offered you. Make sure that a specific number of design rounds is included in the price. This is how many times the design can go back and forth between the designer and the author before incurring extra charges; if this isn't specified, you could end up making the designer do ten different designs or, conversely, he or she could refuse to give you anything but one go. You should also agree in advance whether or not any stock images that have to be purchased are included in the price, or if they're extra.

A *good* cover designer will then prepare a design brief based on questions they've asked you about your book, or you might even prepare one yourself with all your ideas, book covers you like, a synopsis of the subject matter, etc. Have a browse around the internet – Pinterest.com would be a great starting point – for any images that take your fancy, and copy and paste them into a Word document. They don't have to be literal interpretations of your book. It might just be a picture that reminds you of your book, or reminds you of how you feel when you read it. If I was doing this for *Mousetrapped*, for example, there'd be loads of pictures of beaches, sunshine and fireworks, even though only one of those things appears on the actual cover. Think of it less like instructions and more like your book's mood board.

Price-wise, there's huge variation. My guy, Andrew Brown of Design for Writers, has e-book-only packages starting from €200 (about $262 or £160). You can see a selection of the covers he's provided for self-published authors on his Facebook page, facebook.com/designforwriters. Every time I pay it a visit I'm newly impressed by his most recent projects.

How do either of you know what shape and size the cover needs to be? Thankfully, *you* don't need to worry. Once you've decided on your trim size and page count, you can plug the details into CS and they will generate a cover template for you that's already perfectly sized. You send this to your cover designer and they build your cover inside it. CS will automatically add a barcode; make sure your designer knows this so they don't put anything in that area. But we'll talk more about the specifics of this when we come to actually making our POD paperback.

And please, self-publishing people – *pretty please* – step away from the easel and put down the water-colours. While you're at it, lose the oils, the crayons and the Magic Markers.

I get why you think that creating your own cover image is a good idea – it'll be unique and you own the rights to it – but do you get that it's really, *really* not (unless it's for a children's book or a book about water-colours)?

The goal here is to produce a POD book that looks like a real book, one that will be at home on your bookshelves among the traditionally published books, and to date every self-published book I've seen with a water-colour picture on the front has no hope of doing that. Also, look at your shelves! Look at the books on them. What's on their front covers? They're called *photographs*.

(There are, of course, exceptions. Some books on my shelves have illustrations or cartoons on their covers, and they work really well. But they have been done by professional illustrators, cartoonists or graphic designers. Not by you and a paint-by-numbers set.)

Finally, I'll leave you with this thought: covers are important to books, but they are the *most important thing* about self-published books.

If I walk into a Waterstones and see the latest Michael Connelly novel, I'm going to buy it because I know he's a bestselling author (so lots of other people think he's good), he's traditionally published (so an agent and an editor think he's good) and because he's my favourite author (so *I* think he's good). His covers don't really matter to me.

And even if you walked in there and you had no idea who he was or what he'd written previously, you wouldn't have to rely on the cover as evidence that the book is likely to be of good quality.

But what if the same book was self-published? What if it had *just* been self-published, and hadn't yet sold many copies or got many reviews? What if you're looking at it on a shelf, and so you can't see the blurb? What is the *one thing* that is available to you to help you decide whether or not that book is any good?

If you haven't guessed by now, it's the cover.

Make sure you get it right.

How Long Will All This Take?

One self-publisher scolded me for not putting the fact that you should hire a cover designer right up front, like on page one, in a previous edition, because it transpired that my cover designer had a three-month waiting list and this self-publisher felt that he'd wasted precious time reading the rest of my book when he could've been getting himself higher up on my cover designer's waiting list.

Er …

I sincerely hope you're not planning to self-publish this weekend. I presume that you are doing your research well in advance, or incorporating all this into the book you plan to release next, a few months down the line. Because there's no rush. When you rush, you cut corners, and once the book is out there, you can't take it back. So take a deep breath and calm down. Maybe make your next cup of coffee a green tea instead.

This self-publishing business is going to *take time*. I think three months is the minimum – and that's going forward from the point where our manuscript has been rewritten to the point of homicidal rage, copy-edited and proofread. As you'll see in the next part of this book, you need those three months to build anticipation about your title online. Releasing the book is actually one of the *last* things you'll do. If it's already been the first, you may have missed your opportunity to do this thing right.

Going back yet again to our coffee shop, would you open one this weekend? *Could* you? Or would you take some time instead to research, plan and consider everything that will be involved? Which option do you think would work out better in the long run?

Take a breath. *Relax.* And whatever you do …

Don't Mention the War

I don't want to devote much time or space to the whole traditional publishing versus self-publishing, us versus them, The People versus The Man "debate" so I'll just say this: it is all *completely irrelevant*.

When it was announced that J. K. Rowling was going to sell Harry Potter e-books through her own site, Pottermore, self-publishing evangelists couldn't get their "NOW EVEN J. K. ROWLING IS SELF-PUBLISHING!" flags printed fast enough, completely missing the point that Rowling became the world's only billionaire author through a *traditional* publishing deal, and that if she sets up a lemonade stand outside her house and sells handwritten stories on Post-It notes, it doesn't matter to us – it has *no relevance* whatsoever to the average self-published author. Same goes for Beyoncé releasing her "visual album" through iTunes a week before the physical CD was available from stores. It's *Beyoncé*, for fudge sake, a woman who has been recording, releasing and selling records in the "traditional" way for more than 15 years. She's arguably the world's biggest entertainer; what she does has practically zero relevance to the teenage girl just starting out who likes to sing in the shower and hopes to perform in front of thousands one day.

You don't need to "pick a side" in order to self-publish and you'll be a better self-publisher if, instead of shouting your mouth off about how publishing companies are wrong about everything, you spend your time, say, writing better books. And despite the sensationalist headlines, let's not forget that right now, most books sold in the world are:

• Print books

- Purchased from bookstores
- Published by mainstream, traditional publishing houses

Even when we hear things like "e-book sales overtake hardback sales for the first time", that's not a win for self-publishing; it's a win for *e-books*. I think sometimes we self-publishers forget that the two aren't one and the same.

In this book – and in my life and hopefully in yours too – there will be no "Down with Big Publishing!" chants, literary agent-shaped voodoo dolls or rants about nobody even giving my novel about My Little Ponies come to life a proper chance. Yes, sometimes the traditional publishing industry prints a few million copies of a book that isn't as entertaining as the instructions for our microwave oven, but clinging on to that as evidence of the beginning of their end is like being a lunar-landing conspiracy theorist who goes on about the shadows in the photos taken on the moon, and ignores the 400,000-plus people employed by the Apollo program who would have had to keep the world's largest secret for going on 60 years.

Another popular anti-traditional-publishing argument is that they're only interested in making money. *What?* A business is only interested in making the money it needs to keep paying its rent, its employees and the factories that print its products? Surely you're not serious! Of *course* they're interested in making money. So am I. And if *you're* not, then what is this all about? Because self-publishing is a business too, and if you just want to chuck money down a toilet, go chuck money down a toilet.

If you insist on calling yourself an "indie author", then I presume you'll be pressing your own paper, binding your books together with thread and selling them door-to-door? Because the only other option is to rely on one of the largest corporations in the world – Amazon – to publish and sell your books, and some of the largest banks in the world to process your royalty payments. Sorry, but that doesn't sound very *independent* to me.

I'm not self-publishing because I want to beat some kind of revolutionary drum, and I hope you're not either. Because what does it have to do with books? What does it have to do with wanting to be an author? If you really love writing and want it to be your career, then you need to be *making* connections, not burning them away with an ill-informed acid tongue. And do you really think anyone who buys a copy of your book even thinks about what "side" of the so-called war you're on? Do you really think they even *know* there's such a thing? Do you think they *care*?

I'm not a self-publishing evangelist and I don't think you should waste your time being one either.

Even if you disagree with everything I've just said, I'm sure you *can* agree that debating the issue is, at this point, a massive waste of time. And that with an already busy self-publishing schedule, we don't have any time to spare ...

* * *

And so concludes the bit where I try to prepare you for your new career as a successful self-published author, replacing any fanciful ideas you may have had about what lies ahead with cold, hard realistic facts and (hopefully) convincing you that the only way to do this is to do it *right*, i.e. professionally.

What's next? Now it's time to lay the foundations of our online homes, the virtual places from where, later on, we'll do almost all of our promotional activities and through which we'll meet the people who'll be among the first to buy our book.

If you already *have* a functioning blog, Twitter account and Facebook fan page or public profile (as opposed to your personal one where you drunkenly post photos of yourself on holidays) then most of Part 2 will not be news to you, but do stick around anyway. You never know, you might pick up a few new tips or tricks.

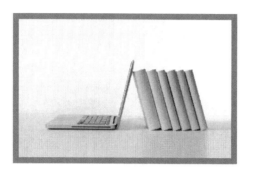

PART 2
Building an Online Platform

Here Comes the Science Bit

(Is "the science bit" too outdated a reference? You know I'm talking about those old L'Oréal shampoo ads, right? Where some gorgeous girl swings her hair while talking about shiny and glossy and weightlessness, and then she frowns and says, "Here comes the science bit!" and a male voice steps in to patiently explain the *why* of the shiny and the glossy and the weightlessness, mostly using made up words, the implication being that women only care about shiny hair and not the stuff in the shampoo that makes it shiny? Well, if you didn't, now you do.)

Here's what's going to happen now: I'm going to tell you how to do all the techie bits of self-publishing: building an online platform, publishing an e-book, publishing a POD paperback. But it'll be later, in the part about *selling* self-published books, that I'll be able to tell you what we're going to *do* with them.

I have a theory about how to sell self-published books. It involves using blogging, Twitter and Facebook to build up a group of supporters, our "first readers", who will then buy our book when it comes out, pushing our book out of the shadows on Amazon and into the light where other people can see it, leading to more sales, and to reviews, which lead to more sales. We'll keep the momentum going by regularly adding new, valuable content to the internet that will both grow our author platform and get people interested in buying our book, and we'll build a fan base using a mailing-list service so that when our *next* book comes out, we have an added booster rocket to get things going.

But I can't go into too much detail about it at this stage, because you may not have a blog. You may not have a Twitter account, or you may have one but not know how to use it right.

And, crucially, you don't yet know how to self-publish your books, or how long it'll take to publish them, and if you've been reading this book straight through without stopping, you might also have forgotten your own name because I've bombarded you with so much stuff that your brain is flashing "Error: Insufficient disk memory to complete this task."

So I'm going to tell you all that stuff first and save the Big Theory of Everything Self-Publishing for later, when you're familiar with all the key players. Think of it like learning how to play the guitar: you start with the individual chords, so that later we can put a few of them together and play a song. This section is about how to **create and maintain a blog, build a mailing list, use Twitter** and **create a Facebook fan page**. In other words, the basic foundations of an author's online platform.

What we're going to *do* with these things in order to sell our books will come a bit later on.

The "What Are You Trying to Achieve Here?" Speech

So I'm about to start telling you how I think you should blog, tweet and use Facebook. This will involve me saying things like, "Don't ask for more Twitter followers", "Don't blog about how your boyfriend just dumped you" and "Don't poke me or anyone else on Facebook", and you saying things like "Don't be such a party pooper!", "I can blog about whatever the hell I want!" and "But I LIKE poking people!"

Let's get something clear right here, right now. I am not here to tell you how to blog, tweet or use Facebook to entertain yourself, connect with friends or become a champion poker player. If those are your goals, you're right: you can do whatever the hell you want. What I'm telling you is how to do it *and sell books* and yes, party pooper or not, this will involve curtailing your poking, because in a professional arena, poking is not only *un*professional but also *extremely bloody annoying*. I'm not trying to put a stop to your fun, or prevent you from talking about your loser boyfriend with your Twitter friends, or implying that blogging about quilting isn't worthwhile. All I'm doing is telling you what works for me as both a writer and a reader, and trying to help you to sell your book.

So hold off on the angry "But a blog is SUPPOSED to be personal!" and "But what's the point of Twitter if you don't TALK to people?" e-mails. For the moment, anyway. At least wait until the end of the book to see if there's anything you can be *really* annoyed about.

Chances are, I will also tell you not to do things that some of you are already doing, and then you will take this personally and imagine that I've been reading your blog and that that's where I got the idea to tell everyone else not to do it from. (Rest assured that even when I seem to be talking about specific people, I have in fact drawn on details from several people and/or changed all identifying details, in order to avoid this very event. Except for that bit where I was talking about *you*.) You might argue with me in your head something along the lines of, "Well, *I* do that and I have loads of followers" or "I actually *prefer* bloggers who do that" and in doing so, you'll be missing the point.

For instance, I'm going to say that those chain-letter style blogger awards (Most Pink Blogger and the like) bestowed upon bloggers by other bloggers, who are then obligated to bestow it upon a specified number of other bloggers, have no place on the blog of a professional writer, or a writer who is trying to look professional. Now, I've received a number of these, and maybe you even sent me one, and if you did you'll have seen that while I appreciated the acknowledgement, I never put another link in the chain and I certainly never put the little MS Paint "award" image in my sidebar. Do I think if you do this you'll never sell a single book or make a living as a writer? No. But do *I* do it? No. And what is the whole point of this book? Telling you how *I* did what I did.

If things are going really badly, you might also get the impression that I want to drain all of the fun out of your blogging, tweeting and Facebooking and make it a clinical, dry and boring experience. Nothing could be further from the truth. I don't do anything that isn't fun for me – or at least, I don't do it for very long (see *dieting* for more examples of this) – and I certainly wouldn't have ploughed so much time into this if I didn't enjoy it. I truly love blogging, I have some fantastic Twitter friends (some of whom have even become friends in real life) and whenever Facebook isn't threatening to sell my home address to the highest bidder, I like Facebook too. I have a *great time* with social media. It's enriched my life. But I use it without doing things like asking for more Twitter followers, blogging about the terrible date I had last night or virtually poking you, and I find it works better that way.

What's with the Be Professional Thing?

Why do you need to act like a professional? Why can't you smear your emotional crap all over the place? Why can't you do whatever it takes to get to a nice round number of Twitter followers? Why can't you virtually poke me in the eye, especially when after reading this far, you really, *really* want to?

You Have Something to Prove

Self-publishers, in the eyes of the discerning reader, start off fairly low on the book ladder. In fact for some, we're not even *on* the ladder. The ladder is leaning against a house and we're across the street and five doors down from it. Before the discerning reader will give our book a chance, we have to convince him or her that we have the potential to be just as good as anything the top-selling, most heavily lauded, international-superstar authors have to offer, and that just because we're associated with a group known for bad quality doesn't necessarily mean that we've gone down that road as well.

How can we do that? By sending *I'm-not-crap* signals at every opportunity. On the book, this is the cover. On our Amazon listing, this is the product description. And online, this is how much our blog looks like the website of a professional author, maybe even one who has someone else to make and maintain their website for them, i.e. a website manager.

(The dream!) When you're a self-published author, everything you do online is a reflection of the quality of your book. *Everything*. Because even when no one is watching, Google is.

The More ... the Merrier?

When you first start blogging, you feel like it's just you and the screen. Then a few people leave comments, and you feel like it's just you and them. Even though you know, intellectually, that whatever you type on those posts is entering the public domain, it doesn't feel like it at the time. Even when your site stats say a couple of thousand people are visiting your blog on a regular basis, it still feels like a little group of friends, gathered together over a coffee every morning, chatting about quilts or whatever. It's nice. It's intimate. It's *safe*.

It's only when something from the real world pierces the bubble of your blogosphere that you realise how many people can, potentially, read your every blogged thought, and who some of those people might be. Maybe you write a post about how your family don't believe in you, and then Aunty Joanne brings it up at your cousin's wedding. Maybe you tell people the name of the resort you're going to on holidays and, while you're there, someone comes up to you by the pool and says, "Are you the Quilting Queen of the Universe? I read your blog!" Or maybe you bitch about how your boss is clearly a devoted disciple of Satan, and then the next day you get fired. Not to get all serious and sinister, but a lot worse can happen too.

Your social media presence requires your personality, but it shouldn't include your personal life. The easiest way to ensure that we keep one but exclude the other is to behave ourselves, and act the same way a professional writer – who knows, right from the outset, that lots of people, including reporters, agents and editors, are reading his/her every word – would.

We've all heard the advice "dress for the job you want, not the job you have", right? The same applies to your online presence. Even if today you are unpublished, unknown and (for now) just talking to yourself, act online like you are already a bestselling author.

A Few Words About Being Nice

Another great rule in life, treat others as you would like them to treat you, is especially important in social media. You'll only get out of it as much as you put in, and that isn't confined to blogging on a regular basis or always responding to any comments your posts may get. I'm talking about *outside* of your blog, or *outside* of your own Twitter profile. Always be nice, kind and generous. Hopefully this will lead to people being nice, kind and generous to you.

When author Talli Roland (*The Hating Game*) started building her blog following a year before her book came out, she knew how important it would be to read other blogs and comment on the posts. In fact, whenever someone left a comment on her blog she would make a point of reciprocating. In the beginning she was visiting an average of *70 blogs a day*! Now that's dedication, and it paid off: *The Hating Game* was an Amazon bestseller on the day of its release.

A Few Words About Being Genuine

As I'll be explaining – and hopefully *proving* – in more detail later, I believe that the best chance of self-published success is a promotional strategy that involves an online platform, i.e. a blog, a Twitter account that sends traffic to it and a Facebook page that taps into already assembled groups of potential readers. It's the only *free* way to do it that I know of.

I also believe that the best way to maintain that success and to enjoy the fruits of it is to have a direct connection with your readers through the same tools, and that blogging, tweeting and using Facebook is *fun*. (*Way too much fun, sometimes*.)

With so much of our time spent online these days, author platforms are becoming increasingly important, especially in the traditional publishing world where marketing budgets are being cut and competition for review space is fiercer than ever.

That's why, every now and then, a traditionally published author who has previously shied away from every internet-related activity except e-mail and booking cheap flights feels forced to sign up for Twitter and steps, blinking, into your stream with something like, "Erm, my new book, *I Don't Want To Be Here and Resent The Fact That I Feel I Have To*, is out on July 18. So ... buy it?"

There are also certain books and seminars out there encouraging writers to abuse online platforms, i.e. write specific types of blog posts and send tweets worded in a specific way to hoodwink readers into connecting with them and their books. This is just plain dishonest and manipulative. Social media is all about making a connection, and that connection *has* to be genuine. Please don't do this if you don't want to. Don't do it just because I said you should. Now, I'll be honest with you: I don't know how you can do this without an online platform.

But I *do* know that it definitely won't work if your heart isn't in it. The rest of us will be able to tell.

The Internet = Real Life

You will be fine so long as you don't do anything on the internet you wouldn't do in real life.

I'm disturbed and dumbfounded on a near daily basis by the behaviour of people online. On the innocent-but-annoying end of the spectrum, you have the scourge that is The Praise Repeater. This person constantly tweets nice things other people have said about their work until their Twitter stream becomes variations of "ANOTHER 5-star review for my novel, *Are You Unfollowing Me Yet?* [insert link no one will click]" On the other, more sinister end of things, you have The Creep who turns innocent content, e.g. details gleaned from my profile photo, into e-mails that make me want to take a shower, e.g. "My dearest Catherine, your husband must be so proud of you and your success." (Eh, what? I don't have a ... Oh, wait. I get it. You saw the ring on my finger in the profile photo on my blog, didn't realise that it was taken using Mac's Photo Booth program and so is flipped around, and you thought the ring I wear on my right ring finger was in fact on my left, and so was a wedding ring. And then you time-travelled back to the Fifties when pat-on-the-head-for-you-little-girl, chauvinistic statements like "Your husband must be proud of you" were all the rage. *Ugh.*) In the middle you have the people who left their manners behind them when they came to sit at their desks or swipe their phone's screen – the ones who, despite having never talked to you before or interacted with you in any way, demand help without so much as a please or a thank you.

I used to think that the internet merely brought out the crazies, but after meeting people in real life who I first came to know online – and coming to know online people who I first met in real life – I know now that the truth is different. Sometimes people just behave completely differently online. With a screen in the way, they engage in behaviour they *never* would back in the 3-D world.

There's an author I've met a few times in real life who, in person, is perfectly lovely. She's sweet and pleasant and she can crack a joke. But her Twitter account is the stuff of nightmares. Tweet after tweet *after tweet* about how wonderful her book is according to other people. Nothing else: just repeated praise. Why would anyone follow that? What would be in it for them? And why does she do it, when in real life she's too humble and self-effacing to ever even mention such a thing? I just can't figure it out.

Here's a tip: the people who succeed at social media do so because they are being genuine. That means being yourself at all times. Don't do anything online that you wouldn't do in real life.

Privacy Issues

Back when I was living in Florida I came home to Ireland for a visit to find that the family PC had about fifteen new icons on the desktop. Turns out that in my absence, my parents had hired some cowboy to come and "spring clean" the computer to speed it up and he'd managed to convince them to pay him to install a whole host of anti-virus, anti-malware and anti-spyware software. My parents, not knowing enough to realise that the best way to avoid viruses was to refrain from clicking on things called "happy.exe" and the like, readily agreed, and now our PC was so clogged with anti-virus programs (there must have been upwards of ten things just auto-running at start-up) you couldn't use the internet anyway, as you'd have to wait half an hour for every page to pass their anti-virus scan and load. That was a few years ago now, and these days the Really Scary Thing about the internet has become privacy, or lack thereof. But while invasion of privacy is a genuine concern online, chances are you're worried about the wrong *kind* of invasion of privacy. And all you need to do to avoid this kind is to exercise some common sense.

If I write a Facebook status that I think will only be seen by my Facebook friends and Facebook dump it out into the internet at large, allowing Google to catalogue it so that it shows up in their search results, that is an invasion of privacy. That is something to *actually* be worried about. (Although whenever Facebook does something like this behind its users' backs, the beady-eyed among us get all angry and riled up, and they get it sorted for the rest of us. So we don't *really* need to worry about it.) But someone getting your credit card details because you've signed up for Twitter? Publishing your home address online because you've got a WordPress blog? Finding out about all those knitting books you bought from Amazon through your Facebook fan page? Um … *no*. Those are things we don't need to worry about, unless we're stupid enough to, say, post our home address in the About Me section of our blog.

I often hear social-media-phobes say things like, "I know I should have a blog, but I don't want one. I don't want people reading every little thing about me" or "I'd sign up for a Facebook page, but I don't want everyone knowing where I am all the time." The eye-rolling I then indulge in – behind their backs, because I'm a coward who hates confrontation – is nobody's business. *You* control what goes on your blog. *You* control what you tweet. *You* control what goes on your Facebook fan page and it won't be connected in any way to your personal Facebook profile if you don't want it to be.

Don't do a Hollywood actor on it and say that you're only "interested in the art". You'll *have* to be interested in something other than the art if the art doesn't pay any money, and people can't go to see movies (or buy books) if they don't know they exist, so you're just going to have to go tell them about it.

Don't Be Scared

I know from experience that telling authors they need to use social media to help sell their books usually brings on heart palpitations and sweaty palms. How in the heck are you supposed to use the Twitter machine and the Facebook thingy to convince people to read your book? The only thing in your life that ever goes viral is the sniffles in your house during flu season. And *blogging*? How can there *possibly* be a connection between people reading your recipe for cookies-in-a-cup and then going to Amazon to shell out $3 on a copy of your book?

First of all, take a deep breath.

Second of all, I'm going to let you in on a little secret.

Today, social media is a great way to sell books. It's the best way for self-published authors who don't have access to, say, bottomless pits of cash or traditional media, for the most part. But guess what? It's nothing new. The thing that sells books today is the same thing that has always sold books: *word of mouth.*

All the novels you see sitting pretty atop the bestseller charts have one thing – at least – in common: they're the kind of books people talk about. The kind you read, you love and then implore your friends to read too so you can meet up to discuss the ending or just bask in the warm and fuzzy feeling you have for the characters. The kind that the bookseller enthusiastically recommends to you while you wander around the store looking for the 3 in your 3 for 2. (I weep for 3 for 2. Waterstones customers will know what I'm talking about.) The kind of book you buy extra copies of to give away as presents. Word of mouth is the fuel in the engine of what sells books.

Selling books with social media is not anything new, strange or startling. All it's done is moved the word of mouth process online and multiplied the numbers. A few years ago if I loved a book, I might tell four or five people, i.e. my book-loving real-life friends. Now I might tweet about it to more than 4,000 people, gush about it on Goodreads to more than 600 virtual book-loving friends and champion it on my blog which goes out to more than 14,000 subscribers.

That's what we're talking about here. That's *all* we're talking about. People finding out our book exists, caring about it enough to buy it and read it, and then liking it enough it to recommend it to their friends. Doesn't that sound perfectly doable?

Don't be scared by terms like "social media", "viral marketing" or "SEO", or be put off by self-designated "social media experts" (disclaimer:

I have been called this by other people, but I would never claim to be one myself) who will pull out chart after graph after chart that definitively prove that 17.03 GMT is *the* best time to tweet. DRAMATIC EYE ROLL. Who the hell cares about crap like that? *We* certainly don't. We're just out to sell books, and sell them by a method that's been proven to work: word of mouth.

So let's get going.

Blogging

The blog is where it all starts. This is the main hub of your online platform, the place where people can come to find out more about you, to hear more from you or, let's be honest, satisfy their curiosity about what you look like. It's one big advertisement for you as a writer, and a snapshot of your personality in HTML.

Why start a blog? Because blogging is so much FUN. You get to tell people what you think about things and they can't interrupt you. It doesn't cost anything but your time, if that; I write most of my blog posts while simultaneously watching TV. (True story: I'm writing the first draft of these very words with one eye on a late night showing of *Jackie Brown*.) The true magic of blogging is that you have no idea of the fantastic places it'll take you – new friends, free stuff, bestseller lists, speaking engagements, VIP events – but rest assured, it *will* take you somewhere.

The Best Things in Blogging Are Free

Don't pay for anyone to design, host (store) or maintain your blog, website or blogsite (a term I'll explain in a second) – at least now, here at the beginning. You don't need to and the less money you spend, the more of your profit you get to keep.

Right now I have a WordPress blog that also acts as my website. (See? A *blogsite*.) It's adorable. I love it, everybody else loves it too and it's all free.

The blog is free, the space online for the blog is free and the theme (the design or the template) is free too.

The only thing I pay for is called a customised URL upgrade, and it costs about $17 a year per blog. This allows me to take the free URL that came with the site (www.catherineryanhoward.wordpress.com) and change it to something I want (www.catherineryanhoward.com). You don't even have to do this, but I recommend that you do. I'll explain why and how later on.

Blogger.com is free too, but I think in most cases it looks it. I recommend that you use WordPress. You may find it a bit tricky to use in the beginning especially if you've been using Blogger.com, but stick with it because it is so worth it. I have never seen a Blogger.com blog that looks as good as a WP one can.

(You might hear people talking about WordPress.com versus WordPress.org. "Org" is the self-hosted version of WP; you use their software but you pay for your blog. We're going to stick with WordPress.com, the free version.)

The Benefits of a Practice Run

The best way to figure out how to use social media effectively is to start *using it*, as you'll quickly get an intuitive sense of what works and what doesn't. We all make mistakes right out of the gate, and there's a wealth of articles online called things like "10 Things I Wish I'd Known When I Started Blogging" because the top bloggers learned everything they know on the job. Still, you might not want to make all your rookie mistakes on the blog you've just worked incredibly hard to get thousands of people to visit, which is why it's best to have a bit of a practice run in semi-private first.

I started Catherine, Caffeinated on 1 February 2010, but I started The Scribbler in September 2009. You can still go have a look at it now, if you like (www.cathryanhoward.blogspot.com) but before you all run off, I've already deleted the most embarrassing bits. So there. A list of things that were wrong with it includes but isn't limited to: a name that implied this was a hobby, an unattractive colour and design, mismatched widgets, no focus, no regular schedule. Luckily no one was reading it except for real-life friends I forced to on pain of death or being forced to watch my Floridian memories DVD *again*, and one teenage boy who seemed oddly obsessed with me. So even though I was doing the blogging equivalent of flailing about in the water and screeching "I can't swim!" (fun fact: I actually *can't* swim), only a couple of people were around to see it and thankfully none of them had smartphones.

Crucially, it was only after I started The Scribbler that I started reading other people's blogs, something I *insist* you do before starting your own. You wouldn't attempt to write a book without reading as many as you could first, right? The same goes for blogs. Sign up for something like Feedly (www.feedly.com) which enables you to subscribe to as many blogs as you'd like and then delivers their new posts to one convenient place – your Feedly account – each day. (This is the only way I can read blogs; visiting them all individually would be a nightmare and *so* time-consuming.)

When I knew I'd be self-publishing *Mousetrapped* and thus raising my own blogging stakes, I decided to take everything I'd learned from reading other people's blogs and having no one read my own, and move to WordPress.com where I'd start a new, free and very pink blog, Catherine, Caffeinated:

Today that blogsite is the hub of all my online activities. It's where people come if they want to find out more about me, find out more about my books, sign up to my newsletter, contact me and/or read my blog posts, current or past. And it costs me next to nothing, as you'll see in a minute.

Books and blogs have another thing in common. Just as you should write the book you want to read (but don't see on the shelves), you should create the blog you want to read (but can't find on the internet). That's exactly what I did with my blog, and I think that's largely why it's been so successful. So try to imagine the kind of blog you'd like to read. What would it look like? What would the tone be? What topics would it cover? Then think about how *you* can create that blog.

With regards to separate websites and blogs, I don't believe in them. Many authors have static websites, where not much changes on a weekly or even monthly basis, and then entirely separate blogs. I think they should be together, in one spot. (Or at least *look* like they are.) I don't want to go to the trouble of looking up an author online, finding their blog and then having to make yet another hop onto their website. And if someone does land on our website, why wouldn't we entice them to read some of our latest musings by having them right there? Attention spans are getting shorter; we have to do what we can as *quick* as we can to keep browsers interested.

Make things easy for your visitors and yourself: have everything together, in the one place.

Get Yourself a Blog

Signing up for a free WordPress blog is easy and can be done in less than a minute. Simply go to **www.wordpress.com**, click the Sign up Now button and on the page that appears, fill in:

- Your desired blog address. This should be your writing name, e.g. catherineryanhoward. As soon as you type it in, WP will run a check to see if it's available. If it's not, try putting the word "writer" after it, or stick in a middle initial. We're going to upgrade this once our blog is up and running, so we'll be changing it eventually anyway.
- Your username. Keep this the same as what you've entered in the box above. When you comment on someone else's WP blog, this is the name that will appear, so it's not a good idea to have that saying something totally unconnected to your own blog, like "angelwings1980" for example.
- A password.
- An e-mail address.

After you click Submit you'll be brought to a second page that tells you to go check your e-mail. It also prompts you to fill in some profile information, but we're going to leave this for now. Instead, go to your e-mail account where there should be an activation message from WordPress waiting for you. Click on the link in it.

Then, congratulations! You now have a free WordPress blog. Go back to WordPress.com and log in to it. At the very top of your screen you'll see a black bar that begins with the WP logo (a "W" in a circle). Next to it should be the name of your blog. If you move your cursor until it's over it, a menu should appear. Click Dashboard.

You are now on your WordPress Dashboard, the nerve centre of your blog. If this is the first time you've seen it, a yellow box will be prompting you to watch an introductory video, read tutorials, etc. But we don't want an overload of information, so look for the Hide This link in the bottom right-hand corner.

You will now be looking at your Dashboard as you'll normally see it every time you log in. This is your blog's mission control. It's here we'll return to whenever we want to do something to our blog over the rest of this section.

What's in a Name?

Unless you're already a household name, you're going to need a name for your blog. Consider that most people find new blogs to read in lists of recommended blogs on other people's blogs ("blog rolls") that look like this:

Blogs I Like:

John Smith's Blog
Jane Murphy
Claire Richardson's Musings
The Blog of Edward May

Now I may be looking for new blogs to read but I don't have the time to click into all those links to see what those blogs are about, or if they're the kind of thing I'd like to read. But imagine if the blog roll looked like this:

Blogs I Like:

Girls Who Love To Read
Help! I Need a Publisher
The Rejectionist
Pimp My Novel
Organic Growing Pains

How much more inclined would you be to click on those blogs? They're already sinking their blogging teeth into you with their clever and pithy names, telling you that they're exactly what you need and have been looking for. So give your blog a name, something short and sweet, and either informative (How Publishing Really Works) or funny and cute (High Heels and Book Deals). You can even incorporate your own name if you like (Catherine, Caffeinated) or award yourself a subtitle (Coffee and Roses: Life as an Eternal Optimist). This really is a shortcut to lots of blog readers, because most people *don't* do it. They just call their blog after themselves, e.g. Mary Smith's Blog. BOR-ing!

And While We're on the Subject of Names ...

I have a confession to make: my name isn't Catherine Ryan Howard.

It's actually just Catherine Howard, but I added in *Ryan*, my mother's maiden name, because there's another Catherine Howard, and she gets a *lot* of Google search results.

Catherine Howard was the fifth wife of Henry VIII of England, and if you google "Catherine Howard" you get over 1,000,000 results. I haven't checked, but I'm fairly certain that if I do pop up anywhere, it's so many pages down that anyone looking for me and not her would give up long before they got to it. Google "Catherine Ryan Howard", however, and you get me, me and more me. The top results are all links to my blog.

If you have a very common name or you share your name with someone famous, seriously consider changing it or adding something in. Even an extra initial might do the job. Whatever you do you need to make absolutely sure that if someone knows your name, all they have to do to find you is enter that name into Google – and by "find you" I mean find *you* (and not another author with a similar name) through a link on the first page of returned results (before they give up out of frustration). You *must* make Google your friend so that people who are interested in you and/or your books can find you as quickly and as painlessly as possible.

This is why I despair when I see authors – traditionally published authors, I might add, whose publishing houses should know better – recycling titles, using titles already used for movies, famous song lyrics or even other books, e.g. *Some Like it Hot*. This is a bit silly in the Google Age, but it's downright stupid when the movie or book they're borrowing from is infinitely more famous than theirs, and has been around for a long, long time, thus allowing years and years of Google friendliness (links, pathways, etc.) to build up. It also makes it difficult for potential readers to locate the title online, because Amazon sells music and DVDs as well as books. For traditionally published authors, however, this isn't that big of a deal. They're also in bookstores. There'll be plenty of other chances for us to find out about their books.

But for self-published authors, we're *only* online. If someone has just the title of our book and Google doesn't help them find us, they may never encounter a mention of us again. Just something to think about before you name your book and your blog – and yourself.

Getting a Customised URL

WordPress offers you the opportunity to take the free URL they gave you when you first signed up (that has the word "WordPress" in it, e.g.

www.catherineryanhoward.wordpress.com) and upgrade it to a customised URL that can say anything you want, provided it is available.

I strongly recommend that you do this, and that the URL you upgrade to is www.yourfullname.com, where the name is the same as the one you're going to put on your books. Why?

- Let's be honest: having your own domain name feels good, doesn't it? It's like having a little home of your own on the magical interweb
- It's easier for people to remember a yourname.com address
- It fits better on a business card, the back of your book, a poster, an advertisement for your "using social media to sell books" workshop and on the forearm of someone who loves your blog so much they want to get its URL tattooed on their body
- Having a .com address is more – what's that thing, again? – oh, yeah: PROFESSIONAL!

This way, if someone googles the hilarious name of your blog, they find your blog. If they google your name, they find your blog. And if you meet them in the street and tell them your blog address, they'll remember enough of it to find your blog when they get home.

Upgrade to a Customised URL

To upgrade to a customised URL, go to your WP Dashboard and look for Store → My Domains on the menu on the left-hand side of your screen. Click on it. On the new page that appears you will see a big blue button that says "Register a New Domain Name", and – yes, you've guessed it – you're going to click that too.

Now you'll be asked what domain you'd like for your blog and there'll be a box for you to type it in. Click on Go when you're done so that WP can check if that domain name is available. If it's not you'll just have to try again. When you're happy, click Register Now.

Please, please, *please*: stick to a domain that ends in dot com. Don't be getting any fanciful notions.

All that's left to do is fill in your personal information and pay the fees: $18 a year for the domain name alone, or $26 for the domain name plus privacy protection.

What's privacy protection all about? The domain registry, i.e. who owns what URLs, is a public one. If you subscribe to a service like Who.is, you can look up the real people behind the websites you see online. This is supposed to facilitate the purchasing of domains. For instance let's say I had a very savvy premonition and registered www.twitter.com a decade before Jack Dorsey and co. founded the social network we all know and love today. If they'd still wanted to use Twitter.com, they'd have had to come to me and make me an offer for it. (It's a great way to make money if you got in early. The biggest domain sale ever was for Insurance.com: over $35 million back in 2010.) In order to do that they'd have had to contact me first – and they'd have had to make sure they were dealing with the actual owner of the domain and not some con-artist who just said he was. Hence the publicly accessible domain registry. But you don't have to appear in it and for an extra $8, WP will make it so.

Once you've purchased your domain, wait a minute or two for it to kick in. In my experience, it'll go live almost immediately and at most, it'll take five minutes. If you'd rather manually renew this domain when it expires in a year, you can click the Disable Auto Renew button now. Don't worry – WP will send you plenty of reminders! Then change your primary domain to the one you've just purchased (i.e. check the box next to your new domain, leaving the button next to your old one empty) and click Update Primary Domain.

NB: The $18 price is broken down into registration and mapping. Registration is, not surprisingly, the registration of your new domain name to you. Mapping basically means redirecting. If you already own your own domain, you can just purchase the mapping service from WP. Prices are correct at time of writing and are of course subject to change.

Say No to Rainbows: Your Blog's Appearance

Now for something a bit more fun: picking a theme for your blog and then making it look pretty. Professional-looking themes are WP's strong point and you'll have plenty of them to choose from. But we have three requirements for our theme that are non-negotiable:

- We need a customisable header (we need to be able to insert our own picture at the top)
- We need a theme that is readable (no navy blue text on a slightly lighter navy blue background)
- We need a theme that allows us to put "Pages" (i.e. sections) across the top or down the side

If you've ever visited my blog, you'll know that it's colour coordinated to within an inch of its virtual life. (And if you've ever seen my house at Christmas or received something gift-wrapped from me, then this will come as no surprise.) This isn't just me being anally retentive; I'm pushing what my free WP blog can do to the max. Visitors might not be able to say exactly why, but they'll leave my blog thinking, *well, doesn't that look nice?* (Or perhaps, *why does that blog look like something you drink when you're nauseous?* But let's hope it's the first one.) If you had a website designed by a professional website designer, do you think he or she would give you a red background, purple text and a blue header? Of course not. They'd give you a site whose elements match, coordinate or complement each other. So because we're aiming for that same professionalism, we're going to make ours match as well.

The easiest way to do this is to find a header photo that not only reflects the content of your blog, but also matches the colour scheme, e.g. the pink typewriter. (You can find these on the same stock photo websites you went to looking for cover images. Or take one of your own.) I also got really lucky, in that WP happened to have a free theme ("Bueno") whose header was in the same font (Impact) as the title on the cover of *Mousetrapped.* Yes, you can imagine how much *that* discovery satisfied my coordination-loving soul. Many WP themes even enable you to change the colours of the theme; try to pick one that does. Then you can *really* take your colour coordination to the max.

If colour coordination isn't your thing, I couldn't give a monkeys. Don't fall into *The House Doctor* mentality where you think that just because *you* love your Barbie-pink kitchen units, every potential buyer coming to your open house will too. Aim for *cohesiveness.*

It's also worth remembering that blogs aren't set in stone. Play around with them. Change them up until you're happy.

Customising Your WP Blog: Title, Theme and Header

First things first: if you haven't already given your blog a snazzy name and tagline, here's how. On the Dashboard, scroll down the left-hand side menu until you come to Settings → General. Click it. On this page you can add the title of your blog (e.g. Catherine, Caffeinated) and a short tagline that gives the reader some idea of what it's about or who you are (e.g. "Writer, astronaut, skinny: Catherine Ryan Howard wouldn't mind being any of those things …"). You should also set the blog to your local time zone so that when you schedule a blog post for 9 a.m. on Tuesday, it posts when it's 9 a.m. on Tuesday wherever in the world you are.

When you signed up for your blog you were assigned the default theme by, um, default. Now you can go back to your Dashboard menu and find Appearance → Themes. Click it. You will now be on the WP Manage Themes page. Browse the themes to find the one you like best for your blog. (I actually hate looking at this page because they add new themes all the time and I'm always SO tempted to change my site up with a new one. But no, I must resist!) When you find one you like, click Activate.

For the purposes of these instructions we're going to activate the "Sketch" theme and use it to make a blogsite for a Disney World fanatic. Once we do, a dialogue box will appear inviting us to customise our new blog. Say yes! On a blue menu running down the right-hand side of your new screen, you'll see options that include Colors, Header and Site Title. We'll work from here.

Tip: do you see the little black rectangle with little icons in it at the bottom centre of your screen? That's a nifty little tool that enables you to preview what your blog will look like on different screens: a desktop PC or laptop, a tablet such as an iPad and the small, narrow screen of a smartphone. These days everyone accesses the internet from all these devices, so while I would focus primarily on what your blog "really" looks like – i.e. the desktop PC or laptop screen view – it's important that everything is readable on the other screens too.

Start with the **header**. This is where you select and upload your own photo to serve as your (colour-coordinated) header photo, i.e. the picture that runs across the top of your screen. I recommend picking something that (a) looks good – full colour, high resolution, etc., (b) has something to do with the topic of your blog and (c) has a predominant colour in it that you can then match in your blog's background. Once you've upload and cropped the picture and it's proudly strutting across the top of your homepage, go to the **colour** section and make the background a complimentary shade.

Close this "Customize" screen by clicking the X in the bottom right-hand corner. You will now be returned to your blog's homepage with that black bar running across the top of the screen. Select "[Your blog name] → Dashboard to get back to Mission Control.

Creating Sidebars, Footers & Widgets

Depending on the theme you've chosen, you may have a space called a **sidebar** running down one or both sides of your blog and possibly a **footer** running along the bottom as well. These are spaces for **widgets**.

Have you seen *Office Space*? In this *very* close to the bone comedy about 9-to-5-induced despair, Jennifer Aniston plays a waitress at a TGI Fridays-style establishment where, in addition to her uniform, she is expected to wear a number of pieces of "flair" – shiny little pins and buttons, the kind you see Hard Rock Café staff and Disney World Cast Members wear and sometimes swap with guests. Widgets are your blog's pieces of flair and when it comes to them, you should make like Jennifer Aniston's *Office Space* character: stick to the minimum required. Use too much of them and your blog will soon be an all-singing, all-dancing, disco-light-flashing eyesore that looks like the Las Vegas Strip and a website from 1996 made a baby. Does that sound like it could be the blog of a professional writer? Me thinks not.

Each widget has its own functionality. For example, I might have a *countdown widget* that fits neatly into my sidebar, into which I have entered (behind the scenes) an important time and date, e.g. the date my book will be released. It will then count down to that date without any further input from me. Or I might install an *image widget*, where I can permanently display a picture to one side of my blog. I can *embed a custom URL* in it too, which means that if someone clicks on that picture, they're taken to the internet location of my choice, e.g. a book cover that links to my Amazon listing.

To add widgets to your blog, go to your Dashboard and click Appearance → Widgets left-hand menu. Then it's just a matter of drag-and-drop.

Each widget will ask you to fill in some information, or choose settings. I'm just going to go through the main ones I think you should have, but what you need will of course depend on your blog and preferences:

Twitter widget. Will automatically show your five most recent tweets. Just enter your Twitter username and check the box that says "hide replies." Click Save.

Facebook "Like" box. Displays your Facebook page and enables "liking" to take place right there and then, i.e. on your blog.

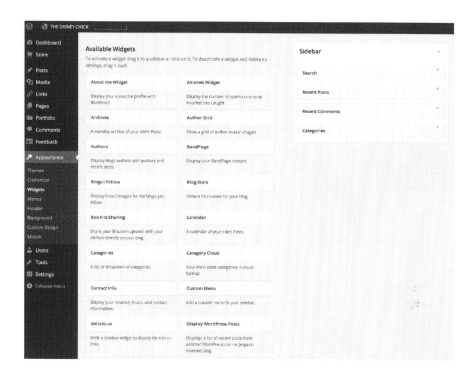

The "Sketch" theme only allows widgets to be displayed in the sidebar, which is the pale box you can see to the right. To the left are the available widgets. To add one, I simply drag it and drop it into the "Sidebar" area. Were a footer available too, it would be displayed into another pale box below the "Sidebar" one.

Blog subscriptions. Add this widget so that readers, should they be so inclined, can click the Sign Me Up! button and receive new posts by you in their inbox.

Text widget. Use one each for your comment policy, disclaimer if applicable and copyright notice. These should go in the footer if your theme has one, otherwise the sidebar will do. (More on these in a minute.) You might also use this for a welcome message at the top of your sidebar.

An image widget. Slightly complicated because you have to upload the image first and then link to it in the widget. To upload the image, select Media → Add New from your Dashboard menu. Follow the instructions on screen to upload a new image and copy and paste the link where the image will be stored. Then paste this link into the image widget where it says "Image URL". You can resize it to fit by altering the width and height, and just below that you'll see a place to enter the link you'd like to take your blog reader to when they click on the image. If you want it to fit in nicely with an existing image in your sidebar, go into *that* image's widget first to check what the size is, e.g. 200 x 300.

A link widget. Again, you have to save the links (choose Links in the Dashboard menu) and then select which ones you want to display. This link widget is what you use for your blog roll, or list of recommended blogs.

Milestone. A countdown to a special day and time – perfect for upcoming book-release dates.

WP doesn't allow most "outside" widgets; you can only display those on offer from your WP Dashboard. I think that's a great thing.

"Outside" widgets – or widgets designed by third parties – invariably look messy. They're hard to size and they don't match. The font, colours and style will be all off because they won't have been designed with a WP blog in mind, let alone your WP blog and chosen theme, font, etc. I detest them. I also think that if you fill your sidebar with them, you're creating the impression that you're an amateur. A couple is okay, but I've been on blogs where there are so many different widgets of all shapes, colours and sizes (and some of them are flashing on and off as well), that it looks like something you'd see on the back of your eyelids after someone punches you in the head.

And yes, to answer your question, I was one of those children who wouldn't allow baby-sized dolls into Barbie games because they weren't the right size. They just WEREN'T THE RIGHT SIZE, okay?!

The Small Print

To protect yourself and your blog, make sure you have all the small print you and your blog require. You can insert these into your sidebar or footer by using *text widgets*. You'll need:

A copyright notice. It should be obvious that stuff you write belongs to you and that if someone else copies and pastes it into an e-book they're charging $9.99 for, it's stealing (although not very profitable stealing, as you and I both know that $9.99 e-books don't sell). Just because something's on the internet does not mean that it's free for anyone to use. But just to make sure, put a copyright notice at the bottom of your page. NOT at the bottom of individual blog posts, mind you, because that will make you look like a bit of a tool. One at the bottom of the site itself is sufficient.

Mine reads:

I've never, to my knowledge, had a problem with this, but it doesn't hurt to put it up there. And guess what else it does? You got it in one: it makes you look *professional*!

A comment policy. This is like a nightclub reserving the right to refuse admission to very drunk and/or aggressive people. On your blog, it's you reserving the right not to publish (or to delete) comments left on your blog by pissy people. I can't say I've had much problem with this, but I do know some bloggers who have had terrible trouble with people who have nothing better to do with their time than verbally abuse people they don't even know, about subjects they either know nothing about or are taking WAY too seriously. Mine reads:

So here's the thing: this is my site. It's not a democracy. Neither is it a place where we discuss The Big Issues of the World Today. Every post is written with a wink; that's why it takes me so long to write them. Therefore if you insist on leaving abusive or annoying comments, I will delete them, because I can. Please note I am also not free advertising for your crappy and/or spammy site, nor am I host to comments run through a translation program and/or written in Adolscnt Txt Msg Englsh. Do NOT put links in your comments unless they are relevant. Even if your book is great and your business is reputable, please don't use my site to advertise them. I reserve the right to remove any links. First-time commenters (or is it commentators?) are moderated. Keep it short – we're already spending too long on the internet as it is. Now, how do the rest of you take your coffee?

My blog is light-hearted, so you wouldn't expect there to be much cause to assert this right – and there isn't. But it *has* happened. And why should you be forced to publish a comment written by someone who is (a) obviously a tad deranged and (b) being abusive towards you? You don't have to *at all*, but it helps to have a bit of a warning about it. Then if they come back a second time to spit idiot bullets about you preventing free speech (DRAMATIC EYE ROLL), you can point them to your comment policy and tell them it wasn't like they weren't warned.

Just to give you an idea of a time when you might need your comment policy, let me tell you a little story. I once wrote a book review about a non-fiction title that detailed a famous crime. The prime suspect committed suicide before his trial could begin, and there are as many people who think he was innocent as there are think he was guilty. Crucially, the FBI and other investigating authorities are in the latter group. Shortly after I posted my review, a man who had never before commented on my blog stopped by to leave a comment accusing *the author* of the book of the crime, and then went on to list "evidence" of his guilt. He was clearly (i) unhinged and (ii) either had a personal beef with the author or was a friend of the prime suspect. Whatever his story, he had no right to accuse innocent people of murder on my blog, so I deleted his comment and then posted a comment of my own saying something like, "[Crazy man]: your most recent comment has been deleted. This is a book review and not a discussion about who committed the crime. See my comment policy below for more information."

A disclosure. If you review products on your blog that you've received for free, are paid by any outside party to blog about specific topics or you are connected with a company or brand in some way that may appear on your blog from time to time, tell people that upfront. If they find out later, trust is broken and your readers will no longer believe anything you say. For instance, let's say you're a mummy blogger who is always recommending a certain brand of nappies (diapers). Your readers love you, believe everything you say and so rush out and buy this brand you're championing. But then it emerges that the company who makes them keeps you in stock of them for free; that puts your blog posts in a whole new light – and not a good one. Be honest from the start. I don't have anything like this on my blog, so I don't have a disclosure. I *do* receive free books to review, and at the end of the review I usually put something like "Thanks to [publisher] for my copy", both to thank the publishers and to alert the reader to the fact that I got it for free.

Creating Pages In WP

A blogsite, as I've said already, is a free blog that masquerades as a website, or a website that incorporates a blog. Ours is going to be a little bit of both.

A blog is an online journal that's updated regularly. You log on, find a pretty picture (a *header*) going across the top of the page, the blog posts themselves taking up most of the space below, with the newest one on top, and a column (*sidebar*) of links, pictures and potentially weird flashy things (*widgets*) going down the right-hand side. This type of thing is fine if you're sharing your adventures in quilting, but if you want to sell books, you're going to need something a tad more sophisticated, or what I call a *blogsite*. What makes a blog a blogsite? One word, people: **pages**.

On Catherine, Caffeinated, you can see my pages running across the top, just below the title and just above my header picture. (See image on the next page.) They are *About Me*, *My Books*, *Self-Publishing*, *Videos*,

Newsletter and *Contact Me* and each one represents a sub-section of my blog where blog posts are *not* displayed. They're static pages that don't change unless I amend them, and they enable us to create extensive, comprehensive online homes for us and our work.

Make sure you choose a WP theme that allows you to display your pages across the top or at the very least, down the side. You want readers to be able to instantly access them without having to go looking.

What pages or sections should you have? This will vary depending on what you decide to blog about, but as a professional writer, aspiring or otherwise, you should always have:

- An "About" page where you write a little bit about yourself, i.e. an author bio and your author photo
- A "Books" page listing all your available books and detailed information about where to buy them
- A "Contact" page. WP allows you to insert a form really easily that will ask people to fill in their name, website, e-mail and whatever else you specify and then hit Submit to e-mail you. You *must* have a Contact page; you never know who will be trying to get in contact with you, and so saying something like "hey, tweet me @thisistotallyunprofessional" isn't going to cut the mustard. You MUST provide an option for people to contact you confidentially

To make pages or sections in your WP blog, go to Pages in your left-hand-side Dashboard menu and click Add New. Whatever title you give your page is what will be displayed across the top of your homepage, so keep it short. You may have to edit their names to ensure they all fit across the screen in ONE neat row. I'm insisting on this. Because please, FOR THE LOVE OF FUDGE people – PLEASE! – do *not* do this:

I CAN'T EVEN LOOK DIRECTLY AT IT. Would a web designer return a homepage to you that looks like that? Only if he or she didn't want to get paid. Maybe I'm a bit OCD about this, but landing on a blog or website that has an overhanging menu like that makes me come out in hives. I'm definitely not sticking around to read it.

When you're about to publish your pages, on the right-hand side you'll see a box with a zero in it labelled "Order". This lets you change what order your pages appear in across the top of your page. When you're done, click Publish.

To insert a contact form, click the last icon in the row of icons after Upload/Insert just above your formatting bar.

You can also create a *hierarchy* of pages. Let's say you have a "Writing" page/section, but you want to split that further into a page/section for each of your two books. Create a new page for each of them, but before you click Publish, select Writing as the "parent page" in the drop-down menu to the right of the screen.

We make our blogsites pretty and well-organised for the same reason we format our manuscript perfectly before submitting it to an agent or an editor: because *we don't want to distract from the content.*

Creating a Customised Menu in WP

I've described above how, by using WP's Pages feature and organising the pages into a certain order, you can create a nice spread of links to sub-sections across the top of your blogsite. But what if you want to put something in that spread that links to something else, something that isn't part of your blogsite? Can you do that? How? WP offers a great feature called *a customised menu*.

You'll find it by going to Appearance → Menus and then clicking Create a New Menu. What you're essentially doing is overriding the spread of links you've just created with one you can create with a lot more freedom. The links on this menu can link to anything, including the pages you've just made and other websites.

NB: Set your newly created menu to "primary navigation" and don't forget to click Save!

In my main menu I use this feature (i.e. having an option on my menu link to anything I like) to create a Newsletter link, which links directly to the sign-up form for my Mail Chimp mailing list but you could also use it to link directly to Twitter, Facebook or Amazon.

I think it's very important to have some kind of mailing list/newsletter sign-up somewhere on your blogsite. Nine years ago I was twenty-three, and most people I knew had a Bebo page. *A what page?* you say. A Bebo page. It was a precursor to Facebook that, for some reason no one has ever quite been able to pinpoint, took off in Ireland quicker than a new way to eat potatoes.

Not long after that, everyone I knew had a Myspace page. When I started blogging, people were desperate for Google Wave invites and the people who *had* them were treated like demigods. Now no one remembers Bebo, no one cares about Myspace and Google Wave has been shut down. So who's to say where the likes of Twitter and Facebook will be a few years down the line? My guess would be still around, but you never know. So what if you devote all your time to building up an impressive and engaged following on Twitter, only for it all to disappear a bit further down the road? What happens to your 50,000 followers then? How do you let them know that you'll still be writing books, and that as luck would have it there's a new one out soon? The only thing we can really rely on to be around forever is *e-mail*. Therefore it's important to establish a mailing list, and to establish it early on.

Sign up for Mail Chimp (www.mailchimp.com), a free service that enables you to build a mailing list and then send newsletters and other announcements out to the people on that list whenever you like. Here you can create a new mailing list and design a sign-up form so people can join it. Mail Chimp's design features are a little tricky to use, I find, but they have "auto-design" wizards that make it a bit easier.

Your sign-up form will have a unique link – put this link in your customised menu so that when people click Newsletter on your blogsite's menu, they're brought straight to your personal sign-up page.

A word or 50 on mailing list etiquette: it's illegal to send people mass e-mails from mailing lists they haven't signed up for. You can't sign anyone else up for your Mail Chimp mailing list – they have to do it themselves, and then confirm their subscription by verifying a link in a subsequent e-mail. Avoid harassing or pushing people into signing up for it. They will if they want to. If they don't want to, they're not going to read it anyway. You also *cannot* collect e-mail addresses and then send out messages to them about your book or anything else manually. That's still spam, *extremely* annoying and 100 per cent guaranteed not to get you anywhere except the top of the Naughty List.

The Author Photo

There is one thing you're going to need across *all* social media platforms and that's a profile picture. Here on your blog, you're going to put it on your "About Me" page. And what am I going to say about this? Yes, you've guessed it: make it a *professional* one.

If you can afford it get one taken, but that's not quite what I mean. I have never had photos taken; every one I've ever had on any of my sites has been taken with the tiny little camera above my Mac's screen. What I'm getting at is don't use that picture of you drunk and making an obscene hand gesture that was taken in Ibiza when you were 21, sunburnt and three (or thirteen) sheets to the wind – unless, of course, that's what your book and blog are about.

A good profile picture is usually a close-up of you; better yet if it's just your head and shoulders. Try and take it against a blank background, or at least one that doesn't interfere with your pretty face.

For maximum Catherine Brownie Points, wear something that coordinates with the colour scheme of your blog. You look ahhmazing, daahling.

Tip: I would avoid using book covers because they change and have little impact in the tiny sizes things like Twitter profile pictures display in.

Keep everything the same and keep everything the same on all your social media accounts.

As ever, Catherine says cohesiveness is best.

Comment Moderation

All free blogging platforms allow you to moderate comments that are left on your blog posts, i.e. hold them for publication until you have a chance to read and okay them. There are several schools of thought on what's the best way to do this, and I can see pros and cons to them all.

You can either (a) not moderate comments; all comments are published except those identified as spam which are held for checking, (b) moderate first-time commentators; the first time someone leaves a comment, you must approve, but if that's approved, all their future comments will be published immediately, or (c) moderate all comments no matter what.

I moderate all comments. As in, every comment must be manually approved by me before it's published. This may sound time-consuming but (a) how many comments do you really think you're going to get? and (b) download the free WP app to your smartphone and do it while you're waiting in queues, stuck in traffic, killing time during the commercial breaks in *X-Factor*, etc.

To change your comment moderation settings in WP, go to Settings and then Discussion. You can then choose the actions you want taken – or not – whenever someone leaves a comment on one of your blog posts. You can also change your settings for receiving e-mail notifications about comments, etc.

To *get* comments, end your blog post with a question. Most of the posts I write don't really invite commentary as they're instructional. But if you want to get a discussion going in the comments, end your post with something like "Have you had any problems with this?" or "Is it just me?"

What Am I Supposed to Blog About?

Oh, yeah. *That.* I can't tell you what you should blog about because that has to come from you. I can only recommend that you read lots of blogs, identify what you'd like to read about on a blog but can't find (or can't find it written in a way that you like) and then get to it. Simples.

Anatomy of a Blog Post

A good blog post has an interesting title, well-laid-out text divided into paragraphs, perhaps with headers if it's a really long post, and a relevant link to something else by the same blogger at the end. For instance, if I write a post about self-publishing, I put something at the end of the post like, "Click here to see all my self-printing posts" or "Click here to find out more about *Mousetrapped*, the book I self-printed."

A lot of bloggers don't do the relevant link and I think it's because they don't think about *where* most people will read their blog posts because, newsflash, it won't be on their blog. Many people use blog feeders (like Feedly) and will never or rarely see your lovely blog with all your links, etc. in your lovely sidebar. If they want to read more, give them a link right there that they can click on to get it.

(If you're asking yourself now why we go to the bother of making our blogsite pretty when most people are reading our posts somewhere else, it's because (i) not everyone is and (ii) that's probably where they first saw one of our posts, and a professional-looking blog will help convince them that the post we wrote and they liked today was not just a one-off – more quality content can be expected from us in the future.)

You'll find loads of social media "guru" posts telling you the best ways to get people to read your posts, down to the font size, number of words and the exact time of day you should post them, but I think that's taking things a tad too far. Just follow this piece of advice instead: make 'em *interesting*. And perhaps don't post them in 16 pt Wingdings.

Also, tag your blog posts with relevant keywords (search terms) so if someone is looking to read about this very subject, they'll find your post. It's also a good idea to sort your posts into categories, which you can create in the Categories section of the Dashboard and then select from the New Post window.

New WP users: remember to delete the "Hello world!" blog post that WP puts on your blog by default. (To post a new blog post in WP, just click one of the many New Post buttons you'll see on the Dashboard. Write it and publish it. It doesn't quite need its own instructional section, now does it?)

The Regularity Rules

How often do you need to blog? It's entirely up to you, but you should consider where you are in your blogging life too. At the beginning I probably posted three to five times a week. Now, four years later, I blog maybe once a month – *but* I make that one blog post count by making it long and informative.

I think if you're just starting off, you should aim to blog once to twice a week minimum or every weekday if you can. The reason I say this is because every time you release a new blog post out into the world, you create a window of opportunity in which people might find you for the first time. You create a new Google search result, someone might post a link to it on Twitter, someone else might repost that link, or you might stumble onto the kind of blog post that suddenly brings a tidal wave of new followers racing to your blog. So if you're only producing one new blog post a week then you're really limiting your opportunity to grow your audience. And just like anything else new, the beginning is when you need to spend the most time on it.

Remember that not every blog post has to be 1,000 words long. You can vary your weekly schedule to include one traditional blog post, an image or inspirational quote you found that you like and a list of interesting links you read during the week. Two of those will only take minutes to post. I usually write my blog posts ahead of time and then schedule them to publish throughout the week, which you can do through WP (choose Schedule instead of Publish when you've finished typing your post). Also: don't overthink it. *It's just a blog post.*

The Blogging Community

One of the best things about becoming a blogger is finding your place in *the blogging community* and making loads of new blogging friends. For now, they'll keep you entertained with their brilliant blogs and start interesting discussions with comments on your blog, and in the future they might write you a guest post, host your guest post on their blog or help you with giveaways, reviewing your book or recommending your blog to their readers. And if you have a blogging-related problem, they might be able to help.

Remember those blogs we added to your Feedly account that you've been reading all this time? Well, start commenting on them. Follow the bloggers on Twitter and chat to them there. Run along now children, and go make some blogging friends.

Before You Get out Your Catherine-shaped Voodoo Doll ...

So now that you know in some detail all the things about blogging I don't want you to do, you are no doubt swearing at me in your head again. Maybe your blog is exactly as I've described in my "don't do this" sections, or your favourite blog is. Or you know of an author who has sold trillions of books and has the most popular blog on the web since the dawn of HTML, and at last count he had 70 widgets in his sidebar and they were *all flashing*. To which I say: good for him.

I attended a talk a few months ago about how to get published, and at it an editor at a major Irish publishing house told the story of how he had received the manuscript of a memoir on dog-eared pages, not only formatted the wrong way but not formatted at all, and filled with grammatical errors and misspellings. He wasn't even going to read it, but he did, and only a few pages in he realised that the story of the author's life was utterly gripping. *So* gripping that he offered the writer a book deal, and put an editor to work on getting the manuscript into acceptable shape. Knowing this, would you send the manuscript of your book to that editor in the same condition? Of course not. You'd make sure it was spell-checked, printed out fresh on bright-white paper, double-spaced and in a readable font. Why? Because you'd want to put your best foot forward and give yourself the best possible chance of getting a "Yes, we'd love to publish this!"

That's what I'm saying here about blogging. No, you don't have to do as I say. No, there is no one right way to blog. Yes, all of this has been poured through a filter called *my personal taste* and yes, all of this is based on just me and my failures and successes. Yes, you can have twenty multi-coloured flashing widgets running down the side of your blog that, if you look at them long enough, will hypnotise you into an LSD-like trance and still get blog followers, or even sell books. Perhaps you've done it before. Perhaps you're doing it right now.

But if you want to put your best blogging foot forward and give yourself the *very* best chance at succeeding at this using social media and selling books thing, I *recommend* that you don't.

So you've set up your hilariously named, all matching, blogsite-like blog and you've been reading and commenting on a few other blogs in an effort to start your little corner of the blogging community going. There might even be a trickle of people stopping by your blog every day.

But how can we turn that into a steady stream?

Welcome, my friends, to Twitter.

Twitter

Unless you already use Twitter or have in the past, you likely have no idea what it is. That's fine. What's *not* fine is dismissing it as a time-sucking, idiot-attracting waste of virtual space where Stephen Fry shares what topping he put on his toast this morning, Kim Kardashian posts endless trout-pout selfies and Justin Bieber fans trade insults with One Direction fans in what you sincerely hope is an attempt at phonetic spelling.

Because it's *so* much more than that. In fact, it's the best thing I ever did for my writing and self-publishing career. When people ask me "What's the ONE thing I should do?" I simply say, "Twitter."

But what the fudge is it?

Twitter is like a 24/7/365 cocktail party. It's always going on, and if you've chosen your guests wisely, it'll only ever be filled with people you find funny, interesting, attractive, into the same things as you are or all of the above. You can dip in and out of it as much or as little as you like, and you can stay for five seconds or the whole day. When you *do* dip in, you can:

- Lurk in the corner, saying nothing
- Join in a conversation
- Strike up a conversation with a particular guest
- Respond to a question a particular guest has asked, e.g. "Where are they hiding the good beer?"
- Whisper something in someone's ear that you don't want anyone but them to hear
- Stand in the middle of the room and say something that does not require a response but is intended to entertain or interest
- Stand in the middle of the room and say something that does not require, but welcomes, a response
- Stand in the middle of the room and say something with an eye to getting a good old heated debate going
- Stand in the middle of the room and show everyone this amazing YouTube video you've found of cats standing like humans (This is where the analogy breaks down somewhat, but you get the idea)

Twitter 101

Twitter, if you look it up, will be described as a "micro-blogging" site, where you have to say whatever it is you have to say in **140 characters** or less. (That sentence was 154 characters, so that'll give you some idea of the length we're talking about.) I don't think of Twitter as having anything to do with blogging though; I think of it more like a chat application.

NB: The easiest way to use Twitter is through an app on your phone or tablet computer, but for our purposes here, we're going to stick with the Twitter website (www.twitter.com). If you've never used Twitter before, I recommend you master it there before trying it out anywhere else.

Where's what on the Twitter homepage (see image on previous page):

1. *Navigation.* **Home** is the homepage; **Notifications** are the things that people have said to you, about you or about one of your tweets; **Discover** can be ignored for now (BOR-ing!) and **Me** is a link to your profile.
2. *Your profile.* A snapshot of you on Twitter: your Twitter username, profile pic and header photo and the number of followers, people you're following and tweets. You'll also see a **Compose New Tweet** box here.
3. *Trends.* Topics that are popular on Twitter right now are said to be **trending**.
4. **Tweet stream.** This is where all the tweets posted by people you follow will appear, one after the other as they are posted with the newest ones at the top.
5. **Search box.** You can search all tweets for topics or hashtags (we'll get to them) using this box.
6. Beside the search box you'll see a little envelope icon: this is where your **direct (private) messages** can be accessed.
7. This is an individual **tweet** as it appears in the stream (see below).

CatherineRyanHoward
@cathryanhoward

What am I going to do without my computer for the weekend? I'm thinking I might actually sit back and relax and - gasp! - READ A BOOK.

↶ Reply ★ Favorite   Buffer   ••• More

You sign up for a free account and **follow** whomever's tweets you want – literally by clicking the Follow button on their profile or under one of their tweets – and so whenever they send out a 140-character thought into the Twitterverse, you'll see it in your Twitter **stream**, an ever-updating list of tweets from the people you've followed.

Hopefully someone will think that they'd like to read what *you* have to say, and so they will follow you. Whenever you tweet, everyone following you will see that 140-character nugget of joy appear in *their* Twitter stream.

If you see a tweet that you think your followers will be interested in – say, the answer to the question "What is the meaning of life?" or a link to a YouTube video montage of cats sitting like humans – you can **retweet (RT)** or repost that tweet, making it appear in your Twitter stream too. Anyone who follows your tweets will see this retweet just as they would one of your own hilarious musings, but they'll also be able to see that it was penned by someone else and reposted by you. To retweet a tweet, all you need do is locate the Retweet button underneath it and click. Some Twitter apps, for example the one you can download to your iPhone, offer you the choice of retweeting (reposting in its original form, like a carbon copy, e.g. "RT@cathryanhoward: "Give me 10ccs of caffeine. STAT!"") or **quoting**, whereby the original tweet is reposted with some added insight of yours, e.g. "RT@cathryanhoward: "Give me 10ccs of caffeine. STAT! ← *LOL. Hilarious, as usual."*

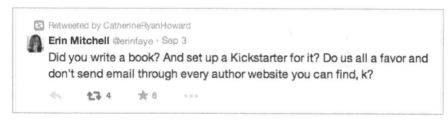

I (@cathryanhoward) retweeted Erin Mitchell's (@erinfaye) tweet about those annoying Kickstarter types who spam every e-mail they can find online, without amending the original tweet. This is how it appears to the people following me. You can also see that six people have marked this tweet as "favourite".

You can also **favourite** a tweet, which essentially means you hit the little star icon underneath it. People do this for one of three reasons: (i) to actually imply that they were impressed with your tweet and so favourited it (yes, that's a word), (ii) to pause or end a Twitter conversation by acknowledging the most recent contribution but not responding to it, the virtual equivalent of a smile and a nod, or maybe a polite laugh, or (iii) to bookmark it so they can come back to it and/or easily find it later. NB: If someone has so much time on their hands that they wonder aloud why you would favourite their tweet but not retweet it too, tell them you're bookmarking it for later. And that they might want to get a hobby or something.

This is how Twitter lets me know that other people have retweeted me, if I missed it as it appeared in my stream. You'll find these under "Notifications".

An "at reply" to me which includes @AmazonKDP. As the tweet starts with my username, I'll be the only one to see this appear in my tweet stream UNLESS someone is following both me and @RobertEdits. @AmazonKDP will see it in their Notifications.

If you see a tweet that you'd like to respond to, you can reply to the tweeter with an **at reply**, so called because to do that you begin your tweet with the @ symbol and then put their Twitter username, e.g. "@cathryanhoward I know all this already. BOR-ing." (If you *do* know all this already, feel free to skip ahead.) This is how you can have a conversation on Twitter, going back and forth with at replies. Your followers will not see these tweets UNLESS they are also following the person you've directed it to.

If you want to **mention** someone in your tweet or direct their attention to a tweet about them while making sure that everyone who's following you can see it too, you do the same thing (the @ symbol followed by their username) but NOT at the beginning of the tweet.

That's a very important point: if you start a tweet with a username, i.e. @cathryanhoward, no one who follows you will see it UNLESS they are also following me, i.e. the person you mentioned. This is why I get the red rage when I see corporate Twitter accounts run by people who should know better tweeting things like "@shakira's new album is out today!" Obviously intended for everyone, no one will see it except the person whose username they've used. *You cannot open a tweet with a username unless you only intend for that person to see it.* Therefore if you must and you don't, add a full stop before it, e.g. ".@cathryanhoward is *really* annoying me now. #facepalm".

Notice the hashtag (#) in that tweet? That's called ... well, a **hashtag**. Hashtags have two main purposes on Twitter: search and comedy.

Let's say you and 50 of your friends want to have a conversation on Twitter. How are you all going to keep track of the tweets? By all using the same pre-agreed hashtag like, say, #writing. (A very popular Twitter hashtag that, by the way.) Then you go to Twitter's search function, plug it in and instead of seeing your usual Twitter stream (of people you follow) you'll see a stream of tweets tagged with #writing. Or say you're watching *The X-Factor* and you want to find out if anyone else thought that last girl was singing like a bag of strangled cats. Search for #xfactor and you'll soon know the answer. (Twitter, while we're on the subject, makes watching reality TV at least *twice* as entertaining as watching alone.) Whenever I post a link to one of my self-printing blog posts on Twitter, I always tag it with something like #selfpublishing or #ebooks, so that if people are interested in those subjects they might happen upon my tweets.

Hashtags are also used for laughs, e.g. "I'm never going to drink again. #liesItellmyself" or "I seem to have forgotten to wear pants today. #imaybearrested" or "I just watched 'Dear John'. What an amazing movie! #sarcasm."

Feel free to make these up. I remember once upon a time I did this – I can't remember what the hashtag was – but a guy who must have been new to Twitter sent me a tweet, deadly serious, accusing me of making up my own hashtag. Um, yeah. Like, *duh*.

A few words of caution on hashtags: they are *search terms*. You can't claim ownership of them because there's nothing to own. But at the same time you shouldn't hijack them, maliciously or accidentally. Take #fridayreads for example. This was started by a book lover stuck at home for the day who was wondering what everyone else was reading, so she asked in a tweet that included the hashtag #fridayreads. It soon caught on, with tens of thousands of Twitter users soon sharing the names of books they were reading every Friday.

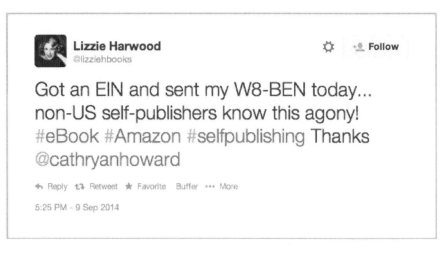

> **Lizzie Harwood**
> @lizziehbooks   ☼   ⚹ Follow
>
> Got an EIN and sent my W8-BEN today... non-US self-publishers know this agony! #eBook #Amazon #selfpublishing Thanks @cathryanhoward
>
> ↩ Reply   ↻ Retweet   ★ Favorite   Buffer   ••• More
>
> 5:25 PM - 9 Sep 2014

@lizziehbooks demonstrates a mention AND hashtags. #Hooray!

You are, of course, free to use the hashtag #fridayreads because it's a search term. (Technically hashtags can be trademarked, at least in the US, but only to prevent other companies who sell the same products as you do from using it to pretend to be you. No one can legally prevent anyone else from using a hashtag. The whole idea of a hashtag, let's not forget, is to have other people use it as much as possible.) But if you were a publisher trying to push a new release, it would be frowned upon if you, say, tweeted "Looking for something this #fridayreads? [Insert link to Amazon]". Frowned upon and completely ineffectual, because everyone would be too busy tut-tutting at your obvious hijacking of what was, up until today, a selling-something-free event. Similarly if your name was Friday and you wanted to start a book review blog, I'd stay away from calling it "Friday Reads" in case you ever need to use that hashtag. Not because it's in use already and so you can't use it too, but because it's in use already for something completely different and so it would be silly for you to use it for this. Are you just out to confuse people? What happens when they mistake your #fridayreads for the other one?

If you're a moron you might also consider hijacking a hashtag intentionally. This is about the most stupid thing you can do, at least in this section of the book. Say J. K. Rowling is doing a live Twitter chat and the "official" hashtag for it – designed to help people find and keep up with the conversation – is #butterbeer, and you have a book that you believe will appeal to Harry Potter fans so, on the same night, you start crazily tweeting links to your Amazon page using the hashtag #butterbeer too.

Please play out the rest of this scenario in your head before you employ this method. What do you think is going to happen when someone looking for J. K. Rowling somehow manages to end up on the Amazon listing for your book (which is itself unlikely, because people will spot what you're doing a mile off)? Do you honestly think the next bit of that story is them buying your book? *Really?*

Oh, for …

(#facepalm)

Finally, if you follow someone on Twitter and they follow you back, that's not only a beautiful thing but you can also communicate with each other by **direct message (DM)**. This is like a miniature e-mail that no one else but you two will see, and you get a whole 160 characters for it. Just make sure you don't do the accidental DM/tweet shuffle; *so* many people have got in trouble for that …

You can actually send a DM to anyone who is following you, but they won't be able to reply unless *you're* following *them*, so if you're not then doing that would just be cruel.

Your Twitter Profile

As well as dropping 140-character gems of knowledge, wisdom and hilarity into the Twittersphere, you'll also have a Twitter profile. This is the little section of information about you that people can see alongside your tweets, and includes your username, actual name, location, profile picture, bio and website address.

First, let's talk about your **username** and **actual name**. There are space limitations (that's why my actual name doesn't have spaces, and my username is cut back to "Cath") and just like our blog address, we want something that's easy for people to remember.

You also have to choose something that no one else is using.

I highly recommend that you stick with your name or some derivative of it, and not something like, say, @oodlesofnoodles. Now is not the time to be cute.

You don't have to put in your **location** but if you do, make sure you make it general. Use the same **profile picture** (sometimes called an "avatar") as you did on your blog.

Cohesiveness, people. Cohesiveness!

My Twitter profile:
profile pic, header pic, real name, username, location, short bio and website URL
plus details about my life on Twitter (how many tweets, etc.)

Along with your tweets, your **Twitter bio** is an opportunity to convince people that you are oh so very interesting and should be followed at once. Take up all the space they give you (160 characters, so only a little bit longer than a tweet) and refrain from using it just for advertising. For example, my bio line used to be something like "author of MOUSETRAPPED, BACKPACKED and SELF-PRINTED." Well, great. But why would anyone follow me? Isn't "Writer, astronaut, skinny …" a much better line and far more likely to convince someone to follow me than a boring bibliography? You might also want to ensure that this line is in keeping with your whole professional-author appearance. Not too long ago I happened upon the profile of a published author that read, "I have publishes 12 novels."

Indeed.

There is only one thing that should be in your **website address box**: your website address. Do not link to a Facebook page and, dear God, do not link back to the very Twitter page the person clicking on the link is already on. (I've seen people do this.) And do put something in there, so if people want to know more about you (and why wouldn't they?) they have somewhere to go.

What Now?

Now you start to follow people. Begin with me (@cathryanhoward) and then, after lurking for a while, you'll find loads of other people you want to follow. You can also search for them by name in the Twitter search box. Each new person you follow might lead you to follow someone else, e.g. you might see them chatting to someone or retweeting a *right* joker all the time.

There is very little point in following celebrities, unless they're particularly funny or something. (Or they're Josh Groban. We're *always* allowed to follow Josh Groban.) Please don't tweet at them, because it almost always comes across as spectacularly amateurish.

It is a good idea to follow people connected with this book world of ours, such as book bloggers, writers, book publicists, publishers, agents and booksellers.

Remember the idea is you follow people who you think will keep you entertained or informed, or who you think you might be able to have a good chat with. Find people you know in real life and say, "Hi! I'm on Twitter now!" You might also want to follow brands you like (they often tweet special offers) or local or national news outlets that will be beneficial to you. Ultimately this is your party and you can invite whomever you want.

Twitter = World

Twitter is completely public. Every tweet you tweet can be read by anybody and may even show up on search engines such as Google. You don't even have to have joined Twitter to read someone's tweets, i.e. even if you're not on Twitter you can go to www.twitter.com/cathryanhoward right this second and see what wondrous musings I've failed to come up with today. But this is what we *want*; we want as many people as possible to find out about us and our writing.

You can **protect** your tweets, which means that no one will see them unless you okay their follower request – which is the same as opening a hotel and then refusing to let anyone make reservations. I'm guessing you can infer from that sentence what I recommend you do about *that*.

Earn, Don't Ask

If you were at a party, would you stand in the middle of room, call for quiet and then say, "Wow! I have *so* many friends. Five hundred and forty-two to be exact. I'm, like, SO popular. Can I get one more?"

Hopefully the answer is *no*. And just as we shouldn't do this in real life, whether we're popular or not, you shouldn't do it on Twitter either. As a general principle (I was very careful there not to use the word *rule*) you shouldn't acknowledge your follower count at all, or only do so in very special circumstances. The reason I say this is not because of how you'll come across or how you'll be perceived or the fact that there are people on Twitter who, as a rule, unfollow anyone, friend or foe, who dares break the fourth wall and draw attention to their follower count (which, I think, is a *bit* of an overreaction). It's because of *what happens when you do*, and how what happens is utterly pointless and no help at all to you or your cause.

Some people are obsessed with getting followers. They follow as many people as Twitter will allow them to (there's a limit based on your follower-to-followed ratio as a deterrent to spamming), hoping that they will follow them back and thus raise their follower number. Others will offer "follow backs" like they're something *to* be offered. They're not. There's the follower-fishing tweet: "I only have 56 followers ... feeling very unpopular here! Can I get 300 by midnight?" and its friend, the friend-follower-fishing tweet: "My friend @pain_in_the_ass has only 99 followers – can we make it 200 in time for her birthday tomorrow?"

We could, but what would be the point? The people who click Follow won't be doing it because they dig your disarming charm; they'll be doing it because you (or your friend) asked them to. They might never read a tweet of yours again, or unfollow you tomorrow. And what's the point of having 10,000 Twitter followers if most of them aren't even reading your tweets anyway?

A sideline to this is the "Follow me and I'll follow you extravaganza", where people either use the offer of following to sweeten the deal – you'll occasionally see in Twitter bios something like "I always follow back!" or "Follow me and I'll follow you back!" – or take offence because you don't follow everyone who follows you. Twitter is about following people you're interested in, not pretending to be interested in the people who follow you. Just yesterday I saw someone I follow on Twitter say, "Having a clear out. I'm following WAAAAY too many people on here who don't follow me back. Time to say bye-bye." To which in my head I said, "What are you, dude, *twelve*?"

And anyway, how many Twitter followers you have doesn't matter. How you engage with the followers you *do* have, or how they engage with you, is all that does. Anyone can have thousands or hundreds of thousands of followers; it doesn't mean anything. (We live in a world where a washed-up, drug-addled TV star in the midst of a mental breakdown broke the record for acquiring the most Twitter followers in the shortest space of time.) We're not here to collect numbers; we're after *engagers*. And you'll get them – without even trying – if you're a tweeter worth following.

You shouldn't have to ask for anything in social media; you should *earn* it.

If you really want to get your friend more followers, do it in an organic way. Twitter-chat to her or mention her in your tweets ("Oh my God @so-and-so and I were SO drunk last night. You wouldn't BELIEVE what she got me to do to that dustbin!"); your followers will see you talking to this new mysterious tweeter and because they think *you're* interesting, they'll assume they're going to find her interesting too. Recommend her as a tweeter worth following. Post an interesting link to something on her blog.

And if *you* want more followers? Try tweeting interesting stuff.

The flip side of this is the "What Did I Do?" tweet which draws attention to the losing of followers, e.g. "OMG I just lost a follower! Maybe it was all those tweets about how many followers I have …" Twitter is constantly in flux: people sign up, people delete their accounts, people get booted off for being spammers, people protect their tweets, people realise that protecting their tweets is stupid and either unprotect them or delete their accounts instead, etc. etc. Your follower number is going to constantly change, especially once you get over a couple of hundred, because the chances that there's a spammer in there who'll be booted off in the coming days is extremely high. So if your follower count drops by one or two, that's what's happened, and you asking why it happened shows not only that you have a tendency to overreact, but also that you have one eye on that follower count at all times.

Just don't worry about it.

The Discerning Retweeter

Be discerning with your retweeting. I retweet things I think are funny or interesting and that I suspect my followers will find funny or interesting too. But keep in mind there's nothing stopping your followers from following the person whose every thought you're copying into your stream and if they *are* following that person, they'll see all those tweets twice.

What if *you* want to be retweeted? Well, just as with followers, don't ask for retweetage. (Unless it's for a good cause or part of a competition or something.) For instance, there is an otherwise lovely tweeter in my stream who, when he posts a blog link, puts "PLEASE RT PLEASE RT PLEASE RT THANKS" at the end of it. I don't retweet them, and not because I find it annoying, although I do. I don't retweet his links because his blog posts just aren't interesting to me.

If you want to get retweeted, tweet something that's *worth retweeting*.

How Do I Tweet Links to My Blog?

You have three options. You can:

- set up WordPress so that whenever you publish a new post, a tweet from your account is automatically tweeted with a link
- click the Tweet button at the end of the post (automatically inserted into your posts by WP)
- do it manually, i.e. copy and paste the link from the address bar into a new tweet

Facebook offers an option to repost all your tweets automatically as Facebook statuses but DON'T do this. Twitter is used more often than Facebook, and so what seems like a handful of tweets may be a ridiculous overload on a Facebook wall. Depending on the content of the tweet, they might also make little sense to someone on Facebook, especially if you're using a lot of hashtags and/or if the person reading it doesn't use Twitter at all.

Let's hop back to WP for a second and set up our blog so that it connects to Twitter in every way possible. Go to your Dashboard and find Sharing in the Settings menu. On that page you can:

- Set WP to tweet links to new posts as soon as you click the Publish button. At the top of the page you'll see a Twitter icon and below it, a link that says "Connect to Twitter". Click it and follow the instructions. Once it's set up, you'll see a check box marked "Twitter" just above the Publish button when you're in the New Post page.
- Add share buttons to your posts. This is very important: it lets other people share your posts on their Twitter pages with just one click. Drag the share buttons you want into the Enabled Services box.

Then click Save Changes at the end of the page.

What Am I Supposed to Tweet About?

To begin with, whatever you want. I always recommend that you "lurk" for a while before you say something, to get an idea of the kinds of things other people are saying on there and how they use the platform.

I will say this: if you have nothing to say then don't say *anything*. Don't force yourself to get on Twitter just because people like me have said it's a good way to build a platform and sell books, because you won't be any good at it unless you're primarily doing it for fun. And the I'm Tweeting Against My Will Brigade stand out on Twitter like sore twumbs. (See what I did there?)

With regards to tweeting about your *book*, we'll get to that later.

Before You Get out Your Catherine-Shaped Voodoo Doll Again ...

When I was 14 my school friends and I merged our "gang" (there was, like, three of us) with a group of boys who lived in our neighbourhood, who we thought were *oh so cool*. They all smoked. One day, one of them gave me a cigarette and because I thought that I too could become oh so cool by smoking it, I put it to my lips and took the shallowest of drags. As a plume of grey smoke left my mouth, one of the Oh So Cool Boys laughed and said, "You didn't even *inhale!*" and in that moment I certainly didn't feel cool, but stupid. I felt like everyone except me knew how to do something. I wasn't in on it. It wasn't a nice feeling, and not just because my mouth was filled with smoke.

Sometimes when people are told to not ask for Twitter followers, retweet too much or protect their tweets, they feel as if there is a Twitterati Club, a sort of Premium Class lounge for clued-up tweeters where they can look out at those who don't know how to tweet the "right way" and laugh. And because these people *do* do things like ask for more followers, they feel like they're in the group being laughed at. They feel like they're fourteen again, not inhaling, and a group of "cool" boys are sneering at them.

It is not my intention to make you feel like Twitter is something that only an elite group of people "get" or know how to use, or make you question whether or not you're using it "right". There is no secret manual to using Twitter and no right way to use it. As I said about blogging, if you want to make your blog one gigantic flashing widget, please do, and if you want to tweet nothing but how many followers you have, please do that too.

What this book is about is how *I* used Twitter, as an author, to effectively build an online platform and then later, sell books. I also spend a lot of time on Twitter as a reader and therefore I see, from the other side, what works for tweeting authors and what doesn't. I've bought a huge number of books because I've encountered the authors on Twitter, but I haven't bought books from all the authors I follow on Twitter and it's not just because I'd be broke if I did. Some of them are just better at convincing me through their tweets that their books are worth checking out. Maybe some of those authors don't care whether or not anyone buys their books after reading their tweets. Maybe for them, Twitter is just a place to chat about *The Great British Bake Off* or whatever, and not to advertise their work. And that's *okay*. But if you just want to use Twitter as a place to chat about *The Great British Bake Off* and don't want to use it to sell books, why are you reading this book? (So don't hate me, is what I'm basically saying.)

Facebook

If your head is swimming with terms like *at replies*, *retweets* and *follow Friday*, fear not, because this section is going to be very short and super sweet.

Let's get one thing straight first: when I talk about Facebook, I don't mean a personal profile where people can add you as their "friend" or send you messages or subject you to 500 photos of their third holiday this year in an attempt to make you jealous.

I mean a **public page**, one where Facebook users click a Like button to say *I'm a fan of this*. Anyone can set up one of these pages for anything at all, as long as it's not offensive or something weird.

And guess what? *You're* anyone!

So let's set up a Facebook fan page.

Separate Yourself

But before we do, let's separate your existing Facebook profile (your personal page) from the new fan page you're going to create.

The thing is, you need to have a Facebook profile to set up one of these pages, but the profile used will be linked to the page as the page's administrator. So set up a new Facebook profile, under your writing name if it's different to your real name, and use *that* to set up the fan page. Why not just use your existing profile? Because trust me when I say that you'll want to keep them separate. It may not seem like a big deal now; it may not seem like a big deal for a long time from now, or possibly ever. But it's better to play it safe, because:

- If you are already connected to your real-life friends with an existing Facebook profile, they do not deserve to be subjected to your book promotion, especially since, if they are really your friends, they'll already know all about the book and have bought a copy for every single person they know.

- People who don't know you in real life will "like" your page, see you listed as the administrator and then request you as a friend. Not everyone will do this (thankfully), but lots will – not least of all because there are Facebookers obsessed with friend numbers just like there are tweeters obsessed with follower numbers. You can ignore them, of course, but that might make you seem mean, and what if the requester is someone you've met in real life, say, at a writing event?

Things can start to get complicated. It is far easier to take your existing profile and set it to private (so that if people search for your name, they won't find you) and then create a new one under your writing name from which you will create the fan page, i.e. the new profile will be the appointed administrator of your fan page. That way, if someone does find you through the fan page and requests to add you as a friend, you can accept without reservation.

NB: I don't *use* the profile I created to make my fan page. It's an empty shell. Everything I do in Facebook as an author I do on the fan page itself.

Creating a Fan Page

Once you've made your new "author" Facebook profile, you can go to the main login page and click Create a Page which is just below the green Sign Up button. Now you have to make a decision: do you want to create a page where people become a fan of you as an author, or a fan of your upcoming book?

Initially I set up a page for my first book, *Mousetrapped*, but when it came time to release another book, I thought maybe an author page would be better instead. But the author page is growing cobwebs and the *Mousetrapped* page is a hive of activity, so I'd say whatever you start out with, stick with. The question is *which one* to start out with. It's easier to build a fan base around your book, if only because you'll be less embarrassed asking your real friends and family who are on Facebook to "like" a page about your book than a page all about you. But then you can put more content on a page about you, because people who "like" your book page will be expecting content about the book. And all the already famous writers have pages about *them*, not their books …

A snapshot of the Mousetrapped *Facebook page.*

Oh, it's a toughie. What to do? I think if you're only planning to release one book for now and that book is non-fiction, then set up a *book* page. Anything else – a series of books, other types of writing or novels – then set up an *author* page.

Unlike a Facebook profile, anyone can see a Facebook fan page. That's kind of the idea. So needless to say, no home address, no telephone numbers and no photos of you on holiday.

Why Do I Need One of These?

There are two and a half good reasons for setting up a Facebook fan page.

Reason no. 1: ***Find one, find them all.*** If your book is about a specific subject, you *have* to infiltrate Facebook somehow because somewhere on there are people who are interested in that same subject and have already organised themselves into groups. These are ready-made readerships that you need to connect with, and Facebook is the easiest way. Even if you have, say, a thriller novel, you can target fans of such books, or similar authors. (And when I say "target" I don't mean in a spammy way. I *never* mean in a spammy way.) One day a Facebooker found my *Mousetrapped* page, posted a link to it on his own page and like magic, I suddenly had 50 new fans and sold about that many paperbacks in one afternoon. Turns out he was a Disney podcaster and all his Facebook friends were huge Disney fans. I'd managed to tap into a group of ready-made readers simply by making a Facebook page.

Reason no. 2: *Everyone's on Facebook*. At a self-publishing conference I spoke at a while back, I asked the 50 or so attendees how many of them had blogs, had Twitter accounts and had Facebook pages. About a third had a Twitter account, about half had blogs but nearly everyone had a Facebook page. My own mother has one, which, considering the fact that she can't work the satellite TV remote, tells me everything I need to know about Facebook's popularity. It's the most commonly used social media platform in the world, with over 1.2 *billion* users who check in at least once a month and almost 800 million users who log in *every day*. (Twitter, by comparison, has an estimated 271 million users who are active at least once a month and 500 million tweets are sent every day.)

Reason no. 2.5: *Roping in friends and family*. When you start your fan page, you can rope all your friends and family who are already on Facebook into clicking the Like button on your page, enabling you to create a customised address and give you a good start.

Getting a Customised Address

Once you have 25 or more fans, you can customise the URL, or address, of your Facebook fan page.

For example, when you first sign up, the page will probably have a URL like www.facebook.com/qetv9984user_wei91 or something equally catchy. But once you get your 25 fans, you can change it to actual words, e.g. mine is www.facebook.com/mousetrappedbook.

Getting More Fans

We've already talked about not being fixated on numbers, but here on Facebook I wouldn't even worry about trying to get fans; it'll happen organically. Put links to your Facebook page on your blog and maybe in your Twitter profile, and between that and your friends and family breaking news of it by "liking" it (an action that will appear on their Facebook walls), you'll soon see your fan numbers go up.

Coming Soon: The End of Facebook

I do have to say this though: I think Facebook is *almost* a complete a waste of time these days.

Mark Zuckerberg and his zip-up-sweatshirt-wearing friends just can't stop tinkering with the site, and every change they make seems to move it further and further away from what people want it to be. Mr Z is constantly second-guessing his users, modifying the site to reflect what he *thinks* they want and not what they *actually* want. The most obvious example of this is his incessant tampering with the News Feed, whereby we're now shown only news updates from people we regularly interact with. Um, hello? The *whole point* of Facebook is to casually stalk people, is it not? The most interesting titbits are from people you never interact with at all. That's the point, Marky Mark. How did you miss that?

On a more serious note, Facebook has fed arsenic to organic-reach and is now pummelling it to death with an old PC. *Organic reach* is just a fancy term for the people who will see my stuff without me having to pay for eyeballs – the number of Facebook users who will see a post I publish on my Facebook page without me spending any money on the Boost Post feature (read: advertising) offered by Facebook. Once upon a time if you had a 1,000 fans, you could post something and maybe 500 of them would see it. Now you'll be lucky if 50 of them will, and if you pay cash to "boost" the post, there's evidence to suggest that the eyeballs you'll pay for will be sitting in a cubicle in a "click farm" in New Delhi. In other words, it won't be worth it. This is all Facebook's own doing.

As an author, I have all but abandoned Facebook now – although I have had great success with it in the past. When I posted about this recently on my blog, a number of commenters said they thought Facebook was still the most effective tool at their disposal when it came to selling books. So what should *you* do?

I'd suggest if you're starting out from scratch, set up a Facebook page and see how it goes. Don't plough too much time into it, and absolutely no money. If it happens for you, great. If not, don't worry about it. If you hate all things social media and are looking to drop a module like a hot rock, it can be this. It cannot be blogging (or least building a website of sorts) or using Twitter, but yes, it can be this.

* * *

Thus concludes the building an online platform bit. By now you should have set up a blogsite, joined Twitter and maybe set up a Facebook page too.

In a little bit I'll be telling you what you need to *do* with them, but for now, while you and your editor are putting the finishing touches to your manuscript, all you need do is get used to using them.

And try not to get *too* addicted to Twitter.

Next up, the main event: self-publishing our books. Hooray!

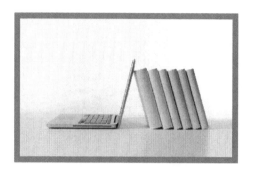

PART 3
Publishing Your E-books

All About E-books

Aren't you excited that we're finally getting to actually *publishing* your book? That makes two of us. (She types at 10 p.m., having sat down to "quickly finish off" Part 2 this morning ...)

Where's your manuscript? By now it should have been edited and proofread. Chances are it's in a word-processing document, double-spaced and on a virtual A4 or letter-sized page. Make two copies of it, marking one "e-book" and one "paperback". It's important you do this now, before you start formatting either of them with a specific edition in mind, and not later, when turning an e-book scroll-type document into a paperback interior will give you a week-long headache. A word of warning: don't start preparing your book for publication until you are *absolutely sure* that it is the final version. Now, if you need to make a change, you do it in one place in one document. But in five minutes' time, you'll have to change it in two places in two different documents that do not resemble each other. Don't make extra work for yourself. Don't start this bit until you are 100 per cent sure the text you're working with is the final version of your book.

We're going to start with e-books. I still laugh at the fact that I "accidentally" published e-books after seeing someone tweet about Smashwords, and now four and a half years later they account for more than 95 per cent of my sales. I think, therefore, there is little point in publishing a paperback but not an e-book. You could be doing yourself out of the majority of your potential sales. And e-books are *so* much easier to sell than their print equivalents, mainly because they're cheaper.

The good news is that producing an e-book is far less complicated than producing a paperback. It's also completely free.

The bad news is that the steps you *do* have to complete are a bit trickier and potentially involve that horribly painful thing you may have already heard about, *formatting*. Ugh.

Formatting Versus Conversion

One little thing while we're on the subject: I may say "formatting our e-book" but I don't *mean* formatting our e-book. Not technically. I mean formatting our MS Word manuscript document so that when we upload it to, say, Smashwords, and they run it through their conversion software, it comes out the other end looking like it should. Like we wanted it to. I mean *optimising our document for e-book conversion*, but that takes ages to type and I'm lazy.

So I'm just going to say formatting, okay?

Why Do E-books Need Formatting?

Why do e-books need special formatting? Why can't you just upload your manuscript as it is now, or use the Word file you just used for the interior of your paperback? Because in e-books, there is *no such thing as the page.*

If you buy the paperback edition of my book and turn to page 36, you'll see exactly what I intended for you to see, which is whatever I put on page 36 when I was making it. But if you buy the e-book edition of my book, there is no page 36 and even if there was, I could only guess as to what would be on it.

E-reading devices – Kindles, iPads, Barnes & Noble's Nook, to name a few – allow readers to customise their reading experience. When they download your book, they don't have to read it as you've uploaded it, e.g. Times New Roman in 12 pt. They can change the font, the font size, the paragraph alignment and the line spacing. They can read it in portrait or landscape view. And before we even start changing things, how many words fit by default on a Nook screen is not the same as how many fit by default on a Kindle screen. In this environment the only way that the book will retain its readability and not descend into total gobbledegook is to make the e-book like a *scroll*. Remove the idea of the page altogether. Make them irrelevant. Let the text *flow.*

The other thing is that there are different e-book formats: Kindle uses .mobi and ePub is the most widely used among the rest. There's also PDF versions to consider. So when you upload your manuscript to a site like Smashwords, it has to put it through its conversion program (Smashwords' conversion program is called, suitably, Meatgrinder) and crank out not one but several different versions of your e-book.

So between the "I can read my e-book however I want" scroll thing and the "my e-book has to be converted into several different formats" thing, your future e-book MS Word document has to go through a lot. And if you've filled it with page breaks, blank lines, seven different fonts, 27 different font sizes, tables, shapes, clip art, headings, sub-headings, sub-sub-headings, a partridge and a pear tree, it's going to end up looking a *right* mess. (Or, as Smashwords puts it, do it wrong and Meatgrinder will turn your book "into hamburger".)

That's why we need to format it in a *very* specific way.

I Feel Your Pain

Formatting your e-book is going to be tough, and not just because it can get really annoying, depending on the complication level of your book and the amount of patience you started off doing it with, but also because it feels utterly unnatural to be removing formatting from your book.

As I type these words in the first draft of this book, I'm not formatting it at all. I'm just typing it. When I have to go onto a new section, I just hit the Return button and start typing. I'm doing this to make it easier for me later on, when I'll take one copy of this document and go off and make a paperback, and use another to make an e-book.

But doing it this way is *killing me*. I am *itching* to copy and paste everything I've done so far and move it into the Word template I've downloaded from CreateSpace, the one that matches the size of my book, and start laying it out properly.

ITCHING, I tell you. But I *must* resist.

If you've never formatted a document with imminent e-book conversion in mind, you'll feel the same way when you start to do it. You'll want to make it look all nice and *pretty*. You'll want to give your chapter headings their own page and centre them, vertically and horizontally, and maybe sprinkle a cute little line underneath it, or insert a piece of clip art. You'll want to put in bullet points and blank lines and pear trees, but you can't. You must resist. Do it for yourself – it'll cut down on the migraines later – and for your readers, who may delete your book in disgust when they find that trying to read it is like staring at the sun.

I Want Out Already

If you've already decided that formatting your own MS Word document for optimum conversion to an e-book isn't for you, I have good news: *you don't have to do it*. You can (a) pay someone else to or (b) pay for a program that will do it for you. Stay tuned for lots of helpful info about this courtesy of my friends at **eBookPartnership**, who I use for the non-Kindle e-book versions of this book because anything more than straightforward text with a few page breaks and I feel a migraine coming on. All you need to do when using them is send them your manuscript, pay their fees and sit back and relax while they take care of the rest.

Alternatively you can pay someone to do the bit I'm about to talk about: formatting your MS Word document. You'll still have to do the uploading bit yourself, but this might save you time and effort and you can find some really reasonable rates. Go to www.smashwords.com/list for **Mark's List** (Mark being Mark Coker, founder of Smashwords), which is a roll call of formatters and e-book designers who'll be happy to help you in exchange for some cold, hard cash.

Another idea is to invest in **Scrivener**, a software program incredibly popular with fiction authors that helps you do all sorts of snazzy stuff including automatically export your book in .mobi (Kindle) and .epub (everyone else) formats. Apparently this is "easy" although I have to admit that although I've managed to convert my manuscript into an e-book with it without much trouble, I find it difficult to make the book look exactly the way I want – something I *do* find easy to do when using a MS Word document and Amazon KDP's automated conversion system. Scrivener costs just $45 (buy it from www.literatureandlatte.com – great website name, no?) which is an absolute bargain, and there are plenty of helpful blog posts online that will guide you through the process step-by-step.

A Word to the Wise

A review of a previous edition groaned about my formatting instructions. "Clearly," one reviewer complained, "the girl can't use a word processor. Anyone who can would never even *dream* of using tabs ..." (I'm paraphrasing.) Another wondered why on earth I didn't just point out that the best thing to do would be to format your book for optimum e-book conversion as you go along – as in, while you write it – as that's so much easier than going back in later and cleaning up the mess.

First of all, I actually have a professional certified qualification in Microsoft Word. Yes, an actual certificate, like on paper and everything. I even had to pay a hefty fee to do the course that awarded it. I mean, yeah, sure, it's about twelve years old and has dust on it, but *still*. I can use the damn program, okay? I can also self-publish. Quite well, in fact. I would even go so far as to say that self-publishing is kind of a specialist subject of mine. That's why *I wrote a 130,000-word book about it.*

Newsflash: *Self-Printed* isn't for me. I already did all this. I'm not writing this book in case I ever suffer from some sort of selective amnesia and forget everything I know about Amazon KDP and hashtag-based competitions.

I'm writing it for the people who *don't* know and in doing so, I have to assume they don't know anything about it at all. That's the only way to make sure that no one is left out, or confused even more because what others may assume is obvious isn't so obvious to them.

And if you think no one out there is using tabs to indent paragraphs, I wonder if (*Friends* reference alert!) your wallet is also too small for your fifties and your diamond shoes are too tight. I used to offer a formatting service and let me tell you: I've seen some things. One client had pressed the space bar three times *and* tabbed across to mark the start of every paragraph. Another had put her dialogue tags *inside* of her periods instead of inside. Another had used section breaks at the bottom of every page, thinking she had to manually move on to the next one. Another had thrown every single formatting style and feature he could find into his document, making it a barely readable mess. Another had –

Well, you get the idea.

If you already know how to do all this kind of stuff, congratulations. I'm melting some gold here for your medal while I type. But just because *you* do doesn't mean that everyone else does too.

As for formatting as you go along, *of course* that is the logical thing to do. But who is reading this book because they're planning on writing a book that they plan to self-publish? I hope the answer is no one because if you are, you're making me nervous. I'd fear that you were writing a book *just* to self-publish, and just self-publishing because you think it'll make you money. I would assume (hope?) that people come to self-publishing because they have *already* felt compelled to write a story, and now they feel compelled to get it out into the world. I would stake a few boxes of Nespresso capsules on that describing the majority of people who are reading this book. So for most, a manuscript *already exists* that needs to be formatted again, this time for optimum e-book conversion. When you write Book 2, you'll know what to do to minimise the reformatting needed later on. But for now, we're going to assume there's an existing MS Word document that needs some serious work.

If you do know all this already, please feel free to skip ahead.

Express Formatting for E-books

Here's the thing though: *getting a good-looking e-book up on Amazon's Kindle is really easy.* No, really. It is. That's because when you go to KDP, nervously clutching your book-baby, all they need to do is convert it from MS Word to .mobi, i.e. change it from *one* format to another. This means that even if you *do* have a partridge and a pear tree in there, chances are it'll still come out looking good at the other end.

In the previous two editions of this book, I advised you to strip back your manuscript and reformat it with an iron fist. I threatened to unleash hell fire if I as much as *smelled* a bulleted list or a footnote. But the fact of the matter is that only Smashwords is the problem. Smashwords, who have to take your book and turn it into several different e-book formats, are the ones who demand this kind of scorched-earth reformatting. Meanwhile, Amazon KDP lets you get away with a lot. You could even, theoretically, upload your manuscript to Amazon KDP's website right this minute and still end up with an okay-looking e-book. We won't do that because we want a *good*-looking e-book, but you could. That's how forgiving Amazon KDP's conversion program is.

This time around, here's what I recommend you do: upload your book to Amazon KDP. Most of my sales come from Amazon and truth be told, neither of my travel memoirs have been available from Smashwords for more than a year. They probably should be because they should be available as widely as possible, but you can survive with just Amazon alone. You can even *thrive* with just them. Offering them digital exclusivity for a time even wins you some promotional benefits, as we'll see in the Selling Your Book section later on.

So how about you publish on KDP for now and then, down the line, after you've collected some royalties, reinvest them in paying someone *else* to do the tricky Smashwords bit (or go to the likes of eBookPartnership, who will get your title onto all other major e-book retailers for no stress at all)? If I'd my self-publishing time over again, this is what I'd do.

Usually when I suggest this, self-publishers panic. "But what about the guy who left a comment on my blog that said he only had a Nook? WHAT WILL WE DO ABOUT HIM?!?!?!?!" I know: right now the idea of losing even *one* sale because you didn't publish in a format the potential purchaser likes is completely terrifying. But don't worry about it. Think bigger than the anonymous guy who happened by your blog one time, who refuses to download the free Kindle Reading App to his desktop or tablet. He can wait a bit.

Meanwhile, we're going to get express formatting our book.

Change Your View

It's easier to resist making everything real-book pretty if you do one simple thing now: *change your view*. Most people use Microsoft Word in Print Layout view or as it will appear on the page when you print it out. Well, when we're trying to ignore the very fact that there is a page, this isn't a good idea. It'll mess with our heads. So instead, go to **View → Draft** to look at your entire document on one, scrolling screen.

NB: I work on MS Word for Mac, so your menus, etc. may look slightly different and there may be a slightly shorter or longer series of steps to complete the tasks. The principles are all the same, however.

Lose the Dead Wood

The first thing we have to do is lose anything that won't work in an e-book and/or has no relevance in an e-book. You can either let them go completely, or leave the bare text in there to do a little workaround on later, e.g. take the text out of any text boxes you've used, delete the text box and put the text back in as an italicised paragraph instead with a blank line above and below it to show that it's "separate".

I would hope that you haven't been writing your book in Comic Sans, but then you never know. Change it now to something simple and straightforward, like Times New Roman. You don't get to decide what font your e-book will be in – the readers get to decide that themselves –

but you should work with a standard font that isn't going to cause any problems down the road. Times New Roman is the ideal candidate for this.

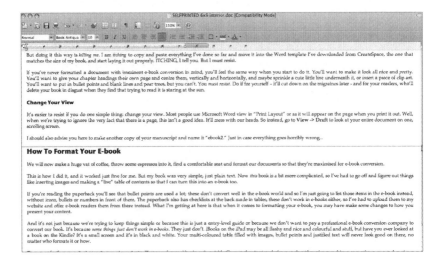

Looking at this page in Draft View on MS Word.

If you've been working with the manuscript as it was when it came home from the Editor Hospital, you won't have much work to do here. But if you're working with something that was once destined to be the interior of a print book, you need to lose nearly all the front and back matter. The following items *have* to go bye-bye:

- Copyright notice (we have to change it)
- Title pages
- Page and section breaks
- Table of contents (numbers only; keep the chapter headings, etc.)
- Extras like headers, footers, page numbers and indexes
- Fancy formatting features like text boxes, columns and bulleted or numbered lists

NB: You can certainly have a list that *looks* bulleted or numbered in your e-book, you just can't use *actual* bullet points or numbers as per Format → Bullets and Numbering. Remove them and enter the numbers manually, or use a dash to create a make-do bulleted list.

Close It Up

Close up your text so that everything is together, i.e. there are only a maximum of *two blank lines* between the end of one chapter and the beginning of a new one, and within your chapters only *one blank line* between the end of one section or scene and the start of another one.

It's unwise to use block paragraph style, i.e. where each paragraph is separated by a blank line. Unwanted blank lines come with e-books like ketchup packets come with fries – whether you want it or not, there's always at least one – so adding *additional* blank lines is a bad idea. Indenting is the most effective way to mark the beginning of your paragraphs, so that's what we're going to do.

This should leave you with absolutely no blank pages and at most, two blank lines together at a time.

Activate Show/Hide and Go Tab Hunting

Word's Show/Hide feature is designated by the ¶ mark in the toolbar. Click it. You will now see all non-printing characters in blue – things like paragraph returns, tabs and section starts. We'll use this feature to help us format our book from here on in.

Formatting e-books makes me feel:¶
¶
→ (a) Stressed¶
→ (b) Angry¶
→ (c) Homicidal. ¶

But first, we need to eliminate every *single* tab in our document. They're nasty little things; even *one* of them can stop our e-book converting correctly. Even if you are 100 per cent positive that you've never used one, check anyway. Remove any you find using the Find and Replace function, putting ^t in the Find box and nothing at all in the Replace one.

Then, just to make absolutely sure, go through your document to double-check there isn't a *single* blue right arrow in it (see image above).

Style It Up

Select all your text (Edit → Select All) and then go to Format → Style. What we're going to do now is make sure that all our text is set to automatic paragraph indent, whereby the first line of every paragraph is indented slightly, out from the left-hand side of the virtual page. The style of your currently selected text (i.e. all of it) will be set to Normal. Look for "Modify" down towards the bottom of the Style window and click it when you find it. A new, smaller window will open, headed "Modify Style". In the bottom left-hand corner of it you'll find a drop-down menu; select Paragraph from it and then make it look like this:

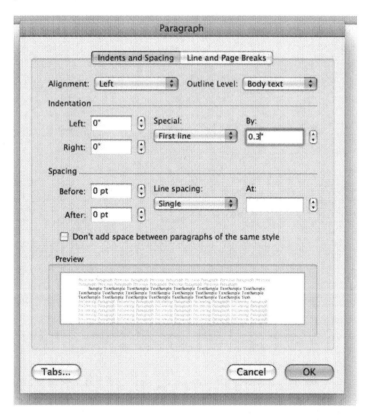

Once you've made your changes, click OK and then Apply. You'll now have set all your text to indent automatically by 0.3 inches at the first line of each paragraph by default, which is what we need for the body of the text.

Why don't we just select all and then go straight into Format → Style and indent all our paragraphs from there? Well, there's a couple of reasons. The first is that Microsoft Word is the devil. It's proved it to me time and time again, throwing things into my document while I sleep –

things that I would never have put it in there. For example a few minutes ago I decided to number the headings in this section; previously there was no number there. So I clicked to the beginning of one of them, typed the number "3" and blinked in confusion as it appeared in Georgia font and light grey. I have no idea *why* it did that. But I suspect it has something to do with the fact that what appears on the screen as you type in Microsoft Word is not necessarily what the program is being told to do in the background by the satanic MS Elves.

Think of this way: when you select text on screen and hit the Centre Text button in the toolbar, you are just dressing up your text in a centred costume for Halloween. But when you do it through *Styles*, you are baptising your text in a Centred church, sending it to a centred school and insisting it lives the centred way of life 24/7 so that it can pass the Centred Citizen test once its old enough. You are making it centred to the *core*.

That's what we need it to be, because e-book conversion will do everything it can to change our text to something else. The second reason is that we will go back to this soon to make other styles for text we (actually) want centred, in a larger font to represent a heading, or not indented at all. Using the Styles feature is quick and convenient, not just in e-book formatting but in manuscript and book-creating in general.

Add Your Sparkly New Front Matter

What goes at the front of your e-book is not the same as what goes at the front of your print edition. You should have (and *only* have):

- The book's title
- Your name
- Whether it's a Kindle or Smashwords edition
- Copyright symbol and date
- Copyright notice (modified to reflect that it's an e-book)
- Licence notes

This text needs to be centred in order to look all fancy and stuff. Create a new style that will (a) indent your paragraphs by 0.01 of an inch and (b) centre your text. Call it "Front Matter" or something like that. Then select the text you want centred at the beginning of your book and set it to that style, just like we did a few steps ago when we changed all our text to Normal.

I'm sorry – 0.01 of an inch? Yes, you read that right. During the MS Word to Kindle conversion, Amazon KDP indents all paragraphs by default. If you've set your line to indent by half an inch or whatever, it'll obey you, but if you've set your line to indent by nothing at all, it'll override you. Some lines should not be indented: titles, centred front and end matter, the first lines of chapters and scenes, table of contents listings, etc. etc. So to combat KDP's compulsion to indent, set the indent to 0.01 – all but invisible to the reading eye when viewed on a Kindle screen.

This is what your front matter should look like:

MY BOOK'S TITLE
by Soon to Be Famous Author, i.e. me
First Kindle edition © 2014 My name
All rights reserved. No part of this e-book may be reproduced in any form other than that in which it was purchased and without the written permission of the author.
This e-book is licensed for your personal enjoyment only. This e-book may not be resold or given away to other people. If you would like to share this book with another person, please purchase an additional copy for each recipient. Thank you for respecting the hard work of this author.
www.myblogsiteURL.com

Note: no blank lines. We do this for two reasons. First, I've already mentioned how during the conversion process, blank lines just *lurve* to appear out of nowhere. Therefore adding unnecessary blank lines is just asking for trouble. Second, e-books allow you to download a free try-before-you-buy sample. If a reader gets hooked on our free sample, they'll pay to read the rest of the book. The more they read, they greater the chance of them getting hooked, and the more likely they are to pay out for the rest when they've already invested a significant amount of time and energy reading the free bit.

So the less space we take up in our sample with stuff that *isn't* our book, the better.

Whip Your Book into Shape

Now we're going to go through our book, working as we go. We're going to:

I don't think so, no. A print copy might be picked up by someone who has never seen our Amazon listing whereas an e-book purchaser *has* to see our listing (where we'll put reviews once it goes live and, crucially, we get some) before clicking that "Buy" button. It also delays them getting to the start of the book. ¶

- **Insert page breaks.** To insert a page break, click Insert → Break → Page Break. It will appear as a thick blue line across the screen that says "Page Break" as in the image above (when in Draft View). If you are also seeing some thin blue lines that don't say anything, don't worry about them. That's just MS Word showing you where your text would split onto another page if you were printing it out, which we'll never do. There are two rules for page breaks: (i) ONLY insert them in between chapters or parts/sections, and in the place where your front matter meets the start of your book and (ii) every page break has to have one paragraph return above it and one paragraph return below it, as in the image on the previous page.

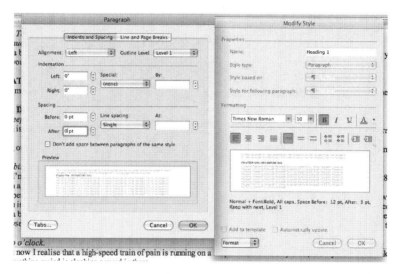

Modifying the Heading 1 style so there's no extra space above or below the text and it's left-aligned.

- **Make chapter headings**. Keep your chapter headings as simple as you possibly can. I usually left-align mine right above the beginning of the chapter, set the font to all caps and make it bold. But remember: we can't just do that from the formatting bar. We need to do it through our old friend Styles. So go into Styles (Format → Styles), find Heading 1 and modify it until it's what you want, i.e. a bigger size (up to 16 pt only!), bold, all caps, left-aligned. Check the Font window to make sure there's no kerning added, and the Paragraph window to ensure that no extra space has been added above or beneath your heading's text. (You'll find these in the drop-down menu, bottom left corner.) The beauty of this is that by setting our chapter headings to Heading 1 style, we're also telling the conversion program that this is where our chapters begin. This means that when our readers download a copy of our book, their e-reader will help them navigate from one chapter to the next based on where we've put our heading styles. Tip: if you have parts and chapter headings, make the parts Heading 1 style and the chapters Heading 2 style to show that they're one level down the hierarchy.

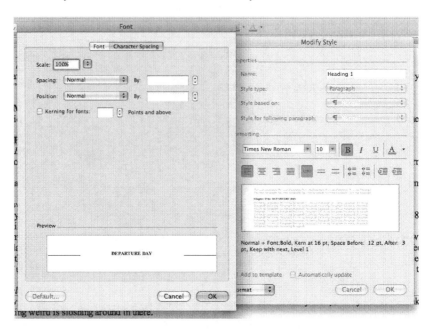

Modifying the Heading 1 style; note the Kerning for Fonts box is unchecked.

- **Remove the paragraph indent from your first lines**. The first line in a chapter or section shouldn't be indented. Create a new style based on your existing paragraph style but with a 0.01 indent. Call it "First Line" or something like that. Then as you go through your book, set the first paragraph of each chapter or section to this new style.

mails, caught up on missed sleep, snacked on things made of high fructose corn syrup and watched BBC World News, the only English-language channel in our room. ¶

I also spent an hour rooting through my backpack for items I could lose, and said goodbye to two impractical T-shirts and the travel hairdryer. ¶ (*Nooooooooooooo!*) ¶

By the time the morning of our third day rolled around, we were restless with cabin fever. Luckily the exhaust fumes we inhaled during the forty-five minute taxi ride out of the city and up into the hills calmed us *right* back down, and so we arrived in Antigua relaxed and ready to *really* start our backpacking adventure. ¶

¶

|¶

¶ -- *Page Break* --

Chapter Three: THE CORRECTIONS ¶

The colonial town of Antigua is nestled in the Guatemalan highlands with only the peaks of volcanoes breaking the blue sky above its brick-red roofs. With its adobe houses, cobbled streets and beautiful Parque Central, it's everything Guatemala City is not: quiet, pretty and relatively safe. ¶

I'd found a hotel online called Casa Cristina, and had booked us three nights there before leaving Florida. We planned on staying in Antigua longer than that, but figured that by the time those three nights were up, we'd have sussed out somewhere cheaper. Of course, Casa Cristina was cheap compared to say, anywhere else of its kind in the Western World, but by backpacker standards it was an indulgence. ¶

It was nice though. A typical Antiguan home from the outside, the doorway led into a tiled hallway filled with natural light. The colours on our room's walls were not, perhaps, what you'd like to see first thing on a hungover morning, but the beds were comfortable, the bathroom was en-suite and there was even a TV. On top of the Casa Cristina was a roof terrace with panoramic views of the town and the countryside beyond, and Parque Central was only steps away. ¶

Memories of Guatemala City's stinky, screeching, smoking metropolis were already fading away. ¶

(Image on previous page)
The beginning of a chapter in my e-book, Backpacked. *Note: one page break with at least one paragraph return on either side (but no more than two), left-aligned bold/caps chapter heading (set to Heading 1 style) and no indent on the first line of my first paragraph, but all first lines indented after that.*

- **Make all hyperlinks live.** The beauty of e-books is that if you're reading one of my books on your iPad, you can click a link to my blog and be taken there immediately by Safari (Apple's internet browser). The Kindle Fire will do the same, and even the Kindle Paperwhite has a browser of sorts built in. But in order for that to happen, we need to make all our links *live*. To do this, select the text, e.g. my website or www.mywebsite.com, and click Insert → Hyperlink. Type the URL into the box provided and click Okay.

- **Reinsert images, if necessary.** Ah, images. I really do wish people would leave them out. Do me one favour, will you? If you're planning on inserting images, mock up a little MS Word document with one of your favourite images in it, send it to a Kindle in PDF and view it on the Kindle screen. And not a fancy new Kindle Fire, but a normal Kindle, one where the screen is in black and white. Now, how does it look? Good? Don't be joking me. It looks crap. It's small, and it's in black and white. Plus, adding images to your book makes your file bigger, and Smashwords has an incredibly small 10MB limit on e-book files. But sometimes you *have* to insert images (as I did in this book), so the way to do it is to insert them from file, i.e. Insert → Picture. You can't copy and paste them – MS Word is the devil and all that jazz. You must also make sure that all your images are set to In Line With Text in the Format box. (Right-click your image and select Format Picture from the menu that appears.) If you can drag them around the screen, they're not. Keep in mind that all e-reading devices have different-size screens and since the user can choose the font size, your book will look totally different on each one. So will the images in them. Make them a reasonable size – I usually stick with 3–4 inches across, max – to give them the best chance of displaying correctly.

- **Remove excess blank lines.** Listen to me VERY carefully: under no circumstances should you have more than three to four empty lines anywhere in your e-book. Trust me, this will be difficult to implement. You'll really, really, *really* want to leave some after your copyright notice, or after the last line of each chapter, but you need to be strong! Don't do it. When you press Return to make a blank line, you'll get a little ¶ mark just as you do at the end of each paragraph. Make sure you have no more than four of these together anywhere in your book. Why? Because some people buy Kindles because their eyesight isn't great, and they make the font as big as they possibly can. Chuck in a few blank lines all together in a big font view and what do you get? A blank page. Just do what you're told and avoid having more than four of them anywhere in your book.

- **Keep all "main" text left-aligned**. Apart from headings, front and end matter and other items we're going to centre, keep all your text left-aligned. Don't use the Justify function, in other words. E-book conversion programmes don't like it much.

Add Your Sparkly New End Matter

Do you have the words "THE END" at the end of your book? If not, type them now. Oh, go on then: you can centre them too. (Using the Front Matter style, needless to say.)

If you have an author's note, acknowledgements and an author bio, put them here and put them together, i.e. only have one line between them. Insert links to all your online homes, and make them work, i.e. Insert → Hyperlink. Then type three pound symbols/hash signs (###) to show that now your book has *really* ended and there is no more.

It should look like this:

And they all lived happily ever after …

THE END

Author's Note
Something very important I have to tell you about my book and not just something I made up because I really wanted an author's note.

Acknowledgements
I don't understand why I have to thank anyone for helping me write this book, as no one did. But maybe I'll sell a few more copies if I put loads of names here, so let's do it. Thanks to Mum, Dad, the guy who sells me my venti lattes in the Starbucks on Market Street, the Mars Foods company for making Snickers bars and the person who invented Sky Plus, without which I'd get nothing done at all …

About the Author
Up until recently, E-Book Author was drinking copious amounts of coffee

and working on her second novel. However, after spending a weekend attempting to format this e-book correctly, she had to be transferred to a secure mental health facility for the safety of the people around her. She's currently considering embellishing her experiences there á la James Frey's *A Million Little Pieces.* Her agent thinks she's on to something … Oh, wait. That should have been *on* something.

Find out more on www.amillionlittleformattingerrors.com

www.myblogsiteURL.com

###

Creating a "Live" Table of Contents

In an e-book there's no point having a table of contents (TOC) unless it *works*, i.e. when you click on or select Part 5: Bubbles, it takes you to Part 5: Bubbles. (Remember there are no page numbers.) So how do we do that? We insert hyperlinks into our table of contents text but, instead of typing a URL, we select one of the headings we've already made.

Although I think it's a complete pile of horse faeces, Amazon KDP and its friends will frown upon an e-book that doesn't have a TOC even if it's a novel. When have you ever bought a printed novel that came with a TOC? I'll tell you: neVAH! Unless it was some arty-farty book that was trying to be all cool and stuff. They just don't need them because novels are read straight through. But – sigh – we have to do what we're told.

Go back to the start of your book, to your table of contents. What we're going to do now is link these to the headings you've created elsewhere in your book.

Highlight the word(s) you want to link the heading to, e.g. "Prepare Your Manuscript" and click Insert → Hyperlink.

What happens next will depend on what version of Word you're using and whether you're using a PC or Mac, but look for Document, i.e. the option that will enable you to link to anchors or points that *already exist* in the document you're working on.

From the list that appears, look for Headings. Then select the heading you want the text to correspond to, linking up to the two.

On the next page is a snapshot of what this process looks like on MS Word for Mac.

If you want to be *really* organised about it, you can also make your table of contents a heading in itself and then link it to a "Back to Top" or "Return to Table of Contents" phrase at the end of every section.

If you do that, consider yourself the teacher's pet in this classroom.

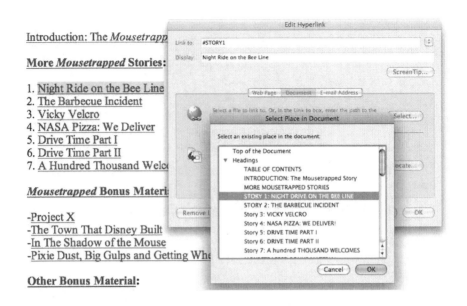

And that's it! Our e-book is formatted – for Amazon Kindle at least.

Now we just need to sort out a cover.

Your E-book Cover

Your e-book cover (also called your Product Image) is just the front cover of your print book. It should be 1,000 pixels wide on the longest side and ideally a height/width ratio of 1:6 for best quality. Amazon recommends 2,500 pixels on the longest side for best quality. I don't know what any of this means; I just pass the information on to my cover designer.

If *you* don't know what this means and you're planning on trying this cover-designing thing yourself (*noooooooooo…!*), then try Catherine's Patented E-Book Cover Resizing Method:

1. Try to upload your cover image. When it doesn't work:
2. Make it slightly smaller or bigger and try to upload again.
3. Repeat until cover image is accepted and uploads.

Remember that Canva Kindle cover we made? Where did you put that?

Uploading to Amazon Kindle Direct Publishing (KDP)

I think one of the reasons Amazon KDP has done so well in convincing self-publishers at all stages of their career to upload, publish and sell their work is that they have an amazing user interface. It is so easy to use, slick to look at and even if you go into the process knowing nothing about it at all, there's plenty of help and assistance on offer along the way. This step of the process is nothing to be afraid of. This is the *nice* bit.

Create a KDP Account

Go to the KDP website (**kdp.amazon.com**) and register for a free account. If you already have an Amazon.com account, you can create your KDP account with that.

Once you've signed in, you'll have to click Agree on a couple of terms and conditions notices and then you'll be brought to the KDP Dashboard, where up in the right-hand corner a yellow box will remind you that you haven't set up your account information yet. Click on Update Now.

 Your account information is incomplete.
To publish a book, you will need to complete this. Update Now

Complete Your Tax Interview – Part I

Now you're on a page headed "Your Account", where you need to fill in your contact details: name, address, phone number, etc. Next you'll see an option to begin your "Tax Interview".

Dum-dum-DUUUUUUUUM!!!!!!!!!!!!!!!!

> ### DISCLAIMER!
> What follows is not intended to be legal advice and should not be considered as such. The author accepts no liability for any loss, damage or other bad stuff. Like, *obviously.*

Since Amazon operates in the US it has a responsibility under US law to ensure that everyone who receives payments from it has provided sufficient tax information, i.e. a tax identification number. Before anyone starts moaning and groaning about red tape and bureaucracy, save your breath – you can like this or you can lump this; those are your options.

Now, pay attention: **if you are a US resident, you will only need your Social Security number (SSN)** to complete the tax interview and all will be well.

If you are not a US resident, Amazon is required by law to withhold 30% of your earnings and give them to the IRS instead. This is called taxation, a process I'm sure you're already familiar with. Again, like it or lump it; those are your options. Unless you want to live off-grid, shun all public services (roads, running water, electricity) and purchase things only by way of a bartering system, getting taxed on money you make is unavoidable, so please spare me your righteous indignation.

Here's the good news: if your country of residence has a tax treaty with the US, you might be able to reduce your withholdings to a lower rate or even avoid having any money withheld by Amazon/the IRS altogether. You can find out the situation for your country at this location:

http://bit.ly/IRStaxtreaties

Self-publishers who live in Ireland and the UK, for example, can avail of a zero per cent withholding rate – as in, Amazon must pay us all our royalties in full once we've completed our tax interviews.

The *great* news is that this process, once a nightmare, is now a dream.

When I started self-publishing, you had to get an Individual Tax Identification Number (ITIN) from the IRS in order to receive the benefits of your country's tax treaty. For me, this involved a trip to a solicitor to have paperwork notarised, over eighteen months of my life and several back-and-forths with the IRS over their impossible paperwork. Then a couple of years ago, my fellow self-publisher David Gaughran (*Let's Get Digital* and *Let's Get Visible*) discovered that there was an easier way: you could get an Employer Identifcation Number (EIN) over the phone and use that instead. But no matter which option you chose, you *still* had to fill out a W-8BEN form (don't ask) for each self-publishing service you were earning money from, and then spend weeks or months chasing the companies for confirmation that they'd received them.

Now – undoubtedly because all these procedures were put in place before self-publishing added millions to the numbers having to follow them – you don't need *any US tax number at all* in order to avail of your country's tax treaty benefits. Amazingly, **you now only need the tax identification number given to you by your own country**. That's a Personal Public Service (PPS) number in Ireland, or a National Insurance (NI) number in the UK.

So all you need on hand to complete your tax interview is information you already have. Isn't that *great*?

When the IRS sends forms back across the Atlantic because you wrote "UK" instead of "United Kingdom", the answer is a resounding YES. Trust me on this one.

Better yet, you no longer need to fill in or post any physical forms. Amazon KDP and CreateSpace allow you to electronically sign a virtual W-8BEN. That's what happens during the tax interview.

You will not need to file "zero balance" US tax returns in the future. The London office of the IRS confirmed this for a helpful blog commenter of mine called Zelah by handwriting "no" next to the questions she put in a letter to them, and that's good enough for me. I've never filed one.

If I've caught you at a bad time and you already have an ITIN or an EIN but you haven't yet completed the tax interviews on Amazon KDP and CreateSpace, my advice is to forget that you ever applied for one. Complete the tax interview using your own country's tax identification number. Entering an ITIN makes things complicated and you won't find a spot in the tax interview in which to plug your EIN.

Speaking of making things complicated, I have to say that I have never in my life come across a process that people needlessly over-complicate more than they do this. David Gaughran gave us all step by step instructions for getting an EIN in minutes back in February 2012 and yet people are *still* visiting that blog post and *still* leaving panicked comments on it. Now it's even easier to get your tax situation sorted. In fact, I don't think they could make it any simpler.

So just do it, don't overthink it and let's all calm the fudge down about it, okay?

Here, in two paragraphs, is the entire situation as summed up by Amazon KDP themselves:

*"If you are claiming a reduced rate of withholding tax under an **income tax treaty** and do not have a U.S. TIN, provide your foreign (non-U.S.) income tax identification number to receive treaty benefits. This number is issued by your local tax authority or government for income tax purposes.*

*If you wish to claim treaty benefits and your country of residence does not provide a foreign (non-U.S.) income tax identification number, you can apply for a U.S. TIN (EIN or ITIN) with the IRS. You can learn more about EIN and ITIN numbers by visiting our Help Page **Applying for a U.S. TIN (Taxpayer ID Number).**"*

I can't imagine how a country could function without providing its citizens with tax identification numbers, but just in case you live in one of them or you never got one because you've never been employed, here's what you need to do to get an EIN which, if you'll recall, is the easier option:

1. CALM THE FUDGE DOWN.
2. Ring the IRS's International and US Residency Certification Service in Philadelphia. Their number is **+1 267 941 1099.**
3. Select option 1 or, in case this changes, whichever number you hear after the recorded voice says "E-I-N" or "Employer Identification Number".
4. When you reach a human, tell him or her that you are applying for an EIN as a foreign entity, as you're self-publishing e-books with Amazon. Answer the human's questions. He or she might ask you for something called a SS-4 form, but technically you don't need this if you're operating as a sole trader, which you are. If your IRS human insists on it, pretend there's someone at the door, hang up the call and ring back. Anecdotal evidence suggests that chances are IRS Human no. 2 will not ask you for it.
5. Have a pen handy to write down your sparkly new EIN.

And that's it. That's all you have to do. A hard copy of your EIN will arrive in the post in a few weeks and, in the meantime, you can move forward with the number you have just jotted down. As for supplying this to Amazon KDP and CreateSpace, you will have some additional form-filling to do. As this has not been my experience, I don't want to offer any advice. I can however recommend **TaxBack.com** who, for a reasonable fee, will add as a go-between for you in all dealings with the IRS, and **BeyondFrontiersTax.com**, whose short e-book is a great source of qualified information. Amazon KDP and CreateSpace also have comprehensive help pages and support via e-mail is available.

What's that? There's a question forming in your mind about being a sole proprietor versus a corporation or who, exactly, is the beneficial owner or what does effective connected income mean because you saw it on a W8-BEN form and now –

For the love of fudge, people, stop the madness. This is what you need to do. This is *all* you need to do. Enter your tax identification number, don't overthink it and let's all move on.

Okay?

Complete Your Tax Interview – Part II

Now we complete Amazon KDP's tax interview.

As I said, not too long ago this was a *right* pain in the arse. We had to download a W8-BEN form from the IRS website, painstakingly fill it out in teeny, *tiny* writing because the lines are like a millimetre apart, snail-mail it to Amazon and then wait weeks for them to receive it and update their records accordingly. Now it's all done online in the space of five minutes. So much easier.

So much easier, in fact, that I don't think it needs an explanation. Just follow the instructions onscreen and input the information you're asked for. (No overthinking allowed!)

If you've broken out in a shivery cold sweat because you need step-by-step instructions with screenshots …

Oh, go on then. You can find them here:

http://www.catherineryanhoward.com/selfprinted3

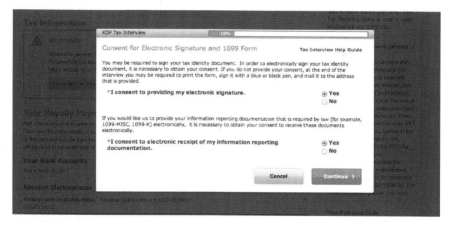

You will also need to provide bank account details so Amazon KDP can pay you by electronic funds transfer (EFT) where possible. If it's not possible, they'll pay you by cheque. Again: like it or lump it. Those are your options.

Don't forget to click Save at the bottom of the page when you're done.

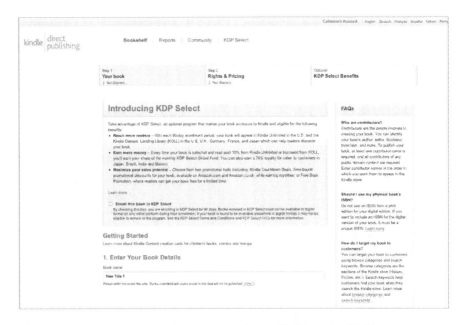

Starting a new title on Amazon's Kindle Direct Publishing.

Add a New Title

If you've just finished entering your account information, there'll be a dialogue box in the middle of your screen inviting you to Start New Title. Behind it will be your Bookshelf, the screen you see when you log in where eventually all your (bestselling!) self-published books will be displayed. Alternatively you can select the Add New Title button to get started. Once you do, you should be met with a screen that looks a little something like the image above.

Now, we start filling things in.

Enrol in KDP Select

When you self-publish with Amazon, you are self-publishing with KDP. KDP *Select* is something else: a special programme that offers you promotional and financial benefits in exchange for Amazon exclusivity. We'll talk about this in detail later on, but this is where you decide whether or not to enrol your book in it. For the purposes of these instructions, we're going to check the Enrol This Book in KDP Select box.

Book Name and Subtitle

Next up: entering the details about your book. These are the very words that will ultimately form your book's Amazon listing, so don't rush through this process. Take your time. You can click the Save as Draft button at the bottom of the page at any time and come back and pick it up again later.

We start by entering the name, or title, of our book. Sounds fairly straightforward, right? And yet, some people will not follow this instruction. I know they won't because I've seen the evidence.

But Catherine, you say, what else would anyone put in this box? What is not a title that could possibly be confused with one?

Oh, *plenty.*

Taglines, most commonly. What is a tagline? Besides being NOTHING THAT BELONGS IN THE "BOOK NAME" BOX, it's a little snazzy phrase that is supposed to entice you to read the book or see the movie. A sort of slogan. You see them on a lot of thrillers and crime novels. They come from Hollywoodland, where no self-respecting movie is released without one. (*Jurassic Park*: An adventure 65 million years in the making. *Jaws*: Don't go in the water. *Finding Nemo*: There are 3.7 trillion fish in the ocean. They're looking for one.) I saw a self-published book on the Kindle Store whose title was *VOLCANO – you need to Run*. Presumably "you need to Run" is the book's incorrectly capitalised tagline, and it has no place being anywhere *near* the book's incorrectly capitalised title.

Once upon a time authors were adding things like "For fans of Patricia Cornwell" to their titles, which was a cute (and highly effective) marketing ploy until Amazon noticed and promptly put a stop to it. So don't do that either.

I would avoid telling people what your book is in the "book name", e.g. *Presumed Dead: A Thriller* or *Talking Purple Unicorns: A Supernatural Steampunk Mystery*. If they can't tell the genre of your book from your book cover, your book cover isn't cutting the mustard and needs to be redesigned.

The only exception I would make here is if you have a novel that might be mistaken for non-fiction. Let's say you've written the novel version of *How To Lose a Guy in 10 Days*. Well, we don't want anyone to purchase our book because they want *instructions* on how to lose a guy in ten days. So in this instance, it would be acceptable to make the title of your book *How to Lose a Guy in 10 Days: A Novel*.

If you were thinking of putting something like "Buy me, please!" in the title box, please:

1.   Read ahead to the end of this numbered list

2. Close this book
3. Hit yourself with it repeatedly

So, enter your title in the Book Name box. Do NOT enter it in capital letters; enter it as it would be written, e.g. Mousetrapped, A Wrinkle in Time, Fifty Shades of Mind-Boggling Levels of Repetition.

If you have a subtitle, enter it in the – yes, you've guessed it! – Subtitle box, underneath. That's if you *really* have one, by the way. Don't make up a subtitle just because you think it'd be cool to have one.

Warning: if on your print edition you used a long subtitle, there's no room for it here. It'll just look weird on your product listing, because Amazon will dump the middle of it to save space and it'll look like this: *How To Lose a Guy in 10 Days: A Dating Plan for … and Leg-Shaving.*

We'll just stick it in our product description instead.

Series, Series Title and Volume Number (Optional)

If your book is part of a series, check the box marked "This book is part of a series" and then put the name of the series in the box beneath it. Add the book's volume number, e.g. which instalment of the series it is, in the Volume Number box, if applicable.

For example, if your book was *Catching Fire*, the name of the series would be The Hunger Games Trilogy, and the volume number would be 2 or II. Or if your book was the first in a planned series about a homicide detective named Harry Bosch (can I stop mentioning Michael Connolly? Seems not!), you could enter the series title as The Harry Bosch Novels or just Harry Bosch and the volume number as 1.

Edition Number (Optional)

Chances are you'll upload newer editions of this book in the future (when you find mistakes, change your website address, produce more books and want to link to them, etc.), so it's an idea to put a 1 in here now and then change it accordingly as you update the book.

Publisher Name (Optional)

Really? You're still going to have your own publisher name? Even after everything I've said?

Oh, go on then. It goes in here.

At least come up with something that doesn't include the words "press" or "books". *Please.*

Description

You now have 4,000 characters (about 700-ish words) in which to convince perfect strangers that they simply *have* to buy your book.

This is where you put the text that, if your book existed in paperback, would appear on the back cover – and *nothing else.*

Your blurb is a very important selling tool for your book. I was at a talk recently where an editor at a major publishing house said that she believed the blurb was even more important than the cover design. I think it's *as* important, but maybe she knows what she's talking about more than me, because she knows how difficult it is to sell all sorts of books all over the world. She even went so far as to say that self-publishers should *hire copywriters* to write their blurbs for them before they think about hiring cover designers, but I can't say I agree with this, especially since blurbs is an area where I see traditional publishing fall down a *lot.* (Just one example that comes to mind: the blurb for *The Drop*, a recent Michael Connelly novel I went to the store on the day of publication to buy, had a blurb that gave away a twist at the end. And crap! There I go mentioning him *again.*)

Sitting down at your desk typing things into Amazon KDP is not the first time your thoughts should have turned to your jacket copy or blurb. You should have been thinking about it, researching it, drafting it, revising it and refining it long before now. Your blurb is under a lot of pressure to perform. Think about it: you've managed to convince someone to go visit your Amazon listing to check out your book (an achievement in itself), then look at the price, think *okay*, they look at the cover, think *okay*, they come to read the blurb. If it's interesting enough, they'll buy it. If it sucks, look at all the time and effort you've wasted getting them to your Amazon listing, only for your blurb to trip you up at the last hurdle.

There is plenty of advice online and in "how to write a book" books about how to write a blurb or short synopsis for your book. You can also seek out books similar in genre to yours and study their blurbs to get an idea of what's the norm, structure, length, etc. It is vital to your success that you have a good one and if you have any concern about your ability to write it, you can hire a copywriter to do it for you.

But personally, I think the best person for the job is the person who wrote the book, because who else knows the story better than you do? Remember, if you followed the instructions in Part 2, you have blog readers and Twitter followers. Chances are, most of them read a lot of books. Why not post your blurb or multiple versions of it and ask them what they think? This is not only helpful to you, but makes them feel involved in your project as well. Do NOT add anything moronic like ***BUY ME PLEASE*** or THIS BOOK IS AMAZING!!!!

Contributors

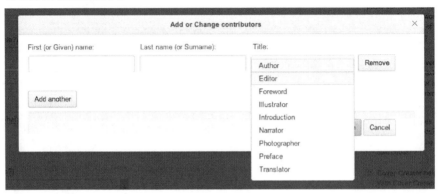

Now we must add the names of the people who contributed to this book. Follow these instructions to the letter:

1. Click on Add Contributor
2. Enter your first and last name
3. Select "Author" from the drop-down menu
4. Click on Save
5. Move on. *Now.* QUICK. Before you add anyone else!

For some unfathomable reason, self-publishers just love abusing this Contributors thing. I've seen it treated as a sort of cast list or, worse yet, the author's acknowledgements.

But it's what will be shown at the top of your Amazon listing for all to see, and that's why it should be your name and your name only. Anything else is a painfully obvious amateur move.

Unless …

You are publishing a collection of short stories or poetry and someone other than you has collected and assembled them. In that case you can add that person's name and then select Editor. *This is what is meant by the role of "editor" in that drop-down list.* It does NOT mean the type of editor who helps you edit your book, okay? While we're on the subject, you don't put the name of your editor inside your book either. I've seen e-books open with things like "*My Novel* by Mary Murphy. Edited by Claire West." No, no, no, no, NO. The *only* place your editor's name should appear in your book is in the acknowledgements where you thank them profusely for all their help. Nowhere else.

You've enlisted someone famous to write a foreword or an introduction to your book. Maybe you've written *Get Rich Quick Writing Novels About Sick Teenagers* and John Green liked it so much that he's agreed to scribble an introduction to it. In that case you *should* add him as a contributor (selecting "Introduction" or "Foreword" from the drop-down list) because his is a name and association that will help sell your book.

If your book contains original illustrations or photographs that (i) have all been taken by the same person and (ii) play a major part in your book. In that case you can add the person's name as being the "Illustrator" or "Photographer" – but only if the illustrations/photos play a major part in the book, e.g. a picture book for children or a collection of travel photography. A recipe book, for instance, would not have the photographer listed as a contributor on its Amazon page. If you are unsure about what to do with your book, look up a similar one on Amazon and see what its listing says, and then copy it.

If your book was written in a language other than English and someone translated it into English for you. Yes, you've guessed correctly: "Translator".

Language

Select the language the book is written in from the drop-down menu.

ISBN (Optional)

You don't need an ISBN to publish on Amazon KDP, so leave this blank.

DO NOT enter any other ISBNs you might have lying around, like the one you may or may not have for this book's paperback version, or the ISBN the book had if/when it was published before. Blank actually means *blank*, you know.

If you happen to have a spare ISBN, I wouldn't waste it on your Kindle book because, again, you don't *need* one to publish to KDP.

(You don't *need* one, okay? Jeez Louise ...)

Verify Your Publishing Rights

Check the box next to "This is not a public domain work and I hold the necessary rights."

Target Your Book to Customers

Choose categories (up to two):

Filter | All | Fiction | Nonfiction

☐ Fairy Tales, Folk Tales, Legends & Mythology
☐ Family Life
⊟ Fantasy
  ☐ General
  ☐ Collections & Anthologies
  ☐ Contemporary
  ☐ Dark Fantasy
  ☐ Epic
  ☐ Historical
  ☐ Paranormal

Selected categories:

Choose a category

Save   Cancel

Were you one of my readers who said "My book isn't in any genre" even after I explained that when it comes to bookselling, *genre* is a shorthand for *category*? Well, come back me after you've done this bit and try to tell me you *still* feel the same way …

This bit is as important as the name suggests. Doing it right means helping readers who like the kind of thing you've written find the thing you've written so they can pay you for a copy of it.

The first thing you have to do is **assign up to two Book Industry Standards & Communications (BISAC) categories**. These are categories standardised throughout the world to help identify books by type and group like with like. Choose from the list available the two best categories that describe your book. It might be something as simple as Fiction → Thriller or it might be more like Reference → Practical Guide → Arts and Crafts → Wool Crafts → Knitting Ugly Jumpers.

Later on, when we become bestsellers (!), it's in these categories it'll happen first. Will I ever forget the day I was No. 1 in Kindle Books → Travel → North America → United States → Regions → South → South Atlantic? (Well, yeah. I probably will.)

Don't be a smartarse here. Pick the correct categories and then move on before you start getting any, ahem, *ideas*. If you've written an erotic novel that features cupcakes, your category is going to be Fiction → Erotica. It's not going to be Cooking → Courses and Dishes → Cakes just because fiction sells in higher quantities than cookery books so you'll have a much better chance of being a No. 1 bestseller in the wrong category than you will in the right one. Putting your book in the wrong category is the same crime as false advertising, and it's not going to help readers find your book. You might also give some little old ladies who like to bake cupcakes a series of coronary events.

Next you have two options that only apply to children's and young-adult books: **Age Range** and **U.S. Grade Range**. If you live outside the US and aren't familiar with their school grade system, click What's This? to find out more. Skip both of these if you haven't written a children's or YA book.

Finally, enter up to seven **keywords** or search terms that will bring readers to your book. Try to imagine how you would locate your book using Google, or find it in the Kindle Store. You can't use terms like "Harry Potter" or "Gone Girl" – I know, right? Damn! – because Amazon doesn't like that kind of behaviour and will remove them. Think of seven other ones and add them here.

Select Your Book Release Option (Pre-ordering)

I used to say that every time a self-publisher wondered whether or not people would be able to pre-order their book, a fairy died. It. Drove. Me. *Craaaaayzee*. That's because, to me, it showed a complete lack of understanding of the differences between self-publishing and traditional publishing – and that the self-publisher was completely unaware of self-publishing's limitations too. A couple of weeks before I finalised this edition of *Self-Printed*, Amazon KDP announced a pre-ordering option so the fairy population is safe for now. (You *still* can't set your POD paperback up for pre-ordering. Don't even go there.)

I like the pre-order feature because it achieves two things. First, it means that if someone encounters news of your amazing book in the run-up to publication, they can go and buy it *right now*, before they forget, change their mind or find something better and cheaper. Second, it means that you have to stick to your self-imposed publication deadline, something I notoriously find hard to do.

What happens if you make your book available for pre-order? You set the date you want it released and then you promise – you *absolutely swear* – that you're going to upload the final version at least 10 days before the publication date. If you fail to do this, you lose your access to the pre-order feature for one year – and, presumably, annoy your readers.

But aren't we uploading our final, ready-to-go, 100 per cent perfect version now? We are for the purposes of these instructions, yes, but normally that's not how you would be using the pre-order feature. For example as I type this, *Self-Printed 3.0* is available for pre-order – but *Self-Printed 3.0* has never been uploaded to Amazon KDP. What I uploaded was actually the text of *Self-Printed 2.0*, which is similar enough to broadly represent the finished product of this book. Ten days before *Self-Printed 3.0*'s Kindle release date, I'll replace the document I uploaded with the right one and that's what'll go out to Amazon customers. If you are self-publishing a novel, you'd upload your unformatted manuscript that perhaps hadn't been copy-edited or proofread yet, open pre-ordering and then, ten days before the release date, update your error-free final edition.

Don't worry: no one will receive the earlier version. Amazon just wants you to upload that because they want to review it before they open pre-ordering for you, to avoid a situation where you decide you're going to write a novel, throw up an Amazon listing for it, have loads of people pre-order it and then fail to come up with the goods.

What happens if you do that, i.e. open a book for pre-ordering and then fail to deliver the goods? I'm afraid that other than losing access to it for a year, I don't know. This feature has just been added and I don't know anyone brave enough or stupid enough to try doing that. Just keep your promise and everything will be fine.

If you don't want to bother with pre-ordering at all, just select "I am ready to release my book now".

Upload ~~or Create~~ a Book Cover

This is your e-book cover that your cover designer has already sent you or you've already made yourself with the likes of Canva. Browse your computer for your image and hit Upload.

(Launch Cover Creator? Um, no. I don't THINK so.)

Digital Rights Management (DRM)

Digital rights management (DRM) is a device that "intends to prohibit the unauthorised distribution" of your book or, simply put, it aims to prevent piracy. And we are not going to add it to our book.

I know that sounds crazy but trust me, we don't want DRM. It will make your e-books more expensive, cut into your royalties and make me roll my eyes in exactly the same way as I do when I see copyright notices at the end of blog posts about choosing a brand of butter, or hear of idiots submitting manuscripts to agents and publishers with trademark symbols on the title page.

Unless you're an internationally bestselling author, the chances of your book being pirated are between so-slim-you-can't-even-see-it and none. You should be so lucky that people think your book is so amazing that they'd go to the trouble of hunting down an illegally obtained copy of it instead of just paying $2.99 to buy the thing.

Puh. *Leeeease.*

I also think inserting DRM is a bit of an insult. You're basically saying to your readers: "Thanks for buying my book, but I don't trust you and suspect that you might steal from me, so I've taken countermeasures." What's next – putting a notice in your print editions prohibiting lending to friends? And that's not all: DRM prohibits readers who *have* paid for your book from reading it when and where they want. Let's say I've bought your book to read on my computer and then I get a present of a dedicated e-reading device like a Kindle or Nook. Shouldn't I be able to transfer that book, seeing as I've paid for it? Indeed I should, but DRM won't let me.

DRM also can affect text-to-speech features – where a reader can set their e-reading device to read your book aloud to them – which discriminates against readers with vision problems who may rely on these features to enjoy your book.

And here's the kicker: *DRM doesn't work.* It doesn't prevent piracy; there are ways around it. So basically there isn't one single reason why you should apply DRM to your book.

If you think you need DRM, you're (a) wrong and (b) suffering from our old friend Peter Paranoia. I wouldn't dream of putting DRM on an e-book and I don't even worry about piracy. In fact, writing this section is the first time I've given it any thought.

It is the scourge of the bestselling author, yes, but it's nothing to do with us. Especially since we're charging such reasonable prices for our e-books.

Upload and Check Your Book

If you have opted to avail of the pre-ordering feature, the first thing you'll be prompted to do here is to tell Amazon if the manuscript you're uploading is the final version or a draft (as in, not completely copy-edited and proofread yet or, in the case of *Self-Printed*, not even the actual book. Ssshhh! That'll be our little secret …). Then browse for your perfectly formatted MS Word file and upload it to Amazon KDP.

Wait for it to convert into .mobi (Kindle) format. Make a cup of coffee for yourself, perhaps. You've earned it.

Now, you need to check your book to make sure that everything is looking a-okay. The first time I self-published an e-book, I got lazy at this point, so exhausted was I after the terrors of Smashwords formatting that I just couldn't deal with spending even one more second thinking about my e-books – which is why the first .epub edition of *Mousetrapped* had 1,300 pages because every paragraph break *somehow* became a page break during the conversion process. Moral of the story? *Check your books.*

---

7. Preview Your Book

Previewing your book is an integral part of the publishing process and the best way to guarantee that your readers will have a good experience and see the book you want them to see. KDP offers two options to preview your book depending on your needs. Which should I use?

Online Previewer

For most users, the online previewer is the best and easiest way to preview your content. The online previewer allows you to preview most books as they will appear on Kindle, Kindle Fire, iPad, and iPhone. If your book is fixed layout (for more information on fixed layout, see the Kindle Publishing Guidelines), the online previewer will display your book as it will appear on Kindle Fire.

`Preview book`

Downloadable Previewer

If you would like to preview your book on Kindle Touch or Kindle DX, you will want to use the downloadable previewer.

Instructions
Download Book Preview File
Download HTML
Download Previewer:
Windows | Mac

You have two options here. Either you can review your book onscreen on a virtual Kindle, or you can download a preview file in .mobi format to your computer and transfer it to your Kindle either by Amazon's e-mail or USB.

You can also download the book preview file and check it in Amazon's free Kindle Reading App, which you can download to your PC, Mac, tablet or smartphone.

I don't think anything beats actually seeing the finished book on an actual Kindle screen. If something's wrong, you'll find it there.

As I said previously, I would very much doubt you'll find much – if anything – wrong with your Kindle edition, as KDP's conversion is really, really good and improving all the time.

Once you're happy, go back to KDP and click Save and Continue. If you've left the process in the meantime, just log back on to KDP and select Edit Book Details alongside the title on your Bookshelf.

On to Page 2: Rights and Pricing!

Verify Your Publishing Territories

This is asking you within what geographical regions you have the rights to publish this work. Since you wrote it and no rights to it have ever been sold, select Worldwide Rights — All Territories.

If you are a traditionally published author self-publishing a book that remains in print somewhere in the world, check with your agent or publisher which territories you can legally publish the e-book in. If it's not all of them, manually select the relevant territories from the list.

Set Your Pricing and Royalty

Here you select whether you want to make 35 per cent off the sale of your e-books, or 70 per cent. It's a toughie, isn't it?

Um, no. It isn't. We want 70 per cent, and as I've already argued I think $2.99 is the right place for each standard-length self-published book to start off from. (Note: when I say standard length I'm talking about not selling pamphlets for $3.00. I'm *not* talking about charging $5.00 because your book is longer than most.) The catch: in order to qualify for the 70 per cent rate, your book has to be at least $2.99 and no more than $9.99, and you'll only get the 70 per cent for books purchased in countries that have their own regional Amazon store (generally speaking). The good news is that in all likelihood, the majority of your sales will come from there.

If your book is 99¢ or $1.99, you have no choice but to go with 35 per cent.

This is also where you enter the list price. If it's more than $4.99 I'll find out, you know.

You can also manually set your foreign-currency prices, or have KDP calculate it automatically based on your US dollar price. In the interests of fairness, I say calculate it automatically.

NB: You *must* select a royalty and *then* a list price, and it will only let you enter a price that agrees with your selected royalty. So if you find yourself unable to enter 99¢ without getting an error message, make sure you've checked the 35 per cent royalty box.

Kindle MatchBook

If you have a print edition of your title on offer on Amazon too, you could enrol both books – paperback and e-book – in the Kindle MatchBook programme. This enables customers who have previously bought your print edition to also purchase your Kindle edition for $2.99 or less. This, obviously, is a great idea, because it encourages more sales but alas, we don't have a paperback yet. You can come back here again when you do and enrol your books if you like.

Kindle Lending Library

Kindle owners can lend a Kindle book they have purchased to a friend and you have to let this happen if you want your 70 per cent. That's why this box is already checked onscreen and you can't uncheck it.

This is another thing that tends to lead to knicker-twisting, but it shouldn't. It's not that different from me buying a book, reading it and then lending it to a friend.

If you enrol your book in KDP Select, you will be compensated for lends from something called the KDP Select Global Fund. This is a six- or seven-figure amount in US dollars that is used to compensate authors whose books are lent out in the Kindle Owners Lending Library (KOLL) during any one month, with the spoils being divided equally.

Let's totally oversimplify things and say that during the month of August, the fund was $100 and 1,000 books were lent out. When we divide the money up equally, we find that one lend is equal to 10¢. Therefore if your book was lent out ten times in this period, you'd earn a whopping one dollar.

Of course, the fund isn't $100 – for September 2014, it's $3,000,000. (You can check the current monthly pot by logging into your KDP account and fixing your eyes on the upper right-hand corner.) But then, there are a lot more than 1,000 lends too.

If you're not enrolled in KDP Select, you won't be compensated for borrows at all but you must allow borrows to happen if you publish on Amazon KDP. So there's not much you can do about that ...

Publish

Once you've completed everything on the page and are happy to do so, click Publish.

What Happens Now?

First of all a little dialogue box will appear telling you that you've successfully published your book and that it should make an appearance on the Kindle Store in 12 hours or so.

If you return to your Bookshelf, you'll see your title has appeared there. It will say "In Review" for a while, and then that will change to "Publishing", and then that will change to "Live". If you've opted for the pre-ordering feature, it'll say something like "Pre-ordering Live".

You'll also see that it has been assigned an Amazon Standard Identification Number (ASIN), which is Amazon's own version of an ISBN, and the reason you didn't need one to publish on Amazon KDP.

So now we wait for our book to appear on Amazon. In my experience it happens a lot quicker than 12 hours. If you go away and have some lunch, it'll probably be up there by the time you get back.

Uploading to Smashwords

As I warned already, it's going to take a bit more work than *that* to get your e-book up on Smashwords, who will sell it directly from their site and push it out to retailers like Barnes & Noble's Nook store, Kobo and Apple's iBooks. Although the principles are the same, there is a lot more nuanced formatting involved than what we've just done to get our book up on Amazon KDP.

Luckily, Smashwords provide detailed instructions in their Smashwords Style Guide, which available to download for free from here:

http://bit.ly/smashwordsguide

Publishing to Smashwords happens in two stages. First, you upload and publish on Smashwords.com, which is similar to the procedure we just did with Amazon KDP. Then, once the book has been published, you assign it a free ISBN – take the free ISBN, remember? – and then submit to Smashwords' Premium Catalogue. This is their name for the books that are pushed out to other retailers via Smashwords distribution and if your formatting isn't absolutely perfect, this is when you'll find it out.

I have to admit that I've just given up on Smashwords – not because I don't think they can sell my books for me, but because I just don't have the time or the patience to jump through the number of hoops their formatting requirements demand. It used to be difficult to get your e-book document perfect for them, but now I find it impossible. So I use eBookPartnership to reach the retailers that Smashwords would otherwise, but you could also go to the aforementioned Mark's List to find a formatter who'll get your book perfect for a few dollars and off you go.

Using an E-book Conversion Service

I've invited Diana of eBookPartnership to explain more about hiring an e-book conversion service who will take your manuscript in any shape at all, sprinkle some pixie dust and then – ta-*daa!* – your e-book is looking great, is available in all major formats and is for sale on all the e-book retailers that count.

I should say that I chose to include eBookPartnership here because they're the service *I* use, and I think they're great. So do the likes of e-book mega-sellers Rachel Abbott and Kerry Wilkinson, and author of one of my favourite books of all time (*Moondust: In Search of the Men Who Fell to Earth*), Andrew Smith, who they can count among their happy clients.

So, over to Diana …

If you would like to manage your own e-book conversion, there is a wealth of advice and resources available to writers. As previously outlined, if you follow guidelines and take advantage of the generosity of pioneer authors like Catherine, Word to .mobi is straightforward. Amazon is continually refining the KDP system, and it is a great tool for authors.

ePub is a slightly different prospect, and can induce a level of frustration that may impact on your writing productivity, but if you recognise this at the outset and invest in the marvellous Liz Castro book *ePub Straight to the Point* you may be able to add e-book formatting to your author toolbox quite quickly. Liz explains the complete process for creating an ePub file from Word and InDesign files. You can also find Liz on Twitter (@lizcastro), and if you follow the #eprdctn stream, you can pick up tips from ePub specialists also.

However, there are several reasons why you may want to enlist the help of a professional e-book conversion service for some or all elements of the project:

- You may have successfully mastered the Kindle file conversion and upload, but would like an ePub file that does not contain any coding errors (which can lead to a title being rejected by a retailer) and allows you to sell on Apple, Barnes & Noble, Waterstones, Kobo and other e-book sales outlets around the world
- Your book has complex formatting, many images, or needs to be converted to a fixed layout rather than a standard flowing e-book.
- Perhaps the terms *html*, *CSS*, or even *zip file* induce instant anxiety and an urge to move away from the PC or Mac
- You would like to simply send the manuscript to someone and get the conversion done quickly and efficiently to meet a specific launch date
- The ePub file you created has been rejected by a retailer and you cannot identify a fix
- The only copy of your book is a print version and you need a scanned version with extracted text that is recognisably English (or whichever language it was originally written in), rather than a collection of unfamiliar characters and symbols
- Your self-publishing company created an e-book version of your book on your behalf, uploaded it to Amazon, and promptly went out of business, or refuses to return your calls or send you the e-book files. Sadly, we have received calls from a number of authors in this predicament in the last two years

These are some common scenarios, but whatever the reason for investigating other options, look for relevant experience in all file formats, including fixed layout. Check for credible client testimonials and do not be afraid to ask as many questions as you need to. E-book conversion is a relatively new field of expertise and there are varying levels of competence.

eBookPartnership.com is a service provider, we advise and support authors, and they pay us for the services they require, rather than enter into a long-term revenue share arrangement. If we also manage distribution for authors looking for wider distribution, we charge a set-up fee and low annual fee, and pay 100 per cent of royalties received from the retailers directly to the writer or publisher. This applies to writers or publishers who do not individually meet new account set-up criteria for Waterstones, or Apple, or Barnes & Noble, for example.

Other companies will offer different levels of involvement and royalty share, and it is vitally important that you understand any agreement before you sign a contract.

Questions to ask your e-book conversion professional:

1. Can you provide a contract and details of terms and conditions?

Obvious, but a good place to start. Make absolutely sure that you retain all rights to your work, that your files are being securely stored, and that any distribution agreement for the e-book is crystal clear. Once converted, you should receive copies of the e-book files, and if you wish to, you can then upload these files to retailers yourself. If you have paid for cover design, the cover then becomes yours, check that any images used are correctly licensed and that the use of the image is not in any way restricted.

2. Will I get a review copy of my e-book?

It is essential that you see the e-book files before publication. Ideally you would view them on a Kindle or iPad, or Kobo reader, for example, but you can use a PC-based reader if you do not have access to an e-book reader.

It is worth emphasising at this point that the file you submit prior to conversion should be the final file, as if it were going to print. If you receive your review copy and decide that you need to make editorial changes, you will be charged for the time it takes to recode the e-book.

Of course, if there are errors in formatting, the conversion specialist should correct these without charge.

3. Are there any extra costs I should be aware of?

Standard pricing may apply to books of a certain length (up to 300 pages for example), or may only take into account a maximum number of images, included in the price. You may have to submit your file in order for an accurate quote to be provided. Images take time to get right – they need to be optimised and placed correctly within the text – so you may find that you incur extra charges for including more than a specified maximum number.

4. Do you help me to promote sales of the e-book?

Do not assume that your conversion company will be able to offer you marketing services as part of the package, unless it is specifically stated. This is a specialist area and one which needs the same focus and research as the conversion. We keep a close eye on industry news and often circulate articles and resources that we find, and our authors and publishers feed back information too.

5. I want to upload my e-book myself to retailers. Can I do this?

Once your e-book files are created, they are yours and you can decide which retailers you would like to upload to. Managing your own account on Amazon is easy, many authors like to take control of this and have access to sales information, and to have the ability to make changes or manage their KDP Select campaigns. This is not the case for all retailers, however, and it may be that you need to use a company like eBookPartnership.com to upload your books via their accounts and have the royalties paid to you by them.

Feel free to call us on +44 845 123 2699 for a chat (or Skype DMHorner). We are delighted to work with authors at any stage of their e-book adventure. Our website has lots more information:

www.ebookpartnership.com

* * *

So there we have it: we've published our e-books. I would love to tell you that the hard part is done, but the hard part is only beginning. (Sorry!) The good news is that next, when we get to work bringing our POD paperback baby into the world, we've already done a lot of the tricky bits, like writing a blurb …

Okay, so we've done *one* of the tricky bits.

Now might be the time to make some more coffee.

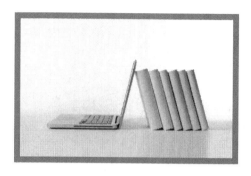

PART 4
Publishing Your Paperback

Welcome to CreateSpace

Oh, the humble paperback! The realisation of our book in the flesh! (Or at least on paper.) None of us grew up dreaming of seeing our name on a Kindle screen but most of us probably *did* dream of seeing it on the spine of a book.

Well, now you get to make that book, and if at any point it starts to feel like hard work, just imagine opening the cardboard package marked "CreateSpace" a couple of weeks from now, seeing your shiny cover for the first time and then calling in sick to work and cancelling all social engagements so you can gaze at it adoringly until the novelty wears off.

(Which it won't. *Ever.*)

For our print-on-demand paperback, we're going to use CreateSpace, the POD service owned by Amazon, because it's at the intersection of quality and value. There is simply *no easier way* to bring a paperback edition of your book into the world, and CreateSpace paperbacks look really good.

I'm not going to tell you how to use other services or recommend that you do because this book is about what *I* did, and I used CreateSpace. I've always been really pleased with their service, especially the quality of my book, their prompt payments and their speedy and helpful responses to any issues I may have had rare cause to e-mail them about. I should say, in case you were getting suspicious, that I have absolutely no ties to CreateSpace other than the ones you'll learn about in a minute, i.e. I published my book with them. I receive nothing in return for telling readers of this book that you should go with them, except the warm, fuzzy feeling I get from helping you. (But I'm not opposed to bribes and should the situation change, I'll be sure to let you know. Promise.)

The order of what follows may seem a bit odd to you, like formatting our interior before we've even seen a mock-up of a cover, but stick with it and you'll see why this is the easiest way.

Create a CreateSpace Account

The first thing you need to do is sign up for a free CreateSpace account. Make your way to www.createspace.com, click Sign Up and then agree to the terms and conditions. You'll have to verify the e-mail address you provide before you can continue, so keep an eye for an e-mail from CreateSpace in your inbox.

Tip: do not click anything that asks for more information or a consultation or in fact anything purporting to be help. You don't need any help; you have already got it, in the form of this book. CreateSpace "help" is in fact a team of pushy sales consultants hawking overpriced cover design and editing services. We're fine on our own, thank you very much.

Once you've verified your e-mail address, you'll be met with a window that prompts you to get started with your first project or to "talk to the pros" (EYE ROLL). Look down the bottom. You see that hyperlink that says "Continue to your Member Dashboard"? As Liz Lemon would say, we want to go to there. Click it.

You should now be looking at a screen like this:

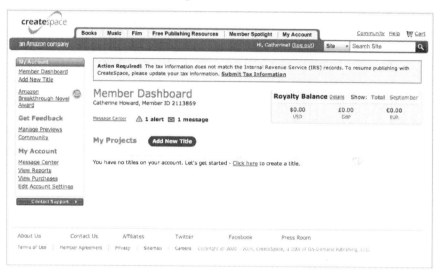

And look who it is, right up there at the top: only our old friend, tax information! Click on Submit Tax Information to get to your Account Settings, where you can start filling in the information CreateSpace needs to pay you.

CreateSpace is slightly different from Amazon KDP in that it offers fewer countries electronic funds transfer (EFT) payments – you can only get paid by EFT if you live in the US, UK, Germany, France, Spain, Portugal, Belgium or the Netherlands. I live in Ireland, which means that for now at least, I receive cheques from CreateSpace in three difference currencies: US dollars (for Amazon.com sales), British pounds (for Amazon.co.uk sales) and euro (for all European Amazons) and I only receive them when my royalties in each currency exceed $100, £100 or €100, the minimum payment threshold for cheques.

If you opt for cheques over EFT, there will be a handling fee of $8/£8/€8 added to each cheque – you'll receive your royalties less that amount – *unless* there is no EFT option for your country, in which case the fee is waived.

Can you guess how much time I have for self-publishers who

complain about any of the above? Yes, you're right: ZERO TIME. Again, your options are like it or lump it. Remember that (a) CreateSpace are providing a service – a fabulous, convenient, efficient service – and that as a business, they expect to be compensated for providing it and (b) *no one is forcing you to do this.*

Now on to the tax interview. CreateSpace are looking for the exact same information you provided to Amazon KDP; this is exactly the same process we went through before.

Yes, the screens will look a little different – but not *that* different, despite a recent commenter on my blog exclaiming that she had "tried" to complete it but gave up because it "made NO sense". Guys, this isn't *Keeping up with the Kardashians*. This is a faux-drama-free zone. Just tell them what they want to know and save the changes.

For those of you in a cold sweat already, you can refer back to the Amazon KDP instructions:

http://www.catherineryanhoward.com/selfprinted3

When you're done click Exit Interview to return to your Account Settings. Look to the list of options on the left-hand side of the screen and find Member Dashboard. Click it. We're now back on the main page of your CreateSpace, the one you'll see whenever you log in. Eventually all your active titles will be displayed here, as well as how much money CS owes you at any particular time (see Royalty Balance in the upper right-hand corner? All showing zeros at the moment but that will change!) Now look for Add New Title and let's get to work.

Title Set-Up

To "Start Your New Project" you need to tell CreateSpace your book's **title** (you can always change this later), the **type of project** you want to start (paperback) and whether you want to do it using the Guided or Expert processes. We're going to go with **Expert**. Don't be scared: all this means is that you're going to work with one page as opposed to being guided through it section by section in a process so over-simplified that it'll drive you crazy. You also won't be able to use this book to get through it. So from now on, consider yourself an expert!

You will then be brought to a screen that looks like the one pictured on the next page. This is the **Setup** screen, where we create our paperback.

We are now going to work our way through this process, but not all at once; when you need to leave the page, find the Save Progress button (scroll down) so that everything you've entered will be there when you return. If you want to access the Member Dashboard at any time, click Return to Member Dashboard (top left-hand corner).

As we begin to fill things in, I want you to keep something in mind: however you do it here is how it'll eventually end up looking on Amazon and any other retailer that sells your paperback online. So all this information is not only telling CreateSpace what you want to produce, it's is going to form your book's online retailer *listings* as well. This means writing titles and names as you wish them to appear – as they *should* appear. That's Best Novel Ever and Bob Bestseller, not BEST NOVEL EVER or *superstar author*, okay?

Title

Fairly straightforward – enter the title of your book. You know what to do.

Subtitle

As with Amazon KDP, only enter a subtitle here if your book actually *has* one. Otherwise, leave this blank.

Primary Author

Think about your book's cover for a second. Visualise the author name on it. Then type that *exact same name* in here.

CreateSpace aren't asking you for this information for the good of their health. This is the author name that will be displayed on your Amazon page alongside your book, so input accordingly. And for the love of fudge, leave those "prefix" and "suffix" boxes empty unless you're Dr Oz III.

I'm probably a bad example to use here, because "Ryan Howard" is made up and the fact that it's not hyphenated confuses people. (Is Ryan her middle name? Her maiden name? If I was filing her alphabetically by surname, would she go in the *R's* or the *H's*? IS THERE NO END TO THIS CONFUSION?) But let's pretend, for our purposes here, that "Ryan Howard" is my double-barrelled surname and the hyphen is invisible. So: "Catherine" goes in the First Name box and "Ryan Howard" goes in the Last Name one. My actual name, Catherine (Mary) Howard, does not get a look in. If I wanted to go by Catherine R Howard, the *R* would go in the middle box.

The name entered here has to match the one on the cover of your book. So if you're a practising medical doctor and your name is Rose Murphy, "Dr" would *only* go into the Prefix box if it also appeared on the front of your book's cover.

Add Contributors

CreateSpace just don't make it easy for people writing "how to self-publish books" books, do they? You could do some damage on KDP, sure, but here you can enter all *sorts* of things: created by, from an idea by, memoir by, preliminary work by, revised by, compiled by, as told by, prepared for publication by, assisted by …

And that's only a *selection* of the fanciful contributor titles they have on offer.

This is because CreateSpace also produces POD audio CDs and DVDs. It is not for you. So just ignore this completely, unless you can prove in a court of law (Catherine's law) that you have a reason that is identical to one of the exceptions to the rule listed when we discussed contributors back on Amazon KDP.

NB: You've already listed yourself as the author in the "Primary Author" bit. You don't need to do it again.

Series, Volume Number and Edition

This is the same shenanigans we dealt with already back on Amazon KDP. If your book is part of a series, check the "part of a series" box and tell us which instalment (volume) it is.

Edition here basically means version. If you have never published a print edition of this book before, enter "1". When I come to CreateSpace the crap out of this book, I'll be entering "3" in this box because it's the third edition.

Leave the language set to English unless you're publishing a book in a different one and also leave the publication date box blank. You can't set it to a date in the future and I see little point in setting it to a date in the past. Leaving it blank will make your publication date the date the book is born (i.e. you complete the publication process on CreateSpace) and that's the right thing to do.

ISBN

Check the box next to "CreateSpace assigned – We can assign an ISBN to your book at no charge".

End of discussion.

Now we'll take a little time-out to ponder the real important stuff: what kind of book do you want? What size do you want it to be? What colour pages do you want? You can't change these later, so now is the time to decide.

Interior Type

Select "Black and White" because that's what you want: a black and white interior. This will make all text black and any images black and white.

The only exception to this is a fully illustrated title, like a cookbook, which is not the kind of the book *this* book is designed to guide you through creating. Full-colour interiors are a lot more expensive, so print-on-demand isn't the ideal way to bring a book like that to life.

Sometimes you see books, particularly non-fiction, that have a number of glossy photo pages in the middle while the rest of the book is black text on plain paper. This is not an option here; all the pages must be the same type.

In the second edition of *Mousetrapped*, I put photographs in the middle but did it on the standard paper, and it looked fine. Not *great* or as good as it would've on photo paper, but it did the job. If you have a print edition of this book, you'll have already noticed all the images appear in black and white.

Paper Colour

You can choose either bright-white or cream-coloured paper. Before we go any further, go to your bookshelves and see what colour the pages are in most if not all of the paperbacks there. I'll save you the bother: they're *cream*. And because we want our books to look as close to "properly" published books as possible, we're going to choose cream too.

There is only one exception, as you may have guessed from the page you're currently reading this on if you're reading the paperback: if your book cover is predominantly white (especially at the edges where it meets the pages), then I'd choose white paper instead, because the cream colour might look dirty or just off-white against a bright white cover.

While we're on the subject of paper, you may be wondering what the paper is like, i.e. does it feel thick or flimsy? According to the CS website, the interior paper they use is 60#. This may mean nothing to you or me, so let me tell you this:

- It's the paper you have in your hands right now if you're not reading this on an e-reader
- It's of a similar quality to mass produced, traditionally published books
- It'll do the job just fine

Self-publishers love using high-quality paper, which, thankfully, isn't an option here. That's not what traditionally published books are printed on. Some books on my shelf have pages so thin you can see through them, and they work just fine. Furthermore, the higher the quality of your interior paper, the heavier it will be, and shipping charges are decided by weight. So pick a colour (cream!) and don't worry about the rest.

Trim Size

Trim size just means the size of your book, i.e. how high it'll stand and how wide it'll be. CreateSpace offers a range of them, but you can't use them all. In order for your book to be eligible for Amazon.com and other online retailers, it needs to conform to industry standards and to do that it needs to be one of the following (all in inches and width x height):

- 5 x 8
- 5.06 x 7.81
- 5.25 x 8
- 5.5 x 8.5
- 6 x 9
- 6.14 x 9.21
- 6.69 x 9.61
- 7 x 10
- 7.44 x 9.69
- 7.5 x 9.25

It'll also have to have a minimum of 24 pages and a maximum of either 828 (for white paper) or 740 (for cream). All of the above trim sizes are also listed in centimetres on the CreateSpace website.

This is confusing, right? Anything with lots of options is. So instead of focusing on all the different sizes you can potentially make your book, think about just one thing: what size do you *want it to be?* If you're about to self-publish a novel, go measure some. See what their trim size is, and then see if it or something similar is available on CS. The same goes for other types of books. (If you can find a book the exact size or almost the exact size as the trim you've chosen, be it traditionally or self-published, hang on to it. We're going to need it in a minute to check something.)

When it came to picking a size for *Mousetrapped*, I ordered a let's-just-see-what-this-is-like proof copy in 6 x 9 because that seemed to be the most popular. But when it arrived, it was thin, floppy and screaming "I'm a crappy self-published book!", because with more space on each page, my page count was under 200. It's hard to judge at this point how thick your book will be, but the smaller the trim size, the thicker it will be. And thickness is just as important to its overall appearance as anything else. I ended up making *Mousetrapped* 5.5. x 8.5, which in turn made it about 230 pages.

This book, however, could not be 5.5 x 8.5, because the number of pages I'd need to use to print at that size would make the book too expensive, both for me to sell and for you to buy. (It's 6 x 9.)

Some self-publishers get fixated on a certain trim size and spit bullets when they discover that CreateSpace doesn't offer POD paperbacks in the exact dimensions that, say, Lee Child's latest offering has been printed in. If this is you, CALM THE FUDGE DOWN and pick the closest trim size to it instead.

The trim size will be set to 6 x 9 on screen by default; if you want something else, click the Choose a Different Size button. A list of the most popular and industry-standard sizes will then be displayed and you can just select whichever one you want.

When you're done, look for Download a Word Template and then, underneath it, Blank Template. Click it to download a blank MS Word document that's been formatted – page size and even/odd margins – to match your chosen trim size exactly. It's this we'll use to create the interior of our book.

Collect Your ISBN

Don't fill in any more information. Instead scroll to the bottom of the screen and click Save Progress. Once your changes have been saved, scroll back up until – *ta-daa!* – you find your sparkly new ISBN-13 and ISBN-10 (the difference between the two being how long they are).

Make a note of both of them and log out of CreateSpace altogether. It's time to make the interior (pages) of our book!

Formatting Your CreateSpace Interior

A quick reminder of how CreateSpace works: we make our book's inside pages in MS Word, convert it to PDF and then upload it to CreateSpace, who print it, bind it, slap a cover on it and ship it whenever someone orders a copy of our book, *Best Novel Ever*. Whatever we upload will be exactly what appears in the finished book – page numbers or lack thereof and all – so tread carefully. We will, of course, order proof copies to make sure everything is a-okay before we offer it for sale anywhere, but the aim is to go through our proof copies confirming our book's perfection. We'd like to get it right first time. You might want to make some more coffee …

Open the blank but perfectly sized MS Word template you downloaded from CreateSpace and save it somewhere you'll find it again easily on your computer. I always name my interior documents for the name of the book followed by something like "6x9interior".

To make doubly sure that everything is as it should be, go to File → Page Set-up to **check that the paper size matches the trim size** you've chosen.

It's important that it does, otherwise your PDF may not print correctly when it's being the inside of your book.

If it doesn't, you will have to create a "Custom Size" to get your paper size to match your trim size. Go back to CreateSpace to get the exact measurements if you like. You could also eyeball your margins: are they different depending on whether you're on an odd (right-hand side as you look at the book) or even (left-hand size as you look at the book) page? They should be.

Next, **decide on a font**. You want a font that is readable, looks good and resembles fonts you have seen used in actual, proper books designed by professional book designers. This is not the time to profess your love for Mistral, Brush Script or a font you designed yourself based on scans of your own handwriting.

Industry standards are industry standards because they *work*. I recommend that you pick one of the following: Times New Roman, Book Antiqua, Georgia or Garamond.

Your main font size should be either 10, 11 or 12 point (pt). Which size you decide upon will depend on what font you pick. For instance, this book is Book Antiqua 10 pt, but if it were in Garamond, 10 pt would be a bit small.

(*Mousetrapped* is in Book Antiqua 11 pt.)

The number one font problem I see in self-published books is that the font is too large. We probably don't realise just how small the text is in traditionally published books – go grab one now and have a look for yourself. In fact, I think the easiest way to get a font and look you like is to find a traditionally published book whose pages you admire and then try to recreate the same style in your CreateSpace interior. One of the best-looking books I ever made was for a client who wanted to create a POD version of a book that had been previously published, which for all intents and purposes would look just like it. (She'd got permission to use the same cover image.) At first glance the pages looked way too "proper" for me to recreate, but I soon found a close font match in MS Word and realised that the chapter headings had been made using Format → Font and then "Expanded spacing" on the Advanced tab, which spread the text out without increasing the font size.

Play around with this a bit. Test your choices. Copy and paste a few paragraphs of any old text at all into the template you just downloaded and print out a page. Then cut the page so it matches the finished trim size and slip it into a "real" book of a similar size to see what the pages will look like. Is the text readable? Does it look good? Will my eyes be hanging out of my head if I look at it for longer than five minutes?

When you've decided how your interior is going to look, open your manuscript document. Select all text and copy and paste it into the MS Word interior template you downloaded from CreateSpace. Remember, this should be your *final* version, save perhaps for a bit of typo-catching. You could also copy and paste the text from your prepared-for-Kindle MS Word document instead. Then:

- Delete anything that may have belonged in your manuscript but does not belong in your book, like contact details or the licence notes if you're copying from your e-book document
- **Justify all text** (Format → Paragraph, select Justified under "Alignment" on the Indents and Spacing tab)
- Set all line spacing to single or whatever you've decided on
- Set it to the font and font size you've decided on too

Do you have inexplicable gaps anywhere in your document? Big chunks of white space that have seemingly come out of nowhere? Has MS Word skipped over the bottom half of, say, page 26, for no apparent reason at all? This is a frequent problem caused by MS Word's satanic ways.

Try this quick solution:

1. Select all text by clicking Edit → Select All
2. Go to Format → Paragraph and select the Line and Page Breaks tab
3. See the little box next to "Keep with next"? Uncheck it (Or check it, if it wasn't checked already. Basically do the opposite of whatever the setting was to begin with)

If that doesn't work, you may have section or page breaks in there that you don't know about. Activate Show/Hide by clicking the ¶ mark and then go hunting for them. If there's one before an inexplicable gap, delete it.

The Front Matter

Pick up any traditionally published book and open its cover. What's on the first page? What's on the second page? And what's on the page after *that*?

The answer is never going to be the first page of Chapter One. Books just don't start like that. There are a few other things that need to go in there first.

My tip for this section is to find a real, live, traditionally published book that's the same as yours, e.g. a thriller novel or a reference book, and then follow its example.

The First Page

I recommend one of two options for your first page.

If this is your first book and it has yet to be reviewed, then put an About the Author on it. This should be short, relevant and written in the third person.

By relevant, I don't just mean leave out the fact that you were Under-8 Munster Disco-Dancing Champion in 1991. (Even though I was, thanks for asking. My winning routine was to that musical classic, *Do the Bartman*.) I mean **tailor it to the content of your book**. For instance, if you've written the next *Bridget Jones's Diary*, you might make a funny joke about how you currently divide your time between Tinder and Match.com. If you've written a thriller, I'd aim for serious and mysterious, with no cute or warm details supplied. If you've written a how-to, you might want to focus on what qualifies you to do so.

Don't give me your life story. Recently I came across a self-published writer whose bio informed me that she currently lives in Idaho with her two daughters and her beloved husband Dave, who she was lucky enough to marry last June after ten wonderful years together and she hopes they have many more wonderful years to come. The woman had published a thriller about a serial killer who stalks his victims while they sleep. How confident are you that she's going to be able to scare you, what with all the puppies and rainbows and heart-shaped balloons in her life?

The shorter your author bio is, the better. Less room for error then. If all else fails, fill in these blanks:

[Your name] was born in [city] in [year]. This is his/her first novel.

The other option is the one I've gone with for the paperback edition of this book: praise. If you have previously released a book or have reviews you can quote for this one, then you can put them on the first page instead. Make sure you attribute them, and *a name is not enough*. You need to demonstrate for the reader why praise from this person is high praise indeed. (I'll be lecturing you more about endorsements in due course.) If you decide to put reviews on this page, we'll relegate the About the Author to the back.

As for *getting* reviews, we'll talk about that later.

The Copyright Page

Your copyright notice should be the next thing to appear, and it should be on an even-numbered or left-hand page. It should begin with both your ISBNs, then your copyright symbol and name, and then the copyright notice itself.

Like this:

If your book is non-fiction, you might need additional lines such as "Although this is a work of non-fiction, some names have been changed by the author." Find a book similar to yours, be it a novel, an instructional guide or a memoir, and see what its copyright notice says. But change it around a bit – don't just copy someone else's copyright notice because the infinity loop of irony would cause the planet to implode.

You can also put things like your blog URL and Twitter username on this page, and maybe even give a shout out to your cover designer. (But NOT your editor!)

NB: Before you can order a proof copy, you'll have to submit your book for "processing", which means that CreateSpace's computers will go through your files checking that your cover file is the right size for the number of pages, etc. They will also check that the ISBNs they assigned you appear on your copyright page, so it's imperative you put them in there and ensure they are correct.

The Title Page

This is an otherwise blank page that just has the title of your book on it. Most books have two of these: one that has the author's name, title and subtitle, and then another later on that has just the title (i.e. the half title). Refer to the real, live book you're using as a model to determine which is the best approach for you.

Also By

If this isn't your first book, you should take the opportunity to list your other titles. These should be on an even page, or on the left-hand side of the book as you open it. Put "Also by [YOUR NAME]" or "By the same author" at the top of the page, centred, and then list your titles underneath it. There should be no other information – no prices, no formats, no special offers. Just the title(s) of the book(s).

Table of Contents

If you want to put a table of contents in your book, do so on an odd page between two titles. Put the chapter name to the left of the page and the corresponding page number to the right, using tabs (yes, you're allowed use tabs here!) so they both line up evenly, like:

If your chapters or sections are numbered and not named, you do not need a table of contents. Nor do you need one if you've written a novel.

Creating Chapters

Make sure that the main text of your book starts on an odd or right-hand side page.

Now we're going to go through the main text of the book checking that all text is justified, new paragraphs are indented and all text is correctly sized.

Use something simple but effective to delineate the start of a new chapter. Here's what I did with *Mousetrapped*:

- Start each new chapter on an odd page
- Press Return until you're approximately 1/4 down the page (check the ruler to see the exact position so you can put it in the same place each time. In a novel, chapters should never start at the very top of a page)
- Type the chapter number in words (i.e. "One") in 12 pt italics. Press Return
- Type the name of the chapter in 14 pt bold, all caps. Press Return twice

- Start your chapter

Try to avoid being overly ambitious with your interior text. In a traditionally published book, you might see some artwork or an illustration accompanying chapter headings, or chapters beginning with a drop cap, where the first letter of a chapter is much larger than the text around it. But those books are laid out by professional book designers; we're just going to concentrate on making ours look good. As we're not professional book designers, this means keeping things simple.

As you go through your book, avoid having pages where only half of one line appears. You can also use MS Word's Widow/Orphan Control function to help you avoid this. Select all text, then Format → Paragraph, and then select the Line and Page Breaks tab. Check the box next to "Widow/Orphan control".

Always start new chapters or sections on the odd page, i.e. the right-hand side. You will end up with some blank pages; this is perfectly normal.

Please don't try to close everything up or use a smaller font just because you want to save yourself a few cents on the extra pages. Not having a well-laid-out interior will cost you more in the long run than the few cents you'll save now by doing that.

The End Matter

The back of your book needs some thought too – typing "THE END" and then having nothing but a cover to close is a wasted opportunity. Imagine you are the reader and you get to the end of (what we hope!) is an enjoyable book that piques your interest in both the author and the subject matter. Don't you want to give them something more?

Author Note

You may want to tell the reader something about the book outside of the book itself. Use these sparingly and only if you have to, i.e. don't try to think of something to put in an author's note just because you want one.

In *Mousetrapped*, I used it to explain that yes, I was aware that Walt Disney World was not "the happiest place on earth" (Disneyland California is; WDW's Magic Kingdom is in fact "the most magical place on earth") but that since "What could go wrong in the resort that has a theme park in it that's called the most magical place on earth?" wasn't anywhere near as catchy a headline, I took some licence with it instead. I also told readers that a number of places mentioned in the book (a movie theatre, a bookstore, etc.) have since closed down.

Acknowledgements

This is where you thank all the people who helped you with the book who, if you don't thank them, will never speak to you again.

Bring Your Readers Online

It doesn't hurt to put your Twitter username or blogsite URL here so that readers know where to find you online if they discovered your book before they discovered you.

About the Author

If you've put reviews at the front, put your About the Author back here.

News of Your Other Books

If you have other, related books available you might want to mention them here, or even include a teaser chapter.

Now if I'm reading a paperback and I see a teaser chapter at the end introduced with something like, "Read the opening scene of Big Author's next novel, coming May 2017", I don't bother reading it, because I don't see the point when I have to wait *ages* to read the rest of the book. But what if the book was out already? I think as long as you're not eating into your profits with too many extra pages, sticking a preview of another book in here isn't a bad idea at all.

Breaking the Spell

Having said all that, there is an argument *against* putting anything after "THE END" except for blank pages: *you break the spell*. A lot of time, talent and tears go into making a reader believe a story you've pulled from the air is actually real. The best novels are the ones whose characters linger with us afterwards, stories that affect us so deeply we find ourselves, days later, daydreaming about what a particular character might be up to now. Sometimes reaching the end of a novel is a wrenching experience, because we don't want to yet let go of the new friends we've made. Sometimes we're pulled so far into the author's imagination that it takes us a while to make our way back to the surface, to blink and look around and realise that we're in the real world once again.

Unless we're met with nine pages of acknowledgements that start with "When I sat down to write this book ..."

That breaks the spell *instantly*, because it's right there in our face: this story was made up. Made up by this author. The one who says that without her best friend, it couldn't have been done.

If you've written a novel, my advice would be to put your About the Author and the acknowledgements at the start and leave your book blank after THE END. Hopefully the reader will stay under your spell, and stay there long enough to go to Amazon and write you a glowing review …

Inserting Images

As I've already said this book isn't aimed at self-publishers looking to produce richly illustrated books (because I don't know anything about doing that, but I know enough about the cost of POD to think you'd be better off not producing your full-colour book this way) but if you want to put a handful of images into your book, you can.

In the second edition of *Mousetrapped*, I inserted about nine photos across five or six pages in the middle of the book. All I did was insert the images as I normally would in any MS Word document, set their layouts to "tight" and after I'd converted to PDF, checked they were all still in the same places. (They were.) Even though they were colour photographs, they of course appeared in black and white in the book because I'd chosen a black and white interior.

Technically speaking, CreateSpace say: "Images may be CMYK or RGB color. All images should be sized at 100%, flattened to one layer and placed in your document at a minimum resolution of 300 DPI." But I have literally no idea what any of that means, so I just Insert → Picture and hope for the best!

NB: Be careful how many images you insert. CreateSpace will not accept your interior file if it's bigger than 400 MB.

Page Numbers and Running Heads

So up until now formatting our interior document has been pretty easy, right? Well now, as we put the finishing touches to it, we have one *ickle* complicated bit that might drive us a tad insane. But it will make our book better and we only have to do it once, so try and stick with it. It'll be worth it in the end.

Our book – obviously – *has* to have page numbers and it *can* have running heads, if you want.

A **running head** in fiction is when the title and the author's name appear in the header of each page, with the title on the even, left-hand pages and the author's name on the odd, right-hand pages. Like this (quite simplistic) example:

> **Backpacked**
>
> gleam from this trip? Would I get anything out of it at all, other than mosquito bites, an increased immunity to malaria and a bronzed tan?
> And how much longer, realistically, could I maintain this pretence of enjoying myself, acting as if I wanted to talk to potentially psychotic strangers, murmuring my consent every time someone suggested white water rafting whilst bound, blindfolded and tied to bricks, and do it all only feet away from the one person who could read me like a book, my very best friend, the person whose trip I'd tagged along on? And do it

> **Catherine Ryan Howard**
>
> my legs. The room is dark, although a faint blue glow in one corner is enough bright to reveal a backpack lying on its side by my feet with a wad of folded paper, a bottle of anti-malaria pills and a Florida licence plate half-in, half-out of it. They must have made a bid for freedom while I slept.
> I prop myself up onto my elbows and see the phone. Having switched off the alarm, I bring it close to my face to read the time.
> 4:00 a.m.

In non-fiction, running heads remind the reader what section or part they're reading, so it might be the book's title on the even page and the current section's name on the odd one.

Page numbers can go in a number of places but for simplicity's sake, I'm going to recommend that you put them in the footer, and that you put them in the middle of it, i.e. centre them at the bottom of each page.

You're thinking, *that sounds simple enough. What's all the fuss about it?* Well, that *does* sound simple enough – but that's only the half of it. The thing is, we don't want a page number on every page. And we don't want our running heads on every page. And on some pages, we'll want page numbers but no running heads. Yet, if you insert a footer or a header into your document, it happily appears on every page.

So what do we do?

First of all, we make another vat of coffee.

We're going to use **the Sections feature of MS Word**. This is theoretically something that's quite easy to do, but in practice it takes a few extra brain cells to master.

Let's make a list of what we need to achieve. We need:

- A header with the title of our book on the even-numbered or left-hand pages
- A header with the author name on the odd-numbered or right-hand pages
- Our page numbers centred in the footer

But we also need to make sure that:

- Page numbers don't start until our book does, i.e. there shouldn't be any page numbers until you get to the first page of Chapter One
- If there isn't a page number, there shouldn't be a running head either

- Blank pages, like the ones we left blank so each chapter would start on a right-hand, odd-numbered page, should be *completely* blank, i.e. no page number or running head
- Title pages in the midst of your book, e.g. "Part 3: My Little Pony", shouldn't have page numbers or running heads
- The first pages of chapters should have page numbers but *not* running heads
- Pages numbers should end when our book does, i.e. there shouldn't be any page numbers after THE END, even if there is something after it

So in practice that means that we're going to divide our book up into the following sections:

- The beginning ←→ the page before the first page of Chapter One
- The first page of each chapter ←→ the last page of each chapter
- The page that says "THE END" ←→ the end of the book
- Each blank page in between will be its own, one-page section

To create a new section, go to the last line on the page *before* you want the section to start and click Insert → Break → Section Break (next page). Creating the next one will "close" or end the first one too.

But if you put a page number in the footer of a page in your first section, it will still appear on the pages in your second section too. This is because unless you tell it otherwise, MS Word assumes you want every page to be the same. Therefore, we need to tell it otherwise.

When you click into or create the header (or footer) in a particular section, you have the following options:

- **Different first page**. This means that the first page of your section will be different from the rest of it, and it's ideal for the first page of chapters, which need a page number but *not* a running head.
- **Different odd and even pages**. We need this so that the title of our book appears in the headers on our even-numbered, left-hand pages, while our name appears in the headers on our odd-numbered, right-hand pages.
- **Link to previous**. Could also be called the Lucifer Lever, because this little thing is what causes *all* the problems. When you create a new section, MS Word assumes you want it to follow the same heading/footer style as the one before it. If you don't want it to – for instance, if the previous sections had page numbers and this section consists of an otherwise blank page – uncheck the "link to

previous" option. These options will be in Edit Header/Footer (right-click in the header/footer) or if you're working on a Mac, in the Toolbox. Tip: *after* you make a new section but *before* you start making changes to it, run ahead and uncheck all the "link to previous" options in the new section. Then you'll be free to amend without inadvertently changing every previous page in the document too. Tip #2: do this all at once. Don't start dividing your book into sections, go have lunch and then come back to finish it later. This is the kind of thing where you need to get into a rhythm to do it effectively. Trust me: if you leave it and come back, you won't have a clue what's going on.

If you've never worked with sections before, I suggest you make a copy of your interior document and practice on it for a while until you get the knack of working with them. After a few sections, you really do get into a rhythm. If you want to keep things as simple as possible, forget about the running headers altogether and just stick with the page numbers instead.

If you need to remove a section break, switch to Draft View. You'll easily spot it as it'll now be visible as a double blue line marked "Section Break". Simply highlight and delete.

For step-by-step instructions for creating your CreateSpace paperback interior using MS Word's sections feature, visit:

http://www.catherineryanhoward.com/selfprinted3

Convert to PDF

The final thing you need to do with your interior file is convert it to PDF. If you're using MS Word, you can just save it as PDF.

Select File → Save As and then select "PDF" from the drop-down "Format" menu.

Collect Your Cover Template

Now that you know how many pages your book is going to be, you can collect your cover template and get your cover designer started on your paperback's jacket design.

Go back to the CreateSpace website and either click Publish → Books on Demand → Cover (tab) → Submission Requirements → Download Cover Templates, or go straight to:

www.createspace.com/Help/Book/Artwork.do

Here you'll find a cover template generator. Enter your interior type, trim size, choice of paper colour and number of pages, and CreateSpace will generate a perfectly sized cover template for your book which you can then download immediately.

In the ZIP file that you download will be a Photoshop template, a PNG template and instructions in a PDF file. Don't worry about what any of these are; just send them off to your cover designer who'll know what to do with them.

There are some stipulations about what goes on your cover. The title and author name must appear *exactly* as they have been entered in the title set-up process, and you need to ensure that there is nothing important in the lower right-hand corner of the back cover, because that's where CreateSpace will insert the barcode for you. (This area will be marked on the template so your designer will know not to put anything there.) If your book is less than 120 pages, CreateSpace recommends nothing goes on the spine. The finished file, i.e. the PDF of your cover that's ready for you to upload, must be **40 MB or less**.

Of course, you may want your cover template before this stage of the process – but you do need to know how many pages are going to be in your book first.

What I do is I mock up an interior file.

I decide on my trim size and download the correctly sized MS Word template. Then I copy and paste my book's text into it, making it the font and size it'll be eventually. Finally I run quickly through the book, breaking up the chapters until they all start on an odd/right-hand page. This gives me a rough estimate of how many pages my book will be. I add in a few more to cover the front and end matter and then I plug that number into the cover template generator.

The downside to this is, of course, that it's not an exact science. The only way to know *for sure* how many pages your book will have is to create the final interior.

Finalise Your Book

Now, armed with our absolutely perfect interior in PDF format and our high-quality, impossible-to-ignore final cover design, also in PDF and supplied to us by our cover designer, we return to CreateSpace to upload our files and finish making our book. You'll find the title in your Member Dashboard. Click on it and you'll be brought back to the Setup screen.

Upload Your Files

Scroll down until you find the next incomplete section: Interior and Cover. Upload your interior file, selecting "ends before the edge of the page" under Bleed. This means your page will appear exactly as it appears in the PDF file, or as we want it to. Then upload your cover file too.

Select Your Cover Finish

CreateSpace offers two options for your cover finish: matte or glossy. Which one you use is entirely up to you. I have to say that I put this book into a matte cover because I don't like the gloss. It collects fingerprints and I found myself wiping down my covers with the little black chamois Apple supplied with my iMac before I gave them to competition winners or reviewers. Don't forget: you'll see what it looks like on your proof copy before you release it to the world. If you hate it, you can just change it for the next proof copy.

Description (Blurb)

Enter the exact same description here as you did back on Amazon KDP.

BISAC Code

Again, pick the same category for your book here as you did back on Amazon KDP. The catch is that while KDP allowed you two, you only get one here. Choose wisely.

Additional Information

Now comes a number of items that, again, we have already filled out for the Kindle edition of this same book, so enter the same details here. These are **Author Biography** (your About the Author), **Book Language**, **Country of Publication** (your own) and **Search Keywords** (you have only up to *five* here though).

Finally, you must tell CreateSpace if the book contains **Adult Content** – this means erotica, not your main characters bumping uglies once or twice, or a swear word – and whether your book can be classed as **Large Print.** (It can't. When it says "Large Print" it means that section of the library where there are special editions of books that cater for those with poor eyesight. It does not mean "Well, I used 16 pt *most* of the time.")

Save Progress

Scroll down to the bottom of the page and hit the Save Progress button. CreateSpace will now upload your files and save all the information you've entered already. This may take a little while if your files are large. You must do this before you can move on to Sales Channels.

Sales Channels

Click on Select Sales Channels and select them all.
That's it. Don't overthink it.

Set Your List Price

Your list price is like the recommended retail price or the full price. Retailers can discount it as they see fit but you will always receive the share of the profits that CreateSpace has promised you, which is based on the list price you set.

I hope back at the start of this book (remember all the way back there? I don't …) we talked about **setting a price that was in keeping with what a similarly sized book would be for sale at in a brick-and-mortar bookstore.**

The first and second paperback editions of this book had list prices of $15.95, which I can tell you barely made me enough to recoup the cost of the caffeine I had to ingest in order to write it. But *Mousetrapped* and *Backpacked* – smaller, thinner books – had each been listed at $14.95, and to me, $15.95 sounded very expensive.

Now, I realise my mistake.

First of all, I was fixated on dollars. Sixteen of them sounded expensive to me, but my 350+ page, 6x9 book was a bargain at around €11. When I go into Waterstones, I find the standard, smaller "B format" paperbacks priced €9.99. We have a phenomenon here in Ireland: we don't have (many) hardcovers. When you go into a bookshop here to buy a new release that has been released in the UK in hardback, you'll find you're only able to buy it in what I think is called C format, which is the size of a hardcover book but doesn't have the "hard" bit. The cover is soft. Essentially it's a sibling of what this book is like in POD paperback. And *those* books are all selling for around €14.99. (Their recommended retail price might be higher, but we're only concerned with what readers expect.) So if you bought this third edition in paperback, you probably paid around $18.95 for it.

CreateSpace gives you the option of automatically calculating a GBP£ and EUR€ price or manually imputing them yourself. In the example in the image below I went manual, just so my prices weren't odd figures like £11.74 or €15.27.

On the right-hand side of that image you can see how much you'll collect from each sales channel or location where the book will be for sale. Now is a good time to remind you that if you were traditionally published, 10 per cent would be a win. If you sell one of these babies from Amazon.com, you get to keep around a *third* of the price. Not too shabby, eh?

Submit Your Book

Once you've completed everything on the Title Set-Up page and double-checked you haven't done anything silly like put an order form at the back, click the Submit Your Book button. What will happen now is that magical CreateSpace computers will check that everything is okay and if it is, they'll invite you to order a proof copy.

What kind of things are they checking are okay? It's kind of hard to say, because there's no list or anything that I know about. There are the obvious things like does the page count fit with the size of the cover, and is your ISBN on your copyright page and correct. Then there are some other grey, blurry things they might be looking for and if they find them, they'll let you know.

In my experience there can be a 24–48 hour delay between submitting your book for processing and CreateSpace coming back, saying everything is okay and inviting you to proof your book.

Proof Your Book

CreateSpace will now offer you three difference options for proofing your book: you can do it onscreen in a virtual viewer-type thingy, you can download a PDF of your interior or you can order a proof copy.

Order a proof copy.

The first option will tell you nothing about what the book actually looks or feels like, and what, pray tell, is the point of re-downloading the PDF you uploaded a couple of days ago? You shouldn't even *entertain* the idea of making your book available for sale without holding a copy of it in your hand.

Further down the line, onscreen proofing will be an option. Maybe in a few months' time I'll change the link to the tax interview information on my blog and I'll need to update the URL I've included in this book. If that's all I need to update out of 128,886 words (and counting – as I type this I still have a whole section to go yet!) then there's really no point in ordering another proof copy all the way from one of the Carolinas (I can never remember which – North?) just to check that the change has been made. But for now, order a physical proof. Don't you want to see it, anyway?

You can't change *anything* after you order a proof copy without having to order another proof copy, so make sure you're good to go before you do.

Your proof copy will look exactly like the finished product EXCEPT that it will say "Proof" on the last page. I was once on a forum for self-published writers when I saw a complaint about this that went along the lines of, "Ugh! My proof copy says 'proof'. Why? Why would they print something in my book I didn't tell them to?" Well, this may come as a shock to you but they did it because *it's a proof copy.*

You can order only up to five copies of any one proof.

I once got an e-mail from a self-publisher chastising me for recommending CreateSpace when, according to him, they were the world's worst self-publishing service. He claimed that on three different occasions he'd sent them a perfect interior file, only to find mistakes in the proof copy that subsequently arrived. Their motivation was to make more money out of him, he said. Guys, a PDF file cannot be changed and at CreateSpace, everything is done automatically. Only a computer sees your interior file before it goes to the printing press, and even that computer can't do anything to change your PDF file. That, if you weren't aware, is the *whole point of PDF files*. So if there's a mistake in your proof copy after you uploaded a "perfect" PDF, it's because the PDF wasn't as perfect as you thought it was.

Publish Your Book

In all likelihood it'll take around a week for your proof copy to arrive on your doorstep. Once it does, you'll have to set aside time to check it thoroughly and then gaze at it adoringly for hours on end while saying "That's my book! *My* book! Look at how pretty it is ..."

When your proof copy arrives, go through it with a fine-tooth comb. Then go through it again. And *again*. Then once more. If you have the time, the money and the inclination, I'd order my maximum five proof copies and give the other four to people who can spot a wayward apostrophe at 50 paces, e.g. your editor, your proofreader and that girl who dumps friends for writing "you're" when they mean "your" or vice versa.

When you're 100 per cent happy with it inside and out, go back to CreateSpace and your book's Project Homepage, take a deep breath and click Approve Proof.

On average, it takes CreateSpace about a week to build your Amazon.com & Friends listings. I say "build" because they don't all appear fully formed at once. You might find there's a delay while the cover appears, for example, or that it takes a full week for your product description to appear.

If you want to order copies for yourself, you'll be able to do so immediately from your CreateSpace account. Select the Order Copies link alongside the title on your Member Dashboard.

* * *

There. You've just *published your book*. Congratulations! So now we've built the foundations of an online platform, published an e-book and published a POD paperback. Phew! I need a lie down. The good news is that you probably could squeeze in a nap. The bad news is that ...

Well, I'm afraid we *still* haven't got to the hardest part. *That's* selling books.

And that's next.

PART 5
Selling Self-Published Books

How to Sell Self-Published Books

So, how do you sell self-published books? Well, isn't *that* the million dollar question …

There are a number of guides on the market right now with enticing titles like *How I Became a Trillionaire in Only 7 Minutes a Day: A Guide to E-books, Message Boards and Jedi Mindtricks* that all promise to contain some hitherto unknown, sure-fire way to sell thousands upon thousands of self-published books. Their advice ranges from common sense to things you could get arrested for in some parts of the world, but they all have one thing in common: the only secret they reveal is how *their author* sold his or her books. In terms of usefulness to other self-published authors, yes, reading them is great motivation and tales of astronomical success always provide great fodder for our wildest daydreams – but that's about it. Because the methods they describe are so grandiose, hyper-specific and time-consuming that the average self-published author neither has the time nor inclination to even half-heartedly adopt them. Even if they *did*, the original results are never replicable; anyone who has sold hundreds of thousands of e-books has *luck* to thank, whether in whole or in part.

I think this kind of thing is overthinking it, which, as you may have established by now, is not my favourite thing. Put it this way: it's like me and dieting. I know, intellectually, that in order to lose weight you have to spend more energy than you consume. Eat less and move more. I *know* this. It's a scientific fact. And yet instead of doing it, I read countless diet books and blogs, watch TV shows, pay for weight management programmes, buy all manner of shakes, bars and Chemical Stuff Masquerading as Food and tell myself that I'm going to start using the treadmill in the garage every single day, come Monday. No, really. This time I will. I *swear*. Why? Because I want to believe that there's some magic secret to weight loss that's just waiting for me to discover it, and I want to believe it because I don't want to do the hard work. So instead of *starting* the hard work, I keep searching for the secret, while in the meantime the circumference of my thighs continues to be in direct proportion to my love of Toblerone cheesecake.

This is exactly what happens to self-published authors, minus the cheesecake. Instead of considering the time, hard work and common sense that has led to hundreds of self-published authors making money but not necessarily headlines, they dream of emulating the handful who did little else than upload to KDP before they found themselves sleeping on mattresses stuffed with cash.

We're not going to do that. We're going to get our arses on the treadmill right *now*.

The Science of Book Selling

If the science of slimming is eat fewer calories and exercise more, what is the science of book selling? What events have to take place in order for someone to purchase a book? What had to happen in order for you to buy the last book you bought?

1. You had to find out that the book existed
2. Something about the book made you care, i.e. made you stop and think, *Hmm. That sounds interesting* (instead of ignoring/not caring about it like all the other books you found out existed)
3. You were convinced enough by the information you had about the book to believe that you'd like it
4. You found a place where it was on sale
5. A combination of the blurb, book cover, price, etc. cemented your decision and you purchased it

Every single book sold has been through this process, unless it was purchased by mistake. It wouldn't be too bad if everyone who was at #1 made it all the way to #5, but of course, that's not the case. The number of readers at #5 are only a *tiny fraction* of the number who were with us back at #1; potential readers drop away at every step.

Let's say that on a particular day 100 people found out that our book existed. Of them, maybe only 50 cared enough to stop and pay attention. Of that 50, only 25 became convinced the book was something they might like. Of that 25, only ten made an effort to find a place where it was on sale and of those ten, only one ended up purchasing our book. That's a conversion rate of 1 per cent, which I'd guess is a heavily multiplied version of what the figure really is in the real world. So how can we improve our chances? The good news is that we can do it easily, and we can do it at every step. Consider, for example, how the conversion rate would be affected if:

- The number of people at #1 was huge
- The people at #1 were established fans of books quite similar to ours
- All the people at #1 were given good reason to think, *Hmm, that sounds interesting*
- The information at #3 was presented in such a way that sent nearly everyone who read it on to #4
- Your Amazon listing (product description, cover, price, etc.) got almost everyone at #4 to #5

We can also set mechanisms in motion that will mean we don't have to be constantly working to inform new people that our book exists – eventually someone *else* will start doing it for us, and doing it for us while we sleep, work on our next book or watch *I Didn't Know I Was Pregnant*. And that someone will make sure *only* to tell people who they know for a fact are interested in books like ours, and they'll promote our book for free.

Actually, buying a book by accident isn't the only way a book sale can bypass this process. I love the likes of Michael Connelly, Karin Slaughter and Belinda Bauer, and I buy every single one of their books when they come out, without steps #1–5. I just buy them.

That's because at some stage in the past I went through the process above and liked the book enough to say to myself, *I want to read all the books this author has written*. When the next book came out, there was only one step for me:

1. Find out about the new book.

That was sure to happen because I had "liked" the author's Facebook fan page, or because I had joined their newsletter mailing list, or because I was a regular visitor to their blog or website. For now we're only selling one book but we have to think of the long term too, so whenever a reader makes it to #5 and reads and likes our book, we need to make it easy for them to find out about future releases. Then when we come to release *that* book, we not only have all the ways we can get to #1 we used with our first title, but also a ready-made audience of #5s just waiting to hear that the book is out.

Wasn't Publishing It Enough?

Once upon a time, a newly self-published author sent me a tweet that said, "How will people find my book on Amazon?" Setting aside for a moment the fact that it's *unbelievably* annoying when people ask you questions via tweet (or e-mail), the answers to which are all over your blog, thus confirming that they haven't bothered to even go look there and instead think you've nothing better to do with your time than to repeat yourself, this tweet is quite frightening. It's frightening because the author seemed to think that the answer could be provided in 140 characters or fewer, just like the questions *What's the URL for Amazon KDP?* and *If I charge $2.99, how much do I get to keep?*

Make your peace now with the fact that this is the hard part. It's going to take time, energy, imagination, dedication and patience to get your book selling. It's entirely *your responsibility*; no one else, Amazon included, is charged with promoting your book.

And as self-published authors – as any kind of first-time authors – we've our work cut out for us because, by default, no one gives a tiny rat's arse about our book.

No One Cares About Your Book, Remember?

I'll say it again: just because you wrote a book does not mean people are going to want to read it. There is no inherent entitlement here; you aren't entitled to readers just because you managed to type 100,000 words. Telling people, "I wrote a book" isn't a strategy. It has to come with something else, and that something else has to be a reason for us to care.

Before you take a *single* step in this book promotion business, you have to acknowledge that. Why? Because this is the kind of thing that happens if you don't:

I am a member of Goodreads (Facebook for readers; we'll be talking more about it soon) and one of the features of Goodreads that self-published authors delight in abusing is the "Events" feature, whereby an author can create a usually virtual event and then invite other Goodreads users to attend it. I'm fairly certain this is supposed to be for things like live web chats with your favourite author, etc. but these days it's a wasteland of free book promotions, blog tours and the like, to wildly varying degrees of success. Recently one self-published author, who shall remain nameless, sent me this via Goodreads Events:

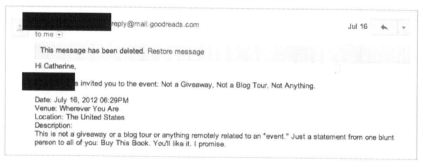

The text reads, "This is not a giveaway or a blog tour or anything remotely related to an 'event'. Just a statement from one blunt person to all of you: Buy This Book. You'll like it. I promise." The book is, of course, the author's own. Underneath that [not pictured] are two endorsements so glowing that I momentarily lost the vision in my right eye – they include words like "masterpiece", phrases like "great American novelist" and the sentence "a saga that blasts away the outer layers so we can gaze into the soul where humanity is one" – but they *aren't attributed to anyone* (!), and underneath them is a fairly unremarkable synopsis.

Are you f------ kidding me with this?!

Now I don't mean to pick on this author; on the grand scale of self-published authors' crimes, he'd get away with merely a warning. He just had the misfortune to send me a perfect example of the point I'm trying to demonstrate here while I was writing the second edition of this book. Because not only is this message spammy, but the author openly admits to their abuse of the Goodreads Events feature ("this is not a giveaway or a blog tour ...") and, most importantly, doesn't give me a *single* reason to go read the book.

This is because the author evidently doesn't know that no one cares about it. He's assumed that because he's written a book, he's already several steps up the ladder of book selling. The lines "Buy This Book. You'll like it. I promise" are irrefutable proof of that. But that's *not* how it works. You have to *make* people care, and care enough to stop and think, *Hmm, that sounds interesting,* to give your book some time instead of just breezing on by it without a second thought like we do with the overwhelming majority of books that enter our line of vision. Just sending them a synopsis and a "buy me!" plea isn't enough.

Why Promoting Your Book Online Is (a Bit) Like *Fight Club*

The first rule of Fight Club is that you do not talk about Fight Club. The first rule of effectively promoting your book online is that you do not promote your book online.

By which I mean, you do not *blatantly* promote your book online.

Some self-published authors take offence at being told that they shouldn't regularly send out tweets like "My book, YOUR EYES ARE GLAZING OVER, is on Amazon now, just $2.99. PLEASE RT! OKAY? THANKS!", or that they should avoid working the title of at least one of their books into every comment they leave on someone else's blog, or that they shouldn't send e-mails to people they don't know or don't know really well trying to flog their book because, even if it's done manually, it's *still* spam. They stubbornly want to do things their way, and that's fine. Maybe a trillion-selling 99¢ e-book author did the same thing and now they're convinced that's the secret to success. Maybe they're just not that bright. Whatever their reasons, leave them to it. But I don't want *you* to do it that way because *that way doesn't work.* Did you hear me? IT DOESN'T WORK. So yes, of course, you're free to do whatever you want. But personally, I'd rather just do stuff that is at least *likely* to work. Otherwise, it seems like it would be a massive waste of time to me.

The reason it doesn't work is because people aren't using social media because they love being sold stuff. They're using it for one or more of the following three reasons:

- Because they want to be **entertained**
- Because they're looking for specific **information**
- Because they want to **connect** with other people (connect as in *virtually meet*, but also as in *relate to*)

From what I've seen over the past four years, both in trying to sell my own books and in watching what other self-published and traditionally published authors have done to try to sell theirs, is that your promotional efforts have to have a value of their own, and that value has to satisfy one or more of the demands in the list above. Online promotion works best when the book actually comes *second* to the content's main objective.

Say *what* now?

To put it another – hopefully clearer – way, **your goal should be to improve the internet**, above all else. Make it a better place to be than it was five minutes ago by writing a great blog post, posting a funny tweet, using a tweet to direct your followers to a great blog post you just found, uploading a video that helps people perform a task, uploading a video that makes people laugh while they're procrastinating to keep from doing that task they're supposed to do … You get the idea.

Adding a mention of your book to this content might also sell a few copies of it for you, yes, but that's secondary. That's not the most important bit. We need to create stuff to put on the internet that would still be something useful and worthwhile even if we took the selling books bit out of it.

Book trailers – good ones, anyway – and other book-related videos are a really effective way to demonstrate what I mean. You can view a selection of my favourites at this location:

http://catherineryanhoward.com/selfprinted3

The book trailer *Love in the Time of Amazon* is one of my favourites. It's a short film about a woman who secretly starts buying copies of her husband's book to raise his Amazon sales ranking and also, what with him obsessively watching his Amazon sales rankings, his mood.

It's also a book trailer that advertises the authors' books.

The point is that if you took the advertising books bit away – if you just imagined for a second that this was just for fun, and that those are actors and those books don't really exist – it would *still* be a video you'd have a little giggle at. It would still be a video you'd post on your blog, share with your Facebook friends and/or tweet a link to. Especially if your friends are published authors, because we can so relate. (And so – added bonus – *connect*.) It's been viewed over 10,000 times; I saw countless links to it on Twitter; I've posted about it myself several times and it got picked up by high-traffic sites like Media Bistro.

My own video, *How Much Editing Backpacked Needed*, is nothing more than a sped-up scroll through *Backpacked*'s manuscript after it came back from the copy-editor. It's been viewed over 2,000 times and passed around numerous editing and writing blogs. At the very end of it, there's some info about the book. But if I didn't name the book that was being edited and took that info at the end out, the video wouldn't lose any of its value. It would still have the same number of views and have been passed around and shared just as much. Because this isn't a video about me wanting you to buy my book. This is a video that, first and foremost, contains useful information and/or is interesting.

The trailer for Mhairi McFarlane's novel *You Had Me at Hello* is, I think, utterly fabulous. It's a fun romp through the corridors of HarperCollins that shows us how books get made – and a fascinating insight into the process from those of us on the outside looking in. It's had over 11,000 views and, if they blacked out the title of the book getting made, we'd still have plenty of reasons to watch it.

My self-printing-themed posts contain information that people need. Fun, chatty tweets that bemoan the pain of having to put words on paper are something any writer can relate to, and over time we might make a connection with the person writing them. Anything that makes us laugh, mutter, "Hmm. Interesting ...", holds our attention for longer than a few seconds or could be considered "just for fun" falls into the entertainment category.

And after they've entertained, informed or made a connection, they've also told a new person that our book exists, which is the first step in getting someone to buy it. (Making them interested in the book is the step in between.) Obviously the number of people who know our books exist is far greater than the number who actually buy it, but as the first number increases, so does the second.

Am I silly enough to think that everyone who reads my blog is going to run straight over to Amazon and buy up all my books? No. I don't think that *anyone* is going to run over there and buy *one* of them. I'm not trying to open and close the deal in the same shot. My main priority is to make my blog a good blog. Above all else, I want new people to keep discovering my blog, and I want the people already reading it to keep doing so, and I want everyone to find it useful with a side of occasional giggles, even if they don't like pink.

Below that on my list of priorities is selling my books. Over time, a very small percentage of blog readers become book readers, but because I have a lot of blog readers, that's enough for me.

How do blog readers become book readers? These are some of my theories:

- They like the way I write; they want to read more
- They want to get my book to see how it's turned out (after reading about its production)
- After hanging around there for ages, they read the About page or My Books, and one of my books catches their eye
- They buy a book of mine as a thank you for me helping them with their book (through my posts)
- One of the above, combined with me telling them I have a free promotion on, and perhaps reading one for free leads them to buy another one
- Then they might write a review, recommend me to a friend, etc. etc. leading to other, "outside" sales
- After reading the blog from the beginning and following me through the release of four books, they just can't resist my Jedi mind tricks any more …

Let's say that instead of writing blog posts, I just stuck up a picture of a book of mine with an Amazon link and a price tag. And I did that every day, without fail and without deviation. Where do you think I'd be then? I'm pretty sure I'd have zero blog readers. But yet people treat Twitter *exactly* this way, and expect people not only to stick around and put up with it, but also to go buy their books. Really? Put down the crazy juice and have a cup of reality instead.

Think about it: what does you tweeting "Another 5* review for MY BOOK on Amazon! Here's the link so you can go read it and marvel at the praise I have received …" achieve out of *entertain, inform* and *connect*? And no, it doesn't fall under inform, because the information provided has to be useful. If you're going on a blog tour and you have five guest posts lined up to send to your kind hosts, ask yourself: are these posts good by themselves? Are they likely to entertain, provide information, have readers relating to them, or is the only point they make something like buy my book and buy it now?

Let's return to the word *rule*. You – I – can't really say "never do this" or "as a rule, don't do that". Sometimes you have to tell the internet something, even if that something doesn't achieve one of our three aims. There's little point, for instance, in your book being free for Kindle for a few days if you can't tell people about it. (Although, in my opinion, the opportunity to get a free book falls into the information category. I'm slow to admit this thought because I just know that someone will take it a step in the wrong direction and assume tweets on the hour, every hour about how his book is "just $1.99" falls into the same category. It doesn't.) And what if you get a review from, like, someone amazing? What if your writing hero says she likes your book and says it on the internet? You couldn't keep news like that in, even if it doesn't do anything but make the rest of us sick with jealousy. So sometimes, it's okay to break the rules or not follow the principles. But only in extreme moderation.

Because remember, the hard sell doesn't work. No one is listening to it because that's not why they're there.

Over time, what's considered valuable information will also change. For instance, if I pick 1,000 people at random and tell them I've released a new book and go buy it now, please, thanks, I'd probably get into trouble for spamming, or at the very least, I'd have wasted my time. But what if those 1,000 people had already read a book of mine and signed up to a newsletter so they could find out about my future releases, and they were happy to hear from me because they were fans of my work? Then "my book is out now!" becomes valuable information to them, because finding that out was exactly why they signed up to the mailing list. BUT – before you bring it up – this isn't the same as me following you on Twitter. I didn't follow you on Twitter to be constantly told about your new book. I'd like to know if you have a new book, sure, but I want it to come on the side with the real reason I'm on Twitter in the first place: to be *entertained*, *informed* or *connected*.

We're Not African Princes

We've all received an e-mail (or three hundred) from some poor unfortunate royal family member on the continent of Africa who'd make us both millionaires if only we'd agree to some shady stuff involving a wire transfer. *Why do they bother?* you wonder. *No one in their right mind would fall for this!* Unfortunately people *do* fall for them – there was a woman on Oprah once who received a fax version at the office and thought it was genuinely from a friend of her boss, who was away on holidays at the time, so she sent the money, thinking she was doing the right thing. And that's the whole point of these spam e-mails: if they send out 500,000 of them and only *one* person falls for it, they've achieved their objective. They've made a profit.

If you're thinking something along the lines of *well, I'd like to sell 1,000 books. If I tell 1,000,000 people about my book, chances are I'll get those 1,000 sales. So why don't I just send a tweet with my Amazon link to the first 1,000,000 people I can find on Twitter? Or collect e-mail addresses from around the web and mail out 1,000,000 press releases at random? Or [insert some other harebrained idea]?*, please stop. We're not going to do any of those things because:

- It's all **spam**, which is at best effortlessly ignorable and at worst, utterly illegal.
- It's a gigantic **waste of everyone's time**: yours, and the people you target.
- The **only sustainable growth is organic.** Going back to our dieting analogy, I could probably drop 20 pounds in ten days if I followed Emily's diet from *The Devil Wears Prada* ("I don't eat anything and then right before I think I'm going to faint, I eat a cube of cheese."), but I'd gain back 40 in five once I started eating normally again. Similarly, I could probably get a few thousand people to buy my book using a variety of shortcuts – like spamming, super-low prices, etc. – but not all of them would bother reading it, and even fewer would remember my name in a week's time. This isn't just about getting as many people to buy our first book as we possibly can. This is about slowly but steadily building a readership over time.

A note: a while back there was a scandal involving an author who had sent out thousands of e-mails in a bid to sell his book. There was a question mark over whether or not he had done it manually or used a mailing list/e-mail collector programme of some sort, and one person (a friend of his, I think it'd be safe to assume) was quite vocal in arguing that if it *was* manual, it *wasn't* spam. This is like saying that because you secured an upright knife to the floor and stuck out your leg to trip your victim causing him to fall onto it, it wasn't murder. The person is still dead, and the "buy my book" e-mail is still something that thousands of people received against their will. Don't waste your time clinging to a technicality. We'll all be *very annoyed with you* and guaranteed *not to buy your book* regardless.

But I Just Want to *Write*!

Just before I wrote this section in the second edition of this book, my fellow "platforming" self-publishers and I were stung by an article in a major UK newspaper that basically said the e-publishing bubble will burst just like the dot com one did, that author platforms are useless and don't work, and that building them eats into writing time and ultimately detracts from the work. It was extremely snarky in tone and used the phrase "self-styled" to describe virtually every self-publishing expert mentioned in the piece.

And it was *completely* wrong.

People who think Twitter et al doesn't sell books don't understand *how* they sell books. The usual anti-using-social-media-to-sell-books argument goes something like this: *Well, Johnny X has 10,000 Twitter followers but he's only sold 500 books. Conclusion: Twitter doesn't sell books.* But that is an observation about *advertising*, not building an online author platform and using social media to sell books.

The clue is in the term *social network*. This, more than anything, is about networking. It's about connecting with other writers, other readers and people who can help us to promote our book without actually buying a copy themselves. It's about meeting the people that matter without even leaving the house. As for how time-consuming it is, that's up to you. Obviously you'll be spending a lot more time on it in the beginning than you will in the long term, and later I'll be sharing some ideas for managing your social media time.

When writers moan about wanting to write all the time, my eyes begin searching for some sort of heavy object I could hit them with while my hands clasp themselves behind my back so I won't if I find one. The *only* way to write all the time is to sell books, and the only way to sell books is to promote them. If you don't sell books, you have to have a job doing something else. And if you have a job, you can't write all the time.

This guide isn't about dropping everything to turn ourselves into lean, mean marketing machines. It's about dividing our time between trying to promote the books we've written and writing more of them.

But you can't "just write". You never could. Because if you don't make money from your writing, you will have to do something else – probably for eight hours a day, five days a week.

Pick a Release Date

Before we start any marketing, we need to know when the book has to be finished by. You need **a release date** for it.

In self-publishing, this is a date you get to pick and, as it's practically impossible to know in advance the *exact* date your book will pop up on Amazon, and it's *actually* impossible to make this coincide with the date your e-book pops up, it's pretty much arbitrary. But you should have one. Remember that we're trying to make our self-published efforts look as professional as possible, and traditionally published books have release dates. So we're going to have one too.

We'll decide on an actual date a bit later on, but for now we'll just work out what month we're aiming to release our book in. It depends, of course on where you are with your book, but assuming that nearly all of the work is ahead of you, your schedule will look something like this:

- Sourcing an editor and cover designer: 1–4 weeks
- Editing your book: anywhere from 1–6 months
- Cover design: 2–4 weeks
- Formatting and uploading paperback's interior: 1 week
- Formatting and uploading e-book's interior: 1 week
- Waiting for e-book to appear on Amazon, etc: 1 day–1 week
- Waiting for proof copy to arrive: 1–2 weeks
- Checking proof copy: 1–3 weeks
- Waiting for book to appear on Amazon sites after you approve proof: 1–2 weeks
- Waiting for book to appear on other retailers: 2–8 weeks

These times can vary greatly and you might be able to do some of these things concurrently, saving time. (For instance, I formatted and uploaded my e-book while waiting for my paperback proof copy to arrive.) You'll also have a much better idea of when you and your book will be ready by the time you get to the end of *this* book.

Or at least, that's the idea, anyway …

Be warned: some people take things like release dates *way* too seriously. Someone once took the time to e-mail me because they'd spotted a book of mine for sale on Amazon even though "it's not supposed to be out until next week?!!?" If you are a regular book buyer – and considering that *you're* considering self-publishing a book you wrote, I sincerely hope you are – you'll know that sometimes, books appear in stores sooner than the author said they were supposed to. It's not a big deal. Your release date is less about availability than it is a focus for your promotional efforts.

I mentioned already that the contents of this book aren't in the *exact* order you need them. Therefore, about half of what I'm about to describe takes place in the months leading up to the release of your book, and half of it afterwards. You'll be doing some of it while simultaneously editing and preparing your book, and for some of it, you'll need proof or finished copies. The bulk of your promotional efforts will take place in the three months before and after your launch date. From then on, it'll just be a matter of maintaining them.

We'll talk more about a specific timescale or schedule towards the end of this book.

So we've talked a lot about what we're *not* going to do. But what *are* we going to do? How are we going to sell our self-published books?

Find Your First Readers

So you have a (colour-coordinated, hilariously named WordPress) blog, Twitter account and Facebook fan page either dedicated to your imminent book release or to you as a writer. You've been finding your blogging feet, making blogging friends and are getting at least *some* non-accidental hits. You've started following people on Twitter, chatted to them, retweeted the links they post to adorable YouTube videos featuring animals acting like humans, and made sure they all know where to find your blog if they want to read longer versions of your priceless witticisms. You've coerced all your friends and family already on Facebook into "liking" your page and then insisted that all *their* friends and family on Facebook do the same. All the accounts have the same profile pic, link to each other and look – here it comes again – *professional*, i.e. the social media presence of a (soon-to-be) world famous author-type.

Fast-forward now to approximately three months before your book launches. You're having the time of your life with your blog readers, Twitter followers and Facebook fans, and you're having it (bonus!) in the comfort of your own home, in your pyjamas and without a scrap of make-up on. (And thinking, *This is the life ...*)

But now we need to tell these people that we have a book coming out, that we are self-publishing it and that, if they come along for the ride, there's at least a *moderate* chance they'll be occasionally entertained.

It's All About You

I've already talked about how much easier it is to get people to buy your book because they're interested in or by *you*, as opposed to the content of the book itself.

When we walk into a bookstore or browse Amazon listings, it's things like the cover art, the blurb, the genre, etc. that help us decide whether or not we'd like to buy a particular book. And no wonder, considering that this is our first contact with the author of the book. But on social media platforms like blogs and Twitter, the first thing we meet is the author in their blog posts and tweets. If their personality shines through and it's a personality we *like*, we might then go and look at their book.

I've bought books I would never have otherwise read in a million years because I've been following the authors on Twitter and either am interested in how their book has turned out (including traditionally published authors) or because I like them and so want to support their writing. I've bought books outside of genres I like just because the author's blog is hilarious. I've bought books because someone I follow on Twitter liked an author's blog and/or book and recommended it to their followers. In all of these examples, the author is my first point of contact; the details of their book (what it's about, who has published it, what genre it's in) comes second.

There are huge benefits to winning readers because of you and your writing rather than because of a specific book. For instance, I love all things NASA so I picked up *Packing for Mars* by Mary Roach, which I found out about after seeing Roach interviewed on *The Daily Show*. She seemed funny and her book was about NASA, so I bought it. I loved Roach's writing. Turns out she's a famous science writer in the States and really funny to boot – an odd combination, I'm sure you'll agree. So I ran out and got all of Roach's other books which, even though they're not about things I'm particularly interested in, I now want to read because I so enjoy the author's writing, and she makes technical details so easy to understand and the science so entertaining that I'm willing to bet that I'll like them too. So with the subject of one of her books, she sold me one book, but with her writing, she sold me the whole set. And if I wasn't interested in NASA or if she hadn't written about it, I might never have picked up any of her books.

Now chances are you and I are not going to get invited on to *The Daily Show* to chat with Jon Stewart, so we need to look for other places we can sell ourselves. That's where your blog, Twitter account and Facebook fan page come in.

Look at my own experience. The weekend *Mousetrapped* – a weird little book if ever there was one – came out, I sold about 50 copies of it. In *paperback*. Nearly all of them were to blog readers, Twitter friends, etc. who had been following my progress and/or chatting to me (about coffee, probably), and now wanted either to see how the book had turned out or to support me by buying it. That really helped get my sales going, right out of the gate.

So how do we advertise ourselves? Well, really it's our *personality*, our *perspective* and our *writing* (or "voice") that we're pushing out into the world. When you write a blog post or type a tweet, you can't help but display all these things. It just occurs naturally.

I was once asked if anyone could sell their books through social media, or if it only suited certain personality types. It was just after giving a talk during which, because it was late afternoon and I was attempting to combat the effects of an exhausting holiday and lingering jet lag with more coffee than a human being should reasonably drink, I came across as "bubbly". Thus the implication for some was that non-bubbly types wouldn't produce very bubbly blogs. And indeed they wouldn't, but there are more than bubbly folk out there in the world (thank fudge) and you certainly don't have to be that way to sell books. Just be *you*.

Be you, be honest and offer something new and/or different, and don't worry about the rest.

... But Not an Annoying Version of You

There is a big difference between introducing the world to us (and by *us* I mean our *personality, perspective* and *voice*) and forcing news of us down the throats of everyone we can find.

In other words, no one likes a shameless self-promoter.

But Catherine, you'll argue now, *isn't blogging in itself a type of shameless self-promotion?* No. Millions of bloggers are out there doing it because they like blogging, and anyway they have nothing to sell. (This is like the argument that by blogging, you're assuming people want to listen to what you have to say and in this way, are a certifiable egotist. It isn't about the listening; it's about the *saying.*) Most people who follow your blog will probably not buy your book, or even consider doing so. They're just there for your blog posts, which is fine because it's a *blog.* Likewise, while I may find out about a lot of books on Twitter, I'm not there to find books. I'm there, first and foremost, to be entertained, encounter interesting people and get links to YouTube videos where animals are acting like humans.

So as we move forward we're going to incorporate promoting our book into our online activities but always politely, in moderation and while still catering to the folks who have been reading our blog or following us on Twitter because of the content we've produced to date, and not because they want to buy our book, now or ever.

Your Unique Selling Point

Any highly trained monkey can start a blog, join Twitter or set up a Facebook page, and writer types are especially good at it. As a result there are thousands if not millions of other people out there doing the social media equivalent of tugging on your sleeve and trying to get your attention, and it's in this environment that you have to find a way to be heard.

Tip: it's not by shouting the loudest or shouting the most often. It's by saying the most interesting, most original, or the funniest things, or if you can't manage that, saying something completely unoriginal in a funny or interesting way. Find a gap and then figure out how to fill it. Work out what will be your *unique selling point.* This doesn't need to be related to your book, but your book needs to fit into it.

My favourite piece of writing advice is "Write the book you want to read." I think this can be applied here too, and in fact it might be the easiest way to find that elusive gap. What's the blog you'd love or need to read? Who's the Twitterer you think you'd enjoy following? What would be on the kind of Facebook page you'd be interested in "liking"?

Back when I had no clue how to go about this self-publishing thing, I did some research online. I quickly discovered that most of the posts, articles and sites about the subject, while helpful, all came served with a large side of evangelism. That is, their authors all championed self-publishing above all else, used the word "gatekeepers" in every other sentence and spoke about the Big Six as if they were minions of the devil himself. If they weren't shouting, "Down with Big Publishing!" they were deluding themselves into thinking that by uploading their book to CreateSpace or Lulu, they were going to be topping the *New York Times* bestseller list by the end of next week. I was self-publishing after traditional publishing had said no, but only as a sideline while I pursued my Real Dream of getting an agent, a book deal and a well-paying job I can do in my pyjamas, and I was brutally realistic about what the results of it were likely to be. So where were the blogs and websites for *me*? Where was there helpful information, good marketing ideas and clear instructions, but relayed with a level head, zero bitterness or resentment and a prevailing mood of sanity?

So I decided that's what I would blog about. That's *how* I would blog. My first post explained why I was calling what I was doing self-*printing* instead of self-publishing, and that set the tone. And it worked. It wasn't related to the subject matter of my book, but it gave me the opportunity to tell people about it. It also gave me plenty of material to blog *about*.

Don't try to tell me that because you've written a novel, you'll have to take a different approach. I've had people tell me this in person about their self-published books and all I can think when they do is, *You're just lacking in imagination*. And since you've written a novel, you must have *some* imagination, so the only excuse that leaves is laziness. There must be *something* about you or your book that's interesting. If you can't think of one single thing, then maybe you have bigger problems than I can help you with. Let's have a little brainstorm.

How did you write the book? Every writer can blog about how they wrote their book. All you need to do here is find a new way to do it. For example, I read a blog by a UK writer who has started a weekly video blog entitled A Year in the Life of a Book, where she'll take us, her blog readers, right along with her as her next novel goes from idea to finished book. I read lots of writing blogs, but hers is the one I make sure to visit every week, because no one else is doing that.

What were you doing before you wrote the book? Were you an astrophysicist in a previous life? Once voted America's Sexiest Man? A NASA astronaut? (If you were all those things, CALL ME.) The story of how you came to write your book might be the interesting thing about you, enabling you to make *you* the real story and the focus of your social media efforts. Let's say you were enslaved in a corporate cubicle and you wrote a novel about being enslaved in a corporate cubicle. Well, you need to start blogging about being in and then finding a way out of a corporate cubicle. Put a satirical slant on it, or write the next *The Four Hour Work Week*. If you do it well, people will be attracted to your book, and now that they know your background, they'll know it's going to be authentic too.

What is the book about? Are you a feisty pathologist who has written something like Patricia Cornwell's *Point of Origin*? A bereaved widow who has written something like Anita Shrieve's *The Pilot's Wife*? A recovered drug addict who has written something like James Frey's *A Million Little Pieces*, except you haven't made it all up? If you can connect your life to your book, then you're golden. Or maybe the fact that you *can't* connect your life to your book is going to be your story. Stephanie Meyer was a Mormon housewife when she started the *Twilight* series, for example, and I'm pretty sure that the lovely Karin Slaughter doesn't commit or investigate murders. Maybe there's something there.

Ask yourself *what makes me different from everyone else?* Maybe your personality is enough of a focus. Or maybe you already have a blog about quilting and you plan to slip mentions of your upcoming book in there, ninja-like, between the photos of your stitching. And it goes without saying that self-publishing your book is something to blog about all by itself.

Whatever it is that you decide on, make sure it's unique. Or at least considerably different from most everybody else.

Meet My Book

When it comes to introducing your online readership to your upcoming book, it's not so much about *how*, it's about *what*. We want content that's about our book but that also offers a value of its own so that a reader who has no intention of *ever* reading a book of ours isn't left behind.

What, why, when, how. The fact that you've decided to write and self-publish a book – or self-publish the book you've been trying to get traditionally published up until now – generates content for your blog posts, tweets and Facebook page in itself. Make an announcement. Tell the story of why you wrote the book. Explain how you came to this decision. Blog about your self-publishing adventures. Start a countdown to publication day.

Share the blurb of your upcoming book. If you're having trouble writing it, ask your blog readers for help. Even if you're not, a focus group would be beneficial and fun. Post a few versions of it; ask for feedback.

Involve your readers, followers, etc. in the self-publishing process. Chances are they're readers too, and their opinions will be highly valuable.

Share your book's cover. *Mousetrapped*'s cover had four incarnations. Before I decided which print-on-demand company to go with, I ordered one proof copy from Lulu and one proof copy from CreateSpace. Each of these had a cover on them generated by the relevant site's cover creation software. I wasn't happy with either of them, so I mocked-up a cover myself using MS Word. Finally that went to the cover designer I hired who turned it into the cover you see on the book today. Not only did I show my blog readers each version of the cover, but I asked them which one they preferred. When my proof copy arrived, I told them how exciting it was (the initial reaction) and then all the things that were wrong with it (terrible paper, weird size, etc.). When I'd decided on one, I "revealed" it on the blog too, and then tweeted links to the post and invited people to *ooh* and *ahh* over it. Blog about how you came to decide on a cover. Share where you or your cover designer got the idea for it in the first place. Tell them what you especially love about it, or how long you've spent gazing at it since you got the final proof. (*Hours*, if you're anything like me.)

Release your first chapter. When your manuscript has been finalised, convert the first chapter to a PDF and upload it to your blog. (WordPress lets you upload PDFs just as you would an image.) Then point everyone in the known universe in the direction of it. This is a *major* advertisement for your book. A number of readers told me that they bought my book after reading the first chapter online and, crucially, liking it. Warning: if you're thinking something along the lines of *I'd rather release my third chapter, because the first one isn't really the best advertisement for my book,* put down *this* book immediately and go back to working on your own, because it's not ready yet.

Book Trailers

A book trailer is essentially a short video (1–3 minutes) that advertises your book in the same way a movie trailer does for an upcoming feature film release. Book trailers are a relatively new addition to the book world and as there's no one way to make a book trailer, nor is there any particular thing you're supposed to put into it. The only limit here is your imagination. They vary in quality from DIY to slick and professional, and you can upload them to video sharing sites like YouTube and Vimeo. After your book comes out, you can also add them to places like your Amazon Author Page and your Goodreads Author Profile.

I don't believe that book trailer views convert directly to sales, but I do think a good book trailer can encourage someone to go look up your book, check your blog or start following you on Twitter and, since you'll have such a stunning-looking book, colour coordinated blog and hilarious tweet stream, *that* might lead to a sale.

Book trailers also have a huge "share" value, i.e. there is a much better chance that someone will post your book trailer on their Facebook wall or tweet a link to it than something plain and unexciting like the text of your preview chapter. Some book trailers even go viral and end up with hundreds of thousands, if not millions, of views.

I love making little movie mementoes of holidays, trips and other experiences with programs like Windows Movie Maker (PC) and iMovie (Mac), so it wasn't that much of a stretch for me to make a book trailer, especially since my book was non-fiction. You can watch it at the book trailers link I provided before.

If you can't use those programs and don't want to learn, there are alternatives. Ask a friend, or maybe find an editor who's looking to build a portfolio. If you want to be really professional about it, write a script, hire a camera and audition actors (who will work for free when they're starting out in exchange for something good they can add to their CVs and show-reels). This is exactly what author Gemma Burgess did for her novel *The Dating Detox*, and the result is a fantastic book trailer that is an excellent reflection of her book. And it's got thousands of views and helped her second book, *A Girl Like You*, become a bestseller.

I don't recommend spending a lot of money on a book trailer, or any at all if you can help it. Buying your camera operator or actors lunch is one thing, but don't go paying a crew of people to produce a three-minute Hollywood-style movie of your book. As I said, I don't think views convert directly into sales and sinking money into something that isn't proven to sell books just isn't a good idea.

A word of warning: I recently saw somebody advertising their book-trailer-making talents online and charging a not insubstantial amount of money in exchange for them. What was laughable was that the trailer they'd made to show how great they were was *terrible*, and something I – or any other person who has figured Windows Movie Maker or iMovie out – could have knocked together in less than five minutes. What was even *more* laughable was that this person's own video book trailer, which they'd made for their novel, was even worse, and in my opinion could only serve to *dissuade* people from buying the book.

When my father turned 60 I made a little movie to play at the party, which basically consisted of a slideshow of photographs I'd scanned into my computer, playing to music. The people watching it thought it was a wondrous thing, but I knew it was just a simple slideshow, something anyone with a bit of patience could do.

When you watch video book trailers, don't get distracted by their apparent shininess or sleekness. Ask yourself, what am I looking at? How was this done? I'll tell you right now, both my book trailers are only *slightly* more complicated affairs than a simple slideshow. So please, don't get conned by people who only know a *tiny* little bit more about a thing than you do. Instead of paying them money they don't deserve, see if you can do it yourself first. You probably can, and you can probably do it better.

Video Blogs

If making a book trailer sounds too much like hard work or is beyond your technical capabilities, consider a video blog. You should be able to point your laptop's built-in camera in your direction (or plug a webcam into your PC), hit record and *go*.

Video blogs (or *vlogs*, if we're being painfully up to date) are just video versions of your blog posts: say what you would've otherwise typed out. The beauty of video blogs is that they can be much more exciting for your blog readers (as there's the novelty of hearing you speak and seeing you in the flesh) and you can show them things, like the room where you write, or the proof copy that just arrived, or your book launch shoes.

You can also work your video blogs into a series. Ali McNamara (*From Notting Hill With Love ... Actually*) started a video diary when she signed the contract for her debut novel and then took her blog readers right the way through the experience until her book launch party. It was fantastic because it showed her meeting with her publicist, seeing her book getting printed and putting her proof copies in the space she'd reserved on her bookcase ever since she'd first dreamed of seeing a book of hers in print. Bestselling chick-lit author Miranda Dickinson (*Fairytale of New York*) made a video blog series called A Year in the Life of a Book, where she took her blog readers from writing the first draft through edits to seeing the cover, proof copies, etc. right up to the book being in stores.

I bought Ali's novel purely because after watching her video diaries, I wanted to see what the book was like, and I bought Miranda's new novel for the very same reason.

Twitter Events

As *Mousetrapped*'s release date got nearer and nearer, I was spending more and more time doing *Mousetrapped*-related things. This, in turn, gave me more and more *Mousetrapped* things to tweet about. Not all of these were promotional in motivation, but I was still afraid that I was bombarding my followers with yawn-inducing self-promotional tweets, or that they'd think I was. So I decided to put a cap on them, limit them to between 3–5 tweets one afternoon a week and label them for full disclosure, which I did with the hashtag **#mousetrappedmonday**.

I was amazed when what started off as a warning about me yapping on about my book (again) became a thing that people actually enjoyed, and got in on. They retweeted my #mousetrappedmonday tweets to their followers, and if I forgot to do it or did it late, they'd ask where it was.

To top everything off, I released the book on a Monday, making the final #mousetrappedmonday its publication day.

(I know. I'm like, *so* clever. Can I have a gold star?)

Twitter is the ideal venue for a virtual party, live discussion or giveaway. Set your imagination to work on how you might use it.

Twitter Graphics

Since the last edition of this book, Twitter made a change to its site that meant photos attached to tweets have started to appear "in stream" instead of just as a URL.

An example of an "in stream" graphic and Canva advertising the fact that they can help you make the most of it, all in one!

So while once upon a time I could only link to my book cover and hope that you would be interested enough to stop at my tweet and click the link, now you'll see it as you scroll through your timeline. This means we can – and should – take advantage of this situation by creating graphics for this specific purpose.

I love **PicMonkey** (www.picmonkey.com), which is similar to Canva. That's what I use for Twitter graphics, but of course you can use Canva too. You can sign up for PicMonkey and use it for free, although some of its premium features require a small annual subscription. You can see some examples of these Twitter graphics in use on the next page.

Scheduling Tweets with Buffer App

Another great idea for Twitter is **Buffer App**. It's free to use in its basic form, but you might consider upgrading to an "Awesome" account for around $10 a month. Buffer makes it incredibly easy to retweet interesting things and you can also queue tweets to post automatically at scheduled times of your choosing. It's a fabulous way to manage your Twitter presence while you're off being busy doing other things.

Meanwhile, on Facebook

The main purpose of your Facebook page is really to get as many interested people to "like" it as possible, and to keep those people updated about what's happening with your book.

Post links to your blog on the days you share the cover, first chapter, etc., upload photos of you proudly holding your proof copy and encourage interaction on the page by asking questions that encourage answers, e.g. *I'm trying to decide on a price for the paperback. What do you guys think? What do you normally pay for a paperback book?* If you have a Real World event like a book launch or signing, you can also list it as an "event" on Facebook. This enables you to invite specific people or leave it open to all, and attendees can RSVP.

Keep in mind that depending on the user's settings and how generous Facebook are being at any given time, if someone RSVPs to an event of yours, it'll be potentially visible to all *their* friends on the profile page and maybe even in the News Feed. The same goes for answering questions, posting comments or "liking" photos and statuses. Therefore the more activity you encourage on your Facebook page, the more likely it is that even more people will find it.

When Does Me Promoting My Book Get Annoying?

Quickly, if you do it wrong. It's been my experience that you are far better off focusing on providing the internet with a quality blog and an entertaining or interesting tweet stream, rather than concentrating on getting people to buy your book. If you do the former well, the latter will take care of itself, to a point.

This is, again, where the idea of getting people to like *you* rather than your book comes into play.

I think there's a line, and you should be able to judge for yourself where that line is. Saying "don't promote your book in your tweet stream" is a needlessly broad statement, as Twitter is a great place to find out about new books I want to read and I wouldn't find out about them if everyone thought there was a rule about not mentioning them. There are also a number of writers I follow on Twitter purely because I want to know about their upcoming releases, signings, TV appearances, etc., because I'm a fan of theirs. But on the other side of the coin, there are writers I'm following because they're funny or they can always be counted upon for animals-as-humans YouTube videos, and if their stream suddenly becomes choked with tweets like "My book is out March 3. Just $9.99. Pre-order it here! PLEASE RT PLEASE RT PLEASE RT THANKS!" then I'll get annoyed.

If you're unsure where your line is, ask yourself:

- Why are all these people reading my blog and following me on Twitter and while I promote my book, *am I still giving them that?* (The most important question)
- What's the ratio of my promotional tweets to my non-promotional tweets? Does it seem high?
- Have I lost a significant number of followers or blog subscribers since I started promoting my book?
- Am I doing anything that when I see someone *else* doing it, it annoys me?
- Am I even starting to annoy *myself?* (Time to rethink your strategy!)

Remember too that all anybody is really interested in is themselves. A cynic's view of the world maybe, but a rule of thumb when it comes to advertising. Think about what your followers will ask themselves: Will *I* like this book? Will *my* money be well spent on it? What's in purchasing this book for *me?* So you have to make engaging in your self-promotion worth their while. This is where the content you're offering becomes an important factor.

I used to work in an office, and every so often someone from a stationery company would come around and try to sell me stuff, or get me to buy stuff in the future from them rather than someone else. Usually it was a guy in a suit with a sheet of A4 paper listing their special offers, or comparing their prices with a competitor. To which I would say, "Yeah, thanks," and then never think of them again. But sometimes a guy would come in with a sheet of A4 paper listing their offers, a glossy catalogue (I

LOVE me a good stationery catalogue) and free stuff: notepads, pens and Post-Its all embossed with their logo and phone number. Since I was getting something out of the deal – free stationery, woo-hoo! – I would think of them whenever I next needed to place an order.

Online, you're selling *entertainment*. Tweeting a link to your Amazon listing is boring with a capital *B* and doing it repeatedly, all day every day, is grounds for unfollowing. But tweeting a link to your book trailer which will give me something to do for three minutes and maybe even make me laugh, or showing me pictures of you holding your book in your hands for the first time (something we all dream of, and understand the excitement of) will entertain and maybe even inspire me, and I probably won't even notice that in doing so, you're trying to sell me a copy of your book.

What's My Goal Here?

Your book isn't for sale yet, so at this stage we're not trying to get people to run off and buy it. Our goal here is to build a group of supporters, friends and fans who will help us launch our book by helping us spread the word about it online, maybe even buying it, or both. (The people who do *that* get gold stars and our undying gratitude.) These are the people who will help pull our book out in front of the millions like it and shine a great big torch in its direction. We'll love them forever, and owe them *lots* of chocolate.

We want to:

- Let people know that your book exists and will be out soon, especially targeting people who might be interested in it because they're fans of that genre or interested in its subject matter
- Get these people to spread the word about our book, tell their friends, etc.
- Bring people along on our self-publishing ride so that when the book is released, they want to see how it turned out
- Build anticipation so when these same people realise the book is now on sale say, "Oh, I must get that! I've been looking forward to reading that book"
- Do all this without annoying, or worse, losing the people who love our blog and tweets but have no interest in buying our book

Do not rush this step. One of the most common mistakes I see self-published authors make is telling us on Monday that they've a book coming out and then telling us on Tuesday where we can go buy it. This part needs *time*. It takes time to get used to Facebook, time to build real relationships on Twitter and with other bloggers, time to have any sort of readership at all stopping by your blog on a regular basis. You wouldn't get the painters in while your builders were digging the foundations, so don't release your book while you're still building anticipation about it. Wait.

One final word of author platform warning: this isn't about telling people stuff. It's about *connecting* with them. Try to remember that *before* you click Send on a "MY BOOK IS OUT SOON PLEASE PLEASE RT PLEASE RT THANKS OKAY LOVE YOU!" tweet.

Launching Your Book

This is crunch time. Sure, you've built a successful (and colour coordinated) blog, a Twitter following and a snazzy Facebook page, and you've produced a fabulous paperback and an e-book that you're confident are as good as they can be, and you are clued up on every aspect of the bookselling experience. (And, most importantly, you haven't used the word "gatekeepers" once during the whole operation. Hooray!) You've even made some new friends who are kind enough to retweet links to your book-themed blog posts, offer support when you moan about the scourge that is e-book formatting and appreciate hilarious cat-themed YouTube videos as much you do. Maybe one or two of them have told you that they're looking forward to reading your book.

But all this will have been for nothing if you don't give your book the launch it deserves and needs. Think of your book's launch as its breakfast: if it ain't a good one packed with fibre, caffeine and that wholewheat stuff that releases energy slowly, then it's not going to set your book up for a very good day.

Rockets Versus Matchsticks

When it comes to your book's launch I have two golden rules for you that I discovered the hard way: (i) don't pick a specific date too far in advance and (ii) don't diffuse your own momentum.

We need to ensure that by the time we're telling people "My book is out March 14th" it'll actually be available to *buy* on March 14th, and that when we come to launch our book, we're lighting the engines of a Saturn V moonrocket and not desperately blowing on a damp matchstick.

If I had my time over again, I wouldn't say anything more specific than "My book will be out in March." If pressed, I'd say, "my book will be out towards the end of March." Then I'd quietly upload my e-book and paperback files, wait for them to appear on Amazon, etc., make sure everything is absolutely perfect and ready to go, and then I'd set a launch date a week ahead, e.g. "My book is launching next Monday, March 29th." This takes the pressure off you, and will save you having many a sleepless night if something goes wrong and there's a not-insignificant delay.

The alternative is disaster. Say my paperback listing *didn't* go live in time for my launch. I would have either had to tell everyone that the launch was postponed, or launch anyway but explain that only the e-book was ready to buy. Doing either of those things would have diffused the momentum I'd worked so hard to build up and turned what should have been an exciting launch into a damp squib. It would have looked amateur instead of professional, and I would've been *mortified*.

On our release date, we want the people we've got excited about our book saying to themselves, "Finally! That book I've really been looking forward to reading is out. I must go and get a copy." If we get enough people saying this, the excitement begins to spread and thus the excitement surrounding our book's release begins to gather momentum. If all we can do is get people to say, "I was looking forward to that book coming out ... but now it's been delayed" or "I was going to buy that book today ... but it's not available yet in the format I want", then you're just sticking a big fat needle in your own balloon.

Don't Diffuse Your Own Momentum

I've seen self-publishers do amazingly well at building up anticipation and excitement around their book and then ruin it all by telling me beforehand where I can go buy their book right now. I know that when your listings go live you want to scream it from the rooftops, but *don't*. Resist the urge and don't tell anyone. If they find it, then so be it, but chances are they won't go looking until you tell them that it's time to. Every day of the week I see a self-publisher on Twitter say something like, "The e-book of [TITLE] is available now – the paperback should be out by my launch day!" and every time they do, they let a little air out of their balloon.

A good balloon needs to be filled with air, and a good launch needs to be filled with *concentrated anticipation*. Save everything for your big day, i.e. the day of its release.

Think of it this way: you're opening a new clothing store and you've set your opening date for May 1st. On opening day you plan to have special offers, free champagne and finger food for customers, and the first 25 people in the door will get vouchers to use in store. You're doing all this because you want opening day to be an exciting event that everyone's talking about, one the local newspapers and radio stations are covering. This will help spread the word about your shop, and ensure a steady flow of customers in your opening weeks. Are you going to open your shop beforehand and put things on special offer? Are you going to hand out those vouchers in dribs and drabs? Are you going to offer champagne and finger food every day? No, because if you did, it wouldn't be anything special. It would just be what you do every day. And what you do every day isn't exciting, and it certainly isn't news.

But That's Not What the Professionals Do!

A traditionally published author will in all likelihood spend their publication date at home, signing for the flowers their publisher sent, drinking a celebratory glass of champagne and then writing 2,000 words of their next book. They'll have told their Twitter followers about their Amazon listing months ago, or as soon as it could be preordered, and they'll have already blogged about their new e-book. They can do this because they'll have a launch party, interviews, TV appearances, signings and other events coming up that will help spread the news that their book exists, and you can now go buy it. Even if they're *not* doing any of these things, their books are still in bookstores, where I might happen upon it during my weekly browse.

You and your book, on the other hand, only have the opportunities you can create for yourself, which will probably be confined – for now anyway – to social media. People cannot chance upon your book; they can either hear about it from you or from someone who heard about it from you (for the most part). You need to grasp hold of anything you can that will give you something to blog about, tweet about or post as a status on your Facebook wall, and this means making an event out of your release date.

The good news is that you can be at home drinking champagne *and* blogging at the same time.

Reviews

Reviews are both the best thing and the worst thing about sending something you wrote out into the world. I've had reviews so wonderful they've made me cry, and reviews so scathing that I've felt as if someone reached into my chest, pulled out my heart and tore it to shreds right in front of me. (And if you're about to tell me not to take it personally, you clearly haven't yet experienced the acidic, burning pain of a bad review.) Thing is, reviews are *very* important to self-published books; much more so than they are to their traditionally published counterparts. With no editor or agent to vet the quality of the work, the potential customer has to look elsewhere for promises of quality. Your cover is one, your blog or website is another – even how your Amazon listing is laid out can sway a person's mind. But none are as convincing (or as condemning) as your book's reviews. A 2012 survey of self-publishers also found that the most successful self-publishers had, on average, won three times as many reviews for their books as their less successful counterparts.

There are four types of reviews we're going to talk about here:

- **Blurbs and endorsements**, where someone important is happy to lend their stamp of approval to your book, usually pre-release
- **Reviewer reviews**, which for self-publishers usually means getting impartial book bloggers to read and review your book
- **Goodreads reviews**
- **Amazon customer reviews**

NB: *Never* pay for a review. There are services out there run by everyone from off-shoots of well-known literary reviews to callous cowboys, offering to impartially review your book for a fee. Not only is this a gigantic waste of money, but the resulting "reviews" are likely to be far less impressive than those you'll get from your actual readers.

ARCs (or Why Cover Creator Isn't *Completely* Useless)

In the traditionally published world, reviewers are sent advanced reader copies (ARCs) or *proofs*. These are rough-and-ready paperbacks put together just so the publishing house has something to send out when the actual finished copies are still months away.

Usually they have a different cover to the finished product, haven't yet been proofread and are marked with warnings like "Uncorrected proof copy – not for resale or quotation". They're likely to have typos or other errors but the reviewers who receive them know this, and overlook them because they know it's an unfinished book. They may also be printed on flimsier paper or cover card than the final book will eventually be.

If you are being a *very* organised and professional self-publisher, you may be approaching reviewers long before your book is finalised. If you'd like to send them paperbacks, here's how to make your own proof:
1. Put your copy-edited but not yet proofread text into an MS Word template provided by CreateSpace, but don't worry about page numbers or any of that stuff.
2. Upload it to CreateSpace as if you were making a "proper" book, but leave all sales channels unchecked and:
3. Use Cover Creator + your Canva Kindle cover to make a cover for

your proof copy. One of CC's many templates is a cover whose whole front is taken up with a photograph and whose spine and back cover can be left blank or just have some text added to it. Insert your Kindle cover as the "front" picture and then type something like "Advance reader copy – not for resale or quotation" on the back. Leave the spine blank. Finalise your book and then order as many of your new proof copies as you like.

Alternatively you could order your maximum five proof copies at the proofing stage and send them to your reviewers. If you need more than five, re-upload your cover or your interior. You'll have to resubmit your book then (even though strictly there haven't been any changes) and once it's done, CreateSpace will come back and invite you to order a new proof (which will be exactly the same!) and there you go: another five copies.

Sending E-books to Reviewers

But physical proof copies cost money, not just for the book but for posting it too. Wouldn't it be easier and cheaper – not to mention quicker – to send your reviewers e-books?

If you only publish on Amazon KDP, you'll only have the book preview file you downloading during the publishing process. You can't download your own Kindle book for free, and anyway it would have to be for sale and published before you could do that.

However if you publish on Smashwords, you can download your own book for free at any time – and you could unpublish it again immediately afterwards, if you were still a few months ahead of your publication date. Then you'd have .mobi and .epub editions of your book that you could just e-mail to potential reviewers like you would any other file. You'll also have them if you have use an e-book conversion service, who'll send them to you when the job is done.

Please don't even begin to worry about the security of sending your book out to reviewers via e-mail. Illegal sharing? Chance would be a fine thing!

Blurbs and Endorsements

Blurbs and endorsements are short quotes from People Who Matter that you can use to convince the book-buying public that your book is indeed the bee's knees. These are normally sought prepublication so that the blurb can go on the cover of the book or inside it. (That's where those advanced reader copies, or ARCs, would have to come in.)

A Person Who Matters, or a PWM, if you will, for the purposes of blurbs and endorsements, is:

- a famous or well-known author, highly-respected and/or selling loads of books
- a highly-regarded expert in a field related to your book
- a well-known, respected newspaper, magazine or literary review

Even though the following people may be important to *you*, they are so *un*important when it comes to endorsing your book that they are basically irrelevant:

- your mother
- your best friend who reads, like, *all* the time
- anyone who the majority of the book-buying public has never heard of (with *one* exception, which we'll come to)

Let's look at some examples of this blurbing business that I found on my own bookshelves:

- On the cover of *You're Next* by Gregg Hurwitz, *New York Times* bestselling thriller writer Harlan Coben says, "Pure stay-up-all-night suspense"
- On the cover of *If I Never See You Again* by Niamh O'Connor, internationally bestselling crime writer Tess Gerritsen says, "Gripping, terrifying. If you like Martina Cole, you'll love this" (which is a double-whammy, because Martina Cole is also a bestselling crime writer!)
- On the cover of *Mennonite in a Black Dress* by Rhoda Janzen, phenomenon starter, recipient of much Oprah love and author of *Eat, Pray, Love*, Elizabeth Gilbert says, "Not just beautiful and intelligent but also painfully – even wincingly – funny"

and finally, in what is by far, far, *far* my favourite example:

- On the cover of *Moondust: In Search of the Men Who Fell to Earth* by Andrew Smith, the late Arthur C. Clarke, author of *2001: A Space Odyssey*, simply says, "Splendid!" (Sometimes just one word is enough if the right person is saying it!)

Thing is, as a self-published author, you can't just run off and *ask* for these blurbs, in that you can't just fire off an e-mail to, say, Stephen Fry, and ask him if he'd read and endorse your book. (Well you *could*, of course, but I'm guessing you wouldn't get a reply.) Chances are you will only get one of these if you know a PWM. Here in Ireland, this might actually be the case, what with everyone being about half a degree of separation away from everyone else, but it might also be the case if you've been making blogging and Twitter friends. Are any of them PWMs? Do you think they'd consider it? Could you ask without not being able to sleep for a week beforehand because you're so sick over the thought of asking? Then maybe you'll get a PWM to write an endorsement for your book. *Maybe.*

I said there was one exception to your PWM being a name recognised by the majority of the book-buying public, and that's if they're an expert or highly-respected leader in a field related to your book. Then whether or not they're a household name doesn't really matter, as long as you can relate their PWM status alongside the blurb. Let's pretend you've written a novel in which the central character has mental health problems, and you deal with that issue in a realistic and sensitive way. In that case, you could get someone prominent in the field of psychology to write a blurb. As long as you could quantify who they were, you could put that blurb on your cover. For example:

"A heartbreakingly sensitive portrayal of manic depression that, while fiction, will surely help the ever-growing number of very real sufferers of this condition out there today."

– Prof. Stephen Jones
Dean of Psychology at Johns Hopkins University

With cover blurbs and endorsements, **it's not so much** *what* **the quote says** (because they're all positive; otherwise they wouldn't be used) **as** *who* **is saying it**. That's what lends weight to the endorsement, and what convinces the potential reader to go ahead and buy.

In my experience, this crucial difference is the bit that self-published authors struggle to grasp, or ignore altogether. You can put the best sentence that anyone has ever said about any book in the history of the world on your front cover, but it won't matter a damn unless we know the person who said it. (And I don't mean know because you tell us. I mean know because they're a PWM.)

Take the professor's blurb above. Using *the exact same review,* here are three ways that this review would sink into irrelevancy on the cover of your book.

"A heartbreakingly sensitive portrayal of manic depression that, while fiction, will surely help the ever-growing number of very real sufferers of this condition out there today."

– Stephen Jones

"A heartbreakingly sensitive portrayal of manic depression that, while fiction, will surely help the ever-growing number of very real sufferers of this condition out there today."

– Stephen Jones,
Undergraduate at Lancaster University's Psychology Department*

"A heartbreakingly sensitive portrayal of manic depression that, while fiction, will surely help the ever-growing number of very real sufferers of this condition out there today."

– Stephen Jones. He reads like, a LOT, so he'd know.

Or take these *actual* "endorsements" I've seen on self-published books (I'm not kidding; these are real. I've changed the names to protect the silly):

"Funny and original. I read it all in one go." *– Jack, aged 16*

"I am your number one fan." – Emily, Manchester

"A magical journey into a wonderful land. Brilliant!" – Person with Same Last Name as the Author

They don't have *quite* the same gravitas, now do they?

Some people know some people who are famous, and they think that getting them to say something about their book is a good idea. If this Someone Famous is in no way connected to books, or is only connected to them because once upon a time they hired a ghost-writer to scribble their autobiography, then no, it's not. And it's not clever either. This is the fictionalised equivalent of a review I saw on a self-published book recently:

"This book has pages in it. Works for me!"

– Justin Timberlake

If you think after reading all that that the chances of you getting a blurb or endorsement for your book that passes the PWM test are between slim and none, then you'd be right. It is almost a certainty that you won't, unless you've had the foresight to make friends with Stephen King in the last twelve months. So why am I telling you all this if there's little to no hope of it applying to you?

Because self-publishers *love* putting blurbs and reviews on their covers by non-PWMs. And putting a non-PWM endorsement on your cover might do worse than just not matter – it might actually *harm* your book's chances of getting read, because the subconscious message you send out by doing it is that you don't know *what* you're doing, and that doesn't bode well for the rest of your work, i.e. the book itself. So unless your blurb is from a certified PWM, don't put it on the cover of your book.

Some blurbs and endorsements are neither irrelevant nor from PWMs. These could be reviews from traditionally published authors who aren't household names, self-published authors who have sold a gazillion books but who nobody's ever heard of, or from bloggers and blogs. Getting these is *great* and we're going to use them to do fantastic stuff, but they don't belong on your cover.

Yes, I know: a lot of the super-famous authors who write blurbs for books are paid to do so, and many of them don't even bother reading the books before they put their names to endorsements of them. They don't have the time, and the publishers don't care what they say anyway – they just want their name on the cover. And if that isn't the case, then the new author is likely to be one of the mega-selling author's friends or have photographs of them that could potentially be very damaging if they ever got out. And, yes, sometimes when you buy a book because your favourite author told you on the cover that it is the greatest book he'd ever read, it turns out to be about as entertaining as a big pile of poo, and even less memorable.

YES, I AM WELL AWARE OF THIS, thank you.

But what has any of this got to do with *you*? You are a self-publishing author, in case you've forgotten, because the making of your paperback and e-book was, like, two whole sections ago, and you need to do everything you can to convince people that your book is better than the majority of self-published books, i.e. not crap, and, on top of that, that it's something they want to read and will hand over their hard-earned cash in order to buy.

Getting Your Book Reviewed

The best way for a self-published author to help launch their book and secure its subsequent success is to offer review copies of their book to:

- book bloggers
- other bloggers
- genre-specific book review sites, e.g. crime or chick-lit websites
- owners of websites related to their book
- Goodreads users
- Amazon Top Reviewers

and put the resulting reviews (if they're good!) on places like a Reviews page on their dedicated book site and in the Editorial Reviews section of their Amazon listing. They can also quote from these reviews on promotional material, such as press releases, or even on a "Praise for ..." page in their next book.

In the first edition of this book, I advised against offering e-book review copies. A year ago most book bloggers, reviewers, etc. refused to accept e-books to review, and I felt that offering them one sent a message to the reviewer that their time wasn't "worth" the cost of one of my paperbacks to me. But things change fast in the book world, so now my advice would be:

- **To offer at least a small number of paperback ARCs** that you've had made by CreateSpace if possible. You could send these to the reviewers who matter to you the most, i.e. a reviewer who you think is likely to actually review your book and whose review would be widely read by people interested in books like yours.
- **To offer e-books, not PDFs.** PDFs are not e-books. They're PDFs. They're difficult to read on most e-reading devices – if the devices read them at all – and the only alternative is to read them on your computer, which is not ideal.
- **To not send anything else.** At least once a week I get an e-mail from a newly self-published author offering me a coupon that will allow me to download their book from Smashwords for free. (Smashwords allows authors to generate coupons offering percentage discounts to readers, including 100 per cent discounts that translate into free books.) Would you send an agent a link to a website where he or she could go read your manuscript? No. You'd just send it to them, because when it comes to them reading and liking your work the odds are already stacked against you, so you don't want to add any additional hurdles that might make things even worse. So don't send coupons. Send the book.

Bad Review Attitude Syndrome

I just took a very deep breath because writing this section is going to be very, very hard for me to do without GETTING VERY MAD and directing that madness at you, dear innocent reader. I do apologise. It's just that I have seen some horrors in my time in this self-published-authors-trying-to-get-reviewed arena, let me tell you, and I have seen for myself the reaction of self-publishing authors' faces when I tell them how they have to go about this business of getting their book reviewed.

A great number of self-publishers I have encountered in my time (and I concede that maybe I just need to change the places where I hang out) have held one or more of the following beliefs about getting their book reviewed:

- By giving away a free copy of my book I am depleting my profit, so I don't want to do it
- If someone wants to read and review my book, they can go and buy a copy
- To save money, I'll only offer PDFs of my book to review – that'll do
- by giving someone a free copy of my book, I am doing *them* a favour
- I only want to give copies to bloggers who have a minimum number of monthly hits; otherwise I'm just wasting my time
- since they didn't even *pay* for my book, the least they can do is give it a positive review

Now that, my friends, is just horse faeces. FACT. And here's another fact: **when you give someone your book and they review it for you, *they* are doing *you* a favour**. It's *never* the other way around.

Think for a second about what the reviewer does. First, they choose to read your book over the piles and piles of other books they've received to review. If you don't believe in the piles and piles, consider this: I'm *extremely* small fry in the book-blogging world, and I currently have six books piled up that need to be read and reviewed. And when you get a book to review, you don't *have* to review it, so the reviewer has decided to spend their limited reading time on your book above others. Then the reviewer spends anything from four to eight hours of their life reading your book, and then another hour or two thinking about what they thought of it, and then another hour on top of that putting those thoughts into words in the form of a written review. If the reviewer is a book blogger, they then have to turn this review into a blog post and put it up on their site. If they aren't strictly a book blogger but just review books as part of their personal blog (like I am and do), then they are giving your book a post that they would otherwise use for their own cause. And even if they *are* strictly a book blogger, they're still doing all this for *free*, and just because they love books and reading them.

And if that doesn't convince you, then let's look at it this way: what do the professionals do? We are trying to come across as professional authors, so let's see what professional authors – or their publishing houses – do to get their books reviewed.

A few months ago I received an e-mail from a book publicist who had come across a review of *The Snowman* by Jo Nesbo that I'd posted on my blog. She said that she too had read *The Snowman*, and thought that if I enjoyed that, then perhaps I'd be interested in reading a crime novel by a debut author that was coming out in a month or two, and a crime novel by an author already established in another genre. She included brief blurbs of both these books, and invited me to e-mail her back if I'd like to receive copies of them to review. She also said that she realised that I was probably "inundated" with review copies and would understand if I didn't get around to them; there was no obligation to ultimately review. I did e-mail her, and she did send them. Each came with a single A4 page that told me a little bit more about the book, a little bit more about the author and logistical details like when it was going to be published, in what format, etc. I never had to contact her again but I did, just as a courtesy, when I posted the review of the first book on my blog. I still haven't got around to reading the other one, but it's not out yet, so I still have some time to get to it. But if I never get to it, it's not a problem.

Now I will acknowledge that there is one major difference between a traditional publishing house and you, a self-published author: *money*. Obviously you do not have the resources to send out hundreds of copies of your book to people who may never review them; you and your budget (and profit) just can't afford to take a hit like that.

But here is what you *can* afford to do, and what I highly recommend: **send between 10–50 copies of your book to people who you think are** *likely* **to ultimately post a review on a website, blog or on Amazon.**

Remember, this isn't "lost" money. Far from it. We're going to get great mileage out of any reviews we get, and that's not even considering how many new readers we may get just by people hearing about our book through these reviewers posting about it on their blogs or websites.

And if you claim you can't afford to send ten copies of your book out to potential reviewers in a move that will practically guarantee that many sales and potentially many times more than that, then I have *no idea* why you got into this self-publishing thing in the first place.

The Reviewing Principles

Here are the principles I strongly recommend you abide by as you seek reviews of your book:

- *There is never any obligation to review.* Never send out a copy of your book in exchange for a review. If they find the time to review it, great, but if not, we'll all still be friends.

- *There is never any obligation to write a positive review.* Do you want a review, or do you want your ego stroked? The whole point of reviews is to find out what books are like. Lies are not only pointless (because they'll soon be found out and then cast a very bad light on both the lying reviewer and the egotistical author) but also dishonest. Book bloggers are very professional people; if they don't like your book, they'll explain why and they'll be more than reasonable about it. Them not liking your book is just a chance you'll have to take.

- *There is never any obligation to be timely, or to work to a schedule.* Yes, it would be nice if they could read and review your book before it comes out or before you send out that e-mail in which you want to put all the quotes, but you can't ask them to. They'll get around to it whenever they can.

- *You find reviewers, reviewers don't find you.* If you send out a tweet saying something like, "Anyone interested in reviewing my book hit me up for a PDF!" then you can be sure that you'll get lots of people reading and perhaps even reviewing your book, but who will these people be? Publishing houses sometimes tweet looking for book bloggers, but as I've already said, you do not have their resources. You need to be a bit more discerning, so you need to go looking for reviewers. Also, don't expect them to do the legwork of finding you.

- *If you use the review, link back to it.* If you put the review somewhere, be it a quote or the whole thing, make sure you link back to wherever the review was originally posted, i.e. the book blogger's blog. Similarly, if you put the review anywhere offline, credit the reviewer and include their blog address, like: "Thoroughly enjoyable. I'll be looking out for this author in the future."– *Romance Central, www.romance-central.co.uk.*

- *Say thank you.* ALWAYS thank reviewers for reviewing your book; being courteous goes a very long way. Either leave a comment on the review if it was posted on a blog or website, send them a thank-you tweet or do your thanking in an e-mail.

Finding Reviewers

The easiest way to find potential reviewers for your book is to google "review" and the name of a recently published book that's very similar to yours. You should be able to see in the search results book review websites and book bloggers who reviewed the book, and then you can e-mail them to see if they'd be interested in reviewing yours.

This is also where your blogging and Twitter friends can be a HUGE help. Offer them review copies. Since you've been subjecting them to blog posts about the book for the last six months, they'll definitely read it just to see how it turned out. (And – bonus – shut you up about it too!)

If your book has a very specific subject matter, search online for websites, podcasts, forums or online magazines devoted to that subject, and then contact them to see if they'd like a copy.

To give you some idea of who I targeted to review *Mousetrapped*, here is a selection of them (not all of them wrote reviews):

- An author who was looking for prizes to give away on her blog; I sent her a copy for herself as well, and she wrote a post about it
- A journalist with a blog that reviewed memoirs
- Two chick-lit review blogs that also review non-fiction
- The book blogger of a site specialising in women travelling
- The editor of a newsletter that lists work-travel opportunities
- The editor of a directory about working abroad to which I had contributed
- A website that reviews all genres of books, TV and movies
- A Disney news blog
- A Disney podcaster

You can find Amazon's Top Reviewers – the Amazon customers who review the most and whose reviews get the most helpful votes – on (surprise, surprise) Amazon. There are two top reviewers lists: the best contributors at this moment in time, and "Hall of Famers" based on all-time contributions. If you go to Amazon.com, you can find both lists here:

http://www.amazon.com/review/top-reviewers

Each Top Reviewer has a profile, and it's links to these profiles that appear in the list. In order to find suitable reviewers for your book, you'll have to investigate the reviewer's previous reviews (to see if they read books like yours) and you'll have to find reviewers who include their e-mail address in their public profiles (so you can contact them). This process, therefore, is extremely time-consuming, but if even *one* Top Reviewer reviews your book, it'll be worth the effort, because not only will you have a review of your book, but that review will be written by someone who Amazon customers know they can trust.

Here is as good a place as any to explain to you why the *New York*

Times isn't going to review your book. Well actually, the *NYT* isn't going to review your book for lots of reasons, so let's just concentrate on a local or national paper where you live instead. Why are books reviewed in the press? It's not for the good of the newspaper's health, let me assure you. No – it's for the readers of the newspaper, just like the rest of the stuff in there. And the space allocated to book reviews is small as it is and shrinking all the time, so why would they review a book that their readers cannot find in bookstores? Why would they review a book that has zero hope of making an impact on the bestseller lists because it's not in bookstores? And why would you, as an author who is almost totally focused on activities online, even pursue this Real World review?

Don't send copies of your books to newspapers and magazines unless it's in a significant number of brick-and-mortar bookstores; that *is* a waste of money.

How to Ask for Reviews

Once you've found your book reviewers, you now need to contact them to see if they'd like a copy of your book. E-mail works best for this; I wouldn't approach reviewers on Twitter or Facebook.

If you can't find an e-mail address, see if they have a Contact page or form on their site. Here is the kind of e-mail you should write:

Dear [first name]

I recently published *Mousetrapped: A Year and a Bit in Orlando, Florida*, a travel memoir of the eighteen months I spent living in Orlando and working in Walt Disney World.

As book blogger for RelevantSite.com, I wondered if you might be interested in reading it?

If so, I'd be happy to send you a complimentary copy. There is, of course, no obligation to review but if you like it, you might consider mentioning it in one of your posts. But as I said, there is no obligation.

You can read the synopsis below and, if you wish, find out more about the book at mousetrappedbook.com.

If you are interested in receiving a copy, please forward a postal address and I will mail one to you immediately.

Kind regards,
Me

or

Dear [first name]

I saw your review of [similar book] on RelevantSite.com and wondered if you'd be interested in a copy of my travel memoir, *Mousetrapped: A Year and a Bit in Orlando, Florida.*

If so, I'd be happy to send one to you. There is, of course, no obligation to review but if you like it, you might consider mentioning it in one of your posts. But as I said, there is no obligation.

You can read the synopsis below and, if you wish, find out more about the book at mousetrappedbook.com. If you are interested in receiving a copy, please forward a postal address and I will mail one to you immediately.

Kind regards,
Me

If you have any proof that you're a good writer or that this book is more likely to be good than bad, put it in here.
Like:

Dear [first name]

I saw your review of [similar book] on RelevantSite.com and wondered if you'd be interested in a copy of my novel, *Title Goes Here.*

If so, I'd be happy to send one to you. There is, of course, no obligation to review but if you like it, you might consider mentioning it in one of your posts. But as I said, there is no obligation.

You can read the synopsis below and, if you wish, find out more about the book at titlegoeshere.com.

A little bit about me: I've been writing short stories for several years, and have had them published in the likes of *Short Story Magazine, Stories People Have Written* and *Snooty Literary Stuff Monthly.* While a student of Very Famous University's English Literature department, I was shortlisted for the Famous Short Story Award and last year, placed second in Equally Famous Write a Novel competition. Famous Author of Books Like Mine, who was on the judging panel, said of *Title Goes Here* that it was "an accomplished début whose ending left me bereft".

If you are interested in receiving a copy, please forward a postal address and I will mail one to you immediately.

Kind regards,
Me

Here is the kind of e-mail you should NOT write:

Dear Blogger,

I really need to get my book mentioned on RelevantSite.com and am wondering if you're the person to make that happen. If you are, I'd be happy to send you a FREE copy of my book, *Mousetrapped: A Year and a Bit in Orlando, Florida.*

Before I do though, I'm going to need a guarantee that you will post a review of it. Perhaps you could send me your passport? I'll send it back after my (positive!) review goes live. I also need you to do it ASAP. Like, yesterday. I got bills, y'know?

I'm also gonna need a signed declaration – notarised, obviously – that you'll accompany my review with links to my blog, website, Twitter feed, Facebook profile, Flickr albums and Goodreads page, and that you won't use any photos of me in which my left side predominantly features.

That's what's up.

LATERS,
Me

And just because I'm still reeling in shock, this is an e-mail I received last week asking for a review – and this is the e-mail in its *entirety*:
Catherine,

My book, *Yes, This is Happening*, needs to be read.

Seriously. That was it. No sign-off, no further information about the book, not even a *link*.
I mean … REALLY?!
If you're being *super* organised about this and have printed up ARCs especially, I would say you'd want to start this review business around three months before your planned release date.
(Was *I* this organised? Excuse me for a moment while I roll around on the floor laughing, would you?)
In reality, any time from then until about a month after your book is published is fine.

Should you say you're self-published? This is a tricky one. Some might not want your book based on this fact alone (and we can't say it's unfair because it is a fact, plain and simple, that a lot of self-published books are stinky poop), and in fact some book-blogging sites specify that they do not review self-published books. But the self-published world is losing its stigma more and more every day, so you never know, it might not be a problem for most reviewers in the future.

I would say check if the site says anything about it, and if they say they don't review self-published books, then don't approach them with yours. Otherwise you don't have to point it out, but don't lie about it either. Notice in my e-mail example I said "I recently published ..." which doesn't contain the phrase "self-published" but is the truth: I'm the one who published the book.

Chances are the reviewer will click on the link to your book site or blog and use what they find there to decide. And because we've all worked so very hard to look *professional,* chances are it will convince them to say *yes.*

Do NOT consider lying. What would be the point?

If someone says, "Why yes! I'd love to read your book!" then send out a copy of your book no later than the very next day.

(It goes without saying that should you not be in a position to send a copy of your book out the very next day, then you shouldn't be sending reviewers e-mails yet! But I've said it anyway.)

If you're sending a paperback, make sure the book is in perfect condition, and new. CreateSpace covers are glossy and collect fingerprints; give it a wipe with a cloth before you put it in the envelope. I even went so far as to buy polybags (the clear plastic envelopes that seal at the top that handmade greeting cards tend to come in) that I then put my paperbacks in before I sent them out, but then maybe you're not as crazy about books being perfect as me. (And polybags add more expense, so just get a cloth!) And while we're on the subject of envelopes, use a big enough one. Don't stuff your book in there because when it's opened at the other end, the corners will be destroyed and the book itself might be bent.

Put what we'll call an *information sheet* in with the book. This is a single sheet of paper that has your author bio, a synopsis and contact details on it. Jazz it up with photos and colour too if you can, but only colours that coordinate (of course!) with the colours of your book. If you're sending an e-book, attach this to the e-mail in PDF.

Never send review copies by registered post or courier service. Not because it's more expensive (although it is) but because packages like that have to be signed for, and if our potential reviewer is out at their 9–5, they'll have to traipse to the post office to pick up your book.

Your Book Getting Reviewed

With any luck, people other than the ones you've sent free copies to will also be reading your book, i.e. the ones who went out and bought it, and chances are a few of them will log on to Amazon afterwards, click that Create Your Own Review button and start typing. Some of these people will have liked your book; some of them won't have. Some of these people will write balanced, fair reviews; some of them won't. And some of them will go on there to give *your book* a one-star review because *Amazon* delivered it a day late, or because even though they haven't read the book, they don't like the sound of it and wished you would write fiction instead.

You'll have a honeymoon period where logging on to Amazon will be a nice experience, one that fills you with warmth. (Or perhaps the sun of a thousand springtime mornings.) Then one day you'll hit the Enter button and something will look different to you. At first, you won't know what it is that's changed. And then you'll see it: your average star review, the one that's on top of the listing next to your title and is the average of all your reviews, will have lost a star. And then you'll scroll down, your stomach churning, your body covered in a cold sweat, your heart thumping in your ears, and you'll see it, right there …

A one-star review.

Someone doesn't like your book. Reading the text of the review, it becomes clear that they didn't just not like your book, they *hated* it. They detested it. They wished that the trees that died so it could live could be reborn and your book could take their place. They feel about you as a writer as they would you as a person if you drowned their puppy and made them watch, and made other puppies watch too. And while you did it you were laughing. *Hard.*

There is nothing that compares to this feeling, and having 4,124 five-star reviews beside it doesn't do anything to lessen the blow. That's the bad news. The good news is that everyone gets reviews like these – *everyone* does – and there are ways in which we can train ourselves not to take too much notice.

Before we move on I should specify that I'm not talking here about negative reviews, or three-star-out-of-five reviews. Your book is not going to be universally liked. It can't be; we don't all like the same things. What I'm talking about here are *baaaaad* reviews, vehement reviews, nasty reviews – reviews that are written in a tone that, you imagine, conveys that the author of the review would rather you die than produce another book.

(Yes, people really do leave reviews on Amazon that read like that. I've even had the pleasure of getting one of them myself. To which I can only say, *it's just a book* and, *have you considered anger management?*)

The only way to avoid these is to write a book that everyone will love and/or avoid reading your reviews. I have yet to encounter a writer who has managed to do either; if you know of one, do let me know.

Here's what I recommend you do to combat the my-world-is-caving-in feeling of reading bad reviews:

- Print out or photocopy a review of your book that you really like from a source you explicitly trust and/or one whom you recall has raved about books you've loved and been blasé about the same books you've given up on. Stick it somewhere prominent, or in multiple somewheres prominent. Maybe even put an emergency copy in your wallet. Force yourself to read it immediately after the encounter of a bad review.

- Look up a book you adored on Amazon and read its reviews. This is always a good one, if only because the reasons people come up with to dislike books never cease to amaze me, not to mention the imaginative insults they heap on it afterwards. Remind yourself that you loved this book and yet BigReader874124 thought it was "not good enough to wipe my arse with in a no-toilet-paper emergency – I'd rather use my hand." You can't please everyone. (And why would you want to?)

- Look up the reviewer's other reviews. On Amazon especially, this can be a very soothing exercise. Maybe they gave *Freedom* one star because it didn't have any pictures, or maybe they slated *Little Women* for false advertising once they discovered it wasn't actually about vertically challenged females. Or maybe they thought *Never Let Me Go*, one of your favourite books of all time ever, was not good enough to wipe their arse with in a no-toilet-paper emergency.

- Write a response. Bad reviews tend to linger with us because we are passionately arguing with them in our heads. *I didn't mean it literally! You took that out of context! I really did do that! You obviously don't understand what I was getting at! Did you even read the blurb? Did you even read the book?!* So put a stop to this by sitting down and typing out a response. Then delete it.

- If all else fails, pour yourself a stiff drink and ask anyone who'll listen, "Did *she* write a book? No. I didn't *think* so."

How *not* to handle them includes but is not limited to: sending severed horses' heads round to these reviewers' homes à la *The Godfather* is frowned upon, I believe. Also it can get kind of messy.

The only thing to do about these kinds of reviews is nothing at all. *Don't* respond to them. Don't get (too) upset about them. And whatever you do, don't start your writing day by rereading them. But what it they're, like, REALLY bad? If a review violates Amazon's review guidelines, you can report the review, either through Amazon Author Central or by clicking the Report Abuse button underneath the review. Common violations include:

- The reviewer admitting that they either didn't read the book at all or didn't finish it, e.g. "I couldn't even bring myself to read past page 5 this book was so terrible."
- The reviewer using the review to make a point about something unrelated, e.g. "I'm never ordering anything from this seller ever again. They delivered it a week late AND they charged me twice for it."
- Revealing crucial plot points or other spoilers. "I was enjoying it up until, three pages from the end, when the main character died."

Amazon also says that making spiteful remarks about the author is a violation of its guidelines, but from what I've seen in my own and other authors' reviews, this is not something they enforce or make any effort to counteract. Or perhaps their definition of spiteful is just different to mine.

Aside from reviews that are really about the company who fulfilled them and spoilers that might well ruin the reading experience for a future reader, I wouldn't take any action against Amazon customer reviews of your book. It's a slippery slope, and you don't want to become the kind of author who does everything they can to keep all but four- and five-star reviews off their books' listings – or worse, become *known* as the kind of author who does. And the people who leave poisonous reviews are not the kind who are likely to take the removal of their poisonous reviews lying down; taking action might make the situation worse, and more widespread as they take their poison pen to their blog, their Facebook page and Twitter.

You also don't *need* to do anything about them, because most customers do not pay attention to extreme opinions, be they good or bad, and Amazon has a pretty good process for sorting the useful reviews, i.e. the balanced and honest ones, from the too-good-to-be-trues and the too-bad-to-be-reals.

When you view an Amazon listing, the review you see at the top is the "most helpful" review by default. This means that other customers have deemed it helpful by clicking Yes next to the "Was this review helpful?" question just below it, or that a greater of number of people have clicked Yes than have clicked No. Comments left on reviews can also be voted upon, although the question is "Do you think this adds to the discussion?" In this way, the most helpful – or fair – review rises to the top in a kind of natural selection, albeit an elected kind.

As an Amazon customer, I know I don't take much or any notice of reviews on a product unless there are 50 of them and they are *all* bad. If I do read the reviews, I tend to side with the middle-of-the-road verdicts, the three-star reviews that say what they liked and didn't like about the book, and say it in a reasonable tone that doesn't make me think the author drowned their puppies and made them watch. And I don't think I've ever gone onto Amazon to purchase a book and then stopped because the product had negative reviews, even if, on a couple of occasions, I lived to regret it.

Finally, getting bad reviews feels terrible, but the only way to avoid them is to not write any book at all, and I don't care what anyone says about me, my writing or the things I choose to write about: I know that that scenario would feel far, *far* worse.

E-mailed Praise

One of the nicest things about having a book out there in the world is opening your e-mail account and discovering messages from readers in far off lands, telling you how much they loved your book. Now I have no idea how many of these messages I've got, but I can tell you this for a fact: it's a hell of a lot more than I've got Amazon reviews.

Now I *love* those e-mails – I print them out and file them in a Break Open in Case of Loss of Confidence in Writing Emergency – but I sometimes wonder, if these people love my book so much and they took the time to e-mail me about it, why don't they take five minutes to give it an Amazon review and tell everyone else?

As I've already said, Amazon reviews are *so* important to self-published authors, I can't stress it enough. They can make or break a sale. And so sometimes, especially after I've just got a bad or low-starred review, I come *really* close to responding to one of these messages and asking, politely, if they'd consider putting their praise in the public domain. But I don't, because I'm afraid that I'll offend them. (And the one time I *did* do it, the praiser never posted a review. So I assumed she was offended, and I never did it again.)

But I *should* and if you have the courage to, you should as well. If someone sends you a praise-filled e-mail, respond, and then at the end of your message put something like:

I really appreciate your praise and I'm so glad you enjoyed the book. If you have five minutes, perhaps you'd consider leaving a customer review on my Amazon listing? As a self-published author, reviews are extremely important to my book as they can make or break a sale. You can visit the listing here [insert link] and click Create Your Own Review to start.

Alternatively, you could ask your praisers if they'd mind if you copied and pasted some of their kind words onto the Reviews page of your book site, or onto other promotional material. This is better because the reader doesn't have to do anything except give their permission.

NB: If someone praises your book in an e-mail, that's private. You cannot reprint it without their permission. If they tweet it, paste it onto your Facebook wall or leave a comment on your blog, that's public.

Review Karma

Having said that, I know *exactly* why the people who e-mail me praising my book don't leave reviews on Amazon, and why I've had the pleasure of a review so scathing my ego wasn't merely hurt, but sandblasted. It's because of my review karma.

I am always e-mailing authors or tweeting authors or telling authors in person how much I enjoyed their book, but I can't remember the last time I wrote an Amazon review. And let's just say that when a certain author got a major book deal a few years back, at a time when my own writing career was as far away from reality as it's ever been, and she was the same age as me and had started writing last week and only after trying her hand at a succession of other jobs, and I had wanted to be a writer for as long as I could remember and was still getting nowhere, and now she was rich and famous and in *Marie Claire* and I was just broke and despondent, and when her book came out and I could only make it halfway through because it was so bloody terrible, I vented my painful jealousy into a scathing Amazon review that could have stripped old paint off walls its tone was so acidic.

What I'm saying is **be wary of your review karma**. Write Amazon reviews. Be reasonable and professional; you don't have to heap praise on every book you read, but there's never any need to get personal, mean or spiteful. If you thought something (e.g. "this book is boring"), explain *why* you thought it (e.g. "most of the chapters didn't move the pace forward, and the multiple narrators only seemed to slow it down even further"). Always review a book *on its own terms*, i.e. don't give the latest Dan Brown one star out of five because you just read something by George Orwell that was a lot better, and don't chastise it for doing what's expected of its genre. For instance, I recently read a review of a romance novel that called the ending (after being kept apart for the whole book, girl and boy get together) predictable. *Predictable? A happy ending in a romance novel?* Surely not!

And if you read a book that you really, *really* don't enjoy, then just keep quiet about it. Have some diplomacy. You're an author now, and everything you do online – including trashing other people's books – can not only be traced back to you, but lasts forever – if someone gets a screenshot of it before you delete it, anyway.

And the universe *always* knows ... Well, it might. Either way, I wouldn't take the chance.

(If you've got a bee in your bonnet now because I've suggested you curtail your poison pen reviews, ask yourself what you want to do here: write, publish and sell your own book, or spend the rest of your life talking about how much you didn't like everyone else's?)

What to Do With Your Reviews

Or what to do with your *good* reviews, I should say. Once they come in (and you've remembered to thank your kindly reviewer) I would copy and paste some or all of them onto the dedicated book page that you (should) have installed for your book on your blogsite. With any luck, this will be one of the top search results generated by Google if someone goes looking for reviews of your book. Remember to credit each one and link back to the original, if applicable.

Next, go to your News page on your blogsite, and enter a new item. You could say something like, "[Book name] was reviewed by Science Fiction Central" and then link to the review.

If it's a *really* good review and it came from a *really* respectable source, you might consider taking a line or two from it and posting it on your Amazon listing as one of your five editorial reviews, through Amazon Author Central (which we'll get to in a minute).

You can also print them out, stick them on your noticeboard and gaze at them adoringly. That's always fun.

A word of caution here: *not all reviews were created equal*. This is something that, along with what matters in blurbs and endorsements (the *who* and not the *what*, if you need a reminder), many self-publishers fail to grasp. For instance, there is an epidemic of self-published writers on Twitter who tweet every time their book receives a five-star review, e.g. "My book, *Annoying, Much?*, just got ANOTHER 5* review on Amazon! Thanks ReadingBunny79!" If they were doing this because they were genuinely excited about getting a five-star review, I'd let them off. But they're not. They're doing it because they think the rest of us will think, "Oh, wow! That book must be *amazing*. I'm going to drop everything I'm doing and run over to Amazon to buy a copy now." (And maybe because they're excited as well. But only a little bit.) And we are never in a million years going to react that way to an "ANOTHER 5* review!" type tweet. How would you react to a tweet that said, "This girl just told me that I'm way better looking than Brad Pitt" or "My boss said if I left the company, he doesn't know how he'd cope" or "My mother just told me that I'm her favourite daughter. Suck it, sis!"? I know I'd be thinking something involving *unfollowing* and *jerk*. But I'm sorry to say that this is *exactly* what you're doing when you tweet – yet again – that you've got *another* glowing Amazon review: annoying us, and sounding like a bit of a tool. Because what's a five-star review on Amazon? Nothing. Nothing at all. It's just one, and we don't know who wrote it. It could be someone who reads a book a year and so has no frame of reference. It could be someone who only reads books we'd hate. It could be your best friend. But what it definitely is is *not important.*

But – and this is a big but – sometimes Amazon customer reviews *do* matter. They matter when there are a lot of them, or when they've been written by a Top Reviewer (and so come from a more credible source). In those cases, you can use them to sell your book. For example, if I told you that my book has over 500 five-star reviews on Amazon, wouldn't you assume it must have something going for it? Wouldn't it be safe to assume that? The #1 Top Reviewer on Amazon.co.uk (who is also the #1 Hall of Famer) gave *Mousetrapped* four out of five stars and said nice things about it. I took a quote from the review and put it in my Product Description, because the #1 Top Reviewer is as good an endorsement as a respected fellow author, or a popular review site.

This goes back to the same point I made in Blurbs and Endorsements: the *what* isn't as important as the *who* who's saying it. In the case of Amazon customer reviews, *how many* are saying it also becomes a factor. But individually, no matter how glowing, they just don't matter in terms of trying to convince me or anyone else that your book is good. I'm sorry, but they just don't.

As for tweeting about reviews, I'd avoid tweeting about Amazon reviews altogether. If a book review site posts a review of your book, certainly, link to it in a tweet. I'd be interested in reading what they have to say about it. If your writing hero says she loves your book, that's a big moment. If you get a write-up in the local paper or in a magazine, that's something to celebrate. But please avoid the "ANOTHER 5* Amazon review!" tweet. They achieve nothing, and we've more than enough of them already.

Goodreads Giveaways

Goodreads (www.goodreads.com) as we've mentioned already is essentially a kind of Facebook for book lovers. In the run-up to and immediately following the release of your book I would schedule some Goodreads giveaways to help publicise it.

The beauty of the Goodreads giveaway system is that you don't have to do much except tell Goodreads how many copies you want to give away, where you're prepared to post them to and how long you'd like the giveaway to run for. They take care of the rest. They run it, pick the winners and send you their addresses, freeing up time for you to develop an obsessive habit of checking your Amazon sales ranks. Fantastico.

Then the winners receive their copies, drop everything to read them and post gushing reviews on the site. Hundreds of other Goodreads users see these reviews and drop everything to go buy a copy. Then they read it and post gushing reviews on the site, and the cycle continues until you're a bestselling author who can pay for life's big purchases in cold, hard cash.

Well, not always …

Usually what happens is you run the giveaway, send out the books and then: nothing. Silence. *Deafening* silence. Your book doesn't take off. The ratings don't change. If you're lucky, one new review might appear on the site in three months' time. But essentially, your Goodreads giveaway disappeared without trace like a raindrop falling into the ocean. So recently, much like Carrie Bradshaw, I got to thinking: is there a way to do Goodreads giveaways better?

Goodreads have a lot of really interesting and helpful guides for authors on their website, including a Guide to Giveaways. In it they say that a month is the perfect length of time to run a giveaway for and that, ideally, you should run two giveaways: one before publication and one after. I completely disagree and the thing that got me started on disagreeing is a graph that Goodreads included in their own Guide to Giveaways, which showed the popularity of Jess Walter's *Beautiful Ruins* on the site during a giveaway held in 2012. Two enormous spikes were immediately obvious, and they occurred at the start and at the end of the giveaway. Conclusion: the real benefit – the *only* benefit? – of running a giveaway comes at the start and the end.

Why is that? Well, let's think about how Goodreads users discover giveaways. They can either navigate to the book's listing on the site and see the Enter to Win button, or they can browse the lists of current giveaways. Scrap the first one, because in order for that to happen we have to somehow send a user to our book's listing in the first place, and that's not what this is about. This is about getting new people to discover for the first time that our book exists independently of any other social media activity we might be engaged in.

Goodreads giveaways are listed in four different charts: Recently Listed, Popular Authors, Most Requested and Ending Soon. Presuming that you're starting from scratch, you won't have a hope of elbowing your way into Popular Authors or Most Requested, so that just leaves Recently Listed and Ending Soon. Clearly, being in these charts has an effect on entries, because of the *Beautiful Ruins* data – that title saw the *most activity it would ever experience on the site* at the beginning and at the end of the giveaway. In short, beginnings and endings are good.

So why in the name of fudge would you minimise the beginnings and endings you have by running one long giveaway? That's just one opportunity to get into Recently Listed and one opportunity to get into Ending Soon – when we know that appearing in these charts is your giveaway's best chance of winning entries. Wouldn't the intelligent thing to do be to construct your giveaway schedule so that you have as many starts and stops as you possibly can?

(Spoiler alert: the answer is yes.)

But Catherine, you might be squealing now, *who cares about how many entries you get?* We're just trying to get a couple of reviews here, right? So what does it matter if 100 or 10,000 people enter my giveaway? I just want the ten who win copies to read them and write a review.

This is not *really* about getting reviews. Would we really go to the trouble of running a giveaway, publicising it and then spending our first royalty payment sending copies of our books to far flung places just to get reviews? I hope not, because there are easier ways. No, this is about informing Goodreads users that our book exists in the hope that some of them will think it looks interesting, add it to their To Read list and then, on a date in the future, purchase it for themselves. That is our goal here: sales. That is always our goal. So, the more entries we get = the more people know our book exists.

When you enter a giveaway, Goodreads even clicks by default a box that adds the book to your To Read shelf, placing a permanent reminder of it on your Goodreads profile whether you end up winning a copy or not.

It's just as well people-knowing-we-exist is what we're really after, because Goodreads say that on average only 60 per cent of winners of giveaways go on to read and review the book they win on the site. I think that's a tad optimistic, if I'm honest. I know in the giveaways I've run in the past, the figure was well below 50 per cent as far as I could tell. And we're self-published authors, remember. Our budgets are not bottomless. We have to pay for the books themselves and the postage, so we just can't afford to give away the 20 or 25 copies we see traditional publishers offering on the site. We're lucky if we can stretch to five or ten. And what's 60 per cent of five or ten? Not bloody worth it.

Don't restrict your giveaways to any particular geographical region. Publishing houses have a genuine reason for restricting giveaways geographically: they only have the rights to publish the book in certain territories. You only have one reason, and it's stoopid: you don't want to stretch for international postage.

Have you ever posted a book internationally? Unless you've written a doorstopper, it's not going to break the bank. You don't have to FedEx the damn thing; Goodreads tells winners to wait for up to eight weeks for their books after the giveaway closes. Don't think of the shipping costs as something separate, which is a mistake I think a lot of people make. They say to themselves, oh, I'll give away 20 copies because that's [my unit cost + cost of shipping books to me] x 20, and then when the postage bill kicks in it seems like a fortune. I say create a budget, e.g. $75, and then work out how many books you can give away and post, potentially internationally, for that price.

Also, you don't have to send your winners books you ordered in from CreateSpace. That's actually kind of a silly idea, when you think about it. Why would you pay to send the books to yourself, and then pay again to send them to the winners? Send them directly from CreateSpace instead. For example if I have a person in the US who needs to receive a complimentary copy of my book, the unit cost of the book plus domestic postage (because CreateSpace is in the US) is half the price my book is to buy. If you live in the US and your winner is in, say, Ireland or the UK, why not get Amazon.co.uk to send them the book? The shipping will be minimal and you'll get some of the price you paid back in a royalty payment. The Book Depository will even ship one book anywhere in the world for free.

The bottom line here is that if our goal is to inform as many Goodreads users as possible that our book exists, you have no choice but to set your giveaway open to all countries.

And personally I think it's rude not to, especially when, as a self-published author, you have world rights. More importantly, when I log into the site, by default I can only see the giveaways that are open to Ireland. So if you exclude me, I can't just not enter your giveaway – I won't even know you're running it. Therefore, cross me off your list of people who'll discover that your book exists.

Once upon a time, I would've recommended you give away ten copies of your book in a single Goodreads giveaway that lasts a month. But *now* I'm saying:

- Give away as few books as you like, because this isn't about the winners. It can even be one.
- Instead of one long giveaway, run three to five shorter giveaways (five to ten days) of varying length to maximise your appearances in the Recently Listed and Ending Soon charts.
- Open your giveaways to all countries.
- If you've published only in e-book, consider making a physical proof-like copy to give away instead.

- Definitely do it, because it's a great way to spread the word about your book.

Does this work though? Going back to Goodreads own Guide to Giveaways, they tell us we should give away at least ten books and run our giveaways for a month. They also tell us the average number of entries is 825.

Now in the last few months I've been trying it my way with one of my social media clients, a major UK/IRL publisher, and the results are clear. Before this, standard practice was to do what Goodreads told us to do: a month-long giveaway for 20 to 25 copies. I took one title and split those 25 copies into five shorter giveaways of varying length for just five copies at a time. These ranged from five days in length up to two weeks. The average number of entries was 1,726. In a six-week period, we won over 8,000 entries over all. For exactly the same number of books: 25 copies in total.

So I would say yes, yes it does.

Release Day

The big day is finally here: your release day.

This is the date, picked by you, on which you "release" your book, even if in reality it's already been on sale for a few days or even a couple of weeks.

What you do on this date will capitalise on all the hard work you've put into building your online platform up until now and set you and your book on the road to success, so make sure you do *something*.

Am I Ready?

By the day of your release:

- Your dedicated book site should be completed
- Your paperback's availability on Amazon, if applicable, should be "In stock"
- Your Amazon Kindle listing should be live

If you are releasing your book on more than one platform, it can be difficult to ascertain exactly *when* they will all be listed and available to buy. I understand; I've been in the same position myself – and I made a bit of a mess of it. I worked out a schedule and figured that March 29th, the eighth *"Mousetrapped* Monday"*, would be the best day to launch the book online. My e-book listing went live a lot quicker than I thought, so that was up and running by March 9th. My paperback took *longer* than I thought it would, because I didn't check my file as thoroughly as I should have and in the first proof there were mistakes. There was then a delay of a week while I waited for another one to arrive, and then an incredibly anxious few days during which I was searching Amazon every five minutes to see if my listing had appeared. It eventually went to "In stock" on March 26th, or just *three days* before my planned March 29th release date.

Yeah, But What Do You Actually *Do*?

What do you actually *do* on your launch day? That's up to you, but I recommend being online for most of it and doing everything you can to spread the word.

On my launch day I:

* Gave away copies of my book.
* Blogged about the book finally being out.
* Held a virtual launch by setting up a Facebook event, inviting everyone to it and setting the location as "online". I then posted a photo of a mojito cocktail. Even a virtual cocktail is better than none!
* Tweeted about the book (talked about it, thanked people who'd bought it, retweeted tweets anyone else posted about the book, linked to video trailers, linked to the first chapter, linked to Amazon listings, linked to other people's blog posts about it, etc. Did this get annoying? Not that I'm aware of. It was actually really exciting for me, and I think my followers saw that, and only wanted to make it more exciting for me as opposed to rolling their eyes and hitting unfollow. This was because I wasn't just throwing things at them; these were people I "knew", i.e. my blogging and Twitter friends. And they knew I would help do the same for them and their books. Plus I also *stopped* doing it again the day after).

I would estimate that I was online that day, with the exception of bathroom and coffee breaks, from about 8.30 a.m. until 7 p.m. when I collapsed (without spilling any of my self-congratulatory Corona, mind you), exhausted but happy, and safe in the knowledge that my book's life was off to a great start.

Contests and Giveaways

The best way to drum up some excitement about your release day is to have it coincide with a contest or giveaway. In fact, this is a great way to build excitement about anything connected to your online presence, be it your blog or your book.

Blog Giveaways

Giving stuff away to your blog readers is so much fun, and really easy to do. Maybe it's a copy of your book, someone else's book or just something fun, but whatever it is, it's worth it. Not only do you reward your loyal readers for sticking with you, but you draw in new readers as well.

Ask people to enter by leaving a comment at the end of the post that announces the contest. Either specify what they should say, e.g. "Leave a comment that says 'Pick me please!' at the end of this post," or tell them that they can say anything at all. It's best if you leave the entry period open for a few days; not everyone reads blogs every day. Then at the end of the specified time, either put everyone's names in a hat or use a random number generator (**www.random.org**) to choose, say, the sixteenth person to leave a comment, and announce the winner on the blog. Ask them to e-mail you with a postal address and send out their prize.

Sometimes a blogging or Twitter friend will offer you copies of their book to give away on your blog. In this case the process is the same, but you send the address of the winner to your friend who then sends the book out.

When I moved from Blogger.com to WordPress.com, I wanted to do something that would guarantee my new blog a decent readership right from the start. So instead of posting every day and hoping that new readers would happen upon it, I decided to spread the word about it instead, i.e. advertise my sparkly new blog.

I asked myself: what is small (and so easy to mail anywhere and at a low cost), cheap (so I could afford it) and connected in some way to either me or my blog that would make a good prize for a giveaway? Cork Coffee Roasters are a company based here in Cork, where I live, who have a lovely little café and roast the beans that make their signature blends. With my blog being called Catherine, Caffeinated and me having espresso for blood, nothing could've been more perfect. Now, a bag of this coffee costs about €6, so I was more than prepared to buy the three bags I'd need, but on the off chance they'd give them to me for free I e-mailed the café to ask first. And they said yes!

On the day the blog "launched" (which was also a Monday, come to think of it!), I put up the first post: Catherine's Coffee Contest. To enter you could either leave a comment, tweet a link to the blog using the hashtag #corkcoffee (which helped me find the entries *and* advertised the brand of the nice people who'd given me the coffee) or retweet a tweet of mine about it. The result was amazing. There were hundreds of entries, and one of the bags ended up in Texas!

Best of all, in the very first month of my little blog it got a very respectable 1,500 hits, a number it would have taken me far longer than a month to achieve otherwise.

Twitter Giveaways

Twitter is a great place to hold a giveaway because as entering only takes a click, you'll be guaranteed plenty of entries.

Entry in a Twitter-based giveaway usually involves doing one of three things:

- retweeting a link about the contest
- using a hashtag, i.e. "Tell us your #faveTVshow"
- following the account that's doing the giving away, or getting it more followers

If you're asking people to retweet a link, make sure that the link is short and that it includes all the relevant information, e.g. "Giving away 3 copies of #Mousetrapped today! RT to enter." Remember: people will see your username, e.g. @cathryanhoward, in the tweet too, and so will find your Twitter profile and blog if they go looking. When you pick a winner, follow them if you're not already (so they can send you a direct message, or DM). Then tell them they've won by mentioning them in a tweet, e.g. "Congrats to @caroline471 who has won a copy of #Mousetrapped! DM me your address."

I like the hashtag idea, because it engages people more and might make a few other people laugh. It will also make Twitter a more interesting place, which is what you should *always* be trying to do. You can either enter everyone who does it and draw someone at random, or award the best.

My next book is about backpacking, so I could have a contest where to enter you have to tell me the worst travel experience you've ever had, using a hashtag like #MyWorstTravelStory. I could be more specific, and ask for backpacker tales, which would enable me to use the name of my book, *Backpacked*, as a hashtag.

A while back, the brilliant blog Slush Pile Hell held a Twitter contest like this where to enter you had to come up with the best worst self-help title ever. It was a fantastic idea that tied in perfectly with the theme and tone of the blog, fitted well inside Twitter's 140-character limit and some of the entries were hilarious. The winner was *A Hypochondriac's Guide to the REAL Diseases You Need to Worry About and Their Symptoms*, but my favourite was *Do It You're Self: A Guide to Self-Publishing*.

So that's retweeted and hashtag-based contests and giveaways, which are both *much* better ideas than follower-related ones, which I think are pretty pointless and a bit annoying for the followers of the people who enter them. Although these are generally orchestrated by companies and businesses, I've seen self-publishers attempt to get in on the act too.

Follower-related Twitter competitions usually look like one of these:

- "If we can get 1,000 followers by 5 p.m. we'll give away a free subscription to one of them!"
- "Follow us and RT this link to be in with a chance of winning [SOMETHING CRAP]!"
- "I'm going to give my 500th follower a free copy of [TITLE]. Who will it be?"

Let's start with the first two, which are basically variations of the same thing: the Help Us Get More Followers and/or Spread Us Around Twitter Like a Virus and Then We'll Reward a Random Person Giveaway. You might get more followers and you might even spread yourself around Twitter like a virus, but in doing so you'll annoy far more people than you'll interest in your product or brand, and tomorrow morning they're all going to *un*follow you. And even if some stick around, they're just a number. They didn't follow you because they want to hear what you have to say; they followed you because you promised them the chance of winning free stuff. Remember how we talked about engagers not numbers? Those people are not engagers. And so what was the point of that? There wasn't one.

The bottom one, the I'll Reward The Person Who Makes My Follower Count a Nice Round Number, is even *more* pointless because why would *anyone* be motivated to follow you unless they saw that *they* were going to be follower number 500? Do people even *think* about these things before they tweet them? Seriously, it boggles the mind. Not only that, but due to the nature of Twitter the chances of number 500 being a spammer or someone trying to sell you something are high, and then there's the embarrassment of falling below that number shortly after you hand out your reward, which is pretty much guaranteed. Its pointlessness cannot be adequately conveyed with the word *pointless*. At least with the Help Us Get Followers stupidity you have a chance of being a trending topic or something.

Free Stuff

There is one worthwhile thing that can be taken from those examples though, and that's the idea of *rewarding* followers, readers or Facebook fans, and doing it with free stuff. This doesn't directly spread the word about you or your book, but it says thank you to the people who are already helping you do that.

Remember those Smashwords coupons? Every now and then I make one that gives the recipient a free download, and I use them to reward the people who make all this possible: blog readers, Twitter followers and Facebook fans, many of whom are also people who have read my book.

The day *Mousetrapped* sold its 1,000th copy, I put a free download coupon on my blog to thank everyone for all their help. (It had a time limit; I'm not stupid!) When my Facebook fan page was at 99 fans, I said "The next person who likes this page, fan #100, will get a free download of *Mousetrapped*!" (Note that I didn't do it when I had 79 Facebook fans.)

For the launch of this book, the third edition of *Self-Printed*, I've organised the "Self-Printed Splash". I asked for participants via my blog, inviting people to send me their burning self-publishing question. I'll send them back the answer to post on their blog, which they have agreed to do all on the same date, about a week after the book is released. In return for taking part, I will send each participant a coupon that will enable them to download a free digital edition of my book. I'm currently up to almost 100 participants, so fingers crossed, come the day of the splash, you won't be able to move for mentions of my book.

Another idea is to offer a prize that can't be bought, e.g. a special edition of your book. To mark the third anniversary of *Mousetrapped's* publication, I decided to make myself a little hardcover edition using Lulu (another POD service very similar to CreateSpace, except for the fact that they offer a hardcover option). While I was at it I decided to make a few extra copies that I could then use as giveaway prizes on my blog. Remembering that anything we can get onto an MS Word virtual page we can get into our book, I added some "special features" to my hardcover edition, including a "signature" and illustrated title pages.

The signature page was created by simply printing out a title page from my CS interior document, handwriting an inscription on it ("Thanks for reading Mousetrapped – I really hope you enjoy it. Best wishes, Catherine Ryan Howard") and then scanning it. I then took this JPEG and inserted it into my Lulu interior document as a photograph the full size of the page. And, like magic, I had created a "signed" copy of my book that anyone could order. Similarly with the illustrated title page, I inserted a photo that took up the full page and put a vertical text box on top of it. Yes, the photo printed in black and white (because I had a black and white interior) but it was still effective.

Giving Giveaways

I've already explained why you need to provide complimentary copies of your books to review, and the same arguments go for providing copies of your book as prizes. It helps spread the word about your book and the person who wins it might well leave you a five-star Amazon review or, at the very least, mention the book to a friend or two. You never know, so take the chance!

You'll find that your blogging and Twitter friends, from time to time, will tweet or post about looking for items to give away on their blog. (You can do this too.) Offer them a copy of your book. If someone asks you to write a guest post for their blog, offer to give away a copy of your book too. This will ensure that that post gets read and so introduces your book to a new group of people.

Blog Tours

To help publicise their book and give their readers an opportunity to meet them in the flesh, traditionally published authors embark on book tours. This involves travelling to a number of cities, sitting at a table in the middle of a bookstore for an hour or so and hoping that someone comes up to you and asks you to sign the copy of your book they've bought and not for directions to the in-store café. Unless you're a Rock Star Author, of course, who has a queue of nervous, giggly fans (Harlan Coben, Paris, 2006: one of them was me) and the local police force on standby for crowd control.

Of this we can but dream. (Of being the Rock Star Author, not of Harlan Coben. Although that's okay too.) Book tours cost lots of money, what with travel and accommodation, and unless your book is actually in stock in the stores you're going to, there's really no point. This counts us self-publishers out, but there is a free alternative that helps publicise our books and doesn't necessitate the leaving of our own homes: a blog tour.

The idea of a blog tour is fairly simple: instead of touring cities, you tour blogs. Every day for a specified period, e.g. the fortnight after your book comes out, you appear on a different blog, courtesy of the blog owner.

What Do I Do on These Blogs?

Generally speaking, you would do one or more of these things on each blog you're hosted on:

- give away a copy of your book
- answer interview questions
- write a guest post (an original one for each blog, mind you!)

For best results, mix it up a bit. So on Monday you could be giving away a copy of your book on one blog, Tuesday you're being interviewed on another, Wednesday you've written a guest post for a different blog *and* you're giving away a copy, etc. etc.

The beauty of blog tours is that different groups read different blogs, so you are guaranteed to reach new readers. You are also having a bit of fun with your blogging friends, and now their blog readers too. And like everything we do online, all these posts are generating more Google search results for your name and your book.

How to Organise a Blog Tour

A blog tour isn't really a tour unless you have at least a week's worth of blogs to hop through, and the more you can tour, the better. The ultimate blog tour, I imagine, would be one where every weekday for a month you pop your mug up on someone's site. (Although I also imagine this would be an organisational nightmare, and require a week's bed rest to recover from.) Ideally, aim for 5–15 blogs (weekdays over 1–3 weeks), and try to make it a mixture of blogs by your friends and blogs by friendly strangers. I say this because if you and I follow the same group of bloggers, I'm going to be reading about your book every day for a fortnight, and great and all as your book may be, that's a bit much. You'll also be preaching to the choir, because I'll have already heard about your book.

You can either ask bloggers if they'll host you, or announce your intention to do a blog tour and then invite people to say, "Why yes! I'd LOVE to have you on my blog. I thought you'd never ask!" Don't pick and choose based on popularity or colour coordination; if someone invites you onto their blog, go. Make a list of your hosts, their blog URLs and their e-mail addresses.

Next, decide *when* you're going to do the blog tour, and then pencil in a different blog for each date. E-mail each host, thank them for offering to host you, check that the date you've reserved for them is suitable and then ask if they'd prefer a giveaway, an interview, a guest post or a combination of two or more. Most will say that whatever works for you is fine, so figure out what that is. (Hint: writing 20 different blog posts about the same subject is *not* what works for you. Trust me on this.) If it's an interview, ask the hosts to send you the questions before a certain date (politely!) so that it's not all one big rush at the end.

Closer to the date – maybe a week before you're due to make your appearance – e-mail each host with the text of your post (if applicable), a high-resolution JPEG of your book's cover, a picture of your beautiful face and any other information they need, like your blog address, Twitter username, etc.

You should also give them the URL of the blog where you'll be appearing the day after you appear on theirs, and ask them to link to it at the end of the post, e.g. "Find out more about Catherine and her book tomorrow on Eva's Book Blog: www.evasbooks.ie." In this way every blog post is linked. You should also list all your blog-tour stops on *your* blog, embedding links to the posts or blogs in the list.

My *Self-Printed* blog splash is just a variation on this theme.

Being a Good Special Guest Star

I've seen a few blog tours in my time and I am always surprised – and, as a blog reader, disappointed – when a blog touring author doesn't *quite* get what the point of a blog tour is all about. Similarly I've hosted a few blog touring authors, and not all of them left me happy to have them back. To make sure that your blog tour achieves all of its aims and that you make a pleasant impression on your gracious host, follow Catherine's Five Steps to Being a Good Special Guest Star:

1. **Write a good post**. The number one aim of it is to *get someone new interested in you and your books*. It seems like that old common sense thing again, but in order for that to happen, you have to be *interesting*. If your book is funny, make your post funny. If your book is about writing advice, give good writing advice. For the love of fudge, do SOMETHING that makes people  say to themselves, "I want to read more of *her*!" You might also want to keep it short and snappy; I once came across a blog-tour post that was 5,000 words. 5,000 words! The average blog post is fewer than 800. Think of your *audience*. You owe them some entertainment while they procrastinate instead of writing their own novels. Your host blog isn't just a soapbox.

2. **Be organised**. Your blog hosts are doing you a favour, so please make doing this favour as easy as you possibly can for them. Send your guest post in a Word document with the links already embedded and a minimal amount of fancy formatting – make it a simple procedure for your host to copy and paste the text into a new post on their blog. Make a list of all the blog tour dates and make sure all the hosts have the right one. Send them a friendly reminder a day or two out.

3. **Promote your visit**. It's not the host's job to promote your guest

appearance – it's yours. You should be sending traffic to the blog you're appearing on, not hoping it'll bring traffic to your site. For the blog tour of my (since unpublished) e-book *Results Not Typical*, I even had my cover designer knock up some fancy graphics: a blog tour list to display on my blog, and a "badge" for all my hosts.

4. **Add value.** Or as a Mob guy might say in a Hollywood movie, *make it worth their while*. If you're not giving the host a copy of your book to give away on his or her blog – or even if you are – offer the host a copy of their own.

5. **Say thank you.** Most importantly of all, after you appear, send a message to your hosts to thank them for helping you to publicise your book, and say that if they ever want to appear on your blog, they're more than welcome.

Launching in the Real World

Up until now I've only talked about launching your book online. But what about the real world? Should you try to get your face in the paper? Attempt to bribe a bookseller into stocking a few copies of your book? Perhaps even have yourself a little party?

Whether or not you launch in the real world is entirely up to you. It's been my experience that having a real world launch is good for publicity and networking, i.e. meeting people who will bring you more opportunities in the future, and it's a *lot* of fun, but it comes at a cost. It also doesn't necessarily translate into sales, which makes the cost even higher.

As self-publishers of POD paperbacks and e-books, **our base is online**. That's where we spend all of our time, how we find our readers and where people have to go if they want to buy our books. Brick-and-mortar bookstores are for traditionally published authors or self-published authors who have used local printers to produce a few thousand copies of their book and then convinced a distributor to sell them to bookstores. And even if we don't have our launch in a bookstore, we still have to order in the stock that we're going to force all our friends and family to buy after we've plied them with canapés and alcohol. But having boxes of our books underneath the stairs or piled up in the hall is *exactly* the situation we hoped to avoid by going the POD route and, because we went the POD route, those books are going to be expensive to us now, even at cost price. Not to mention the fact that before we can sell them, we have to have them shipped to us.

Let's talk about how to go about this first and then I'll share with you my own experience. I'm also going to include the experience of a self-published friend of mine, Sheena Lambert (*Alberta Clipper*) for a dissenting view.

Then you can decide which route is the best for your book.

A Party Versus an Appearance

What sort of book launch do you want to have? Unless you have a few pots of gold you need to get rid of, it doesn't matter what sort of launch you *want*. All that matters is the kind you *need*.

An in-store launch. This is where you spend an hour or so in a bookstore, posing with your book and signing copies for all the friends and family members you've persuaded to show up and pretend to be interested strangers. Its sole purpose is to get your book in the newspapers, and this can be helped enormously by the appearance of a local celebrity. You can even make a speech, or get your local celebrity to, and you can invite as many people as you want, including actual strangers. You'll have to convince the store to stock your book, order in that stock and organise the event, but it'll be worth it if you can get a picture of you holding your book in a newspaper, or your launch mentioned on local radio. Press coverage can lead to more opportunities for you and your book. This is what I call an *economy book launch*. Personally, I think it's by far the best option for a self-publisher.

An in-store launch after hours. As above, but it happens after hours, when the store is closed. This changes two things. The first change is that there will be no one else there except people you invite, i.e. the store will be closed so there'll be no customers, and with locked or closed doors there can be no curious passers-by dropping in to make up the numbers. So if you invite a hundred people and only ten show up, there will only be you plus ten people in the store, which will be a bit cringe-worthy. However, people might be more interested in attending this because it's at night, has more of an "event" feel than its equivalent during the day and there'll be wine and cheese. That's the second thing. If you have your event during the day, you'll be unable to serve alcohol or nibbles because the store will be open (so there'll be no room and it'll be messy). But now you can, and people will be expecting you to. That's great and all, but you'll have to pay for whatever food and drink you serve, which adds to the cost. This is a bigger deal than our first launch, but it's more expensive and dare I say, a tad self-indulgent for a POD self-publisher.

A launch party. As above, but in a private venue like a bar or hotel, and *definitely* with food and drink on offer. Of all the options, this is the one most likely to be attended by the people you invite but it is *by far* the most expensive.

A private party. Just like any other party you might have in your home with your family and friends, but this is to celebrate the fact that you wrote a book. An utterly pointless activity for a self-publisher because it does nothing to help publicise your book, but you might decide you deserve one. If you understand that the purpose of this is fun and celebration, go ahead. But it's nothing to do with the business of selling your book.

I'm going to focus on the first type of launch, the one I strongly recommend you have if you're going to have one.

Approaching a Bookstore

The first thing you need to do is find a bookstore where you'd like to have your launch. It has to be local – so you can be A Local Author – and independent stores are best, for two reasons: first, they're more likely to agree to buy stock from you directly (crucial for your launch), and second, they have owners who can decide whether or not to host your launch without having to consult a chain of middle managers. It also helps your cause if you're a regular customer of the store, or in a somewhat suspicious but fortuitous coincidence, have suddenly become one in the last month …

Armed with a copy of your book and your best friendly smile, ask to speak to the manager. Show them the book first; if you've listened to me (and NOT used Cover Creator), this will be enough to persuade them that you're a professional operation. Explain what you want to do. If you've approached them because you're a regular customer or you have a mutual friend, or because you attended another author event at the store and were impressed, mention it. Play all your cards. And then cross your fingers that they'll say yes.

Chances are they *will* say yes, because you are going to bring customers into their store, get their store's name in the paper and (hopefully!) sell a large number of books through their tills. It's a total win-win for them. Unless:

- **Your book looks like a pile of poo.** (And if you've used Cover Creator, it does.) This is a bookstore. The people who work there are booksellers, potentially highly experienced ones. They know what real books look like, and what crappy little POD-ed pamphlets do *not* look like, and that's real books. They are not going to want to sully their store with a book that isn't really a book, can't compete with the real books already on their shelves and probably won't sell many copies, if any. If your book doesn't sell, hosting your launch holds no benefit for the store. They are running a business, not operating a charitable hosting service for unprofessional self-publishers.

- **Your wholesale price is too high**. All the books you sell the day of the launch will be sold through the store, i.e. you sell it to them and then they sell it to the people who attend your event. Ask them how much of a profit margin they need on your book, and then *agree to sell it to them for that*. Don't argue; you don't know enough about selling books to make demands, and hey, aren't you trying to get this store to host your event for you? When I went to ask my local bookstore owner about having an event there, one of the first things she asked me was how much my book retails for. I told her the truth, which was €10.99 in local currency. She then explained that their profit margin was 30 per cent, so I'd have to sell my stock to them for €10.99 – 30 per cent, making my profit (€10.99 – 30 per cent) – my cost price. If you have to up your list price by a euro (or a dollar or a pound) to make this deal less painful, do. But don't jack up the price so much that you overcharge people for your book, especially since most people who are going to be buying it will be family members or friends.
- **You don't instil confidence that you are capable of pulling this off**. Here comes the P-word again: do you seem like a *professional* author? Do you give the bookseller the impression that you are a highly organised and motivated individual who is going to actually get people to attend this event? That you'll get out there and publicise it? Or do you come across as someone who's just doing this for kicks or, worse, expects the bookstore to do all the work? I did what I thought was the minimum an author should do for their launch (get the stock in, give the store posters to advertise it, get people to come, get the launch covered by the local newspaper), and therefore I was a tad surprised when the bookseller told me I was by far the most organised self-published author she'd ever dealt with. I'm not telling you this to gloat or show off – although if you want to give me a gold star, you can stick it on my forehead – but to prove that just by being professional, you can stand head and shoulders above the rest.
- **They don't buy stock from individuals**. Many bookstores only buy stock through distributors, so they just have to pay one person and don't end up with invoices from a variety of individuals (authors). If this is their policy, they will have to say no to hosting your event. Don't take it personally.

NB: The store will advise you on the best time for your launch. Listen to them.

Selling the Stock Through the Store

Yes, you have to.

No, you can't have a launch at a bookstore and not put your books through their tills.

The only way to avoid this is to have your launch somewhere other than a bookstore, so you can pocket all the proceeds yourself. (After you pay the credit card bill for all the stock, of course.)

All the stock you order from CreateSpace has to be paid for outright and cannot be sent back. All the stock you give to the bookstore will be for sale or return; if they sell them, they'll pay you for them, but if they don't sell them, they'll hand them back. They might keep a couple in stock and maybe one day in the future they'll call you up and ask for more of them, but they might not, and then you'll be stuck with all of them. But what's the only thing worse than being stuck with excess stock of your own book? Having people ready and willing to buy them, and having run out.

Go through your invite list and figure out how many copies you expect to sell. Then add another 20–50 copies, depending on how many Stranger Purchasers you expect. (Not hope for. *Expect*.) Add another ten copies for safety, and then order that amount of stock.

And order it in plenty of time. Remember the volcanic ash cloud that stopped air travel over all of Europe for a week or so? That was the week before my launch, and the week in which my books were supposed to be travelling from the US to Ireland. I was just about to skip town when, *two days* before the launch, which by then had been mentioned in the newspaper and on invites sent to every single person I had ever met, a delivery van arrived with the books. It was probably the most relieved I have ever been in my life.

Fun With Printed Stuff

Stock isn't the only cost involved in this launch, and I'm not just talking about your outfit. You'll have to get invitations printed, get posters for the store and get something to give out on the day to people who come over to see what's going on but don't buy a book there and then.

I recommend a website like Vistaprint (**www.vistaprint.com**) which is really cheap, seems to ship all over the world and makes it easy for you to order different types of paper products that all match.

Printed materials can be very useful when promoting your self-published book, so long as they look professional, contain all the relevant information and get into the hands of the right people. There's no point leaving a stack of postcards on the counter of your local butchers, for instance, if your book is about vegan recipes.

To help promote *Mousetrapped*, I made myself book launch invites that doubled nicely as bookmarks, postcards and posters. I also produced an "info page" to include with complimentary copies of my book so potential reviewers, stockists, etc. would know what it's about without having to read through the whole thing.

Getting Publicity

You have two opportunities to get publicity for your launch: before and after.

To get publicity beforehand, e-mail every local newspaper, free newspaper and community newsletter you can find. It helps in the months leading up to your book's release if you keep an eye out for news stories about other launches, and take note of where they appear and who writes the pieces or does the reporting. Keep a list of people and places to target.

A book launch is not a story; you need to give them something more than that. This is the actual text of the e-mail I sent out to newspapers:

Hi [name],

My name is Catherine Ryan Howard and I'm an author from Douglas. I'd like to invite you to my book launch at Douglas Books, Douglas Village Shopping Centre, on Saturday 8th May at 12.30 p.m.

If there is any opportunity to publicise the book/the launch beforehand, I'd greatly appreciate it.

I've included some additional information below and if you need any more/clarification, please don't hesitate to contact me. My mobile number is [number] or you can contact me at this address.

Kind regards and thanks,

Catherine

Book Launch:

MOUSETRAPPED will be launched on Saturday May 8th 2010 at 12.30 p.m. in Douglas Books, Douglas Shopping Centre. All welcome.

Book Synopsis:

Three big dreams, two Mouse Ears and one J-1 visa. What could possibly go wrong in the happiest place on earth?

When Catherine Ryan Howard decides to swap the grey clouds of Ireland for the clear skies of the Sunshine State, she thinks all of her dreams – working in Walt Disney World, living in the United States, seeing a Space Shuttle launch – are about to come true. Ahead of her she sees weekends at the beach, mornings by the pool and an inexplicably skinnier version of herself skipping around Magic Kingdom. But not long into her first day on Disney soil – and not long after a breakfast of Mickey-shaped pancakes – Catherine's Disney bubble bursts and soon it seems that among Orlando's baked highways, monotonous mall clusters and world famous theme parks, pixie dust is hard to find and hair is downright impossible to straighten.

The only memoir about working in Walt Disney World, Space Shuttle launches, the town that Disney built, religious theme parks, Bruce Willis, humidity-challenged hair and the Ebola virus, MOUSETRAPPED: A Year and a Bit in Orlando, Florida, is the hilarious story of what happened when one Irish girl went searching for happiness in the happiest place on earth.

The MOUSETRAPPED Story:

Catherine wrote MOUSETRAPPED after returning to Ireland in the summer of 2008. She sent it to one agent and four or five publishing houses, and got the same response from each: they enjoyed reading it but felt there was not enough of a market for it to justify publication. Meanwhile, Catherine gave up her job at a letting office in Cork City so she could do something she'd dreamed of for years: write a novel. To help keep her in paper, ink cartridges and coffee while she did, she self-published MOUSETRAPPED.

On March 29th 2010, MOUSETRAPPED launched online, for sale on Amazon.com, Amazon.co.uk and other international Amazons, as well as through Catherine's own website. Catherine blogged about her entire self-publishing experience – the highs, the lows, the headaches – and also maintained an active Twitter account.

About the Author:

CATHERINE RYAN HOWARD is an occasionally delusional twenty-something from Douglas, Cork. As well as working in Walt Disney World, Catherine has been a student journalist, administrated things in the Netherlands, cleaned tents on a French campsite, established a handmade card company and answered telephones in several different offices. Yes, several. She is currently working on her first novel, daydreaming of a US Green Card and drinking way too much coffee. She wants to be a NASA astronaut when she grows up.

Contact Details:

[Telephone]
[E-mail]
www.catherineryanhoward.com
www.twitter.com/cathryanhoward
www.facebook.com/mousetrappedbook

Photos Attached:

MOUSETRAPPED cover
Author photo
Launch invite
(Higher resolutions available on request.)

Some of the people I sent this to just ignored it, but I *did* get a story about my book launch in Cork's *Evening Echo*, the daily tabloid here in Cork and by far the biggest newspaper, circulation-wise, that I'd sent it to. Word of warning: they didn't contact me before they wrote the piece. They only used the information in my e-mail, and the photo I sent. So be careful what you put in your e-mail!

You can get great coverage after the launch if you can convince a social diarist to attend. This is the person who works for your local paper who has to go to events like launches, take loads of photos and chat to the attendees and then, if you're lucky, give you a two-page spread a few days later. Again, keep an eye out for coverage of other launches and events, and look for how to contact the reporter.

This is the actual text of the e-mail I sent to the social diarist of my local paper, Cork's *Evening Echo*:

Hi Martina,

My name is Catherine Ryan Howard and I'm from Douglas.

I've just self-published a travel memoir called MOUSETRAPPED: A YEAR AND A BIT IN ORLANDO, FLORIDA, and I would love to invite to you to the launch.

It will take place in Douglas Books, Douglas Village Shopping Centre, at 12.30 p.m. on Saturday 8th May. I have printed invitations and can send you one if you'd like.

I've included some information below about the book.

Thanks for your time and I really hope to see you there.

Catherine

[Here I put the same information as in the previous e-mail – synopsis, about me, etc.]

This was really successful, because not only did Martina come to my launch, but she gave the coverage of it a two-page spread. I got chatting to her during the launch and offered her a free book. (Remember my free book principle?) She then offered to have me on her radio show, where I got to talk about my book and pick songs to play for an entire hour. Added bonus: there were so many pictures of the launch that another reporter for the paper took a "spare" one for her community news section, and wrote an additional story about my book.

Not bad for a few e-mails, right?

The Day of the Launch

Check with the store to see if they want you to give them a hand setting up; if they say there's no need then show up no later than fifteen minutes before your event is due to start. Explain to your friends and family that this is not a "stop by whenever you can" type of event, but an "everyone has to arrive at the beginning" one. Basically you want them to be an instant crowd, helping to fill up the store, make your event look well attended and make passers-by curious enough to come in.

If you can, wear an outfit that coordinates with the cover of your book. It'll look good in the photos. (Needless to say, I did! And imagine how much it satisfied my coordination needs when I saw that the store had put a blue tablecloth on the table I was to sit at, which matched my top, which matched my book, which matched the postcards, invites and posters. I was in colour coordination *heaven*!)

Speaking of photos, designate an official photo taker. You won't have time, and your attendees will be too busy chatting to each other and *oohing* and *aahing* over your book. You can then post the photos on your website afterwards and attach them to future I-want-publicity e-mails.

How long it goes on for depends on the event itself but an hour is a good length, generally speaking. If someone is going to make a speech or an Important Person is there to take photos, it's best to do this first and then take a seat and sign books. (If only to get it out of the way, and your Important Person might have to dash.) Check with the bookstore before leaving – and don't forget to thank them!

After the Launch

Send the bookstore a thank-you e-mail. If they were *really* helpful, maybe even stop by with a box of chocolates and a thank-you card.

Next, find out how many books you sold. Collect the remainder from the store and then invoice them for the stock they've sold. Warning: bookstores take *ages* to pay.

Wait with bated breath for coverage of your launch to appear in the paper. Keep a copy for your scrapbook, and don't worry too much about your eyes being closed in the photo, or your cousin's name being spelled wrong. As long as your book's name is correct, that's all that matters! Again, send a thank-you e-mail to the writer of any pieces about you that appear in the press. It only takes a second, but it's a nice gesture, and it might make getting publicity for your second book a little easier.

To Launch or Not to Launch

Initially I wasn't going to have a launch at all. I'd wanted to be a writer ever since I found out that real, live people were behind the books I loved and so that first book launch, be it a signing or a party, was a Very Big Deal. I wanted to "save" it and not "waste" it on my self-published book which, don't forget, was nothing much of anything at the time. I wanted my first book launch to be a glittering affair, one that had an agent and an editor on the guest list, complimentary wine and the wearing of an expensive designer dress. (And to be skinny for it, but that's another story …!) I wanted it to be for a novel that a publisher had published, not a travel memoir about working in Walt Disney World, NASA and the Ebola virus that I had produced myself.

I took a baby step and informed my mother we would be having a Florida-themed party in our house to celebrate the book's release. There would be American flag bunting, tropical-themed cupcakes and shortbread cut with a Space Shuttle-shaped cookie cutter. (And it would have been *so* cool.) But we wouldn't be able to invite anyone but friends and family, and that would nix any publicity opportunities; you can't invite your local newspaper's social diarist to a party you're having in your own house. So I decided instead to have it in a bookstore.

I was terrified at the thought of approaching my local independent bookstore, Douglas Bookshop, and asking first, if they'd stock a few copies of *Mousetrapped* and second, if they'd let me have my launch there, but they couldn't have been nicer or more accommodating. And so around lunchtime one Saturday in May 2010, *Mousetrapped* had its launch-style signing in a brick-and-mortar bookshop. It was great fun, but self-publishing is a business, and with that in mind, was the launch worth having? Did it make financial sense? Did it result in sales, or a loss of profit?

The Arguments For

- It felt good. I really enjoyed the day and it made me feel like a proper author.
- It gave my self-publishing operation a sense of professionalism. My books were in a bookstore, I had a well-attended launch and I managed to get some publicity for it.
- The event got good newspaper coverage locally, and led to a radio interview.

The Arguments Against

- It didn't result in any extra sales, and practically all copies sold on the day were sold to family and friends, i.e. people who would have bought copies anyway.
- I made less money from each sale, because instead of selling directly to my family and friends, I sold the books to the bookshop, who then sold them to the attendees.
- It cost money in other ways. I had to print posters, invites and postcards and order in the stock so I could sell it on (incurring shipping charges).

So what should you do? I don't think you should automatically have a launch or signing for your self-published book, but then I don't think there's anything in self-publishing that you should do automatically, without any thought. Every single book is different and needs to be treated as such. I think you need to ask yourself, *What will I get out of doing this?* and when you find the answer ask, *Is that what I want?*

If all you want is to feel like a proper author for a couple of hours, then go ahead and have whatever sort of launch/party/signing your heart desires. Buy a new outfit, hire a photographer and arrange nibbles. Invite all your friends. It'll be great fun, but be prepared for it to cost you money. If what you want is publicity, stick with a signing or "appearance" where maybe you give a little book-related talk and then scribble your name in a few copies. Get in no more stock than you think you can sell and avoid any glossy and expensive extras, such as posters or even invites. Send an e-mail to every editor, radio show producer, social diarist, etc. that you can find and get your face in the paper, preferably with a hand holding your book up just below it. Take plenty of pictures to put on your website or blog afterwards, and maybe even rope a special guest, such as another writer or a local celebrity connected with your book or your book's subject matter, into attending and saying a few words.

If it's sales you're after, you're going to need to do a *lot* of work. Start with everything above. Then calculate all your costs and work out how many books you're going to need to sell to recoup that money. Then, get out and sell them. This means hand-selling them at the launch, forbidding anyone you know from buying a copy beforehand (so they buy it on the night instead) and getting as many people you don't know to attend as people you do.

It won't be easy but it'll all be worth it if it works.

(A sentence that doesn't just apply to this but also to self-publishing as a whole, when you think about it.)

Why Getting Your Book into Bookshops Is Worth It
by Sheena Lambert

I'll be honest. I only self-published my first novel *Alberta Clipper* when I failed to secure a traditional publishing deal for it. It would have suited me better to have the backing and belief of a publishing house behind me. So when I did decide to self-publish *Alberta Clipper* as an e-book and POD paperback, I set myself the goal of getting hardcopies onto physical bookshelves. In physical bookshops. Somehow. But not for the glory of being able to see my book in shop windows (although that was nice) – for that backing and belief. I wanted acceptance by someone in the industry. Affirmation that my book was as good as I thought it was, and that it deserved its place next to traditionally published authors. A professional pat on the back.

Now I could have just approached my local bookshops and asked them to take some copies sale or return. And I did do this. But Ireland is a small country, and so I decided to think big. There are only two major Irish book distributors (Argosy and Eason), and so I wrote to both, including a hardcopy of *Alberta Clipper*, printed by CreateSpace. And when Eason wrote to me saying that they would like to order copies for stocking in their shops – well. It felt almost as good as getting that traditional publishing deal.

From a practical point of view, it meant I had to get busy. A couple of the independent chains and smaller stores I had approached had also expressed an interest in stocking my book, so I had to order (and pay for) almost 500 hardcopies, and personally deliver them to the shops. Most of the shops priced *Alberta Clipper* just over €10. On that basis, I was receiving just over €5 per copy, which sounds great when compared with a traditional publishing deal, until you remember that I was paying CreateSpace €5 for each copy printed.

But I wasn't in this for the money, just the glory. And being able to say that my book was being stocked by (or at least available from) most of the larger bookshops in Ireland was worth the small financial losses I made overall when I took the cost of delivering the books to the shops/distributor into account.

Easons and a few independents did reorder *Alberta Clipper* a few times. Small orders, but orders nonetheless. Each one felt good. When the six months allocated to my book was up however, I had to suffer the indignity of taking receipt of some unsold copies (they now reside in a box under my bed). And that was that. And a year later, I'm still waiting for payment from one or two of the smaller independents. Ho hum.

So, after all that, would I advise another self-publisher to try and get their books onto the shelves of real live bookshops? Well, yes. It's certainly worth a try. If the major distributors in your home country are open to considering self-published books, then why not send them a copy and see what happens? I wouldn't advise putting a lot of time and effort into the endeavour, but if it does work out, you'll be able to put that fact proudly on any future submission you make to literary agents or publishing houses.

Don't expect to make any money out of it, but if you really want to see your book in a bookshop window or if, like me, you just really want some industry acclamation, then where's the harm in trying?

The Amazing Amazon

Between your stunning pre-release reviews, exciting release day, free book giveaways and fortnight-long blog tour, you and your newly published book are doing great. People are talking about it, sales are ticking over steadily and you've even got some (nice!) Amazon customer reviews. If you've had a Real World launch, perhaps this success has even been carried over into the offline world. And well done you, because doing all that was no small feat and a *lot* of hard work.

Now we're going to take some time to make sure that our little corner of Amazon is doing everything it can to help convince people to buy our book, because if enough people start to buy it on a regular basis, Amazon will effectively start promoting our book for us.

KDP Select

When I first released this book, KDP Select – which, let's not forget, is a different thing to just plain old KDP – didn't exist. By the time it came to release a second edition, hundreds of self-published authors were singing its praises. Now, third time around, the general consensus is that you should avoid it. So what should *you* do?

First of all, what *is* KDP Select? Basically it's a programme run by Amazon that:

- Compensates you for borrows from the Kindle Owner's Lending Library (KOLL) – you don't get paid for borrows otherwise
- Enables you to promote your book as free for up to five days out of every 90 OR run a Kindle Countdown Deal whereby you get to discount your book against a ticking clock e.g. 99¢ today, $1.99 tomorrow and so on until it goes back up to full price when the countdown is over.

Translated into Stuff We Care About speak, this means:

- You make a little bit more money, because you're getting paid when someone borrows your book
- You get oodles of free advertising because when your book is free, thousands of people automatically download it
- A countdown deal might help boost sales too
- You get the benefits of increased reviews, higher sales ranks, etc. from the free downloads/new readers

Before we go any further, I want to make something clear: it allows you to promote your book *as* free. This means your book will be advertised as free – sold for nothing – for the days you enrol in the KDP Select promotion. It does not mean anything else, and it *especially* doesn't mean that Amazon will promote your book *for* free while it sells at normal price. Therefore you are not earning *any* royalties when your book is available for free.

What's the catch? Well, there are a few:

- **To enrol in KDP Select, your book *cannot* be available in digital format *anywhere* else.** No Smashwords, no Barnes & Noble, no iBooks – not even a PDF that's free to download from your blog. (Paperback editions being available elsewhere are fine.) They must be exclusive to Amazon for the full 90 days of the minimum enrolment period, even if you withdraw it before the 90 days are up. If they're not and Amazon finds out, they are entitled to withhold any money you've earned under the KDP Select programme, and might even freeze your KDP account.

- Anecdotal evidence suggests that most people who download free books do it just because they're free. They might never read them – there's no incentive to; they were freebies – and if they do, they mightn't finish them, and even if they do, they might not bother reviewing them. The flip side to this is when they *do* read and review them, but then hate them and give them one-star reviews. Why? Because why read the blurb, other reviews, etc. before downloading a free book? When it's free, there's no need to check if it's suitable for me.
- In terms of helping your sales ranks, etc. one free download is rumoured to be equal to about 0.1 paid sale in Amazon's eyes, at the moment. This means that when your book goes back to paid, the "bump" in its sale rank will be minimal.
- The compensation for borrows comes out of a shared fund. This means that the more titles enrolled in KDP Select and the more those titles are borrowed, the less each author's individual compensation, and the compensation might be less than the retail price of your book.

You may be wondering why, with all this bad news, I'm even mentioning KDP Select. The truth is I still like it. I still think it can help self-published authors, *if* they use it wisely and *if* they start seeing it for what – for all – that it is: free publicity.

When to Use KDP Select

Something happens when you set your book to free. It's like magic: one minute you've had ten downloads all month, the next you've had 100 downloads in the last ten minutes. Setting your book to free is like lighting the fuse on a firework: all you need to do is stand well back and watch it soar. But there's no point in lighting that firework unless we're having a party. Otherwise it's just an expensive waste. And that's how you should think of KDP: something to bring out for special occasions, and only when you're prepared to get the most out of it.

I think there are three great times to use KDP Select:

- **To launch your book.** If KDP Select had been around when I'd released *Mousetrapped*, I definitely would've used it. What other way can a no-name author without a shred of credibility to her name get thousands of people to notice her book, and hundreds of people to read it? No way I can think of that doesn't require the spending of lots of cash. Now I know what your reaction will be to this: *why would I give it away for free first? Shouldn't I let everyone* *who'll buy it* buy *it before I do that?* Think about it: how many people do you know for sure are going to buy your book as soon as it comes out? I'm guessing the answer is a number that will be entirely dwarfed by the figure you're likely to score on free downloads. On balance, the reviews, increased awareness, visibility, etc. you'll get from KDP Select will be worth a *lot* more to you. If a lot of people are guaranteed to buy your book when it comes out, you could do the sneaky KDP Select: set your book to free for a few days before you've told a single soul, least of all any of your first readers, that it's out. I'm on the fence about the fairness of this though – you should be rewarding your supporters, not tricking them into paying for something you're offering to others for free.

- **To launch your next book**. Imagine now, if you will, a slot machine making that winning *ding-ding-ding* sound, because the best way to use KDP Select is when the book you want to sell *isn't* the one KDP Selected. Let's say you've written a series, and the second title is about to come out. So to give it a little boost, you set the first title to free for five days with KDP Select. Now it truly is free advertising for your second book, because anyone who downloads the first for free and likes it can skip merrily along and pay for the next instalment.

- **To bring your book back to life**. Back in KDP Select's early days, there were lots of blog posts about it with names like "How KDP Select Saved My Book." You know the way in *ER* and *Grey's Anatomy* they get those human jump-lead thingies to shock people's tickers back to life? Well, KDP Select can be those jump-lead thingies for your book. If it's not selling very well anyway, what have you got to lose by setting it to free for a few days? Nothing. You only have everything to gain.

You don't have to use all of your five free days at once, but I recommend that you do. Each day's downloads will snowball, hopefully pushing you high up the bestseller list of free books. You can't really achieve much in just one or two days of free; the best results come from using them all up together.

As for which *days*, I'd recommend going Thursday to Monday inclusive. Thursday is apparently the biggest day for e-book sales – why? I don't have a clue – and of course more books are sold on the weekends than weekdays, as Kindle owners are at home looking for books to spend their leisure time with.

I only did a Kindle Countdown Deal once and I wasn't exactly bowled over by the response. The free days are much better, and you choose to do just one or the other in each 90 day period.

A word of warning: removing your books for sale from Smashwords and all their Premium Catalogue channels is *not* easy. It can take weeks, and many, many e-mails before the books disappear entirely, and you can only enrol them in KDP Select once all trace of them has disappeared from everywhere else. If I was back at the start of my self-publishing experience again, I'd go exclusively with Amazon for the first three months of my book's life, doing a free promotion right out of the gate, and then only *after* that would I upload to Smashwords and other retailers if I was planning to.

How to Use KDP Select

You can enrol any book of yours in KDP Select from your Bookshelf on KDP Select. To pick your free days, select Manage Promotions.

Before you set your book to free, make sure that your listing *and* your book are both ready for it. Cast a critical eye over your product description, About the Author, etc. and see if there is any room for improvement. Have you recently got a glowing review that might sway a few minds? Well, now is the time to add it in. Think about what's about to happen: thousands of eyes are about to land on your listing for the very first time. If you had just launched a website and were airing a prime-time television commercial tomorrow evening, wouldn't you devote some time to checking that your website was ready for a few million visitors first? Your Amazon listing is no different, and neither is your book. Double-check it's as perfect as possible. Maybe even have another read through to see if you can spot any errors that have thus far avoided detection. Trust me when I say that people who get your book for free will expect far more perfection of it than those who hand over money for it. If there's as much as an *apostrophe* in the wrong place, you'll soon know all about it.

It's also a good idea to maximise the benefits of your free run by arranging some cross promotion for the first day it goes back to paid. Perhaps you could line this up with the beginning of your blog tour, or a Twitter contest you've organised, or maybe even try some paid-for advertising for 48 hours after your book goes back to paid. This way, the sales-rank improvement hangover gets a few vodka shots and next thing you know, it's drunk again.

Or something.

I would also recommend that you *uncheck* the box for automatic re-enrol in the KDP Select program. Unless you've got further book releases planned in the near future, you'll only want to run your book through

KDP Select's 90 days once. If you've checked automatic re-enrol (and I believe that's the default setting), you might well forget to uncheck it again before the next 90 days come around. Instead, I'd recommend that you take your success and build on it by going for full distribution, i.e. making your book available through all possible sales channels.

Your Amazon Listing

One area where a lot of authors fail to take full advantage of the promotional opportunities available to them is on Amazon. They'll haunt the site day and night, clicking Refresh every 60 seconds on their search results and holding their breath as they reload, but once the initial excitement of seeing their book up there wears off, they'll never return to Amazon again except for the occasional "has anyone left me a scathing review" check.

The better your Amazon listing is, the more chance you have of someone clicking the Buy button after viewing it. So let's make it as good as we possibly can.

Amazon Speak

I'm sure you've purchased a book from Amazon before (maybe even this one!) but have you ever really studied an Amazon listing? There's a *lot* of information on there – not just about your book but about similar books and the habits of the customers who buy them. Before we talk about optimising our little corner of the biggest online book retailer in the world, let's have a crash course in Amazon Speak.

Project Image. Your front cover. For your Kindle edition, this is the cover image you uploaded. If a customer clicks on it, they get a larger version. For your paperback, CreateSpace will crop it for you. If a customer clicks on that, they'll get to "Look Inside"(which we'll come to in a second).

Pricing Information. This will usually show the list price (the price you set) and if Amazon are discounting it, the percentage discount and the amount that makes the price now. On the Kindle listing, they might compare the digital price to the print price (which is ridiculous, but anyway) as well as showing a discount, if applicable. NB: If you have a Kindle book on Amazon.co.uk and you are signed in as, say, an Irish or American customer, you won't be able to see your pricing information. It will say something like "pricing information is not available" because only customers in the UK can see or purchase it. Sign out and go back and it should become visible to you. Remember as well that depending on the region, VAT and international delivery charges may have been added to your book; that's why the price isn't exactly the same as the one you set. But you are still getting paid the same royalties, so don't worry.

Customers Who Bought This Item Also Bought. A list of titles also bought by the customers who bought your book. This is a gold mine of information and we're going to put it to good use in a minute.

Editorial Reviews. Under the heading "Editorial Reviews" will be your product description (your back cover blurb), your About the Author paragraph and any editorial reviews you add through Amazon Author Central.

Product Details. The nitty gritty: the ISBN or ASIN (a unique identifier added by Amazon to Kindle books), how many pages in the paperback edition (shown on Kindle listing too), the publisher, whether or not lending is enabled (Kindle only) and your book's sales ranks, if any. They're a whole other story, so they're getting their own section soon.

Customer Reviews. Reviews uploaded by Amazon customers. These can either be your best friend or the reason you're crying yourself to sleep at night. The most helpful review will be shown at the top (as voted for by other Amazon customers; look for the Was This Review Helpful to You? button) and on the right-hand side the reviews will be arranged, on a much smaller scale, chronologically, with the newest review first.

What Other Items Do Customers Buy After Viewing This Item? Again, a gold mine of information. This tells you what people buy after they look at your Amazon listing. This is slightly different from the Customers Who Bought … list because this one contains people who looked at your listing but didn't necessarily buy your book.

Tags Customers Associate With This Product. This is where customers can help tag your book so that it's easier to find on the site. And guess what? *You're* an Amazon customer, so you can tag your own book. Tip: if you have a Kindle edition and it's $2.99 or less, tag it "cheap Kindle books". If it's more than that don't, because regardless of what *you* may think, it ain't a cheap Kindle book.

Look Inside. This allows customers to look inside your book. They can choose from Front Cover, Copyright, First Pages, Back Cover or Surprise Me! (And yes, they spell it with an exclamation mark.) Customers can also search for keywords inside the book using this feature.

Frequently Bought Together. If your book is frequently purchased with one or more other books, Amazon will sometimes offer all of them together in a discounted bundle. If this happens, great! Make sure you have a look around at books in your "Customers Who Bought …" list as well to see if *your* book is being offered in a FBT bundle with any other titles (paperback only).

Popular Highlights. (Kindle only) This is one of my favourite Amazon listing features, if only because it's like looking over the shoulder of your readers as they go through your book. The Kindle allows users to highlight sections of text in any Kindle book, enabling them to mark sentences they liked, books mentioned they want to check out or words they don't know the meaning of and want to look up. That's great and all, but what's even better is that Kindle then compiles these highlights and puts the most popular ones on your listing. Hilariously, *Mousetrapped*'s popular highlights includes the phrase, "if the world was inhabited by third cousins of Chucky from *Child's Play*, all of whom wear traditional dress and follow your every move with their soulless black eyes of toy darkness". Out of context, that sounds a bit weird, doesn't it? Well, fear not: I'm talking about the little animatronic dolls in the Magic Kingdom's It's a Small World attraction. Makes sense now, eh?

Where's My Listing?

Your Amazon Kindle listing will go live on Amazon.com as soon as your book says it's "live" in your Amazon KDP Dashboard. It will also be visible to any Kindle user who accesses the store through their Kindle device.

Your Amazon paperback listing will take a little longer, although you should be able to find the first signs of it after about a week by using the site's Advanced Search feature and searching for your book by its ISBN.

Amazon listings are made up of many components and they won't all appear at once. For example when your listing first goes live, it will likely only show the product image, title and product details (like how many pages). It will also say something like "Temporarily out of stock". Then a few days later the product description will appear and the stock update will change to something like "Usually ships in 1–3 weeks". One of the last features to appear on it will be Look Inside.

Don't direct people to your listing until it is *ready*. This doesn't mean complete, but it does mean functional. Your listing is ready when:

- Your book is listed as "in stock"
- Your product description has appeared (your back cover blurb)
- You can find the listing by typing the book's name into Amazon's search box

POD books are not always "in stock". Amazon has a range of stock statuses, and from my experience they go something like this:

- In stock
- Only x left in stock … order soon (more on the way)
- Allow an extra 1–3 days

- Usually ships in 1–2 weeks
- Usually ships in 3–4 weeks
- Usually ships in 1–2 months
- Temporarily out of stock
- Available from these sellers

I'm guessing this is because Amazon keeps a specified virtual number of your books in its computer system and then depletes this virtual number accordingly. This is a *good thing*, because if your stock starts to deplete (virtually or otherwise) it looks like your book is hot property. And if a customer sees "Only 1 left in stock" they might buy it now rather than later.

I wouldn't concern myself with stock levels UNLESS it goes to "Available from these sellers", which basically means Amazon can't get your book. This is unlikely to happen unless you put a hold on your book with CreateSpace, which you need to do if you want to make changes to your book after publishing. Amazon is a huge operation and minute, temporary fluctuations in stock levels are just the norm. There's no point in stressing.

Back in the early days when I was watching my Amazon listing 24/7, there were times when it went to "Usually ships in 3–4 weeks" and I had a minor heart attack, only to see it pop back to "In stock" an hour later. Likewise, my Amazon.co.uk listing could be relied upon to go from "Only 5 left in stock ..." into a countdown (only four left, only three left, etc.) all the way down to one, when it would go to "Usually ships in 1–2 weeks" before popping back up to "Only 5 left in stock" so we could do the whole thing again.

So don't stress about your stock levels. What really matters is that people can order your book, not how long they're going to have to wait for it after they do.

Amazon Author Central

Once at least one of your listings is live, you can sign up for Amazon Author Central. There is an Amazon.com Author Central and an (inferior) Amazon.co.uk Author Central, but we're just going to concentrate here on the .com one, and because the tendons in my fingers are hurting and I've practically typed my fingerprints away, I'm going to call it AC from here on in.

You can sign up for an AC account and page at **authorcentral.amazon.com** using an existing Amazon account (or the one you used for KDP) if you wish. You will have to fill in your information and identify what books of yours are on the site, and then Amazon will say thanks very much, we'll be in touch. They'll go away and verify that those are your books and, a couple of days later, come back and say hooray! You're an Amazon Author now.

The Perceived Benefits of an AC Author Page

If you have an AC page, customers can click on your name on your book's listing or the More About the Author section and go to a page that's just all about you and your books. This is what they'll see, depending on how many features you've activated:

- **Bibliography**. All your books in one place.
- **Biography**. An author bio and photograph.
- **Blog posts**. Your blog posts can be automatically fed to this page.
- **Events**. You can list upcoming signings, appearances, etc.
- **Videos**. Upload video blogs or book trailers.
- **Customers Also Bought Items By**. Authors that people who like you like too.

Behind the scenes, you'll also be able to see all your **customer reviews** listed (sort "Rating: Highest to Lowest" – it's best for the soul) and **sales data**, such as where in the US were those people who bought those six copies last week, and what your sales rank looks like over time on a graph. I have yet to find a use for this information, and looking at it too often can become an obsession. (And seeing my sales rank on my listing is bad enough, obsession-wise.)

Now as a customer, the only time I have ever looked at an AC page is to see how many books a particular author has published. And even then, I looked at nothing else but the bibliography. And since you can put your blog URL in your product description, you already have an About the Author, you don't want to see your customer reviews, thanks very much, and you have enough obsessive-compulsive behaviours without adding Nielsen BookScan data to the mix as well, what is the point of signing up for it?

Well my friends, I shall tell you.

The Actual Benefits of an AC Author Page

There are two reasons you should sign up for Amazon AC – because *you can edit and thereby enhance your listing* and *you can contact Amazon.com.*

Now of course, anyone can contact Amazon.com. There are Contact Us and Leave Feedback buttons all over the site. But this particular contact button is on AC, making you an author and not just one more cranky customer among millions. If you have a problem with anything, don't e-mail Amazon through the site, contact them through AC. I've had nothing but positive experiences communicating with Amazon – even when they haven't been able to solve a problem for me, at least they've told me so really quickly. I've also corresponded with them as a customer and for whatever reason, it's always taken a lot longer. So assert your author-ness and use what clout you have whenever you can!

And as soon as your AC account goes live, you *need* to e-mail them to tell them to link your paperback edition with your Kindle edition like, yesterday. Always be very clear when you're contacting them about products. Include the ISBNs or ASINs and links to the listings in question, if applicable.

But back to editing your listing. This is a superb feature because it not only enables you to update information, but also to put extra stuff in there. (Very exciting, I know.)

The first thing you can do is **edit your product description**. This is a great feature that allows you to format your blurb, i.e. add bold and italics. It's also what you can use to update your product description if you get a better idea for it a few weeks after launch, or if you need to update it with new information. For me, this is the best feature of Amazon Author Central.

Your product description is vital to the success of your book. What is the point of going to the effort of informing me that your book exists, getting me to stop and think about it, motivating me to find out more and eventually leading me to your Amazon page, the final hurdle, only to have me leave again without buying anything? There is no point, only time-wasting.

I personally believe your product description should have the following key elements, preferably in this order:

- **The answer to the question** *what is this book?* **in one sentence,** ideally with an incentive to buy, or at least to read on, thrown in too. The average Amazon browser is flicking through tens of books a minute and so we need something that they can read in a second that will (hopefully) stop them in their tracks. In the description of *Backpacked* above, this is the line "The laugh-out-loud new travel memoir from the bestselling author of *Mousetrapped: A Year and a Bit in Orlando, Florida.*" This promises: (i) a funny book, (ii) a book from an author who has already sold books and so, presumably, can write as opposed to merely type and (iii) something fans of *Mousetrapped* will like too.
- **A tagline.** Yes! We can actually put our tagline here! I know; I

must be going soft in my old age. This answers the question *what is this book about?* in a sentence or three, without giving away any key plot points. If the potential purchaser of our book didn't stop reading at the sentence that describes what kind of book we have here, this line that tells them what it's about shouldn't stop them reading either – it should encourage them to read on. For *Backpacked*, this is "Catherine Ryan Howard prefers bathrobes to bed bugs, lattes to lizards and mini-bars to malaria. So why is she going *backpacking*? She doesn't know either ..."

- **Your blurb**. Again, don't just throw up the first thing that comes into your head; work on it. And once it's up there, play with it a bit. Try out different ones. Is one more successful than the other? Could it be improved at all? Bestselling self-published e-book author Mark Edwards attributes his No. 1 bestseller success on Amazon.co.uk to changing his product descriptions.
- **An endorsement**. Because the editorial reviews are much further down the page – further than most potential purchasers will read, in my opinion – it won't hurt to put one or two endorsements into our actual product description.
- **Any other relevant information**. If your book was shortlisted for an award or has been No. 1 in a major Amazon category or has sold over 100,000 copies, I'd put a mention of it here.

Then we have **editorial reviews**. These are not so much reviews as quotes or blurbs excerpted from reviews. These should be from named, reputable sources (i.e. not your mother), limited to one or two sentences and up to 250 characters or about 50 words in length. You can add up to five of them, and they should look something like this: "[Catherine] writes with wit and humour about her time in Orlando. Thoroughly enjoyable and a great read!" – Talli Roland, author of THE HATING GAME.

You can also **edit your author biography** from this page, and you have 2,000 characters in which to do it, which is about 400 words. This is a good feature that you should think about whenever something major happens to you, like you win something or you're on the radio or in a national newspaper. (Writing-related, I should add!)

All you need to do to add or edit any of these items is to sign in to Amazon AC, click on the book's image in your bibliography and start typing. You'll also be able to edit these items in the future.

I know being able to put all this information about ourselves on Amazon is heady stuff, but don't lose sight of what you're actually trying to achieve here: you want to convince people to buy your book.

So avoid:

- Coming across like a jerk ("I just *had* to write this book – to save the world!")
- Irrelevant information ("I love bunnies!")
- Too much information ("I started writing page 3 at 10 p.m. on Tuesday 2nd March ...")
- Hyperbole ("This is the greatest book ever written" – Person Nobody Has Ever Heard Of).

Amazon Sales Ranks

Your Amazon Sales Rank is that little (or big) number you see on your listing next to "Amazon Bestseller Rank" even though, ahem, you might be the furthest thing from a bestseller. When someone buys a copy of your book, the number goes down. It'll then rise steadily (as the sales of other books and their improving ranks push it down – or up!) until someone buys another copy. Thus, the lower the number, the better. No. 1,042,181? Very bad. But No. 201? Pretty amazing.

But of course it's not that simple, and it wasn't all that simple anyway what with a number that goes up as it gets pushed down. (My brain hurts.) These numbers are determined by all sorts of mysterious, secret algorithms, change all the time and are *not* straightforward bestseller ranks.

If my book is currently ranking at No. 1,505, it doesn't mean that based on the numbers of copies of all the books on Amazon that have been sold in the last few hours, I sold the 1,505th most. It's more like taking into account all of the books sold on Amazon in the last few hours, the books that are like mine that sold and how my book was selling before this number was updated, I'm the 1,505th most popular book on Amazon at this moment in time.

(Or something.)

Let me put it another way: multiple factors affect your sales rank, and they are not directly related to how many copies of your book you've sold. If your sales rank is No. 1,000 on Friday and the purchase of one copy makes it go to No. 800, doing the same thing when your sales rank is No. 1,000 on Saturday won't have the same effect. It might make it No. 100, No. 1,500 or it might not change it at all, because Amazon also takes into account sales of books that are related to yours *and* the sales of all other books. And so maybe the site was quiet on Friday, giving you an advantage (or a better sales rank) with the sale of one book, but on Saturday it was busy, with plenty of other authors selling copies too, giving you no advantage and keeping your sales rank practically unchanged.

(Is this section over yet?)

Sales ranks can take two to three hours to update after the sale of a book has taken place.

Does Your Sales Rank Matter?

Only if it's *really* good or *really* bad. If it's really good, congrats! Your book must be doing really, really well, especially if it breaks into the top 1,000. (Or, dare we dream, the top 500. Or, dare we delude ourselves, the top 100.) Make sure you take a screenshot for posterity. The benefits of having a low (or good) sales rank is that your book becomes more visible on the site – higher up on bestseller lists, higher up on search results, more frequently recommended, etc. – and therefore has a better chance of selling even more copies; this is why sales lead to more sales on Amazon.com.

If you don't have a sales rank, no one has ever bought a copy of your book. At least not from Amazon. And if your sales rank is 1,000,000 or more, it means no one has bought a copy of your book in ages, and neither of those scenarios make you or your book look very good.

The Power of One Sale

You'd be surprised, however, how as little as one sale can vastly improve your sales rank. Sometimes my paperback is hovering up around 500,000 (after maybe four or five days of no sales at all), and then one person buys one copy and it drops to under 100,000. If more than one or two people buy a copy within the space of a few hours, you can see your rank drop to less than 10,000, which would be brilliant for a self-published POD book. Kindle is even better because a) you sell more copies and b) there's less competition, a situation that makes for very good sales ranks indeed. I've seen my Kindle edition of *Mousetrapped* drop below 250 on Amazon.co.uk, which was quite the coronary-inducing moment, let me tell you.

Don't Even THINK About It

Since sales ranks are so easy to affect, some people get the idea to artificially raise (or lower!) them by organising mass purchasing of their book in a very short space of time, pushing it into the bestseller ranks, making it more visible around the site and securing its future as an Amazon bestselling book, even if it's in name only and the very next day the book drops out of sight.

The most popular way to do this is to enlist friends, family, people who signed up to your mailing list, yourself and anyone else you can find with an Amazon account to all go online at, say, noon on the day your book launches and buy one copy. There is even a book (for sale on Amazon, of course) that describes in detail how to do this.

This and stuff like it is completely dishonest, pointless, desperate, moronic and pathetic, times ten. Is that really what you have to do to get your book selling? Make all your friends buy it? Buy copies of it yourself? Boy, I bet *that's* a good book.

The Non-Moronic Way to Improve Your Sales Rank

When author Talli Roland (*The Hating Game* – you've met her already) released her e-book, she "took on Amazon" with a blog splash. She got as many people as possible to blog or tweet about her book on the day it launched. Let's be clear: she didn't *ask* anyone to buy it. Not once. She just said "my book is now available on Amazon" across the platforms of her online presence and those of her blogging and Twitter friends and fans. At the end of the day, her Amazon.com sales rank was 460, and her Amazon.co.uk was a staggering 24! She can now say her book was an Amazon bestseller on the day of its release, and she didn't have to buy a single copy of her own book, or ask anyone else to.

Category Bestseller Rankings

And anyway, where you rank in your book's categories is far more fun, and a hell of a lot more straightforward. You'll see these in the same place as your sales rank, although they'll only appear there if you're towards the top.

Will I ever forget the joyous day I saw *Mousetrapped*'s Kindle edition go to No. 1 in Kindle Store → Books → Non-fiction → Travel → United States → Regions → South → South Atlantic? (I knew I'd made it then, let me tell you.) But here's the thing: that makes my book an Amazon bestseller, even if the category is so hilariously specific I'd never recall it from memory. And yet at the time my sales rank was 3,489, or not exactly setting the world on fire. The moral of the story: don't worry too much about your sales rank.

And DON'T buy copies of your own book.

Setting up Your Own E-book Store

It used to be the case that all roads led to Amazon – or that they should, at least. When your book came out you wanted everyone to buy it from there, so that every single sale had a chance to elevate your sales rank and therefore also improve your visibility on the site, possibly leading to more sales. If someone went instead and bought your book from, say, Smashwords, that was a lost opportunity. It was a sale, yes, but also a chance missed to make *another* sale because of it.

At the beginning of your book's life, I would say this is still the case. We still want anyone who's planning on buying our e-book to do so from Amazon if they can, i.e. if they have a Kindle. But further down the line you might want to sell your e-books directly and keep almost all of the list price.

You can do this through your website. I use a company called **Gumroad** (www.gumroad.com) which helps me sell files – and let's not forget, e-books are just files – securely online. They take just a tiny fraction of the price I set and put the rest in my PayPal account. All you need do then is link to your Gumroad listings from your blog, Twitter account or Facebook page, and we're all off to the races. They'll even imprint your PDFs with an e-mail address so if the document is illegally shared, the perpetrator's name is at the top of every page.

You can ONLY use e-book files created either by an e-book conversion service like eBookPartnership or by you with a program like Scrivener. You CANNOT use files made by Amazon KDP or Smashwords – you don't have the right.

While we're on the subject of sending people to buy your book from certain places, please don't attempt to micromanage this – and please, please, PLEASE don't be greedy about it. I'm sure it didn't escape your attention a million pages ago that you get the biggest chunk of POD profit if a reader purchases your paperback directly from CreateSpace via your own CreateSpace eStore (basically one page, like an Amazon listing, from where your book is for sale). But when I see authors even mentioning their eStore to people, the RED RAGE descends.

We'll never know whether or not a tree that falls in the woods when there's no one around makes a racket, but we do know that only on sites like Amazon do paperback sales lead to other paperback sales. A sale made on a CreateSpace eStore is accompanied only be a complete and total silence. Furthermore it is extremely inconvenient from the point of view of the purchaser. Unless they self-publish with CreateSpace too they'll have to create a new account and sign in with it, and the shipping costs will be higher than they're used to. But if they go to Amazon or The Book Depository, for instance, they might get free shipping AND, thanks to a boost to your sales rank, them buying your book might lead to someone *else* buying it this evening.

Turning the Wheel

Haven't we been busy bees, eh? We decided to self-publish, we self-published, expertly built an online platform, used it to spread feverish anticipation about our book (or at least, got people to go, "Hmm. *Interesting ...*"), launched our book like a moonrocket and maximised our Amazon presence so that anyone who makes it all the way to our listing will be so overcome with conviction that they'll not only buy our book, but *multiple* copies of it.

Or maybe just the one.

Maybe only a few copies a day, but still. Copies are being downloaded in exchange for cash. We are published authors, and people are reading our work. Hooray! But, um, what happens now?

The first three months after you release your book are a crucial time in which you have to work to ensure that your book doesn't disappear back into the abyss as quickly as it appeared from it. You won't be working as hard or as much as you did in the three months running up to publication, but you'll be working harder than you'll need to three months from now. Our main goal at this stage is to get Amazon to sell our books *for* us.

How does Amazon sell your book for you?

- By recommending it to their customers in e-mail shots
- By displaying it in features like Customers Also Bought ... and You Might Also Be Interested In
- By displaying it higher up search results

There's no ethical way to *make* this happen, and it takes time for it to happen organically. For example, if you sold 20 copies of your book on Amazon today, that's an amoeba-like speck in Amazon's ocean. But if you sold 20 copies of your book every day for 90 days, you'd at least be visible to the naked eye. (Just bear with me here ...) The sales data and mysterious Amazon algorithms have been laying down tracks for three months now, making connections between more and more customers and more and more books, and so the 20 you'll sell tomorrow will have a much more significant impact on your Amazon presence. Meanwhile, the reviews you've been collecting and the ones left by Amazon customers are telling both *other* Amazon customers and Amazon itself that not only is this book selling, but that it's selling because it's *good*. Think of your Amazon presence like a watermill (without the grinding grain bit!): the water is the people you're sending Amazon's way, and the wheel represents sales of your books. The speed at which the mill is turning is how much help Amazon is giving your sales figures, how much work it's doing on your behalf. The more water you can direct at the wheel and the faster you can direct it there, the faster the wheel turns.

The key to this period in the life of your book is **consistency**. It doesn't matter if you only spend 30 minutes a day online or that you sell fewer than ten books a day, so long as you're spending 30 minutes online and selling ten books a day *every* day. So what do you actually *do*?

Maintain a Workable Social Media Presence

Figure out how much time you can comfortably spend online a week – leaving plenty of time for sleeping, eating and writing your next book, of course – and then plan how you're going to use it.

Map out your **social media week**. When my books were still toddlers, this it what mine looked like:

- *Blog posts*: between one and three hours. Write them over the weekend with one eye on the television. Try to keep them under 1,000 words and then schedule them to post on Mondays, Wednesdays and Fridays, preferably. I try to have at least one that could spark a self-publishing-themed discussion of some sort, and I keep guest posts/advertising/news of events, etc. to a minimum. My blog is my main focus. Even if I'm extremely busy and drop everything else, I make sure that I update my blog. I think of it like my online "hub"; all roads – or URLs – lead to it. Downloading the free WP app to your smart phone will enable you to moderate and respond to comments on the go.

- *Twitter.* Back when *Mousetrapped* came out, I was on Twitter *all the time*. That was perhaps a tad unnecessary, but you do need to tweet often in the beginning, both to get used to using Twitter and to make some Twitter friends. But there are ways you can do this without developing a separation anxiety disorder whenever you're away from your phone. I use Twitter in three different ways. First, I use the Buffer App to tweet interesting links. This makes up the majority of my tweeting. Whenever I find an interesting blog post or a share-worthy piece of news or a hilarious YouTube video that I think my followers will get a giggle out of, I add it to my Buffer account. Then at times I've pre-specified on my Buffer Dashboard, these links get tweeted throughout the week until the tweets I've "buffered" run out. I do this Monday to Friday, and I make sure to spread them out to cover all time zones. This means that I can have a valuable Twitter presence without actually having to be there. Second, I downloaded the Twitter app to my smartphone so that in those time-to-kill moments – queuing, commercial breaks, bouts of insomnia – I can mark any tweets I want to respond to, retweet or investigate further later as "favourites" and come back to them later when I have more time. Third, I tweet-chat, meaning that I use Twitter to catch up with both real life and online friends.

- *Facebook.* The least demanding aspect of your social media platform will be your Facebook page. A few minutes a week should do it. Post an update about what you're up to (or if you're up to nothing much, post a link to one of your newest blog posts), or perhaps ask a question ("What was your favourite chapter/character/scene in *My Book*?") and respond to any comments that your lovely Facebook fans have left for you.

- *Blog reading and commenting.* Don't forget to read other people's blogs and to leave comments when you feel you have something to add. This will keep you up to date with what's happening in the blogosphere, provide you with fodder for your Buffer account and hopefully make some new blog-friend connections too.

It is of the utmost importance that while you're busy promoting your book, you don't neglect the blog readers, Twitter followers and Facebook fans that will *never* buy it. An empty shell of a blog that only exists so you can remind us that your book is just $2.99 is never going to work, neither as effective book promotion *nor* a blog. Your social media presence, like everything else in this operation, has to be *genuine*.

And no matter what happens you need to continue to produce quality content (i.e. blog posts, etc.) and do so regularly. Far more people are interested in my blog – and have found me by way of it – than my books, and by some significant margin. I need to keep them interested, because they might eventually buy my book or, if they're not at all interested in it, they might buy the next one. Even if they *never* buy a book, their support will still be a huge help to me when I'm trying to sell it to other people, and spread the word that it exists. Also, I love blogging. I really do. And knowing that thousands of people are reading it makes it even sweeter.

Your blog shouldn't just be about your book but you should use it to keep people updated of its progress. If someone posts a review of your book or mentions it on their blog, or if in the Real World you're written about in a newspaper or interviewed on the radio, or if you hit a big sales milestone like 100, 500 or 1,000 copies, put it on your blog. Don't be concerned that it'll read like, "Look at me! Look what I've done!" Remember: this is *your* blog. It's all about you by default.

You may also have collected readers purely because they're interested in your self-publishing adventure and want to see how it's going for you. Let them know.

Shooting for the Moon (or Why You Shouldn't Just Listen to Me)

When it comes to ideas for ways we can attract new readers and keep the ones we have entertained, self-published authors tend to look to other self-published authors for ideas. This is fine, but you shouldn't *only* look to them. The bestselling authors in the world are all traditionally published – and yes, that includes our old friend *50 Shades* – so why not look to them too?

Here are some ideas I've, um, borrowed from some of my favourite traditionally published authors:

Michael Connelly's Photo Submission/Review Contest. Michael Connelly is my favourite author and I am glued to his website and Facebook page for updates. A few books ago – it may have been *The Brass Verdict* – his webmaster asked readers to send in photos of themselves reading his book. If you did, you got your picture on his website under a section called Look Who's Reading [BOOK TITLE] and if you were one of the first 1,000 people to do it, you got sent an exclusive little book about how he created his two main characters, Harry Bosch and Mickey Haller, that wasn't available to buy. When *Mousetrapped* came out, I invited readers to do the same thing with Look Who's Reading *Mousetrapped*. I didn't reward them with anything but I *did* get some great content to add to my Facebook page.

Karin Slaughter's Newsletter. You may know Karin Slaughter as the author of gripping and occasionally gory thrillers like *Faithless*, *Fallen* and *Broken*, but did you know she has the funniest newsletter around? You know how it is: you find a new author you like, you sign up for their newsletter because you think you're going to want to hear from them, but then whenever it lands in your inbox you yawn and click Delete. Well, trust me when I say you won't be doing this with Slaughter's. They. Are. HILARIOUS. And she writes them in plain text! They don't even have any bells, whistles or fancy HTML. Sign up on her website to receive them so you can learn how it should be done. Then you can use MailChimp's wizard to design a simple newsletter template to send your own.

Miranda Dickinson's Video Blog. Miranda Dickinson is the author of bestsellers *Fairytale of New York* and *Welcome to My World*. In the lead up to the publication of her third novel, *It Started With a Kiss*, she kept a video blog/diary of the entire process: from writing the first draft of the book right through to publication, launch, etc. We're all fascinated with how other writers write, so to see a successful author at work is incentive enough to watch these videos, but you also can't help but keep tuning in to see what excitement is coming up next. (And of course, you ultimately want to buy the book whose birth you witnessed too.) Another idea: Miranda's e-book edition of *It Started With a Kiss* contains "bonus features" like deleted scenes and commentary! Intriguing.

Ali McNamara's Breakfast with Ali. Ali McNamara is the author of *From Notting Hill ... With Love Actually* and she (or someone clever she knows) has had a great idea to help publicise her book *Breakfast at Darcy's.* "Breakfast with Ali" is a challenge: Ali must eat something different for breakfast every day for 30 days – and blog about it, of course. I think it's great fun and something different. Plus, it's the kind of thing a self-publisher could easily replicate.

What NOT to Do

I could write a whole other book on what not to do to promote your book, but as we're already up to way over 100,000 words, I'm going to keep it short and sweet here. Kindly refrain from doing any of these things, okay? Thanks.

Indulge in Hyperbole

I could devote an entire book to this subject alone, but I'm going to do my best to keep it short here. When you self-publish, everyone knows that whatever is on the book's cover or inside its pages was put there by *you*. Therefore you should refrain from making grandiose claims, including quotes that say your book is the best thing since people started using the phrase "the best thing since sliced bread", and comparisons to other authors, living or dead, or indeed to other books. Don't sell yourself short, but don't be a jerk either.

And jerk is a very nice version of the word, or combination of words, that I'm using for this type of person in my head.

And whatever you do, don't make up a review or get a friend to say something glowing, because guess what? We can tell that's what you did. If I read a review that says Hemingway would have never written a word if he'd read any of your work because he would've known, instantly, that he could never do better, and then I open your book and the first paragraph reads like something an automated translation program coughed up while it was malfunctioning, I'm going to know something's up. Furthermore, I'm going to think you're dishonest, a liar and have your head so far up your own arse that when you open your eyes you see the back of your teeth.

This is a review I recently read on the press release of a self-published novel I had the misfortune to receive a copy of. I've changed it enough so the author can't identify it (hopefully!) but I haven't changed its level of cringe-inducing, I-got-paid-to-write-this, my-best-friend-is-the-author or I'm-not-real-the-author-made-me-up super stinky BS *one little bit.*

(I should also point out that this "review" is attributed to someone I've never heard of, with no explanation of who they are. I don't think anyone else knows who they are either, because when I googled them I couldn't find anything. So.)

"When an advanced reader copy of *The Best Novel Ever Written* arrived at my door, I was filled with the warmth of a thousand sunny springtime mornings, so grateful was I for this opportunity to feast my eyes on and direct my synapses towards this wondrous tome, one I am certain will take its rightful place on the bookshelves of every forward-thinking man, woman, child and household pet across all lands, societies, races, continents and dimensions. I was on page 13 when it struck me: this is not a debut novel. It just *couldn't* be! Based on the facts with which I am presented and the calibre of the writing before me, I could only surmise that the author had devised a clever way to turn back time, write several novels before this and then return to the present to begin work on *The Best Novel Ever Written;* that is the only explanation for the skill, wisdom and experience he shows in putting one word after the other. *The Best Novel Ever Written* is not only an entertaining novel that fans of Dan Brown will find a significant and pleasing improvement on the work of their favourite author, but also an allegory for the state of the world yesterday, today and tomorrow. It not only illuminates the path we must now all take as we move into the future; it shines new light on the past as well. It's *multi-tasking.* It should be required reading for every human, and broadcast into space by NASA in binary code so every other being can read it as well. And yet within its shining diamonds of pages lies unexpected humour, a brand only seen in comedy classics like *Fawlty Towers* and *30 Rock.* But there is real emotion too; I am reluctant to admit I had to send the butler out for Kleenex on page 341 and again on page 1,394, but will do so to comprehensively explain to you the stirrings I felt in every last molecule of my self as I read this book, although "book" seems like too small a word to describe the experience I just had with *The Best Novel Ever Written.* Truly a masterful, important, entertaining, amazing, hilarious, touching, dramatic and intelligent work. I recommend it with the conviction of a thousand convinced men. Superb."

Indeed. (And for the record, I read a bit of this book. Maybe 25 pages. And the only thing I was convinced of was that this "reviewer" clearly read some *other* book.)

Promote Your Book Offline

I've worked with a number of self-published authors who have been traditionally published in the past, and the number one mistake I see them making is trying to promote their self-published work in the same way their publishers did their traditionally published work. They hire publicists, hand over wads of cash in exchange for polished press releases and badger newspaper editors, radio show producers and even TV stations in the hope that news of their book will get a mention in print or on air.

No, no, no, no, NO. Just *no.*

When you self-publish, your book is either predominantly or only for sale online. Therefore advertising offline is a *complete* waste of time, and a very expensive one.

I wouldn't even bother pursuing offline attention, such as reviews and interviews in newspapers. If it comes to you, great. By all means take advantage of it. But I wouldn't spend too much time chasing it, because if you're not in bookshops, it's worthless to you.

If I hear about a traditionally published book on the radio or see an ad for it on TV or in print, I might think to myself, Oh, that looks interesting. But I need to see that book again, on the shelves of a bookshop, to be reminded and nudged into purchasing it. With self-published books, there is no such reminder.

As for public relations people and publicists, no one can sell your book like you can, and they can't sell self-published books at *all.* They don't know how. They can only model their efforts on what publishing houses do and hope for the best. What self-publishing success do you know of that came via a PR company, eh? There aren't any.

John Locke, the first self-published author to sell 1,000,000 Kindle books, famously spent a small fortune on the traditional promotional efforts he believed would help sell his book (newspaper and TV advertisements, press releases, even ads in movie theatres) and *none* of them worked. It was just a gigantic waste of time and money. So instead he turned to blogging, Twitter and building a mailing list of fans – all of which are free to do, I might add – and the rest is history.

In my experience, newspapers and radio shows only come calling when your book is *already* a success, because that's a story. "Author publishes own book" is not.

Hire Someone to "Do" Your Social Media

Again, no one can sell your book like you can, which is the first reason you shouldn't hire someone else to do your online promotion for you.

The second is that the best blogs, Twitter accounts and Facebook presences make a direct connection with their readers, followers and fans, and this is impossible to achieve if there's a "social media guru" between you and them. It's like paying someone else to give your friend a hug.

Thirdly, it's stupid. Social media isn't rocket science. You don't need any special training or experience to do it and you only need to be pointed in the direction of the people who do it well to do it well yourself. Books like these can get you set up with the basics and offer you little tips and tricks, but there's no major skill involved. So why waste money paying somebody who pretends there is? Not only can you do it yourself, but the results will be infinitely better if you do.

Let Your Friends Defend Your Honour

A few years ago a friend of mine self-published a book and submitted it to a very popular book blogger for review. I'd been reading this book blogger's posts longer than I'd known of my friend's plans to self-publish; it's one of my favourite book review sites. It's not anything fancy: the blogger just reads the books, tells us what's they're about and then gives us a verdict out of ten based on how much she liked it. Sometimes I totally disagree with her, but she's always fair, and when she has to criticise she'll always add an apologetic "this just wasn't my kind of thing" or "remember, this is just my opinion". In other words, she's a balanced, professional book blogger.

Who didn't particularly like my friend's book. She didn't *not* like it; she was on the fence. She gave it six out of ten and amongst plenty of praise for the writing, humour and descriptions, said that she didn't like the main character and didn't find her actions believable.

My friend was momentarily upset that the review wasn't glowing, but she wasn't devastated. She knew – as I did – that not *all* reviews can be glowing, and that this was just one book blogger's opinion, and that in the scheme of things, not that many people would even read it. She sent the blogger an e-mail expressing her disappointment that she didn't like it more, but also thanking her for taking the time to review it and promising to keep her on the review copy list for her next book. The blogger replied with a thank you and said there was a lot about the book she *did* like and that she'd love to receive a copy of the new book. In other words: perfect author behaviour.

But *friends* of my friends didn't take it as well. One of them took it upon herself to leave a comment on the review refuting the blogger's criticisms, and not in a polite way. She also referred to the author in such a way that it was clear to everyone that the two were personal friends. The blogger responded, defending herself, and the defending friend left another comment, this one much nastier and full of insults, including a line about how the blogger was probably just a failed writer herself who was so jealous of everyone else's success that she couldn't write positive reviews. The situation snowballed out of control and within hours, people in my Twitter stream were posting links to the exchange saying things like, "How NOT to respond to a review … Yikes!"

It was embarrassing. I don't actually think my author friend appreciated just *how* embarrassing, or how badly it reflected on her. I think she thought that because she wasn't the one commenting it was okay, but of course anyone with half a brain would conclude that she was friends with the person who *was*.

Clearly, my friend's friend thought she was doing something good. She thought she was defending her friend's honour, and letting everyone who read the review know that, actually, the book was good. But all she was doing was turning people off ever reading my friend's book, this one or the ones she releases in the future. She was making my friend look like a complete amateur who didn't know how to behave in public.

So rein in your friends. Explain to them that the internet never forgets, and that the only way to respond to a negative review is not to. The same goes for any other "favours" they might think to do for you: sending e-mails about your book to everyone they know, writing suspiciously glowing Amazon reviews, tweeting links to your website every 30 seconds. All they'll be doing is making *you* look bad.

Release Multiple Books Simultaneously

There's a school of thought that says don't do anything to promote your book until you have several books to promote. The idea is that if you manage to find a reader and convince them to buy one of your books, there are another two or three or more for them to buy immediately afterwards, thus converting the effort of promoting one book into the sale of several.

Seems like a good idea, right?

It's not. At least *I* don't think it is. In fact, I completely disagree with it. I believe you need to release your books one at a time with space in between, and market, promote and sell them that way too. Here's why.

We've talked already about the science of bookselling. Let's say now that getting me to buy your book involves at least three steps. You need to:

1. Tell me about it
2. Pique my interest
3. Give me a reason (i.e. make me care enough) to buy it

Let me give you a real-life example of how this 1–2–3 process led me to buy a self-published e-book. One day I was reading a blog post about how some self-publishers had been adding things like "For Fans of Dan Brown" to their e-book titles and how Amazon had now moved to crack down on their clever (and a bit cheeky!) use of their system. The post mentioned two UK self-publishers, Louise Voss and Mark Edwards, who had done this to great effect with their e-book *Catch Your Death*. So that's how I found out the book existed – through a blog post. My interest was piqued when I read that the thriller was partly set at the Cold Research Unit in Salisbury, because anything that involves viruses is a winner for me. (In another life I wanted to be a virologist.) So I went to look it up on Amazon, where a combination of what I already knew, the synopsis and the pair's writing credentials gave me reason enough to buy it. And so, because Mark and Louise had a good book that was the kind of thing I liked to read and they'd designed a convincing Amazon listing, the only real work they had to do was inform me of their book's existence, and it's this that marketing multiple books simultaneously – or waiting until you have multiple books to market – cripples.

You want to create as many worthwhile opportunities as possible to inform new readers that your book exists, without boring the arses off the readers who are already along for the ride, i.e. your blog readers, Twitter followers, Facebook fans, newsletter recipients, etc. The way to do this is to squeeze every last bit of Interesting Juice out of each book, and then give everyone a chance to recover before you go at it again with your next title.

Take *Mousetrapped*. I started building anticipation about that book approximately three months before I released it. Here's some of the things I did:

- I blogged about my decision to self-publish it
- I blogged about the logistics of self-publishing it
- I shared my cover design process and other milestones such as the finished blurb
- I made two book trailers (see the Videos page)
- I offered copies to book bloggers
- I was interviewed by book bloggers and other sites
- I wrote guest posts for other blogs
- I had #MousetrappedMondays on Twitter where I made a thing of containing my self-promotion to three to five tweets every Monday in the lead up to its release, and then I released the book

on the final #MousetrappedMonday, March 29th, 2010

- I posted photos of my first proof copy, my first box of books, my bookstore launch, etc.
- I set up a Facebook page, asked friends to like it, and posted updates about the book on the wall
- I gave away copies on my blog
- I tweeted links to all of the above

And in these ways, I told people that *Mousetrapped* existed and I managed to get some of those people to buy it when it came out, to recommend it to friends and family and to mention it on their own online homes. And here is the key: when *Backpacked* came out more than a year later, I was able to do all those things again and more besides. Why? Because I now had a completely different title that generated new material for me to blog about, etc. and because enough time had passed for (i) the people who had been around since the beginning to forgive all my *Mousetrapped* talk and (ii) a whole new audience to turn to face my way, i.e. new Twitter followers, new friends of my Facebook fans, new blog readers of my blog friends, etc. Enough time had passed for me to reach loads of new people using the same methods as I had before – and to do it without pissing people off.

What if I had released all of my books at the same time? I would only ever have reached that first, small group. My original readers. The ones who came on board at the beginning. Now maybe they would've been loyal enough to buy all of my books, but what then? I can't continue to churn out post after tweet after post about the same old stuff, so I can't blog about my books. No one likes "My book is on Amazon. Buy it!" tweets, so that's out too. And what are all my lovely fans going to do after they've read all my books? What now?

I know the temptation to get the next book out there right now is overwhelming, especially if it's already written and ready to go. If someone sends you an e-mail saying "Just read *Your First Book* – loved it!!! When is the next one out? Can't wait to read it!" there's a reptilian part of your brain that considers going to KDP right that minute to upload the book, just so you don't lose that sale. Because that's the Big Fear, isn't it? That that reader will have forgotten all about you by the time your next book comes out. Well, guess what? I have to wait a year between books for *all* of my favourite writers – because that's the speed at which the publishing world works – and I manage it just fine. I never forget about them. Instead, I wait anxiously for their new books to come out. The waiting makes the reading sweeter. I've spent 364 days of every year waiting for a new Michael Connelly novel for almost half my life, and somehow I manage. I also buy every single one of his books. And if I do forget? Amazon reminds me in my recommendations whenever I visit the site. Sometimes they even e-mail me too. If that fails, I still have his Facebook fan page and newsletter to remind me of it.

You have to look at this in the long term. Yes, the person who e-mailed you might not buy your next book because by the time it comes out six months from now, they'll have forgotten about it. But the people who will find out about you for the first time when you put a full launch effort into your next title is a far greater number.

As I've already said, organic growth is always better. You promote this first book well, you focus entirely on the one title, and hopefully you carry a lot of the readers you gain with you to the next book. You repeat the process in a few months' time, and now you're carrying forward the readers from the first and second books, and they all read both of them. And so on and on. I think those readers, thanks to the longer relationship they'll have with you, will be a lot more likely to stick around in the long term that someone you managed to sell three 99¢ books to and then never interacted with again.

One of the people I follow on Twitter released three different books in rapid succession (I'd say, all within the same month) a while back. They were all quite different titles, and he'd never released anything before. He didn't blog really, so Twitter was his main online home. At the time of the release, there was a lot of Twitter talk about it, but that soon dropped off, like a rock dropping off the edge of a cliff, once the third book had been released. Since then? Nothing. Nada. Not a word. There's nothing new to report, and he's nice enough not to use his tweets for advertisements, so now he's stuck. And so are his sales.

If he'd spread out those releases, he might be heading into the summer now with a brand new book to promote – and so, new things to tweet about (like how he came to have his cover design, what a headache e-book formatting is, what he's doing different this time around, etc.) – and I'd be willing to bet that he'd definitely get more sales. He has more Twitter followers now than he did when he released those books, and I – and all his other followers – are likely to have more people around us too, and so if I retweeted one of his book links, his audience would be much larger now than it was then.

So, he should have waited. He should have spread out the release dates of his books.

What I'm basically trying to say is this:

- Each title release creates a wealth of material you can use to promote your book
- Putting this material online is one of the ways people find out that your book exists

- Informing people that your book exists is the first step in getting them to buy it
- You can't constantly use your online platform to promote your book, and it's not much fun to do that anyways
- Different people are following you and your followers than will be in six months' or a year's time
- The only way to maximise (i) how much material you get out of each book and (ii) the new people who see that material is to spread out your books
- What you sacrifice in "I just finished the first I'll buy the next one sales", you'll more than make up for with new, more loyal readers in the long term

Forget Your Manners

Some self-published authors seem to be stricken with a mutant strain of highly resistant Entitlement Syndrome. Symptoms include: thinking that everyone is just *dying* to read their book; sending book reviewers e-mails like "My book *needs* to be read"; sending e-mails to *everyone* saying something similar; being controversial about publishing just for the sake of it; more than occasionally using words and phrases like "gatekeepers", "the Big Six" (or the Big Five, as it is now), "revolution", "tenant farming", "Stockholm syndrome" and "indie" while also not knowing what they're on about having never been traditionally published OR self-published for a full week yet; offering self-publishing advice at a price when their own sales are in the three digits, pronouncing the death of (i) print books, (ii) bookshops and (iii) the evil corporate entities who man the gates between our dreams and reality; responding to negative reviews with a tone that says "*You* don't know what you're talking about"; never commenting on someone else's blog without at least *three* hyperlinks to places where their own book is on sale, and a really serious, not-at-all-casual mention of their book in said comment, e.g. "I know what you mean about KDP Select. When I was promoting my 3,103-5*-reviewed steampunk dystopian love story, *All This and a Bag of Android Cats*, I found that ..." At the time of diagnosis over 90 per cent of sufferers are given less than three months to continue selling books, and some are warned that they are only moments away from a catastrophic career implosion. There's no known cure – although swift smacks upside the head have been known to be effective in temporarily alleviating the symptoms – leaving only one sure-fire method of protection against this devastating syndrome: *abstinence*.

The Role of Luck

One thing that we can be certain plays a role in whether a book ends up on the bestseller list or in the remainder pile is *luck*. Now while I don't subscribe to the notion that we make our own luck, I *do* think you can position yourself so that you're first in the queue to receive some of it. The best way to explain this – and everything else I've been talking about – is to share with you what's happened to me.

I released *Mousetrapped* in March 2010. Sales steadily ticked over for the first six months of its life, but the proceeds were barely keeping me in coffee grounds, let alone ink cartridges.

By September 1st I'd sold the grand total of 531 copies, or an average of 88 copies per month. I was happy with this because that was almost exactly my goal: 100 copies in a month, 500 in six months, 1,000 in a year. I'd been chronicling my self-printing adventures, as I called them, on my blog, and had promised readers a breakdown of my royalties and sales figures after six months, so I posted them.

These posts brought a lot of traffic to my blog, and as a result my sales kicked up a notch. In September, October and November 2010, I sold 184, 174 and 180 copies respectively. My sales had more than doubled, but the growth was all in e-books. With me getting to keep over $2 from every $2.99 e-book sold, I wasn't complaining.

In the meantime, something happened in the real world: I was invited to speak about how I used social media to sell my book at a self-publishing conference in Dublin. How did this happen? Back in January when I was preparing to self-publish my book, I got chatting to a woman called Vanessa on Twitter. Vanessa, it turned out, was the owner of a company that runs writers' workshops and offers services like manuscript critique. A lot of the other Irish writers I was talking to on Twitter knew her as well, and I went along to one of the workshops to meet up with them all. When I found out Vanessa was organising a self-publishing conference, I decided to attend and booked a place. I thought it would be a great learning and networking opportunity. Then, a couple of weeks before the conference, a problem with a keynote speaker arose. Vanessa, knowing about my self-publishing story and knowing that I was going to be attending anyway, asked me if I would fill in. I was only too happy to, and (luckily!) it went really well. Not only that, but I was quoted in an article in *The Sunday Independent* newspaper the week before the conference, which talked about the self-publishing success of the conference's keynote speakers.

Next: Christmas happened. Santa must have brought lots of people new Kindles, because my e-book sales suddenly spiked. I'd sold 180 copies in November but in December, I sold 422 – and hit 1,000 copies sold, four months ahead of schedule. But then something even crazier happened: in

January, I sold nearly a thousand copies. Now every month for three months, I'd sold double what I'd sold the month before.

One day I sat down at my desk, went to WordPress and wrote a blog post basically saying "What the hell just happened to my e-book sales?" I included some charts and told everybody how, between Christmas Eve and the end of January, I'd sold more than a thousand copies of my book – having taken *eight months* to sell the thousand before that.

This post proved popular, and Eoin Purcell, the then editor of the Irish Publishing News website, asked if he could repost it on IPN. I said yes, and he did. *The Bookseller*, the biggest publishing trade publication on this side of the pond, put a link to the post in their morning briefing e-mail. This increased my blog traffic but other than that, I didn't think too much more about it.

Three days later an e-mail arrived in my inbox with an e-mail address ending with "-sunday-times.ie". It was an enquiry from a writer for the Irish edition of *The Sunday Times* newspaper expressing interest in writing a piece about my e-book success. He'd seen my post on IPN. *The Sunday Times*?!?! I couldn't say yes quick enough. The story was about how, having been rejected by traditional publishing based on the non-existence of a market for my book, I'd turned to self-publishing, which provided me with access to a global market and used outlets like social media to get people interested in my writing as opposed to the book. I was so excited the day the story came out, thinking that surely, it couldn't get better than this. But the following week there were e-mails from no fewer than *five* different radio shows asking me to come on and talk about my self-publishing success story. One of them was the most listened-to weekend radio show in Ireland, with over 400,000 listeners. Big-name traditionally published authors (or their publicists!) would kill to get on the show, but somehow, I'd been invited on to it.

This was all in February 2011, and it bumped up my sales another few notches. But luck hadn't abandoned me yet. In February of 2012 I was asked to deliver Faber & Faber's first ever self-publishing course at their Faber Academy. This was a big gig – Faber had their reputation to uphold, and they were already taking a chance offering a self-publishing course when they were better known for literary courses like writing novels, short stories and poetry. They needed a self-publisher who (a) could speak in public, (b) wasn't one of the "down with the gatekeepers!" brigade but was actually quite sensible about self-publishing and (c) had had some success. The course was being organised by a friend I'd made on Twitter and when he mentioned the course to a friend *he'd* made on Twitter, she suggested that I'd be a perfect fit – because she was also my editor and had seen me speak back at the self-publishing conference the year before.

A few months later I was invited to meet with the Irish office of the world's biggest publishing house and before I left I had a freelance gig promoting their books through social media. I've been working for them ever since. I've also appeared on television, delivered a Guardian Masterclass, taught a social media "how to" to the Irish publishers' trade association, travelled to appearances at book festivals and writing weekends all over the country and, this summer, used all of this to prove to Trinity College Dublin that I was worthy of one of just three places on their English studies degree course set aside for mature students.

My days, from sun-up to sun-down, are spent doing *only* book-related things: writing them, selling them, promoting them, getting paid to promote them for someone else, talking about them, studying them and – of course – reading them.

Now you can read that and say to yourself, "She was just *really* lucky." I *have* been lucky; I don't deny that. But in all those things I've just described, the luck accounted for only about 5 per cent of the reason things happened. I had control over the other 95 per cent, and you do too. You can be ready for luck. You can point it your way. You can *make luck your only variable*.

How?

Selling Books

My e-book sales took off by themselves, without any help from the press coverage or appearances. (The proof: most of them were in the US and in the UK. All my press, with the sole exception of a mention of my blog in *Writers' Magazine*, has been here in Ireland.) I did it through producing a good book with an attractive cover, maximising my Amazon listings, behaving professionally at all times, blogging, tweeting and using Facebook.

Becoming The Story

People are interested in my success because it has a few interesting angles. I went to work to Disney World, I successfully self-published a book that got rejected by traditional publishing, even though I've successfully self-published I'm still pursing traditional publication and I managed to promote my book for free. These are all more interesting stories than the one about me writing a book and self-publishing it. Find yourself an angle and then push it.

Doing Things Well

If someone is thinking about writing an article about self-publishing and your name comes up, that's not luck, It's your hard work paying off. You've been recognised as a good example. And if this person then goes to your blog and sees it laid out like the website of a professional writer, they know you're the person to help them with their research. If they see some multi-coloured widgets and a book cover that looks like crap, they'll find someone else. Similarly, because I was successful at my first speaking engagement, I got another one. And so on and so on. When I'm invited on to a radio show, I always arrive prepared and do everything I can to give a good interview. Then, the next time someone is thinking of using me as a subject, they know they can rely on me to deliver the goods.

Saying "Yes"

When Vanessa asked me to talk at the self-publishing conference, I said yes without even thinking, despite the fact that the last time I'd spoken in public was more than ten years before and during a debating class in school. I had no idea what I would say or how I would say it, and on the day I just noted some reminders to myself on a legal pad, got up and told my story. Not all speaking engagements pay but most do, and some are worth doing even if they don't pay, purely because of how much they'll raise your profile and the people you might meet there. If you can, say yes. You can't even *imagine* what opportunities may arise.

Networking

I always used to imagine networking as going to yuppie-filled events where you have to wear name tags and shamelessly swap business cards with the other yuppies, and therefore something I could never bring myself to do. But what I've learned in the last year is that just using social media is networking. (The movie was called *The Social Network*, wasn't it?!) It's chatting to people at writing and book-related events you go to. It's just being friendly. It's offering to help people out with something, like an article they're writing or a giveaway they're trying to organise, or sending out complimentary copies of your book. Do you know how many of the opportunities I've got have come, directly or indirectly, out of me using Twitter? I'll tell you: *all of them*. (Although, I *do* recommend you get yourself some snazzy business cards!)

And finally, throughout all this I'm still doing what I've always done – blogging, tweeting, using Facebook – and I will always continue to do it.

I always remind myself that among my blog readers is at least one person who bought and read my book a year ago, when it came out, and who doesn't need to hear anything else about it when they come to my blog. They want new content and if they don't get it, I'll lose them. Moreover, you never know who that new content will bring to your blog, and what opportunity they'll bring to you.

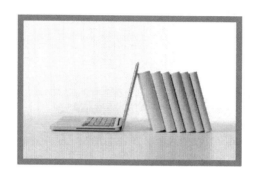

PART 6
Everything Else

Sales Reporting and Payment

How do you know if someone has bought your book? How do you know when they bought it and from where? And why hasn't CreateSpace sent you that $2.05 they owe you from the copy of your book that your grandmother bought yesterday morning?

CreateSpace

Whenever you log on to CreateSpace and see your Member Dashboard, the number of copies your book has sold to date this month will be displayed next to its title. This updates not far off real time, in my experience, but only for Amazon.com and eStore sales. If you sell a book through any retailer in your Expanded Distribution channel (i.e. any retailer that isn't an Amazon site) it can take weeks to show up in your reports. Infuriatingly, you won't be able to see when or where those sales occurred – only that they have.

You can also run reports to look at your sales data from a specific period or overall. You can run these reports by title or sales channel, or you can run a report showing your payment history.

CreateSpace pay royalties 30 days after the end of the calendar month during which you earned those royalties, e.g. you get paid for sales that occurred in January at the end of February. Depending on your location this payment will be made via direct deposit or by cheque.

Since CreateSpace started selling in Europe as well, they now pay in three different currencies: dollars, British pounds and euro. The minimum payment threshold is $100/£100/€100. If you don't meet this threshold, your royalties will be carried over to the next month. All payments are sent with remittance advices.

Remember, when you're running sales reports that unless you provide tax information, the amount you get paid will be that less 30 per cent.

Amazon KDP

You can see your monthly sales to date by logging on to Amazon KDP, clicking Reports at the top of the screen and then Month-to-Date Unit Sales. There's a separate tab for the Amazon.com, Amazon.co.uk, Amazon.de etc. Kindle Stores. It's been my experience that these update in almost real time.

You might also see refunds listed in your sales reports. Don't get too upset about them – it's incredibly easy to accidentally download a Kindle book, especially on the Kindle itself, and this is normally why customers request refunds. I think the most I had was five in a month of eight hundred or so sales in total, so it's not a cause for concern.

If your title is enrolled in KDP Select, you'll also see "Borrows" and "Free" (books downloaded during your free promotion days) columns.

You can also access the last six weeks' worth of sales and royalties, which is a feature I've never understood considering payment periods are only ever a month long. (So seeing royalties from a six-week period is just needlessly confusing.) You can generate MS Excel reports for previous months, which are available after the fifteenth of that month.

You will receive three different sets of payments from KDP: the Amazon.com royalties will arrive by US dollar cheque (or direct deposit if you live in the States), the Amazon.co.uk royalties will arrive by British pound cheque and the other European Amazon stores will arrive in a euro cheque. Depending on your location, you might be eligible to receive direct deposits.

Payments are made 60 days after the end of the calendar month in which the royalties were earned, so at the end of February I got paid for what I'd sold in December.

KDP has minimum royalty thresholds too, such as:

- $10/£10/€10 for electronic funds transfers (EFT)
- $100/£100/€100 for cheques

If you don't make these thresholds, your royalties will carry over to the next payment period. All payments are sent with remittance advices.

Calm the Fudge Down

Kindly refrain from doing silly things like sending registered letters to Amazon KDP HQ threatening them with legal action because your friend told you that they bought your book from Barnes & Noble last Tuesday and even though you've waited patiently for *four whole days* you still haven't even been notified of this sale, much less paid for it, and if they don't hand over that $1.83 right this minute you'll have no choice but to instruct your lawyer to initiate proceedings.

Each of the services we're dealing with here clearly state on their websites that sales data is NOT reported in real time (although CreateSpace and KDP do an excellent job of reporting in *almost* real time). They are crystal clear about when they pay. They are not stealing your money, or hiding your sales. Chillax.

Honestly, my advice is not to give any of this any thought at all. It is just absolutely *impossible* to match up your sales as you see or suspect them to have occurred online with the data you see in your sales reports. For instance, I unpublished the second edition of this book just last week, and now Amazon.com is showing "Only 4 left in stock ... Order soon". Have I already been paid for those four copies? Or will I get paid when they sell? I don't know and it doesn't matter. If you have time to worry about this kind of crap, you'd better already be a member of the Kindle Million Club (authors who've sold over 1,000,000 Kindle books) because otherwise you have *far* more important things to be doing.

Trust that these companies are telling you the truth. They are.

Keeping Accounts

You are now essentially running your own business and, unfortunately, that comes with a *lot* of paperwork. Your responsibilities will vary depending on where in the world you live, but most of us will have to file a tax return of some sort that tells our government:

- how much we earned from our books
- how much we had to spend to earn that money
- how much tax we owe on the difference

In order to give them those figures, we need to know them ourselves. This is why keeping organised and accurate accounts is *so* important. Back in 2010 I wasn't even thinking about this but let me tell you that after having to go back and do it, I'll never make the same mistake again. Here's a very simple system that I use for my own income and expenditure:

Create an Income/Expenditure Spreadsheet

Open a new Excel document and create four columns: Number (format: *text*), Date (format: *date*), Description (format: *text*) and Amount (format: *currency to two decimal points*). Now merge the top row of each of those four columns and label it "Income". Copy and paste so you have an identical set of columns immediately after them, and label those ones "Expenditure".

When you receive, for instance, a royalty payment, enter it in the first available space in the Income columns, making it the next available number ("10") and recording the date it was received, where it came from ("CreateSpace – July") and the amount it was for. Then take a red pen – I only use Sharpies – and write the number on the physical item (in this case the remittance advice) as well.

So let's say I bought some ink cartridges, and this was the tenth thing I had spent money on during my self-publishing operation thus far. I'd write "10" on the receipt in red, and enter the date I bought the cartridges, the word "ink cartridges" and the amount on the receipt in the corresponding row on my spreadsheet.

Make an "Accounts" E-mail Folder

All e-mail programs, be they web-based or on your computer, allow you to create folders. Create one now for your accounts. Then whenever you book a flight to travel to a speaking engagement, order a proof copy or purchase supplies online, you can send the confirmation e-mail directly into this folder where it'll stay safe until you have a chance to print it out.

Try to keep your income/expenditure spreadsheet up to date as things happen, as opposed to waiting until the items are printed out. This way it'll be in chronological order at the end of the year.

Buy Yourself Some Office Supplies

Is there anything more exciting than stationery shopping? If there is, I've yet to discover it. And there's nothing better than having a Staples spree when you actually *need* the stationery or office supplies in question. (Me needing the stationery I'm buying is *quite* the rare occurrence.) So go forth and purchase yourself an accordion file – one of those document holders with five or six separate compartments, ideally with a flap that closes with a snappy clasp – and a sturdy ring binder with some flashy dividers.

Label the divisions something like Royalty Statements, Other Income, Bills, Receipts, Tax Documents and anything else you think you might need. This is where we're going to store all our paperwork until we prepare our accounts at the end of the year; it's easy to throw a receipt or a remittance advice in here when we're in a rush, and we know it'll be safe there until we need it.

What's a Business Expense?

As a general rule, your taxable income will be your income minus your business expenses, and evidence of those are the most important documents you'll keep on file.

It's up to you to decide – and maybe, to prove – what's a business expense, but here are some of mine to give you an idea:

- Anything directly linked with self-publishing my books: cover design, editing/proofreading services, proof copies, stock, etc.
- For a while I rented a "hot desk" in a shared office; that was decidedly a business expense
- My phone bill
- Business cards
- Membership fees of any professional body, e.g. The Society of Authors
- Postage, including postage on contest/giveaway prizes
- My WordPress personalised domain upgrade
- A new computer and word-processing software
- Office supplies
- Travel to/from speaking engagements, associated accommodation and food expenses
- If you work from home, you could feasibly add in *some* of your energy bills

End of Year Accounts

If you manage to stay organised until the end of the year, you should find yourself with an up-to-date income/expenditure spreadsheet, and all the relevant documents, if not yet printed out, then ready and waiting for you to do so.

Then all you need to do is file them sequentially in your fancy ring binder, along with a printout of your tallied spreadsheet. I also like to print out bank statements so I can see how much the British pound cheque for x was in my own currency. And that's it: you should be all set for your accountant or, if you're feeling patient, tallying your tax obligations yourself. Good luck!

Workshops and Speaking Engagements

I can't really tell you how to start getting speaking engagements, because there's no simple, five-step process, and anyway, frankly, not everyone deserves to get them.

It's kind of like writing a book. Just because you managed to write 100,000 words does not mean that that book should be published, and just because you figured out how to self-publish does not mean you should be paid to explain the process to other people. Good speakers not only have the knowledge, they're good at delivering it too. Essentially, that means that they're entertaining. This doesn't necessarily involve cracking jokes and doing a little jig at the top of the room, but it does mean that you can – you must – keep your audience totally engaged for anywhere from one to six hours without them feeling bored, confused or like they're back in school, and that you have the stamina needed to do it.

If that sounds a bit scary, it should, because most of the time the events you're speaking at aren't free, and in fact some of them can be quite expensive. This is because it's presumed that for whatever amount of time the workshop or seminar is on for, the participants are getting to listen to – and ask questions of – an expert. Are you an expert?

Speaking engagements tend to pay really, really well, when you consider the time involved, i.e. €x amount for 90 minutes of my time, and this is why they can seem oh-so-attractive to self-publishers who only have e-book royalties coming in. Except that's not what you're getting paid for. The time involved is not just the amount of time you're scheduled to speak for, but the years of your life you've put into collecting the knowledge that qualifies you to speak, and the hours or days you spent preparing for the talk – which, if we're talking about a full day's workshop, could mean weeks upon weeks of devising, designing and practising the delivery of a PowerPoint presentation. Consider that too.

I may sound a bit doom and gloom about this, but it's only because I think people have a rosy view of getting paid to talk about self-publishing (or anything, for that matter), and this leads them to thinking they should be doing it when really, they're not right for it. And who will suffer then? The people who paid to listen to them.

On the flip side, if you've figured out how to do this self-publishing business, you've achieved more than most. It's easy for me to format an e-book from a Word document, for example, but if someone rarely sends an e-mail, it's going to seem like an Everest climb to them. They might relish the idea of getting a real, live person to patiently explain how to do it, instead of trawling through online articles and books full of terms they don't understand. So if you are suitable for speaking about self-publishing, you should do it. There's definitely a demand there, and it can be oh so much fun.

The first time I ever spoke about self-publishing was at the One Stop Self-Publishing Conference in Dublin in 2010. Here's the funny thing: I really didn't treat it very seriously. I wore jeans, and walked to the top of the room with my notes scribbled on a yellow legal pad. I thought about nothing other than telling my story, and telling it within the time frame: about half an hour, with fifteen minutes for questions. But I had a huge advantage before I even spoke: the person before me had been very technical and spoke in a bit of a monotone. I'd also noticed that, during the day, the speakers the audiences seemed to enjoy the most were not the ones with the technical knowledge, necessarily, but the ones who told their personal stories. For example, a professional cover designer had imparted fantastically useful advice, but the self-published children's book author before her was way more popular with the crowd, even though he "educated" us very little.

I'd been in a room with endless free coffee since 9.00 a.m. and I only *had* my personal story. So jeans or no jeans, I knew I'd do well. And I did. My little 30-minute giddy ramble about my self-publishing experience went down like a six-figure KDP Select Fund bonus, and it was the best feeling ever. I wanted to do it again.

In the audience (and also speaking) that day was Sarah, who I'd hired to copy-edit *Mousetrapped*. Almost two years later, she'd bump into Ben, another Twitter friend and fellow Apollo nut, who had just pitched the idea of doing a social media workshop to Faber Academy. They loved it, and suggested adding a self-publishing element. Did Ben know anyone who could do that? He thought of me, but he'd never seen me speak. When he met Sarah the subject came up, and she assured him that I could do it. That's how I got to do Faber Academy. One of the participants at the Faber Academy workshop the first year was the lovely Alexandra, a traditionally published author who was looking to e-publish her backlist. A few months later she'd get in touch to invite me along to another London event she was chairing: an e-book seminar for Women in Journalism (UK). So that's how I got to do that.

And so on and so on. I meet people through Twitter (good old-fashioned networking, if you want to be fancy about it); they invite me to speak; me speaking leads to more opportunities. So if I had to answer the question *How do I get speaking engagements?* my absolute shortest answer would be Twitter!

(But then that's pretty much my shortest answer to everything got to do with self-publishing success, so there you go.)

You'll probably want to know how much to ask for/expect, or even how I much I ask for/expect. Well, I'm not going to tell you. It's private, and it's also not going to be of any use to you, because any figure would only be an example of what I get and absolutely nothing to do with you, with your events, your environment, etc. I will tell you this though: if you're doing this right, you won't really need to worry about it.

I really believe that if you can, you should aim to get invited by an established company/event/festival/etc. to speak at something they're organising, as opposed to organising your own workshop or seminar. It's so much easier. And if they're a professional operation, they'll tell you the fee, and this fee will be what they pay all their speakers, a kind of standard.

A less professional – or less reputable – operation might ask, well, how much would you do it for? Because they're trying to get away with paying you as little as they can.

I can tell you that in two and a half years of doing this I've never been asked how much my fee is. I've just been presented with what's on offer, and either agreed or disagreed to take part. (Actually, I've never disagreed, come to think of it. But then I've been very, very lucky.)

Compensation for speaking engagements usually falls into one of these categories:

Charity. That's what the organisers seem to think you are anyway, because there's no compensation whatsoever: no expenses, no fee and no feeding. They might say something like, "We don't offer a fee, but our previous speakers have really enjoyed themselves." Um, riiiiight. How wonderful. But will my credit card company take enjoyment in lieu of this month's minimum payment, eh? I doubt it somehow. I would only do something for free if it was (i) likely to raise my profile and/or look good on my writing CV, (ii) for an *actual* charity, (iii) not going to cost me any money in terms of travel, preparation time, etc., (iv) not going to make any money for the organisers outside of their costs and (v) going to be fun for me.

Expenses only. I have never done a speaking engagement at home; almost all of them have been in Dublin (three hours away by train until I moved here seven days ago!) or London (an hour away by plane). Therefore I always incur travel expenses. Many events will not offer a fee but will offer reimbursement (or partial reimbursement) of how much it costs you to get there. At this stage in my speaking/self-publishing career, this is perfectly acceptable to me, especially because I genuinely enjoy these events and see them not only as an opportunity to travel but also to meet loads of interesting people and talk publishing over free coffee.

Expenses + a fee (AKA cha-CHING!). The best case scenario is that you would be paid a speaking fee and offered x amount towards a reimbursement of your expenses. When this happens, it's a beautiful thing.

Whether it's expenses only or expenses plus a fee, there's a game to play. Let's say you're getting paid €500 for a full-day workshop, but that's it; no expenses. Or let's say there's no fee at all for participating in a panel discussion, but they are willing to give you £200 towards the expenses you incur travelling to get there. Well, in both these cases the less you spend, the more you make. (Amount paid – expenses incurred = profit.) And so begins the challenge of budget travel.

I have this down to a fine art by now. Here are some tips for saving on your travel expenses:

Book your travel as soon as possible. Flights, train tickets and even hotel rooms get more expensive as availability declines.

Prepay for lower rates. Most hotel chains offer prepay rates which are

10 per cent or more cheaper than what you'll pay if you book now and settle the bill on check-out. The only downside is that these are normally non-refundable, so make sure you're definitely going before you book. Failing that:

Search for good deals. I love Booking.com because you don't have to pay in advance but you can still avail of great rates. But here's a tip: all the hotels that sell rooms on sites like that have to pay the site a commission. So if you're feeling a bit cheeky, you could ring the hotel and say you want to book with them direct, and what's the best rate they could do for you. For example, could they give you the Booking.com rate for a standard room, but upgrade you to a superior one? That's a good deal for them, because you're saving them commission.

Stick to public transport, if possible. Avoid taxis.

Sign up to mileage and loyalty schemes. Nearly all hotel chains and airlines have loyalty cards for their customers; sign up for them. You won't be able to take advantage for a while but one day you might get a free night or a free flight and, hey, you were buying them anyway.

Ask the organisers. If this is an event that has run in the past, the organisers will probably have a list of accommodation options, and they might offer a discounted rate for attendees/speakers.

Get creative. This isn't a holiday, it's a challenge: spend as little money as possible while still being sufficiently sheltered, fed and watered. For instance, on a trip to London a few months ago I made it my mission to spend as little as I thought a person possibly could without hitching and youth hostels. I flew with Ryanair to Gatwick with only carry-on luggage; I took the EasyBus from Gatwick to Earl's Court tube station (for only £2!); I ordered a visitor's Oyster Card online so I could avail of cheaper tube fares; I stayed in an EasyHotel (a fraction – a tiny, *tiny* fraction – of the cost of staying anywhere else in London); instead of eating out I got takeaway foods from places like Sainsbury's and Starbucks. Now if I was on holiday, I wouldn't want to start it with the stress of a Ryanair flight and an hour-long bus ride into London. But I wasn't on holiday, I was working. And my entire two-night London visit came to less than £200, which isn't at all bad for accommodation + transport + food in one of the most expensive cities in the world.

Of course, I ruined it all by spreeing in Paperchase, Foyles, etc. while I was there, but, hey, nobody's perfect …

Some events pay on the day but most pay afterwards in response to an invoice you've sent them. Remember to keep all your receipts and evidence of your travel expenses such as booking confirmations, etc. I don't send these to the organisers unless they ask for them; I just bill them the amount. But I do say something like "Receipts are available on request."

Some practical tips about *getting* speaking engagements:

- If you're unsure whether or not you're cut out for this, start by simply sharing your self-publishing story with other people. Find an opportunity to just do that. It may be in the form of a short talk (like my break was at the One Stop Self-Publishing Conference) or it may be by participating in a panel discussion where two or three people discuss topics put forth by a chairperson. If all else fails, post your own videos on your website. If you have a popular web series going on, why wouldn't someone want you for the live, 3-D version?

- Say yes to everything, within reason. If you get an invite to speak at an event, find out everything you can about it before you answer. Google is your friend. Does it seem like the real deal? Who else will be there? Have they done this before? If they've asked you to speak for free, check: are they charging for tickets to your event? Because if they are, that might be a red flag. Why are they making money when you're expected to do this for nothing? The main questions to ask yourself are: (i) Will this cost me money? (ii) Is this a networking opportunity? (iii) Is this likely to further my profile? Sometimes you might want to do something just because it seems like it'll be fun, and that's fine. Go ahead. But go into everything with eyes wide open.

- Be good. Almost every speaking engagement will lead to another speaking engagement – if you're good and impress the organisers and participants. No one will invite back someone who underwhelmed, or who made the workshop attendees' brains turn to soup. Ditto for being unprofessional, late, making diva demands or being otherwise annoying.

- I'm sure many writers would see speaking engagements as an excellent opportunity to sell copies of their own books, and I'm sure it is – but I never do it. The first reason is that as a POD paperback self-publisher, I avoid ordering stock of my own book like the plague. Second, I always travel to these events, sometimes by plane, always by public transport, and lugging a box of books there and back is just not feasible. Third, I would feel cheeky trying to sell a €10 or €15 "how to self-publish" book to someone who's just spent €125 to hear what was advertised as everything I know about self-publishing. Instead, I bring little business cards or postcards so that if people do want to purchase the book, they have all the information they need to do it when they get back home.

- Be flexible. The summer before last I was sitting in my back garden one Friday afternoon, covered in sunscreen and halfway through a great book, when the phone rang. The Irish Writers' Centre were holding a seminar on how to publish e-books the following day and the speaker had had to drop out because of illness. Would I be available to fill in? "Filling in" meant (i) curtailing my sunbathing, (ii) having to put together a PowerPoint presentation in a few hours and (iii) travelling up to Dublin the following morning on the 6.00 a.m. train so I could arrive at the centre in time to hold a workshop on a day I thought I was going to spend lazing around in my PJs. But I said yes, and not only did the day go off without a hitch, but they invited me back to do another seminar – only this time with a bit more notice!

About the presentation itself:

- If you are booked to talk for longer than an hour and you can, use a visual aid. For most people, this will take the form of a PowerPoint presentation. It should serve both as eye-fodder for your listeners and notes for you. (And if you have a brand, extend it to your slides – mine have a pink colour scheme.) Arrive in plenty of time so you can ensure that everything is working perfectly before the attendees arrive.
- The hardest thing to get right is timing, especially if you're doing a whole day. Start by dividing the day into blocks, e.g. start to first coffee break, coffee break to lunch, after lunch to mid-afternoon break, mid-afternoon break to Q&A time, Q&A time. Then divide your talk into sections, e.g. Overview, Why Self-Publishing, E-books, POD Paperbacks, Social Media, etc. and match them up with the blocks of time. Try not to straddle a subject across two blocks of time if you can avoid it; you'll lose momentum and the participants might lose out. I do an initial practice in which I quickly run through the talk – and yes, this involves talking to yourself – but keep in mind that it will always take longer on the day as people interrupt to ask questions, seek clarification, etc.
- Break up the presentation in the afternoon. Post-lunch, people will be at the most sluggish – including you. I usually talk about book trailers at this point, which allows me to spend half an hour showing funny YouTube videos. A break for my participants from concentrating, and a break for me from speaking. Hooray!
- Start with an overview. For example, "First we're going to talk about why you should self-publish, then move on to e-books, then …" etc. etc. This prevents people from asking questions that are going to be answered later on.

About delivering it:

- I would always recommend that you aim to get invited to speak as opposed to creating your own workshop or seminar. It's so much easier. There's already an established company (and so probably an established customer base), they'll take care of everything from logistics to lunch, and they'll pay you. They'll also likely be a great contact for future invites.

- Whenever I do a long-ish workshop and always when I do a full day, I tell my participants right at the start that they don't need to worry about taking notes because the entire PowerPoint presentation and a page of all the links I mention will be on my website from Monday. (These things are always on a weekend.) Then I make a new page on my website, like http://www.catherineryanhoward.com/faberworkshop, upload the PP file and any links, etc. and make it password protected. I give the participants the password and the URL, and then they – and only they – can access the information afterwards. (Why not make it public? Because how are the participants, who paid money to attend, going to feel when they discover that anyone can now see the presentation for free?) This way they don't stress about writing every single thing I say down, and listen to me instead. Everyone's a winner.

- Always, always, always have two back-ups. My presentation may be on my laptop, but just in case I bring it on disk as well, and just in case just in case, I put a copy in my Dropbox folder, which can be accessed from anywhere there's internet.

- Tailor your talk to your audience. A writers' group who have invited you to share your self-publishing experience will probably be okay with an informal chat, but if people are paying serious money to learn everything they need to know about self-publishing, they're going to want their money's worth.

- If you are doing a day-long workshop where lunch is provided for everyone, don't stay for it. Or at least, don't stay for all of it. (You do need to eat!) Get away for a while. Go for a walk. Get some air. Check your e-mails. But stop talking.

- Thanks to a haunted hotel room, I once had to do a full day's workshop on two hours sleep. Two hours! I didn't think I'd make it, but an emergency raid of the venue's vending machines got me through. You should always have: (i) water … um, obviously, (ii) a bottle of Lucozade or some other energy drink and (iii) chocolate – a couple of squares on the coffee break, along with coffee of course, makes a world of difference.

When It Doesn't Work

If your book doesn't sell or sells for a while and then drops off the radar, then you potentially have one or more of the following problems:

Your Book Looks Like a Pile of Poo

It doesn't matter if you've written the next *Cloud Atlas*, *Room* or *The Time Traveler's Wife*. If the cover looks like something your cat threw up and then another cat threw up *on*, it's not going to sell.

Think of all the hard work you have to do just to get me headed to your Amazon listing with an idea that, hey, I might actually buy that book. But then I get there and see a cover that assures me you're a self-publisher, putting a huge question mark over whether or not your book is any good. (Call this unfair all you want; it's *reality*.) And if I can tell you've self-published just by the quality of your cover, i.e. how much it looks like one of those crappy Cover Creator templates, then I can also tell that you haven't self-published very well and my money will stay in my pocket.

Same goes for clicking your Look Inside on Amazon and seeing that the first line of your book is at the top of page 1, and it says "Chapter One." I'm not looking for perfection here, but I am looking for a sense of what a book is supposed to be like, i.e. *professionalism*. I want a quality product in exchange for my money and if you can't give me that, I'm not going to give you my money.

The biggest tragedy here is that some really good self-published books don't get read because their covers are rubbish or their listings don't have the right information or the author's blog is a mess. Writing a good book is the hardest part. How would you feel if, having mastered that, everything else you did – or didn't bother to do – let you down? What a wasted opportunity.

And please, spare me the "people aren't giving my book a chance!" excuse. No, really. *Please.* Your job is not to convince people to give your book a charitable chance. Your job is to convince people that they want to read it.

You Haven't Worked Hard Enough

Self-publishing is a business, and you need to treat it as such. You are selling a product, even if your ultimate goal is not financial. To become a successful self-publisher you need to consider yourself an entrepreneur.

If you were talking to someone who is single-handedly starting up their own business, what kind of things would you expect them to say? I would be surprised if they didn't tell me they'd worked all the hours that were in the day to get their business up and running, sacrificed time with friends and family and focused all of their energies on one thing: achieving success. Does this sound like a description of you getting your book to sell?

While you were writing the book, you were a writer. You could live *la vie bohème,* hang out in Parisian-style cafés smoking Marlboro Reds and talk about how you'd spend your last euro on a book instead of food because art nourishes you more. (Or, if you're me, spend much of the day in your PJs dreaming about hanging out in Parisian cafés drinking tiny espressos.) This was allowed because you were a writer: a creative, head-in-the-clouds type. But once you turned your scribbles into a book, slapped a price tag on it and encouraged/begged people to buy it, you got into business. You became that entrepreneur.

I'm continually amazed at stories of self-publishers who lob their book up on Amazon, set up a static website and then sit back and relax, expecting the readers to come to them. A website is not a shop window; people will *never* happen upon it unless you send them there.

As for self-publishers who refuse to send out review copies or will only offer PDFs because they "can't afford" it, well, I have a special place reserved on my People Who Have Annoyed Me list for *you.* If you didn't have any money at all, would you still open a restaurant or try to bring a new product to the market? No. Of course not. And as I've shown in this book, the money you do have to spend isn't that much at all, especially if you're creative (which, as a writer, I'm assuming you are!). But you *do* have to spend it.

E-books are exploding now, and the self-publishers who got in on the act are reaping the rewards. As I type this, the magical interweb is whispering about a mega-selling e-book author in the US who is poised to sign her name to a *seven-figure book deal* by the end of this week. Reading these stories, it's easy to come to the conclusion that uploading an e-book to Amazon guarantees sales and success, but this isn't true. It's never true. If you ever read a story like this, I'd encourage you to ignore the sensationalist headlines, find the author's blog and see what *they* have to say about the reason for their success. It's always a variation on the same thing: *lots of hard work.*

If you want to treat self-publishing your book as a hobby, feel free. Just don't expect me to pay for what this hobby produces.

You Haven't Worked Hard for Long Enough

You have to give this thing at least a year. Self-publishing is not a sprint, but a marathon. You're not going to sell every single copy you'll ever sell in the first week, and you can't expect to sit back and relax after just a month.

Self-publishing expert Aaron Shepard says that a POD book takes a year to reach its full potential. Now while I think e-books skew this a bit, it's still essentially true. It's certainly been my experience that after almost a year of slogging away and having good results, everything came together and suddenly became *great.*

This has a lot to do with Amazon, I believe, where as I've already said, sales lead to more sales. Imagine a year's worth of purchases, recommendations, appearances in Customers Also Bought ..., reviews, etc. etc. Every day your book is getting more and more primed to sell. Just hang in there.

You Haven't Done It Right

Somewhere along the way, you've ignored something I recommended. This won't work if you do everything except instead of a blog you just create a website. Or you do everything but you price your e-book $9.99. Or you do everything except put your book on Amazon's Kindle Store because you don't like the company.

These are the most common areas, I think, where self-publishers make mistakes:

- **Pricing.** They price their work too high – it needs to be priced to sell
- **Cover.** I think we've already covered that – no pun intended!
- **Delusions of grandeur.** Symptoms include saying things like, "I know if someone just gives my book a chance, they'll love it" and embarrassingly gushing, ahem, *reviews,* that compare it to Hemingway, Orwell, etc. Also known as Coming Across as a Jerk No One Wants to See Succeed Syndrome

Your Book Doesn't Have Appeal

There's a cautionary tale floating around the traditional publishing world, a kind of "if you don't go to bed early the Boogie Man will get you" scare story for aspiring writers.

A debut writer signs with a superstar agent and bags a six-figure, headline-grabbing deal for her first novel. Everyone's happy and the book is steeped in hype. Then, a year later, it finally comes out and ... Nothing. It doesn't hit the bestseller charts. It doesn't even *sell* in any great quantities and the reviews are lukewarm. The publishing house is out a ton of money – the book will never earn back its advance – and the writer is so humiliated that she can hardly face sitting down to start Book 2. It's a disaster all round. But whose fault is it?

The self-publishing evangelists will climb over each other now to scream that it's Big, Bad Traditional Publishing's fault. They don't know what they're doing! Most of the books they publish fail! They've never known what sells books and what doesn't and they're all quaking in their boots that self-publishers are about to expose their secret!

Publishing is a business and books are their product. Newsflash: products fail. Think about it: how many movies, TV shows, breakfast cereals, fashion trends, restaurants and boy bands have been launched into the world to great fanfare, only to disappear again without a trace? Even the biggest spender on advertising *in the world* has got it wrong (New Coke, anyone?). Why? Because people just didn't want to buy the product. Everyone involved in its inception, design and delivery thought they would, but they didn't. The general public are a fickle bunch. Yes, you can attempt to figure out in advance what they might like with market research, but even that doesn't always work. (*Seinfeld*'s pilot episode was one of the worst test-audience screenings the network ever had.) And the same happens with books. I've seen it myself from behind the scenes. The commissioning editor is in love, the sales team can't wait to get out there and push the title and the publicity department is just brimming with ideas for how they can connect readers to this book. But in the months leading up to publication it becomes increasingly clear: people are just not liking the book. Or they *are* liking it, but not with any great enthusiasm. It's just not getting any traction with book bloggers, reviews and readers. No one knows exactly why, because how could they? The same things that were done with last year's bestseller were done with this. People just didn't want to read the book. Nor did they want to go see *John Carter* (estimated to have lost Disney in the region of $100 million despite a "can't move for hearing about it" PR campaign) and they didn't want to watch *Believe* (a TV show created by *Gravity* director Alfonso Cuarón and executive produced by *LOST* co-creator J. J. Abrams that was cancelled by NBC after only one season).

Maybe your book isn't selling because it's *just not something other people want to read.*

Harsh, I know, but this could well be the truth. That's not to say that your book is bad. It's not to say that it doesn't have worth. It just means that at this point in time the tastes of the general reading public and the content of your book are not in alignment.

What can you do about that?

You can't do anything about that if that really is the case, but make sure your problem *isn't* that you haven't properly communicated with the general reading public in the first place. I told you back at the beginning: *find your book's appeal.*

Let's say you've written a crime/thriller novel with a serial killer. That's the kind of book I and many other people like to read (i.e. there's an established market for such a novel). So once you've informed me that it exists (through social-media-powered word of mouth), how can you be sure that you've done everything you can to convince me to read it?

- ✓ Are your cover design and title in keeping with the genre? I won't pick it up if I don't get that subconscious message that it's like this other book I really liked.
- ✓ Do you have a killer (ha!) tagline, e.g. *Don't bother locking the door. He's already inside …* and an intriguing blurb/product description to match? The books I buy have blurbs that ask questions I feel I MUST find out the answer to.
- ✓ Have you presented the story in the best possible light? I can't say I'd really be all that interested in a story about a mother and son who run a little bed and breakfast. But tell me you've got a polite young man running a motel out in the middle of nowhere that has spy holes in the walls, and a beautiful young woman seemingly murdered by that polite young's man controlling mother – and that the young man denies knowing anything about it when people come to ask – and you've me chomping at the bit to find out what's *really* going on. What is the question your novel asks? Present me with it in the blurb/product description and make sure it's one I simply have to know the answer to.
- ✓ Is your price enticing? Is it encouraging me to give you, an unknown with no track record that I've never read anything by before, a chance?
- ✓ Does your book both fit in *and* stand out in your genre? I know it sounds like doublethink, but your book must simultaneously (a) look like it belongs among the bestsellers in Crime/Thrillers and (b) catch my eye over all the others. Do your title, cover, tagline, price and product description – and even your author bio – work together to do that?

Don't forget that at any given time, the best thing you can do to boost your self-publishing career is write another book. Don't forget that we got into this business because the thing we love to do the most is to tell stories. So make (another!) pot of coffee, sit down at your desk and get telling a new one.

5 Frequently Asked Questions*

(*That haven't already been answered elsewhere in this book)

1. Um, hello? Children's books?

I don't know a lot about self-publishing children's books because of course I've never done it myself. However if anyone doubts that there's a way for self-publishers to make it in the children's book market, google "child thinks magazine is broken iPad" and watch the videos that come back. All the little people I know love to leave fingerprint smudges all over their parents' tablet computers – they're a great way to keep them entertained with interactive e-books and videos.

If I was self-publishing a children's book I'd use the newly launched **KDP Kids** programme (https://kdp.amazon.com/kids) to make a very snazzy illustrated Kindle edition of my book that's going to look great on a Kindle Fire HD screen, and **Blurb** (http://www.blurb.com) to make a fixed-format ePub version for the iPad. Fixed-format means things will stay where you put them, so if you want an illustration to be on page 3, there it'll go. Blurb's service also enables you to add interactive features like video.

Speaking of **video**, that's what I'd use to promote my book. Kids love YouTube – and YouTube loves kids. There's a wealth of entertainment on there for them, including sing-a-longs, short animations and educational tools to help them learn. If you have a computer, it'll cost you nothing except time to get a video on YouTube. Why don't you read your book into your webcam and upload that? Call it Storytelling Time. Or create bonus material for the children who are already reading your book. You could approach "mummy bloggers" and parenting sites and offer review copies.

Another recommendation I'd make is to think of the **gift market**. In the run-up to Christmas lots of big people are looking for cool things to buy the little ones. Why not create a stunning hardcover edition of your book and sell it directly from your website, with an offer to personally inscribe it to the recipient and gift-wrap it for free?

2. British or American English – which one should I use?

If you live in the US, this probably isn't something you've thought about, but for those of us in, say, Britain and Ireland, this is a RIGHT pain in the arse.

We consume Things Made in America all the time, including books, movies and TV shows. Therefore we are familiar with the differences in the language. We know what those other words mean. We don't moan or groan when we find them in a book or a magazine article or on a blog post, because they've always been there.

But, without wanting to offend anyone, it doesn't always work the other way around. In fact, there seems to be a significant problem with readers who perhaps aren't used to British English mistaking our different grammar and spelling rules for errors and typos – and talking about them in Amazon reviews. I know several self-published authors who've encountered this problem, including myself.

And really, you can't blame the American readers, because practically all traditionally published books written over here are modified before they cross the Atlantic. They're not used to seeing British English in the books they buy.

Sometimes though, it gets a little farcical. I've encountered readers, for instance, who thought that although I was writing in British English, because my character was American she should *say* "color" and not "colour". This, I'm afraid, is just ridiculous. When you read translations of Jo Nesbo's books is all the dialogue in Norwegian? Then there are the people who think that because most Kindle books are sold in the United States they should all be presented in American English. But why should I modify *my own mother tongue* because of where the book might ultimately be sold? Should I tell my story differently too? Change my plot? Change my politics? Where does it end?

The *only* thing to do, in my opinion, is to write your book in your own language. If you have money to spare, you might want to create a British English edition and an American English edition, but if I did have money to spare I'd rather spend it on something else.

If you are an American reader, please, consider us over here on this side of the Pond. What's different or unfamiliar isn't always wrong too. I wonder have any of you winced every time your eyes landed on the word *copy-editor*? Did you shake your head at all *my* fist-shaking about hiring editing professionals when I had a wayward hyphen in there all along?

This is a comment exchange between a blog reader of mine and editor extraordinaire, Robert Doran, on a post Robert wrote for my blog about the importance of professional editing.

The reader says:

"I hesitated to mention this, but it is highly likely the first thing a copy editor would do is take the hyphen out of 'copy-editor'. AP and Webster's say it is two words, and Chicago says it's one word, so which style guide says it's hyphenated? If it had been some other compound word or phrase in your article, I wouldn't have noticed because I wouldn't have read it, but it's in the title! So even just seeing a tweet about the blog post made me notice it. [emoticon] Peace."

To which Robert replies:

"I use Butcher's Copy-editing: The Cambridge Handbook for Editors, Copy-editors and Proofreaders. The Society for Editors and Proofreaders (UK) also prefers 'copy-editor', so it's fairly common for writers and editors working with UK English to hyphenate this one. Thanks for reading!"

Thom
October 22, 2013 at 14:47 Edit #

I hesitated to mention this, but it is highly likely the first thing a copy editor would do is take the hyphen out of "copy-editor." AP and Webster's say it is two words, and Chicago says it's one word, so which style guide says it's hyphenated? If it had been some other compound word or phrase in your article, I wouldn't have noticed because I wouldn't have read it, but it's in the title! So even just seeing a tweet about the blog post made me notice it. 😊 Peace.

REPLY

Robert Doran
October 22, 2013 at 22:39 Edit #

I use Butcher's Copy-editing: The Cambridge Handbook for Editors, Copy-editors and Proofreaders. The Society for Editors and Proofreaders (UK) also prefers "copy-editor", so it's fairly common for writers and editors working with UK English to hyphenate this one. Thanks for reading!

REPLY

3. But what if my book *really* isn't in a genre?

Don't confuse genre with the way it's used in terms like "genre fiction". Genre is the category of books that your book will sit amongst in the bookstore. These are: Literary Fiction, Women's Commercial Fiction (chick-lit), Men's Commercial Fiction (lad-lit), Young Adult, Children's, Romance, Crime/Thriller/Mystery, Comic, Erotica, Historical Fiction, Science Fiction, Fantasy, Reference, Manuals and Handbooks, Biography, History, Travel/Adventure, Self-Help, Popular Science, Mind/Body/Spirit, Comics/Graphic Novels, Memoir, Short Stories, Poetry, Film and Theatre (including stage plays and screenplays). Even special little snowflakes can find a home in this list. Pick one.

I was recently asked a question about "mainstream fiction". What in the name of fudge is *that*? You're going to need to narrow it down somewhat. Is it aimed predominantly towards men or towards women? Is it commercial or literary? Funny or sad? What is the plot like – is there a thriller element in there?

Don't be an "18 to 89" Person. These are the people who, when pitching products, services or TV shows, claim to have created something that will appeal to everyone from age 18 to 89. This is not *possible*. Things that appeal equally to everyone within that age range *do not exist*. You are selling a product, and the first thing you need to do is figure out who to sell that product to. *Everyone* is not an answer; the goalposts will be too far apart. Also: just because you're saying your book is women's commercial fiction does not mean there's a ban on men buying it. It just means that's where you're going to focus your promotional efforts. You're making things easier for yourself by giving yourself a target.

(You can still be a special little snowflake too. Don't worry.)

4. How did you find out everything you know about self-publishing?

Last year I met up with two self-publishing friends, Shannon and Toni of Duolit (http://www.selfpublishingteam.com) in real life – and in Walt Disney World! – and we joked that there should be an annual Self-Publishing Experts Day Off, whereby we shut down our blogs, e-mail accounts and Twitter feeds and put this up there instead:

Because that's how I – and Shannon and Toni and everyone else who self-published back in the day – found out everything we needed to know in order to self-publish. We googled and then we did it and then we googled some more. We corrected ourselves. We made mistakes and learned from them. We kept learning, because we were genuinely interested. And eventually, we knew everything we needed to know.

That's why I'm constantly dumbfounded that people send me e-mails asking me questions whose answers are not only available online, but are available on my blog, the very blog they had to be on to send me the e-mail. Why don't they just look it up? You have this book. You have my blog. You have all the other blogs too. If you run into a problem, type the question you want answered into Google.

But the best way to find out how to do this is to *do it*. Just go ahead right now: make a cover on Canva, mock up a quick interior and order a proof copy from CreateSpace just to see what it's like. Grab a notepad and write down every idea you have for promoting your book online. Start a blog tonight. There's only so much I can explain to you. The rest you have to find out for yourself.

5. What's the ONE thing I should do to help make my book a success?

If you've already done everything you possibly can to ensure that it's a great one? Then I'd say Twitter.

And That's All, Folks

And that, my friends, is that. I hope I've helped you self-publish and sell your book, kept you mildly entertained for however long it took you to read this book or, at the very least, persuaded you not to ask Amazon – and therefore, me – for a refund.

If you've read this book all in one go and before you've even finished *writing* your book, I'm sure it sounds like an awful lot of work. But most of it is *fun*, and when someone sends you a message saying how much they've enjoyed your book, or you get a cheque for money your writing earned, or you get called *a writer*, it all feels worth it. And I don't want to get all dramatic and emotional now, mere sentences before the end, but doing this could even change your life. It's changed mine.

I'll leave you with the five biggest lessons I've learned since I self-published my book:

1. Everything takes much longer than you think it's going to take
2. You can't edit your own book
3. Twitter is amazing
4. All the hard work is worth it – eventually!
5. No matter what happens, hang in there for at least a year

And if you were wondering what you do once a year has passed, well...

Then you release another book, and do it all over again.

Good luck!

(You can do this.)

Some Useful Stuff

Useful Websites & Services

Social Media

wordpress.com
twitter.com
bufferapp.com
facebook.com
goodreads.com
pinterest.com
instagram.com
feedly.com

Print-on-demand (POD)

createspace.com
lulu.com
blurb.com

E-books

kdp.amazon.com
smashwords.com
ebookpartnership.com

Manuscript Assessment & Editorial

inkwellwriters.ie
bubblecow.co.uk
sfep.org.co.uk
epani.org.uk
robert-edits.com
averillbuchanan.com

Financial

xe.com (currency converter)
gumroad.com (sell e-book files)
taxback.com (tax/IRS assistance)
paypal.com (online payments)

Graphic/Cover Design

canva.com (DIY Kindle covers)
picmonkey.com (Twitter/blog graphics)
designforwriters.com (Andrew – he does my covers!)
istockphoto.com (Buy stock images)

Video Sharing

youtube.com
vimeo.com

Printing Services

vistaprint.com
moo.com

E-book Reading Apps

adobe.com/products/digitaleditions
amazon.com/gp/kindle/pc/download
amazon.com/gp/kindle/mac/download

Mailing Lists & Newsletters

mailchimp.com

More About Me

catherineryanhoward.com
twitter.com/cathryanhoward
facebook.com/mousetrappedbook

Find all this and more at:

catherineryanhoward.com/selfprinted3

Books I Recommend

Writing the Book

How Not To Write a Novel: 200 Mistakes to Avoid At All Costs if You Ever Want to Get Published, Howard Mittelmark and Sandra Newman, Penguin, 2009

Save the Cat: The Last Book on Screenwriting You'll Ever Need, Blake Snyder, Michael Wiese Productions, 2005

Nail Your Novel: Why Writers Abandon Books and How You Can Draft, Fix and Finish With Confidence 2nd Edition, Roz Morris, Kindle Media and CreateSpace Independent Publishing Platform, 2011

Promoting the Book

Aiming at Amazon, Aaron Shepard, Shepard Publications, 2007

Wannabe a Writer We've Heard Of?, Jane Wenham Jones, Accent Press, 2010

Tweet Right: The Sensible Person's Guide to Twitter, Nicola Morgan, Crabbit Publishing, 2012

The Writing Life

On Writing: A Memoir of the Craft, Stephen King, New English Library, 2001

The Forest for the Trees: An Editor's Advice to Writers, Betsy Lerner, Riverhead Books, 2010

Other Publishing Guides

The Naked Author: A Guide to Self-publishing, Alison Baverstock, Bloomsbury, 2011

Publishing for Success, Anne Tannahill, NIPR, The National Collection of Northern Ireland Publications, 2014

Just for Fun

How I Became a Famous Novelist (A Novel), Steve Hely, Corsair, 2011

Self-Publishing *Backpacked*

In 2011 I published a blog post on catherineryanhoward.com listing every step I'd taken in self-publishing my second travel memoir, *Backpacked: A Reluctant Trip Across Central America*. This isn't really a checklist – I made a dedicated website for the book, for example, which is something I'd advise against doing now, and some of the other steps are out of date – but I include it here to give you an idea of (i) how much work is involved and (ii) the order in which you need to do that work. **Please keep in mind however that this is just an *example* and not at all an instruction.**

1. (February 2011) Decide to write and release the book
2. Decide on a release month (not enough information for release date yet)
3. Register a new free WordPress blog to act as *Backpacked's* dedicated book site
4. Upgrade free blog URL to "backpackedbook.com"
5. Set site to "private" while it's under construction
6. Take "scrapbook" picture to go on the cover
7. Start new "scrapbox" for *Backpacked*; I use one of these for each book
8. Mock up front cover design in MS Word
9. E-mail cover designer mock up and ask for quote
10. E-mail copyeditor and ask for quote
11. Blog about decision to write and self-publish it
12. Update Twitter profile, etc. with news of *Backpacked*
13. Write a synopsis
14. Blog the synopsis
15. Get e-book (front) cover from designer to use for promotion
16. Construct backpackedbook.com and set it to public
17. Rearrange catherineryanhoward.com to make room for links, etc. about *Backpacked*
18. Share cover design with blog readers and Facebook fans
19. Write the book (Um yeah, that only comes now…)
20. Edit first draft
21. Send book to Sarah, my copyeditor
22. Send book to Sheelagh, my best friend who's *in* the book, so she can okay it
23. Mock-up rough interior to get page count
24. With page count, determine manufacturing cost using CreateSpace's calculators
25. Use manufacturing costs to determine list price

26. Get cover designer to build an online bookstore so readers can pre-order signed copies for a limited time
27. Mock-up design, liaise with designer to perfect online bookstore
28. Set online bookstore to live and start to advertise it
29. Download full cover template from CreateSpace
30. Send template to cover designer along with instructions for back cover
31. Send update to *Mousetrapped* page Facebook fans re: pre-ordering *Backpacked*
32. … and to everyone in my e-mail contacts list…
33. … and to everyone who ordered a copy of *Mousetrapped* from me…
34. … and to everyone the More *Mousetrapped* mailing list…
35. … and blog a reminder too, just for good measure.
36. Answer interview questions for Alyssa Martino's blog.
37. Close online bookstore.
38. Make a list of books ordered and print out receipts from PayPal.
39. Upload 70+ photos to Backpackedbook.com to make slideshow and…
40. … write captions for every single one of them while watching *Outnumbered.*
41. Ok *Backpacked*'s paperback cover design.
42. Work out remaining timeline and set release date.
43. Set up new title on CreateSpace.
44. Upload finished PDF cover file to CreateSpace.
45. Work through copyeditor's suggestions, accepting/rejecting changes.
46. Create two copies of MS – one destined to be e-book, one a paperback.
47. Download CreateSpace interior MS Word template.
48. Copy and paste in edited text and format interior.
49. Insert free ISBN provided by CS onto copyright page.
50. Go through interior again, fixing errors.
51. Upload interior file to CreateSpace and submit for review.
52. Order a proof copy so I can see for first time what cover, font, etc. looks like.
53. Create a PDF version of *Backpacked* to send to blogger friends.
54. Make this video about editing.
55. Go through proof copy looking for errors and adjust interior file with corrections.
56. Send interior file to copyeditor for proofreading.
57. Buy envelopes for sending pre-orders.

58. Take e-book MS and prepare it for upload – one for Kindle, one for Smashwords.
59. Smashwords version won't convert properly; try again.
60. Smashwords version won't convert properly; try *again*.
61. Figure out only way to make it work is to "go nuclear", i.e. strip out all formatting then go back and put it in.
62. Upload/publish this new file to Smashwords.
63. Upload/publish this new file to Amazon KDP too, so they match.
64. Upload proofread interior file to CreateSpace.
65. Order proof copies of this final version.
66. Download .mobi version from Smashwords and send to friends/reviewers.
67. Purchase royalty free music for book trailer.
68. Use JING to record video for book trailer.
69. Make book trailer using iMovie.
70. Upload book trailer to YouTube and Vimeo.
71. Check second – and final – proof copy.
72. Click "Approve Proof" on CreateSpace (i.e. publish).
73. Pay for ProPlan upgrade on CreateSpace.
74. Order enough stock to cover pre-orders.
75. Send "Out now!" message to everyone on my mailing list and the More *Mousetrapped* mailing list with MailChimp.
76. Post "Out now!" status updates on *Mousetrapped*'s Facebook page.
77. Add book trailer to Smashwords listing.
78. Add book trailer to Goodreads Author Profile.
79. Set up new Google Alert for "Backpacked" + my name
80. Add new section for *Backpacked* to my sales data spreadsheet
81. Add *Backpacked* to bibliography in Amazon Author Central.
82. E-mail Amazon to get them to link paperback to Kindle edition.
83. Update *Mousetrapped* e-books with links to *Backpacked's* e-book.
84. Update *Mousetrapped* paperback interior with Backpacked in the "Also By…"
85. Update *Self-Printed* e-books with links to Backpacked's e-book.
86. Update *Self-Printed* paperback interior with *Backpacked* in the "Also By…"
87. Update blog, booksite etc. changing "Coming soon" to "Out now!" and links to buy.
88. Update Goodreads author profile.
89. Write 5 x launch day blog posts (including this one); schedule them for posting
90. (Today) Keel over.

Self-Publishing: a Checklist

If you did want something in the form of a checklist, I'd recommend starting with something that looks like the list below.

1. Write the book
2. Get your US tax issue sorted, if applicable
3. Check you've money to (potentially) lose (ahem, *invest*) in the bank
4. Create a marketing/promotion plan for your book
5. Start blogging about the book, i.e. building anticipation about it
6. Research reviewers, make list of potentials
7. Research and decide on prices
8. Find and hire an editor
9. Edit book, meanwhile:
10. Find and hire a cover designer
11. Mock-up paperback interior to determine page count
12. Download cover template from CreateSpace and:
13. Send cover template to cover designer
14. Proofread book
15. Create two copies of the manuscript
16. Create interior PDF for inside of paperback from Copy A
17. Okay cover design from cover designer
18. Upload files to CreateSpace and order proof copy
19. Format Copy B for e-book conversion
20. Upload files to Amazon KDP and Smashwords but publish ONLY on Smashwords (leave KDP in 'draft')
21. Download ePub and Mobi files from Smashwords and immediately unpublish (so no one can buy the book for now)
22. Check e-book files using Kindle App for PC/Mac and Adobe Digital Editions
23. Check proof copy paperback, publish if all okay but set to 'Private' (so no one but you can order it and it doesn't go out to retailers)
24. Order x amount of paperbacks to send to reviewers
25. Contact reviewers, offering paperbacks or e-book files. Send them.
26. Two weeks before launch date, publish paperback
27. One week before launch date, publish on Amazon KDP and Smashwords
28. Wait for Amazon listings to go live
29. Sign up for Amazon Author Central, email them to get them to link Kindle and paperback listings
30. Announce to the world on your (chosen by you) launch day that the book is now available
31. Start writing your next book.

Acknowledgements

Special thanks first of all to what I like to think of as the *Self-Printed* Team: Andrew Brown, Averill Buchanan, Robert Doran and everyone at eBookPartnership.com. You are all *so* generous and lovely – and, let's be honest, probably glad I don't update this 130,000-word monster too often…

Thanks also to Alison Baverstock; Sally Clements; Kitty French; Joel Friedlander; David Gaughran; Lena Goldfinch; Michael Harling; Sheena Lambert; Katie Mack; Marcela Martinez Millan; Nicola Morgan; Roz Morris; Vanessa O'Loughlin; Martin Turnbull; David Wright; the lovely people who read my blog, books and tweets; and my Nespresso machine which was under *so* much pressure during the updating of this third edition that it ended up in the Nespresso Hospital. (Longest two weeks of my life. FACT.)

Mel Sherratt deserves a special mention for plugging *Self-Printed* every chance she gets – I've said it before and I'll say it again: lady, you should be on commission!

Finally thank YOU for reading.

Now kindly go tell everyone you've ever met in your life about this book.

(Joke!)

(Well, sort of …)

About the Author

CATHERINE RYAN HOWARD is a writer, blogger, coffee enthusiast and one of Ireland's most successful self-published authors.

Catherine self-published her first book, a travel memoir called *Mousetrapped: A Year and A Bit in Orlando, Florida*, in March 2010, after her tale of Space Shuttle launches, humidity-challenged hair, Bruce Willis, the Ebola virus and an Irish girl working in Walt Disney World failed to find a publisher. Since then Catherine has also self-published *Backpacked: A Reluctant Trip Across Central America* and *Self-Printed: The Sane Person's Guide to Self-Publishing*, now in its third edition.

Catherine's success story has been featured in the likes of the *Irish Independent*, *Sunday Times* and *Irish Examiner* newspapers, and Catherine has been interviewed on numerous radio shows and even appeared (briefly!) on national TV. She's delivered workshops and seminars for the likes of Irish PEN, Publishing Ireland and Guardian Masterclasses, and has appeared at events such as ChipLitFest, Mountains to Sea and Dublin Book Festival, among others. In 2012 she was chosen to deliver the first ever self-publishing course run by a traditional publisher, Faber Academy's 'Bring Your Book To Market', and she continues to be a guest tutor there.

Since late 2012 Catherine has been working as a freelancer with Penguin Ireland, a division of Penguin Random House, helping them devise and execute social media campaigns for their commercial fiction titles.

She's currently reading for a degree in English Studies at Trinity College Dublin.

Before all this, she worked as an administrator in the Netherlands, a campsite courier in France and a front desk agent in a hotel in Walt Disney World, Florida.

She wants to be a NASA astronaut when she grows up. (She's 32.)

www.catherineryanhoward.com

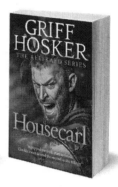

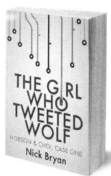

EDITOR | COPY-EDITOR | PROOFREADER

ROBERT DORAN

WWW.ROBERT-EDITS.COM

Let's make your book
the best it can be ...

Ab Averill Buchanan
Editor & proofreader

www.averillbuchanan.com

Made in the USA
Charleston, SC
13 February 2016